Hong Kong Management and Labour

Hong Kong: world city or Chinese society? To what extent will management in Hong Kong now reflect westernisation or Chinese culture? What is the impact of economic, social and political change on Hong Kong's management and labour?

This book considers the highly topical and rapid changes over recent decades in Hong Kong's labour market in order to answer these questions. With waves of immigration and emigration, an improvement in the level of skill and education, and increasing participation by women, Hong Kong's labour market is changing. This book examines the economic, social and political factors affecting labour markets, management style, employee participation and trade unions in recent years, and examines enduring influences such as the Chinese cultural stress on family collectivism and many changes such as deindustrialisation following the transfer of manufacturing to the Chinese mainland. Moreover, these far-reaching changes look set to continue in the new Hong Kong Special Administrative Region of China.

Hong Kong Management and Labour argues, in a series of previously unpublished, completely up-to-date contributions, that economic and social change has been ongoing in Hong Kong for many years, and political change is perhaps less important for labour and management in the region. This book is written bearing in mind the concerns of policy makers and managers – particularly human resource managers, and those interested in labour relations, trade unions, labour markets, labour law, and comparative management.

The editors: Patricia Fosh is Professor of Human Resource Management at Cardiff Business School. She is the author of a number of books including jointly writing *The Last Colony: But Whose? A Study of the Labour Movement, Labour Market and Labour Relations in Hong Kong.* **W. Chan** is Assistant Professor in the Department of Management at Hong Kong Polytechnic University, and most recently published *Managing Human Resources in Hong Kong, second edition.* **Wilson W. S. Chow** is Assistant Professor in the Department of Professional Legal Education at the University of Hong Kong. **Andy Ed Snape** is Professor of Human Resource Management at the University of Bradford Management Centre; he most recently co-authored *Managing with Total Quality Management.* **Robert Westwood** is Senior Lecturer in the Australian Graduate School of Management at the University of Sydney.

Routledge advances in Asia-Pacific business

Hong Kong Management and Labour

Change and continuity

Edited by Patricia Fosh, Andy W. Chan, Wilson W. S. Chow, Ed Snape and Robert Westwood

London and New York

First published 1999
by Routledge
11 New Fetter Lane, London EC4P 4EE

Simultaneously published in the USA and Canada
by Routledge
29 West 35th Street, New York, NY 10001

Routledge is an imprint of the Taylor & Francis Group

© 1999 Patricia Fosh, Andy W. Chan, Wilson W. S. Chow, Ed Snape
and Robert Westwood for selection and editorial matter; individual
chapters the contributors

Typeset in Times by
Exe Valley Dataset Ltd, Exeter, Devon, England
Printed and bound in Great Britain by
St Edmundsbury Press, Bury St Edmunds, Suffolk

British Library Cataloguing in Publication Data
A catalogue record for this book is available
from the British Library

Library of Congress Cataloguing in Publication Data
Hong Kong management and labour : continuity and change / edited
    by Patricia Fosh ... [et al.]
        p.   cm. — (Routledge advances in Asia-Pacific business)
    Includes bibliographical references and index.
    1. Management—China—Hong Kong. 2. Labor—China—
    Hong Kong. 3. Hong Kong (China)—Economic conditions.
    4. Hong Kong (China)—Social conditions. 5. Hong Kong
    (China)—Politics and government—1997–   I. Fosh, Patricia.
    II. Series.
    HD70.C52H854   1999
    330.95125—dc21   99–31957
                                                                 CIP

ISBN 0–415–22269–9

In memory of Bert Turner 1919 to 1998

Contents

Figures

Tables

Contributors

Anne Carver, Senior Lecturer, Department of Professional Legal Education, University of Hong Kong.

Andy W. Chan, Assistant Professor, Department of Management, Hong Kong Polytechnic University.

K. F. Chan, Associate Professor, Department of Management, Hong Kong Polytechnic University.

William Chan, Lecturer, School of Economics and Finance, University of Hong Kong.

Frenda Cheung, Assistant Professor, Department of Management, Hong Kong Polytechnic University.

Randy K. Chiu, Associate Professor, Department of Management, Hong Kong Baptist University.

Warren C. K. Chiu, Assistant Professor, Department of Management, Hong Kong Polytechnic University.

Wilson W. S. Chow, Assistant Professor, Department of Professional Legal Education, University of Hong Kong.

Howard Davies, Professor, Department of Business Studies, Hong Kong Polytechnic University.

Patricia Fosh, Professor of Human Resources Management, Cardiff Business School, Cardiff University.

Kit-chun Lam, Associate Professor, Department of Economics, Hong Kong Baptist University.

Theresa Lau, Assistant Professor, Department of Management, Hong Kong Polytechnic University.

Chris Leggett, Professor of International Employment Relations, Division of Business and Enterprise, University of South Australia.

Alicia S. M. Leung, Assistant Professor, Department of Management, Hong Kong Baptist University.

Pak-Wai Liu, Professor of Economics, Department of Economics, Chinese University of Hong Kong.

Hon-Kwong Lui, Associate Professor, Department of Marketing and International Business, Lingnan University.

Clifford Kei-fung Mak, Research Associate, Department of Management, Hong Kong Polytechnic University.

Thomas W. Y. Man, Research Assistant, Department of Management, Hong Kong Polytechnic University.

Ng Sek-hong, Reader, School of Business, University of Hong Kong.

Catherine W. Ng, Assistant Professor, Department of Management, Hong Kong Polytechnic University.

Harriet Samuels, Senior Lecturer, Department of Law, University of Westminster.

Margaret Shaffer, Assistant Professor, Department of Management, Hong Kong Polytechnic University.

Ed Snape, Professor of Human Resource Management, Bradford Management Centre, University of Bradford.

Coryn Stokes, Independent Consultant.

Wing Suen, Senior Lecturer, School of Economics and Finance, University of Hong Kong.

David Thompson, Associate Professor, Department of Management, Hong Kong Polytechnic University.

Robert Westwood, Senior Lecturer, Australian Graduate School of Management, University of Sydney and University of New South Wales.

Abbreviations

ADPL	Association for Democracy and People's Livelihood	E&LR(MA)O	Employment and Labour Relations (Miscellaneous Amendments) Ordinance
AFL-CIO	American Federation of Labour–Congress of Industrial Organizations	EEOC	Equal Employment Opportunity Commission
AGM	Annual General Meeting		
APEC	Asia-Pacific Economic Cooperation Forum	EGM	Extraordinary General Meeting
ASEAN	Association of Southeast Asian Nations	EO	Equal opportunities
BORO	Bill of Rights Ordinance	EO(A)(No.4)O	Employment (Amendment) (No.4) Ordinance
CC	Consultative Committee		
CCP	Communist Party of China	EOC	Equal Opportunities Commission
CEDAW	Convention on the Elimination of all Forms of Discrimination against Women	EPZ	Export Processing Zone
		ERRCCBO	Employee's Rights to Representation, Consultation and Collective Bargaining Ordinance
CFL	Chinese Federation of Labour		
CIC	Christian Industrial Committee		
CLA	Council of Labour Affairs	ExCo	Executive Council
		EU	European Union
CPF	Central Provident Fund	FCO	Foreign and Commonwealth Office
CTU	Hong Kong Confederation of Trade Unions	FKDTU	Federation of Korean Democratic Trade Unions
CUEPACS	Congress of Unions of Employees in the Public and Civil Services	FKTU	Federation of Korean Trade Unions
DAB	Democratic Alliance for the Betterment of Hong Kong	FLU	Federation of Labour Unions
		FSDO	Family Status Discrimination Ordinance
DD/HR	Deputy Director/Human Resources		
DDO	Disability Discrimination Ordinance	FTU	Hong Kong Federation of Trade Unions
		GDP	Gross domestic product

GMAS	General Manager for Administrative Services
HA	Hong Kong Hospital Authority
HACC	Hospital Authority Consultative Committee
HAHO	Hospital Authority Head Office
HK	Hong Kong
HKIHRM/ IHRM	Hong Kong Institute of Human Resource Management
HKSAR / SAR	Hong Kong Special Administrative Region
HR	Human resources
HRAM	Human Resources Administration Manual
HRD	Human Resources Division
HRM	Human resource management
HRPM	Human Resources Policy Manual
HRPS	Human Resources Payroll System
HSD	Hospital Services Department
ICCPR	International Covenant on Civil and Political Rights
ICFTU	International Confederation of Free Trade Unions
ILO	International Labour Organisation
IRRC	Industrial Relations Reform Commission
JCC	Joint Consultative Committee
KMU	Kilusang Mayo Uno
LAB	Labour Advisory Board
LegCo	Legislative Council
LRO	Labour Relations Ordinance
LSD	Least Significant Differences
MIT	Massachusetts Institute of Technology
MLO	Malaysian Labour Organisation
MOFERT/ MOFTEC	Ministry of Foreign Economic Relations and Trade/Ministry of Foreign Trade and Economic Co-operation
MOWIRT	Meaning of Work International Research Team
MTUC	Malaysian Trade Union Congress
NAFITU	National Federation of Independent Trade Unions
NAFTA	North American Free Trade Agreement
NCIR	New Conception of Industrial Relations
NIE	Newly Industrialized Economy
NMI	New Management Initiatives
NPC	National People's Congress
NTUC	National Trade Union Congress
NUPW	National Union of Plantation Workers
OECD	Organisation for Economic Co-operation and Development
PAP	Peoples' Action Party
PE	Personnel and Emolument (Budget)
POO	Public Order Ordinance
POSCO	Pohang Iron and Steel Company
PRC	People's Republic of China
PTA	Professional Teachers' Union
QWL	Quality of work life
RTU	Registrar of Trade Unions
SBMS	Serikat Buruh Merdeka Setiakawan (Solidarity Free Trade Union)
SBSI	Serikat Buruh Sejahtera Indonesia (Indonesian Prosperous Labour Union)
SCMP	South China Morning Post
SCSC	Senior Civil Service Council

SDO	Sex Discrimination Ordinance	TU(A)O	Trade Union (Amendment) Ordinance
SDR	Staff Development Review	TUC	Hong Kong and Kowloon Trades Union
SEZ	Special Economic Zone		Council
SHRM	Senior Human Resources Manager	TUO	Trade Union Ordinance
SO	Societies Ordinance	TURO	Trade Union Registration Ordinance
SOE	State-owned enterprise	TURR	Trade Union
SPSI	Serikat Pekerja Seluruh Indonesia (All Indonesian Workers' Union)		Registration Regulations
		UK	United Kingdom
		UN	United Nations
		US/USA	United States of America
TFP	Total factor productivity		
TQM	Total quality management	VGCL	Vietnam General Confederation of Labour
TU&TDO	Trade Unions and Trade Disputes Ordinance	WEAP	Women Employee Assistance Programme
TU(A)(No.2)O	Trade Union (Amendment)(No.2) Ordinance	WFD	Women-friendly dimensions

Part I
Hong Kong after the transition

1 Hong Kong at the end of the twentieth century

Management and labour trends

Patricia Fosh, Catherine Ng, Ed Snape and Robert Westwood

Introduction

This book is a collection of research papers discussing the characteristics of management and labour in Hong Kong at the end of the twentieth century:[1] it seeks to analyse the key environmental factors affecting management and labour, to assess to what extent the characteristics of management and labour have endured or been moderated, and to examine the implications for management practice and for management–employee relations. The book also aims to place Hong Kong in its East Asian context.

This collection takes as its starting point two earlier books on labour relations and their context in Hong Kong written by Bert Turner and his colleagues (Turner *et al.* 1980, 1991). The first study, which covered the 1970s, was requested and sponsored by a British Labour government's Foreign and Commonwealth (FCO) Secretary, as an informal solution to pressure from the then politically influential British trade unions to investigate a supposed threat to employment for British workers in several industries because of 'unfair competition' from cheap and allegedly exploited labour in Hong Kong (Turner *et al.* 1991: 1). The study was updated a decade later, with academic sponsorship, in the light of significant legal, economic, political and social changes The present book, focusing on the end of the 1990s, continues this tradition but widens the scope of the earlier work to include a greater emphasis on management issues in general, and on women in employment in particular, and also draws on the now considerable strength of home-grown university research in Hong Kong on labour markets, management policies and practices, and labour issues.

This study charts continuity and change in Hong Kong, both in terms of the characteristics of management and labour, and in the city's relationship with the rest of East Asia and the West. In political terms, the reversion of sovereignty to China on 1 July 1997 and the end of British colonial rule has dominated the landscape, and the political future of the new Hong Kong Special Administrative Region (HKSAR) looks uncertain at present. Whilst Hong Kong's fate will be increasingly tied to that of its motherland, the SAR government is likely to lead the rest of China in the development of democracy. These changes will have a direct impact on management and labour as the growth of participation in the political dimension is accompanied by calls for reform in labour market and welfare policies. The recent sharp downturn in the economy and the rise of unemployment to relatively high levels for Hong Kong,[2] coming on the heels of the chicken flu epidemic and the 'red tide' pollution problems, has imposed considerable strain on the new SAR government. The success of the pro-democracy parties in the 1998 Legislative Council (LegCo) elections ensures that democratic development will remain an issue of public debate and indicates that the government must be cautious of being too one-sided in its pro-business stance. The situation is such that neither continued authoritarianism, nor a rapid and smooth progression towards greater democracy, can be taken for granted.

However, significant economic and social changes are also going on in Hong Kong. It is important to recognise that these predate the return of sovereignty. Social change has been rapid: no longer is Hong Kong dominated by a 'refugee mentality'. Unlike in the initial years of industrial growth, the majority of today's citizens were born in the territory and have a sense of belonging to it. Notions of civic pride and a wish to have a say in the future of Hong Kong appear to be growing. Social change has been accompanied by a substantial increase in public and social services. There has also been a greater emphasis on equal opportunities with the growth of pressure groups calling for greater rights for women and the disabled; there is also the beginning of an interest in racial issues.

In terms of economic change, Hong Kong has experienced rapid deindustrialisation since the mid-1980s as manufacturing has moved across the border into Southern China, and particularly into Shenzhen. Hong Kong companies have been leading investors in China and in the other economies of South East Asia, and the SAR now stands at the hub of an international manufacturing complex, as a key provider of finance, logistics and business services support. Not surprisingly, such developments have been accompanied by major growth in the financial and business services sectors and the associated up-grading in occupations has been assisted by a rise in educational standards. Distribution and tourism also experienced rapid growth, although there have been a slump in the latter in the post-transition period.

This chapter introduces the reader to the rest of the book while, at the same time, linking the present collection's interests to those of the earlier studies by the Turner team and providing the general reader with necessary background on management and labour characteristics in Hong Kong. A number of influences occur and reoccur in these chapters. These are (i) government intervention or abstentionism in business affairs; (ii) the impact of Chinese cultural values on management and labour as mediated by the influence of modernisation and westernisation; (iii) reverberations in Hong Kong of events in China and the resulting deep political divisions in the territory; (iv) the increasing politicisation of ordinary Hong Kong-belongers; and (v) the increasing role of women in Hong Kong society – the last two being concomitants of increasing levels of education and occupational attainment.

The parts of the book

Part I sets the scene for the book, analysing continuities and changes in the legal, political and economic spheres in Hong Kong since the second Turner study.

Chow and Fosh in Chapter 2 discuss the impact on the representation of labour of the complex political and legal changes that took place in Hong Kong at the time of the transfer of Hong Kong's sovereignty to China, thus setting the scene for the book's analysis of the on-going changes in Hong Kong's labour market, management practice and management–employee relations. This chapter introduces the 'China factor' and its part in the development of the deep political divisions in Hong Kong, both in the colonial era and in the new SAR, and also discusses the impact of the increasing politicisation of ordinary Hong Kong-belongers.

Chow and Fosh examine the sequences of changes in the legislative process, particularly in the composition of the Legislative Council (LegCo), and the legal framework for trade unions, and their reversal, or partial reversal, by the incoming SAR government. Much of the controversy surrounding the changes introduced during the late 1980s and the first half of the 1990s centred on the question of whether Hong Kong law should remain unchanged from the date of the Joint Declaration in 1984 or from the date of the transition on 1 July 1997. The authors consider future developments of importance to trade unions, specifically the impact of the Confederation of Trade Unions' (CTU) successful complaint to the ILO's Committee on Freedom of Association and the possibility of a reintroduction of statutory collective bargaining rights.

Turning to the question of Hong Kong's development strategy, we note the importance of the government's adoption in the colonial era of a policy of social non-intervention and economic *laissez-faire*. While social development in the last several decades pushed the government into intervening to provide the necessary social facilities and services for an increasingly complex society, the administration confined its economic function to the provision of a viable political and physical infrastructure in order for the economy to prosper; it has resisted almost all calls for a more interventionist role in this sphere (Lau and Kuan 1988: 22–4). An important question in the new SAR is whether the new Chief Executive, Tung Chee-hwa, will continue this policy of economic non-intervention or whether he will seek actively to change Hong Kong firms' production strategies.

Howard Davies in Chapter 3 introduces the reader to the increasingly lively debate in the new SAR on structural change and the future of manufacturing. Davies questions the widely publicised argument propounded by Berger and Lester that the new SAR should become a 'world class industrial power' competing on the basis of rapid innovation in high-technology manufacturing, and he doubts whether the requirements for the take-up of high technology are consistent with the objectives and behaviour of the Chinese family businesses which predominate in the Hong Kong manufacturing sector (Berger and Lester 1997). Instead, he envisages an economic future based on the SAR's 'merchanting capability' with an emphasis on trade and manufacturing-related services.

Part II looks more specifically at labour market issues. Turner and his colleagues included detailed discussion of labour market issues as part of the context for labour representation, highlighting in particular the growing inequality in Hong Kong between capital and labour and the simultaneous narrowing of income differentials between white-collar and manual workers (Turner *et al.* 1991). The chapters in this part of the book review the continuities and changes that have taken place in the nature of the labour market since that time, focusing on labour supply and adjustment, and also on labour market outcomes in terms of income distribution.

We begin our discussion with William Chan's and Wing Suen's analysis in Chapter 4 of the impact of major sectoral shifts in the Hong Kong economy on the social structure of the labour market. These authors discuss the impact of job losses in the manufacturing sector with the transfer of much of Hong Kong's manufacturing function/facilities to Guangdong, and the impact of the rise of jobs in the services sectors, particularly financing, insurance, real estate and business services. Also discussed are the related changes in the distribution of occupations and of wealth and income, and in the extent of structural unemployment and worker displacement. A further matter of interest is the contrary problem of labour shortages in specific industries and the demand for professional workers – these shortages and demands have waxed and waned according to the state of the economy and the extent of political uncertainty surrounding the transition. Further, these authors address questions of whether the labour market in Hong Kong is competitive, to what extent its workers are mobile across industries and occupations, and what role wage flexibility plays in adjustments to economic crises such as the present one.

Hon-Kwong Lui in Chapter 5 takes up the question of the impact of income inequality on the labour force. The Hong Kong labour market adjusted relatively smoothly to changes in labour demand caused by the structural shifts discussed in Chapters 3 and 4, and there has been an impressive increase in GDP per capita and median employment income since 1976. However, the author argues that these increases conceal a considerable widening of income dispersion between workers of different educational levels. As Turner and his colleagues (1991: 17) commented earlier, this is contrary to what would normally be expected with economic growth. Lui's analysis, however, considers the increases in income inequality for different periods and relates this to the increasing government provision of education, variations in the emigration of skilled and professional workers, and crises of political confidence. In doing so, he comes to a different conclusion from Chan and Suen as to whether there will be a shortage of educated workers in Hong Kong in the future. Lui questions the idea that the service-oriented labour market in twenty-first century Hong Kong will be dominated by skilled workers, given the continued development of IT which will allow less skilled workers to undertake previously skilled jobs.

Chapter 6, also by Hon-Kwong Lui, addresses the gender gap between men and women workers in Hong Kong and is the first of our three chapters addressing women's issues. In order to place these chapters in context, we need to chart briefly the recent pressures for greater equality for women.

Until very recently, anti-employment-discrimination legislation was largely absent from Hong Kong's legal system: government's and employers' preference for a free labour market led to firm opposition to anti-discrimination laws (Ng 1994: 652). The only protection for women was contained in the Employment Ordinance and the Women and Young Persons (Industry) Regulations. The focus of this legislation was on issues such as minimum wage, working conditions, working hours, holiday pay and maternity leave.

The first hint of anti-discrimination legislation came in 1990, when the Bill of Rights Ordinance (BORO) was passed. However, to the disappoint-ment of women's groups, the Ordinance bound only the government and public authorities (Petersen 1997: 328). The rapidly uniting feminist groups then took the initiative in lobbying policy-makers into introducing anti-discrimination legislation. These groups persuaded Emily Lau to move a motion in LegCo in 1992 to extend the United Nations Convention on the Elimination of all Forms of Discrimination against Women to Hong Kong. This success pressurised the colonial government into issuing in 1993 the *Green Paper on Equal Opportunities for Women and Men* for public consultation.

The women's movement in Hong Kong continued to grow in strength, acquiring significant support both in the legislature and from the general public (Petersen 1997: 331). In July 1994 Anna Wu introduced a Private Member's Bill (Equal Opportunities Bill) in LegCo containing proposals to outlaw discrimination on a wide range of grounds in a broad range of activities. To limit the remit of legislative changes, the government chose to table its own more conservative Sex Discrimination Bill in October 1994 which provided much narrower protection.[3] This Bill was enacted as the Sex Discrimination Ordinance (SDO) in July 1995. In May 1996 the members of the Equal Opportunities Commission (EOC) were appointed and they began work in September of the same year. In December 1996 the Code of Practice on Employment under the SDO came into operation.[4]

In the legislative rush that took place just before the transition, two additional Bills were published. One was a Private Member's Bill sponsored by Christine Loh, enacted as the Sex and Disability Discrimination (Miscellaneous Provisions) Ordinance on 20 June 1997, which made significant amendments to SDO including, *inter alia*, the lifting of the ceiling for damages and, most importantly, the provision of reinstatement as a remedy for an aggrieved person who has been dismissed.[5] The other Bill, introduced by the government, focused on family discrimination.[6] This was enacted as the Family Status Discrimination Ordinance on 24 June 1997 and was accompanied by a Code of Practice which came into force in May 1998.

In his second chapter, Lui considers three indicators of the position of women in employment in Hong Kong for which empirical evidence is available: these are earnings, participation rate in the labour force, and occupational segregation by gender. For earnings, the author reviews the variance over time between men's and women's earnings that cannot explained by socio-demographic differences between men and women. Lui also charts the increase in women's participation in the labour force but notes that any interpretation must take account of the availability in Hong Kong of affordable domestic helpers, mainly from the Philippines. He links this increase in participation to the rising educational level of girls, in turn a product of changing Chinese values on the desirability of educating girls. Finally, in terms of working women in Hong Kong climbing the occupational ladder, Lui considers the changing proportion of women working as professionals and managers. His suggestion that women's inequality is resolvable through women investing more in their careers through spending greater periods of time in the labour market is contested in Chapters 11 and 12 which outline the conflicts and barriers faced by working women in Hong Kong.

Turner and his colleagues (1991) in their mid-1980s study paid particular attention to the impact of the sharply increasing migration rates on Hong Kong's labour market and the final chapter in Part II assesses the situation in the late 1990s. Chapter 7 by Kit-Chun Lam and Pak-Wai Liu addresses the issue of immigration and emphasises its importance to Hong Kong as a major source of population growth since the Second World War; each wave of immigrants boosted the labour supply in Hong Kong and sustained the development of labour-intensive industries. The authors assess the impact of the government's decision in 1980 to abolish the 'reached-base' policy towards illegal immigrants after which the flow of immigrants markedly reduced, and only migrants with legal status were permitted to stay. The authors note the impact on the labour force, in the immediate and long term, both of this reduced flow of immigrants and of the immigrants' different socio-economic characteristics. Lam and Liu also discuss the impact of the sharply rising emigration rate in the late 1980s and early 1990s, particularly detrimental being the loss of the youth, educational qualifications and linguistic abilities of the emigrants. However, the authors also point to the beneficial effects of sharply increased return migration from 1992 onwards. The authors believe that the SAR government should free up immigration in order to increase the number of professional and skilled workers in Hong Kong: this returns us to the debate over Hong Kong's future need for professional and skilled workers.

Part III moves on to consider issues at management level and organisation level. Research on management practice in Hong Kong has focused on two areas, the first is the distinctiveness of Chinese business and management practice relative to Western approaches, and the second is the use of particular management techniques.

Research on the distinctiveness of Chinese management and business practice has emphasised low formalisation, personal control by family members, reluctance to place outsiders in key positions of authority, and a generally paternalistic, even authoritarian, approach to the management of employees (Whitley 1992). The relatively authoritarian nature of management styles in Hong Kong extends beyond the family business sector and employers, in general, have resisted unionisation and employee participation.

Turning to the second issue, the use of specific management techniques, Hong Kong employers have been characterised as backward in human resource management (HRM) compared with their counterparts in other countries, especially in terms of the typically low levels of investment by employers in training and staff development (Levin and Ng 1995; Kirkbride and Tang 1990). This has been seen by many commentators as a factor threatening the long-term growth potential of Hong Kong, limiting the ability to move into higher value-added activities. Past surveys have confirmed this relative underdevelopment of the HRM function, certainly outside the public and foreign-owned sectors. However, Hong Kong has since the 1980s witnessed an interest in management innovations such as quality circles, total quality management and culture change initiatives, and the use of such approaches appears to have been spreading. Interestingly, just as in the West, there have been debates about whether or not innovations with their origins in Japanese management practice can be implemented in the Hong Kong cultural context (Kirkbride and Tang 1994; Fukuda 1993). In more general terms, there is evidence that Hong Kong is developing better-educated and more professional managers. There is a growing interest amongst Hong Kong managers for professional development and the membership of the Hong Kong Institute of Human Resource Management (HKIHRM) has been increasing in recent years, reflecting a growing sophistication in HRM practice. Thus, whilst a 1988 survey suggested that only 59 per cent of Hong Kong companies had a specialist personnel function, compared to over 90 per cent in a comparable UK study (Kirkbride and Tang 1990), a 1994 survey found that over 80 per cent of Hong Kong companies had such a specialist function (Tang *et al.* 1995). The two Hong Kong surveys are not matched in terms of sample composition, but they are at least suggestive of a growing sophistication in HRM, especially when we note that even amongst firms with fewer than 200 employees, by 1994 over 67 per cent had a specialist HRM function.

A critical influence on management in Hong Kong has been Chinese cultural values as mediated by modernisation and westernisation. Culture plays an important part in differentially shaping approaches to economic affairs, transaction relationships, organising and managing. This has become widely acknowledged, although the relative contribution of cultural versus non-cultural factors is hard to unpack and remains contested. It can be argued that there is a degree of commonality in the cultural context of Mainland China and Hong Kong despite radical differences in political economy, and historical and economic development. It has certainly been maintained that the cultural values and traditions of the Chinese display remarkable persistence and continuity across time and place (Bond 1986; Lim and Gosling 1983; Wang 1991). A strong and widely shared cultural heritage, comprised of core assumptions and values rooted in the religio-philosophical precepts of Taoism, Buddhism and especially Confucianism, is held to provide cultural coherence. Furthermore, whilst common ethnicity does not secure cultural homogeneity, the concept of 'Chineseness' is trenchant, pervasive and persistent across Chinese communities. However, we need to make it clear in the ensuing discussion of Chinese culture that Hong Kong and Mainland China are not culturally identical, a fact which is understandable given their different development. Hong Kong has been subjected to an intensive and sustained colonial experience and been more exposed to the forces of modernisation and westernisation. In organisation and management terms, certainly, Hong Kong organisations have been subject to an increasing level of Western (and Japanese) influence, leading to the adoption or adaptation of approaches and techniques that are now an integral part of the commercial landscape. These have not, however, supplanted more indigenous approaches based on Chinese cultural values and traditions (Chen 1995; Redding 1990; Westwood 1992; Whitley 1992).

Any attempt to summarise Chinese culture here would be presumptuous, but some cultural values with a bearing on organisation and management and worker orientations can be signalled. In terms of formal dimensions of cultural values, both China and Hong Kong are large power distance and collectivist cultures (Hofstede 1994). The commonality in terms of power distance rests on the acceptance of firmly hierarchical relationships rooted in patriarchal systems. In organisational terms, this entails high levels of centralisation and leadership styles described as 'paternalistic headship' (Westwood 1997a) or 'benevolently autocratic' (Redding 1990). Within the vigorous capitalism of Hong Kong, high power distance relates to acceptance of large disparities in wealth and wage differentials. China's ideology of equalitarianism has, of course, militated against that orientation.

The collectivism is expressed in a strong 'utilitarian' familism (Lau 1982). The family unit, traditionally in its extended and clan form, remains the pre-eminent social structure and needs to be viewed as a socio-economic unit and not only as a socio-emotional one. The family has high cohesion and generates significant in-group to out-group delineations. Family members have an obligation to contribute to the family good so as to secure financial security and enhance family wealth, both now and for future generations. In the Hong Kong context the greatest security, since it represents relative independence and control, rests in owning one's own business. Chinese businesses, even the large ones, are still primarily family businesses and there has not been the same level of separation of ownership from control that has characterised the Western corporate world. This ethos was brought to Hong Kong by the waves of immigrant traders, merchants and business-persons who escaped from communist China in the late 1940s and early 1950s. The 'heroes' of Hong Kong society are those business tycoons who arrived there after the revolution and through hard work and astute business acumen made their fortune. Hierarchical, patriarchal structures, engendered and legitimised by traditional cultural values, are a model for organising social relationships and are replicated in organisations. Heads of organisations have a status, role and function that parallels that of the family head, hence the high levels of centralised decision-making and pertinence of the notion of 'paternalistic headship'.

Collectivism and other cultural aspects also entail a very strong relationship orientation. The need to sustain harmonious relationships in the workplace is critical and a good deal of energy needs to be expended in establishing, building up and maintaining good interpersonal relationships and social networks, both within and outside organisations. This is a prime requirement in organisations in both Hong Kong and China, although the types of relationships and the reasons for their cultivation may vary. Business relationships are facilitated by and often dependent on *guanxi*, which describes the quality of relationships that are developed over time and which centre on the social rules of favours and their return, reciprocity and mutual obligation. *Guanxi* networks are an essential feature of doing business in Hong Kong and the Mainland.

Relationships in both contexts are diffuse rather than specific (Trompenaars 1993), that is relationships are not confined in time and place to the specificities of a particular context, rather they are expected to persist across time and to have extensionality across situations. The issue of diffuseness also tends to mean that life spheres are less differentiated and fragmented than in western, specific cultures. In this regard, work, as a life sphere, is not so readily distinguished from other life spheres such as family or social activity. This is very apparent in Hong Kong where people are prepared to engage in work-related activities at any time and in any place, particularly if they are connected to one's own business.

According to Hofstede (1994), Hong Kong is a 'masculine' culture. China, by contrast, is more towards the middle of the 'masculine–feminine' continuum. For most Hong Kong people the prime motivators have been economic security and advancement. Even the traditional value placed upon education has been transformed into an instrumental one as educational opportunities expanded and securing a decent education was seen as a viable way to attain desired material ends. Financial independence and material success are major status markers and, partly as a result, Hong Kong society has developed a culture of conspicuous consumption. In

China, although its traditional patriarchal structures suggests a masculine orientation, there has been rather less emphasis on competitive attainment and the socialist doctrine expresses humanistic tendencies and a concern for people's well-being: more feminine values according to Hofstede. It is anticipated that the changing conditions in China are likely to release nascent masculine value orientations. Materialism, acquisitiveness, competitiveness and invigorated consumption can be seen emerging in China in the post-1978 period.

Hong Kong recorded one of the weakest uncertainty avoidance index scores on Hofstede's dimension, whereas China is depicted as again being more towards the middle of the dimension (Hofstede 1980, 1994). It could be argued that people in Hong Kong, given its inherent uncertainties, dependencies and transitoriness, have developed a rare tolerance for ambiguity and uncertainty. In China, political, economic and natural vicissitudes have rather cultivated a sense of anxiety and insecurity, which in turn may account for a greater dislike of uncertainty. Chinese organisational regimes have tended to promote rule following and the avoidance of mistakes, rather than initiative, experimentation and risk-taking. Political monitoring and overtly imposed socialist values, sanctioned by a punishing regime, have generated something of a conformist mindset. In the employment context, Hong Kong workers are used to functioning in a free labour market and to trading their skills in it. In China, an expectation of virtual lifetime job security has been established along with other guarantees colloquially collected under the notion of the 'iron rice bowl'. Furthermore, in Hong Kong, people are used to work settings in which organisational flexibility is considered a premium and levels of work and organisational formalisation are kept at a low level (Redding 1990; Westwood 1992). In China, an extensive degree of bureaucratisation has been a feature of state-owned enterprises.

Orientations towards time and activity in time constitute another cultural variance dimension. Hong Kong and China are presumed to have similarly strong long-term orientations (Hofstede 1994; Hofstede and Bond 1986). This in part deals with the processes of deferment (of rewards and gratification), persistence (for example with respect to tasks) and thriftiness which have implications for people's orientations towards economic activity. These long-term orientations have also been discussed as important components of a distinctive work ethic (Hofstede and Bond 1988).

Chinese culture is also characterised by high levels of pragmatism and this is related to the cultural dimension of particularism (opposed to universalism) (see Trompenaars 1993; Lane *et al.* 1997). Actions and events – actual, intended and perceived – are judged and evaluated with respect to the particular features of the context in which they are enacted, especially relationships, not via reference to some internalised universalistic principles. It is in part this particularism and pragmatism that has allowed the notion of market socialism and socialism with Chinese characteristics to emerge. High levels of pragmatism in Hong Kong have enabled the adoption of management and organisational practices from around the world and a ready adaptability to new technologies, new work methods and new systems of trade. This has lent vibrancy to the economic system and considerable flexibility to organisation form, management systems and regimes of work. Workers are used to rapid changes in these areas and are very adaptive to them. It is also suggested that Chinese cultures have a relationship to the environment orientation that is characterised more in terms of 'harmony with' than the western 'dominance over' orientation. This has implications for the perceived capacity to intervene proactively and determine outcomes. At the more personal level, people are rather more fatalistic and stoical than in the west.

An essential element in the discussion on continuities and change in Hong Kong Chinese culture is the meaning of work and working. The meaning of work in Hong Kong and how it compares with that in other countries is the subject of Chapter 8 by Bob Westwood, Alicia Leung and Randy Chiu. As these authors point out, the meaning of work has highly pragmatic concerns: the meanings people attach to work have relevance for their motivation, satisfaction and performance, and have an impact upon concrete associated outcomes such as productivity, turnover and commitment. Thus, an understanding of what work means to people is of central importance in managerial, organisational and economic terms. In Hong Kong, there have been rapid shifts in organisation form and strategy, managerial outlook and practice, and the technological context of work following the wider macro-economic and industrial organisational changes as the economy matures into a fuller service economy and into a trade hub for its hinterland. In China, the changes in political, social, economic and institutional contexts have been even more rapid and radical. Westwood and his colleagues make a significant empirical contribution to this area through their investigation of the meaning of work for workers in Hong Kong, contrasting and comparing this with the meaning for workers in China. The authors seek, utilising and adapting the Meaning of Work International Research Team model and method, to establish the centrality of work to Hong Kong and Mainland Chinese workers, to discover whether any importance attached to work is of an instrumental or intrinsic nature, and to assess the desire for career opportunities, promotion and development. The impact of changes in the meaning of work and working is of crucial importance to Hong Kong managers in the development of motivational strategies to increase the performance of their workforces in the new SAR.

The next two chapters in Part III focus on the adoption of HRM practices in Hong Kong. The first evaluates the development of the HRM function in a large public sector organisation in Hong Kong and the second has a more general focus – the study of the relationship between HR strategy and business performance in the private sector.

In Chapter 9 David Thompson, Ed Snape, Clifford Mak and Coryn

Stokes present the results of a case study of the Hong Kong Hospital Authority (HA): this chapter introduces the unfamiliar reader to many of the concepts and issues in the process of introducing structural and cultural change in an organisation. The HA management was intent on utilising HRM policies and procedures to assist the achievement of a patient-centred culture that emphasised the empowerment of staff, teamwork and the continuous improvement of service quality. This chapter assesses how far the HA achieved these objectives through the decentralisation of the HRM function to hospitals and line managers, combined with an increase in HRM professionalism and a proactive approach towards the development of management competencies and of staff commitment to the new management style and HA mission. The study suggests that the key challenge for HRM in the years after the transition is the extent to which it is able to develop in terms of autonomy based on its professionalisation and confidence.

In Chapter 10 Margaret Shaffer, Ed Snape and Frenda Cheung examine the importance for Hong Kong firms of viewing HRM strategically and of adopting a coherent package of HR practices in order to underpin the achievement of organisational objectives and to build sustainable competitive advantage. The authors make the telling point that much of the research on the effectiveness of specific HR practices misses the point, since what is important is the overall HRM strategy, and the use of a particular technique cannot be evaluated in isolation. The authors utilise a sample of multi-national firms to test two models of HRM – the 'one best way' approach and the 'strategic fit' approach – to establish which model is the most likely to achieve effectiveness in multi-national firms in Hong Kong. This study has several implications for managers in the years following the transition when the uncertainty surrounding Hong Kong's reversion to Chinese rule could moderate the relationship between HR practices and firm performance.

Chapters 11 and 12 contribute specifically to the book's interest in equal opportunities and the position of women in Hong Kong, building on the material on gender-based differences in income presented in Chapter 5. A key issue in women's life chances and their role in the Hong Kong economy is the extent to which their opportunities are constrained by the admixture of Chinese and western values.

The Chinese cultural context has significant implications for women in the workforce. We noted above that Chinese culture has strong patrimonial, patriarchal and patrilineal traditions enshrined in the Confucian social ethic, which still inform societal values and structures. An example is the principle of the Five Cardinal Relationships, or *Wu lun*, which specifies sets of hierarchically ordered relationships entailing power inequalities but also mutual obligations and responsibilities: emperor–minister, father–son, husband–wife, older brother–younger brother, friend–friend. The patriarchal system gives significant power and authority to the male head of the family. It is incumbent upon other family members to exhibit deference, respect and obedience to the patriarch. Thus, there is an established hierarchy within the family in which females are in subordinate positions relative to males. The Confucian doctrine also promotes the Three Obediences for women: to obey the father before marriage, the husband after marriage, and the eldest son should they become widowed. The traditional role of women has been primarily in the reproductive sphere and, given the importance of patri-linearity and familism, particularly to bear sons and perpetuate the family line (Jackson 1980: 48). The status of women was perniciously tied to their capacity to produce a son. Before marriage a woman's status was very low and certainly secondary to any male offspring. After marriage her status was still fragile until a son was delivered (Libra 1980: 1). Typical divisions of labour occurred in the family with males primarily assuming the productive roles and providing the means for the family's survival and progression. Women were consigned to domestic and reproductive duties. The well-documented practices of female infanticide, feet binding, and the selling of daughters into prostitution, servitude or concubinage further index the low status of women in traditional society.

Of course things have changed in the encounter with modernism and industrialisation, but some of these traditional values are entrenched in social structures and perpetuated in weaker forms through socialisation. Gendered structures, differentiations and attitudes are in part constituted and reflexively reconstituted by familial socialisation. To the extent that families are embedded in patriarchal structures and gendered patterns, norms and attitudes, so family socialisation practices play a part in recon-structing them. Gendered social norms and expectations with respect to sex-typical or sex-appropriate roles and options are transmitted in this process. In Chinese contexts this may well remain more fundamental given that Chinese cultures retain strong values and structures of familistic collectivism, as noted previously. Thus, whilst Hong Kong has embraced a vigorous form of pragmatic capitalism, it retains elements of familistic collectivism. The chief consequences for women are that economic expan-sion has given rise to greater opportunities in the productive sphere and the pragmatism means that business opportunism overrides gender politics in many instances. Nonetheless, gendered attitudes persist and Hong Kong organisations are still masculinist and patriarchal to an extent. Patriarchal values and gender stereotypes persist and continue to be an impediment to women's advancement. It is also apparent that the increased proportion of women in the workforce is no guarantee of their penetration into positions of power and authority.

In China, communist ideology has proclaimed gender equality, but there are many indicators that the ideology is not realised in practice. The situation in China continues to evolve as the turn to the market continues. The impact of these developments on the position and status of women is not yet clear. In our estimation they have initiated differential trends. On the one hand, the turn to the market has freed up employment and business opportunities and liberalised the labour market. Some women have moved to take advantage of that and there are a growing number of female entrepreneurs. On the other hand, the reduction in political and ideological control over organisations, and the increasing determination of business decisions by the market has left organisations free to make employment-related decisions in a more unfettered way. Given the starting point of continued male dominance in organisational management and governance, and the resurfacing of traditional and patriarchal values, women may increasingly find themselves recast into traditional roles and marginalised from power sources within contemporary organisations.

In Chapter 11 Catherine Ng and Warren Chiu discuss the barriers to women's participation in the labour force in Hong Kong, identifying the most important of these as gender stereotypes, work–family conflict, tokenism, and biased HRM policies, procedures and practices. In their empirical study of the reports by members of the HKIHRM on their employing firms, the authors sought information on the adoption of women-friendly HRM practices in Hong Kong, on the opinions of a sample of HR managers (both male and female) on the contribution of these practices to the quality of life at work of their firm's employees, and on the extent to which the presence of one women-friendly policy is associated with the presence of another. A particularly important contribution of this chapter is the authors' comparison of the adoption of women-friendly practices by firms of different national origins. The authors question whether the women-friendly practices extolled in the literature are of value to Hong Kong women in their particular socio-economic circumstances – for example the availability of affordable domestic workers, as noted in Chapter 6, frees Hong Kong women from many aspects of house work and child care, diminishing their need for flexible work arrangements.

In Chapter 12 Bob Westwood and Alicia Leung build upon the work by Ng and Chiu, focusing on the status, role and experiences of Chinese female managers in Hong Kong compared to Chinese female managers in China. This chapter pays particular attention to gender differences in management style, attributes and behaviour. The authors explore whether the communalities for women in management, such as under-representation, career constraints, discrimination and the burden of family care, prevail over the differences in the form of patriarchy and the availability of business opportunities between Hong Kong and China.

The arguments in these two chapters in Part III focusing on women's participation in the labour force, their role in society and their experiences at work, together with those in the earlier chapter by Lui on gender differences in income, raise questions as to the future for women at work in the new SAR. Westwood, in particular, asks whether with the return of Hong Kong to China, Hong Kong women will lose some of their modest but hard-won advancement with the spill-over of re-emerging traditional gender values in post-reform China.

Small businesses make up the overwhelming majority of Hong Kong firms and play a vital role in its economic growth: the generation of entrepreneurship in such businesses is a key issue in Hong Kong's future development. Theresa Lau, K. F. Chan and Thomas Man take up this issue in Chapter 13. The small firms that predominate in the Hong Kong economy are characterised by family involvement and control, short-term orientation combined with speed and flexibility of action, extensive subcontracting, and strong transnational skills. These authors' discussion of the importance in the development of entrepreneurship of values such as pragmatism and materialism links up with our earlier discussion of Chinese values. Lau and her colleagues seek to develop a model of managerial and entrepreneurial competencies that can be used to link certain combinations of personality traits, skills and knowledge with small business success. They develop a specific methodology – that of carefully identifying and exploring critical incidents experienced by these owners/managers of small firms – and they utilise their model to investigate a number of small firms selected from three of Hong Kong's leading industries. The findings from their study allow inferences to be drawn for the enhancement of these smaller owners' and managers' entrepreneurship in the recession conditions following the transition through a combination of encouragement and specifically designed training.

Part IV looks at issues in employee relations. In spite of the increased dominance of business interests in Hong Kong, labour representation is likely to be a key issue in the years ahead. At this point we need to acquaint the reader unfamiliar with Hong Kong with the legal framework for labour relations, the development of trade unions in terms of their density, size and political fragmentation, and the roles the trade unions themselves have elected to play.

We begin with the role in labour relations adopted by the government in the colonial era. The administration's economic *laissez-faire*, noted above with respect to industrial development, extended to wage determination. Thus in 1999 there is no legal support for collective bargaining, no centralised wage machinery, no presumption of legally binding collective agreements, no minimum wage, and no unemployment insurance (Chow and Ng 1992; Ng *et al.* 1997).[7] Additionally, the colonial government did not introduce a right to seek redress for unfair dismissal until the last few days of its rule and it consistently ignored trade unions demands for protection for striking workers from dismissal by their employer. As a consequence of this voluntaristic approach, and the frequent presence of employer hostility towards trade unions, collective bargaining coverage in Hong Kong is very low, covering less than five per cent of the private-sector workforce. Public-sector workers and those in a few large private-sector companies are covered by joint consultation arrangements, but most of the private sector lacks any formal mechanism for employee representation and involvement.

It is not surprising, given the weakness of the trade unions and the hostility of employers, that the level of industrial conflict in Hong Kong is low. The Commissioner for Labour described labour relations in Hong Kong as 'characterised by its peacefulness' and 'industrial harmony' (Commissioner for Labour 1995: 34). However, authors such as England (1989: 228) point to the existence of unexpressed discontent and of unredressed injustices. The lack of effective workplace representation means that there are few opportunities for ordinary employees to make their opinions known to their manager or employer, short of voicing them on an individual basis in person and, for cultural reasons as noted previously, Hong Kong workers are reluctant to voice their grievances, preferring instead to suffer in silence and perhaps even to quit.

In contrast to its abstentionism in terms of wage determination, the government in the colonial era adopted a strongly interventionist approach towards the protection of labour from employer exploitation. The administration introduced a steady flow of regulations to improve industrial safety and to provide a range of benefits for workers such as severance pay, compulsory rest days and paid holidays, together with compensation for injured workers and measures to protect women and young people (Turner *et al.* 1980: 11).[8] In terms of trade union organisation and activities the government, motivated by a perceived need to protect trade union members from political agitators or fraudsters, and the desire to obtain information on protest movements and industrial feelings (England and Rear 1981: 120–38) was again strongly in support of intervention, laying down requirements for trade union organisation and administration in the Trade Unions Ordinance (TUO) and for trade union demonstrations in the Public Order Ordinance (POO).

Turning to the Hong Kong trade unions themselves, these were at the time of the transition characterised both by relatively low density and small size, and by political fragmentation as the legacy of historical events in China. Table 1 demonstrates that trade union membership rose to over 400,000 in 1977, with a density peaking at 25 per cent in the previous year – a rise related to the labour unrest of the late 1960s, associated again with events in China. This was followed by a period of declining membership, due to the recession of the early 1980s and to the decline of sectors and firms where trade unions had traditionally been organised (Turner *et al.* 1991: 57). Indeed, for much of the 1980s, the growth in union membership barely kept pace with the growth in employment, and density stagnated at around 16 per cent. Only in the late 1980s did membership growth start to rise and density to increase, a trend which has been sustained into the late 1990s.

Until the 1970s, Hong Kong's trade union movement was dominated by two main federations: the traditionally pro-Beijing Federation of Trade Unions (FTU) and the pro-Taiwan Trades Union Council (TUC). The loss of membership from the late 1970s was particularly marked amongst FTU affiliates, reflecting the waning of the pro-Communist fervour of the earlier post-war era and poor morale amongst FTU cadres during the period of

Table 1.1 Union membership in Hong Kong

Year end	Number of unions	Membership	Density %
1973	283	295,735	21
1974	292	317,041	22
1975	302	361,458	24
1976	311	388,077	25
1977	313	404,325	24
1978	327	399,995	23
1979	340	399,392	21
1980	357	384,282	19
1981	366	345,156	16
1982	378	351,525	16
1983	382	352,306	16
1984	384	357,764	16
1985	391	367,560	16
1986	403	367,345	16
1987	415	381,685	16
1988	430	416,136	17
1989	439	437,939	18
1990	452	468,746	19
1991	469	486,961	20
1992	481	525,538	21
1993	491	543,800	21
1994	506	562,285	21
1995	522	591,181	21
1996	535	624,327	22
1997	538	647,908	22

Sources: *Report of the Commissioner for Labour*, and Registrar of Trade Unions *Annual Reports*, various years.

political infighting in the Chinese Communist Party (England 1989: 123–125). FTU membership has recovered in recent years, rising to over 200,000 by the late 1990s, due to a more proactive approach to recruitment and servicing of members, and possibly also to the FTU's close association with the new administration (Snape and Chan 1997). The TUC's declared membership has held up surprisingly well at around 30,000 despite some loss of membership in the mid-1980s, perhaps reflecting the impact of the Joint Declaration in 1984 on this pro-Taiwan organisation, and a sharp dip during 1988–9 due to temporary disaffiliations.

However, since the 1970s, the main growth in trade union membership has come from the development of trade unions affiliated to neither federation and this has been largely, but not exclusively, in the public and social services. Growing anxiety at the prospects for job security and career advancement, concern about salary differentials, and a wish to be involved in the decisions which affect their lives, have combined to lead to the growth of white-collar trade unionism (Leung 1992). Even amongst the blue-collar workforce, there has been some new organising and, from the late 1970s, the Christian Industrial Committee was active in promoting workers' rights and in helping organise trade unions. In 1990, several of these so-called 'independent' unions formed the Confederation of Trade Unions (CTU), which has been associated with the 'pro-democracy' parties in LegCo.

An enduring feature of Hong Kong trade unions throughout the post-war period has been their fragmentation (Turner *et al.* 1991). Thus, as unions developed in the civil and public services, large numbers of new unions were registered – the continually rising number of trade unions can be seen in Table 1.1. The mean union size has remained at around a thousand members throughout this period, with the bulk of unions having significantly fewer members. The small size of unions is to some extent a reflection of the historic political divisions between unions, with some companies having competing unions of different political persuasions. The relative ease with which small unions may register must also be a factor. In the civil service, it appears that some staff are members of the service-wide Chinese Civil Servants Association and also of a small grade or department-specific union. There must be some concern about the viability of the smaller unions, with many having just a few score members and being too small to employ full-time staff. However, the federations are arguably playing an increasing role in the provision of membership services, in organising, and even in the conduct of industrial disputes, thus compensating for the small size of many of their affiliates.

There is a link between the political fragmentation of Hong Kong trade unions, the lack of collective bargaining, and the Labour Department's assumption of the mantle of labour protection. This link is the Hong Kong trade unions' definition of their role. Indeed, the focus of the Turner team's two studies was the puzzling absence in Hong Kong of a trade union movement oriented towards the raising of labour's share of wealth, towards representing the less privileged sections of labour, and towards the achievement of social goals for the wider community (Turner *et al.* 1991: 99–101). They explained this absence by pointing to the particular characteristics of the two powerful concentrations of employee organisations, the white-collar trade unions organising workers in the government service and associated social services and the transport and communications trade unions affiliated to the FTU. Turner and his colleagues viewed the two groups, both of which enjoyed high pay and procedures for the regular determination of pay increases, as forming a 'labour aristocracy'. Neither of these prestigious groups possessed wider trade union aims. The trade unions organising the civil service and associated social service workers served their members well in material terms but their economic concerns were inward-looking and they displayed little enthusiasm to encourage the spread of trade unionism outside their vocational area. The second FTU-linked group adopted an approach of 'self-preservatory industrial quiescence' on account of its wish not to disrupt Hong Kong's economy and thus offend China, but also on account of the disarticulation of its links with China following the political upheavals of the 1970s.

With China's 'opening to the world' in the late 1970s, the FTU was encouraged to adopt a more public position in Hong Kong. However, instead of the FTU becoming a mass labour organisation agitating for greater trade union autonomy and for legal support for collective bargaining, it assumed a doubly ambassadorial position – as promoter and advocate of the future SAR's 'prosperity and stability' and of 'constructive dialogue' with employers as the means to that end (Turner *et al.* 1991: 101–2). Instead, the pro-democracy and civil liberty-oriented CTU appears to have assumed the change-maker role.

Since the Turner team's studies there has been a considerable body of published research on trade unions and industrial relations in Hong Kong. Stephen Chiu and David Levin have explored the lack of development in the 1990s of industrial democracy, despite the extension of political democracy in the 1990s. As did Turner and his colleagues before, they reject culturalist explanations and see the lack of trade union pressure as a key factor explaining the limited development of collective bargaining and employee participation (Chiu and Levin 1996). Ng Sek-Hong has analysed the nature of the employment relationship in a series of papers and has reviewed the impact of democratisation and of the 'China factor' on Hong Kong trade unions and industrial relations in the period to 1997 (see for example: Ng 1997). Snape and Chan (1997) examined the character of Hong Kong's unions, comparing the FTU's alleged industrial pacifism with the apparently more assertive CTU, and finding some evidence for such stereotypes. However, they also detected a more active approach to labour representation on the part of the FTU during the early 1990s, perhaps as a response to the growing popularity of the CTU as labour issues became increasingly politicised.

The three chapters in Part IV present the findings of some of the most recent studies on labour relations in Hong Kong. The first of these chapters reviews the provisions and administration of the legal framework for trade unions and the other two chapters are concerned with the representation of labour in Hong Kong: representation by trade unions in the second chapter and representation through joint consultation in the third chapter.

The Joint Declaration 1984 guaranteed that trade union law, as other law, would remain unchanged in Hong Kong for 50 years. In Chapter 14 Patricia Fosh, Anne Carver, Wilson Chow, Ng Sek-Hong and Harriet Samuels examine the odd mix in the legal framework for trade unions in the late 1990s of British *laissez-faire*, with few positive rights for trade unions and employees, and close paternalist supervision of trade union organisation and activities. However, the actual control exerted by a government over trade unions' organisation and activities depends not only on what powers are granted to the authorities by law, but also on what policy the authorities adopt in the administration of those powers. While Turner and his colleagues (1980: 107) in their study of Hong Kong in the mid-1970s regarded the legal constraints on trade unions as 'no longer significant', Fosh and her colleagues in the late 1990s are less certain. The latter analyse the extent to which the colonial government chose to use its powers to supervise trade unions from the introduction of TUO in 1948 to the time of the transition. They go on to assess the likelihood of changes in the pattern of enforcement after the transition on the basis of the findings of an interview survey of representatives of different interest groups in Hong Kong. The authors suggest that the extent to which the Chinese government will tolerate a critical trade union movement in Hong Kong depends on the continued success of the territory's economic performance.

Chapter 15 by Ed Snape and Andy Chan is perhaps the chapter in our book linked most closely to the concerns of the earlier studies by Turner and his colleagues. This chapter seeks to evaluate the role of Hong Kong trade unions during the late 1990s and to identify the key constraints faced by unions, in particular in the pursuit of their job-based or workplace-representative function. The chapter includes a considerable empirical contribution to the debate over appropriate trade union roles, presenting the results of a survey of trade union leaders on the provision of different kinds of services to their members, and an analysis of Labour Department files on industrial disputes in the first half of the 1990s. Snape and Chan reject the argument that Hong Kong trade unions are destined to be ineffective by virtue of the Hong Kong Chinese workers' culturally based avoidance of confrontation and the acceptance of authoritarian management. While they acknowledge the problem of member apathy and the presence of a 'free-rider' mentality towards union membership among non-members, they attribute many of the difficulties faced by trade unions to employer attitudes, government policy and the political context. They include here the important constraint imposed by the strategies of the trade unions themselves, repeating the earlier observations of Turner and his colleagues on the trade unions' general reluctance to press for workplace representation. However, Snape and Chan conclude that labour issues are still of concern to the electorate, as evidenced by the results of the 1998 LegCo elections, and whilst trade union moderation and responsibility may be necessary to retain public support, the trade unions' future may depend on their willingness to push for workplace representation more energetically than has been the case hitherto.

The weakness of trade unions at the workplace and their uncertain willingness and ability to participate in formal collective bargaining, together with an apparent general scepticism among employees of that process as a viable route to improvement, lead to a gap in workplace representation and a distinct lack of industrial democracy in Hong Kong. One of the two main recommendations that Turner and his colleagues made to the FCO after their 1970s investigation, and repeated in both of their major publications, was for the extension of joint consultation.[9] The Labour Department had pursued a policy of promoting joint consultation in Hong Kong, especially after the disturbances in 1967 linked to the Cultural Revolution, but the Turner team recommended that a legally encouraged workplace consultation system should be established at least in large and medium-sized enterprises. (Turner *et al.* 1980: 162–5, 1991: 108–11). Turner and his colleagues asserted that joint consultation would provide a substitute, but non-competitive, equivalent to a normal labour movement when the trade union organisation was inhibited from acting as one. They also felt joint consultation would fit with the Basic Law which gives a right to strike but not a right to bargain collectively. This leaves it uncertain how disputes are to be settled. Since most workplace disputes involve small numbers of workers at particular enterprises, a workplace system of representation would clearly provide an important means of conciliation in such disputes. For Turner and his colleagues, Hong Kong's ultimate economic success and political acceptance depended, *inter alia*, on a reasonable balance between employers and labour, and the direct representation of the latter in the determination of economic and social policy.

In Chapter 16, Andy Chan and Ed Snape examine the presence of joint consultation in Hong Kong and consider whether its practice is a genuine channel for employee representation or whether it is a managerial strategy of union exclusion. They demonstrate that joint consultation is wide spread in the public sector and, in the civil service, provides a basis for trade union involvement and relatively effective representation. They contrast this with the restriction of joint consultation in the private sector to a few large organisations in transport and the utilities, pointing out that even here joint consultation is essentially one element of an employee communications strategy, with trade union substitution or marginalisation figuring as an objective. They illustrate this use of joint consultation with a case study of a private sector company. The authors discuss the future for joint consultation schemes in Hong Kong, noting the possibly deleterious impact in the public utilities of changes in management policy designed to improve organisation efficiency and customer service.

Part IV concludes the book and our final chapter, Chapter 17, by Chris Leggett, places the research findings on Hong Kong management and labour in an East Asian context, making links with developments elsewhere in the region. Leggett examines the various frames of reference that have been used to explain the economic achievements and rapid industrialisation of the East Asian countries. He then goes on to consider the influences of regionalisation and globalisation on economic development. He identifies some of the critical characteristics of employment relations in Hong Kong's most important East Asian neighbours, discussing these in order of their stage of industrialisation. Leggett begins his discussion by highlighting the characteristics of employment relations in Japan, continues with those of the newly industrialised economies (NIEs) at the same stage of development as Hong Kong – Singapore, Taiwan and South Korea – and then turns to those of the third generation of industrialisers comprising Malaysia, Thailand, the PRC's Special Economic Zones, finishing with the fourth generation of industrialisers – Indonesia, Vietnam, the Philippines and the provinces of the PRC. This discussion picks up the contrasts and comparisons with Hong Kong, emphasising the diversity of the economies and employment relations of these East Asian countries which are linked to their differing political history, culture, technology and government policies and ideologies. There are some commonalities, of course, perhaps most notably in the transition to a higher skilled and better educated workforce in the more advanced economies in the region, and also in the tendency for democratisation and independent labour activism to go together in some countries at least. What also emerges from this analysis is that the development of the region offers both challenge and opportunity for Hong Kong. Challenge, for example, in that the availability of low-cost land and labour in the industrialising regions of the PRC contributes to deindustrialisation and job loss in Hong Kong, but opportunity in the scope for Hong Kong to develop as a services and logistics centre at the hub of a regional manufacturing system.

Notes

1 In this book authors use the term Hong Kong to refer both to Hong Kong when it was a British-governed territory and to Hong Kong as a Special Administrative Region of the People's Republic of China (PRC). The PRC is also referred to as China, the Mainland and the Chinese Mainland.
2 The unemployment rate reached 6 per cent in February 1999, a 25–year high, *South China Morning Post*, 16 March 1999.
3 The government also introduced a Disability Discrimination Bill which was enacted in August 1995 as the Disability Discrimination Ordinance (DDO).
4 Note that small businesses (those employing five or fewer employees) were exempted for three years from the duty not to discriminate.
5 Amendments to DDO were also included in this Ordinance.
6 'Family status' is defined in law as having responsibility for the care of an immediate family member. 'An immediate family member is a person who is related by blood, marriage, adoption or affinity.' (EOC 1998: 3)
7 The Comprehensive Social Security Assistance Scheme provides a safety net for those proven in need of financial assistance and the Social Security Allowance Scheme provides for the elderly and severely disabled.
8 Furthermore, Turner *et al.* 1980: 11 point out that such regulations are as scrupulously administered as lies within the Labour Department's power.
9 The other recommendation made by the Turner team was for a simple minimum wage fixed at a level sufficiently above the Public Assistance scales to cover the additional costs of going to work.

2 Political and legal parameters for the representation of labour in Hong Kong

Change and counter-change[1]

Wilson W. S. Chow and Patricia Fosh

Introduction

In the Joint Declaration of 1984, the British and Chinese governments agreed a set of 'basic policies' towards Hong Kong that the Chinese government would uphold. The basic policies guaranteed that, after the change of sovereignty on 1 July 1997, the existing social and economic system of Hong Kong and the people's lifestyle would remain unchanged and that rights and freedom would be ensured by the law of the Hong Kong Special Administrative Region (SAR). This is the 'one country, two systems' formula guaranteed to remain unchanged for fifty years (Basic Law Article 5 and Joint Declaration Article 3(12)). Serious discord soon arose between the British and Chinese governments over whether the Joint Declaration implied that Hong Kong law should remain unchanged from the date of the Joint Declaration or from the date of the transition.

In this chapter we shall examine two issues of relevance to labour representation in Hong Kong which were closely related to the growing rift between the British and Chinese governments. The first of these is the changes to the legislative process, particularly to the composition of the Legislative Council (LegCo), introduced by the government in the run-up to the transition, and the reversal of these changes introduced by the new SAR government. The second of these is the changes to the legal framework for trade unions introduced by the former government and the reversal of these changes by the latter.

The analysis presented here differs from other analyses that have been made of the political and legal changes in Hong Kong in that our focus is not on the impact of these changes on political parties such as the Democratic Party, nor on the constitutional and human rights impact of the changes to Ordinances such as the Public Order Ordinance (POO). Our focus is on the impact of these changes on those organisations representing labour. The labour movement in Hong Kong is split along ideological lines with some organisations closely aligned to the SAR government and some not. This means that the political and legal changes we shall discuss are both differently viewed by, and have different consequences for, trade union groups according to their relationship with the government in power. This analysis of these complex political and legal changes, and the impact of these changes on the representation of labour, sets the scene for the book's analysis of the on-going changes in Hong Kong's labour market, management practice and management–employee relations.

Change and counter-change in the legislative process

During the closing stages of the Sino-British negotiations over the future of Hong Kong, the British government made a belated attempt to install a more democratic constitution and greater safeguards for civil liberties before the Territory's sovereignty was transferred to China. According to Miners (1995: 23)

> The British government was well aware that the surrender of 5 million people into the hands of a communist state without their consent was completely arbitrary to the principles of self-government and self-determination which Britain had followed when granting independence to all other parts of her empire.

The complete absence of any moves towards elections and self-government in Hong Kong appeared to reflect a deference to China's wishes, although this has never been publicly stated (Miners 1995: 22–3).

In Hong Kong in the colonial era, the Governor was the representative of, and appointed by, the British sovereign; his delegated powers were circumscribed by the general limits set out in the Letters Patent, the Royal Instructions and Colonial Regulations, and by instructions from the Secretary of State for Foreign and Commonwealth Affairs (Miners 1995: 68). Miners (1995: 69) describes the Governor's powers as 'awesome': he was obliged in most cases to consult the Executive Council (ExCo) but was not obliged to act in accordance with its advice, he could suspend any ExCo member, he had the right to refuse assent to any legislation passed by LegCo, he could dissolve LegCo at any time and, until 1985, he controlled the appointments of LegCo members. ExCo was composed of the Commander of the British Forces, the Chief Secretary, the Attorney General and the Financial Secretary *ex officio*, and further officials (i.e. civil servants) and unofficial members (usually business and professional leaders) were appointed by the Crown, although in practice the Governor's recommendations were invariably accepted. No change was made to the powers of the Governor and few changes were made to the composition of ExCo in the run-up to the transition. However, significant changes were introduced to the composition of LegCo. These changes from 1985 onwards are summarised in Table 2.1. Prior to 1985, LegCo was composed of seventeen officials (including the Governor and the Attorney General, the Financial Secretary and the Chief Secretary *ex officio*) and thirty 'unofficial members' (again mostly business and professional leaders) appointed by the Governor.

Reform to LegCo began in 1985 with the introduction of twenty-four elected members, though these were not elected by universal suffrage. There was a heavy emphasis on functional constituencies, described by Miners (1995: 117) as a rarely used system of 'special representation for the richest and most privileged sectors of the community' (see Table 2.1). However, this process of democratisation was halted when China made it clear that in its opinion the British government had violated the Joint Declaration (Miners 1995: 115).

After the shock of Tiananmen Square in 1989 and the subsequent widespread protest by Hong Kong-belongers, the British government increased the speed of Hong Kong's progress towards more representative government. Most emphasis was laid on the granting of full British citizenship with right of abode to a substantial number of civil servants, and business and professional people. However, a Bill of Rights Ordinance (BORO) incorporating the provisions of the International Covenant on Civil and Political Rights (ICCPR) into Hong Kong law to ensure respect for civil liberties after the transition was introduced in 1991 and the administration promised to speed up the reforms to LegCo (Miners 1995: 27). The final version of the Basic Law (April 1990), which was to replace the British Letters Patent and Royal Instructions, provided that the 1997 LegCo (elected in 1995) would have twenty directly elected seats, thirty elected by functional constituencies and ten chosen by an election committee: all official and appointed members would be removed.

As soon as the decision of the Basic Law Drafting Committee was known, the Hong Kong government introduced nine geographical seats electing two members each by one vote per person for the 1991 LegCo; this increase was compensated for by the removal of the ten members elected by the District Boards, the removal of all officials except the three sitting *ex officio*, and a small reduction in the number of appointed members (see Table 2.1). As each geographical seat on average consisted of 200,000 voters, this represented a considerable enfranchisement of the people of Hong Kong (Miners 1995: 1170). There were also now twenty-one functional constituencies, including Labour which had two members.

With the government's belated democratisation, political parties began to form and to organise (Lee 1996: 272–86, Yeung 1997: 51–2). The United Democrats of Hong Kong (forerunner of the Democratic Party) was formed in 1989 and won twelve out of the eighteen directly elected seats in 1991. As a result, there was considerable criticism of the dual member constituencies as producing a 'coat-tail' effect with a popular Democratic Party candidate pulling his/her running mate to victory (Lo and Yu 1996: 99–100). Leading pro-China supporters responded and formed the Democratic Alliance for the Betterment of Hong Kong (DAB) and, in turn, business interests formed the Co-opt Resources Centre, the predecessor of the Liberal Party. In 1985, the grass-roots Association for Democracy and People's Livelihood (ADPL) was formed which came to challenge the more middle-class oriented Democrats.

Table 2.1 The composition of LegCo 1985–98

	1985–1988	1988–1991	1991–1995
Ex officio and Official Members	3 HK Govt. *ex officio* (Attorney-General, Financial Secretary & Chief Secretary) Additionally, the Governor served as President	3 HK Govt. *ex officio* (Attorney-General, Financial Secretary & Chief Secretary) Additionally, the Governor served as President	3 HK Govt. *ex officio* (Attorney-General, Financial Secretary & Chief Secretary) One of members elected to serve as Deputy President and generally presided as the Governor no longer attended regularly
	7 Official Members (appointed by the Governor)	7 Official Members (appointed by the Governor)	No Official Members
Unofficial Members	22 Unofficial members (appointed by Governor)	20 Unofficial members (appointed by Governor)	18 Unofficial members (appointed by Governor)
Elected by functional constituencies	12 Functional constituency members (elected, first past the post voting)	14 Functional constituency members (elected, first past the post voting)	21 Functional constituency members (elected, first past the post voting)
Elected by geographical constituencies	None	None	18 Geographical constituency members (elected, first past the post voting, dual constituencies)
Elected by Election Committee (electoral college)	12 elected by Election Committee[1]	12 elected by Election Committee[2]	None
Total seats	57	57	60

Notes
1 The Election Committee was elected by the District Boards, Urban Council and Regional Council.
2 As note 1.
3 These were elected by the District Boards.
4 These were elected by 800 permanent SAR residents representing four sectors: (1) industrial, commercial and finance; (2) the professions, labour, social services and religious; (3) members of Provisional LegCo, Hong Kong deputies to the NPC's Congress, representatives of the Chinese People's Political Consultative Conference; and (4) representatives of the district-based organisations.

1995–June 1997	July 1997–June 1998	July 1998–2000
None One of LegCo members elected as President	None One of LegCo members elected as President	None One of LegCo members elected as President
None	All members elected by 400-member Selection Committee appointed by the Preparatory Committee to represent 4 sectors in HK	None
30 Functional constituency members (elected, first past the post voting, increased franchise with corporate voting largely replaced by individual voting)	N/A	30 Functional constituency members (elected, mixture of preferential elimination voting system and first past the post voting, marked reduction in franchise with largely corporate voting)
20 Geographical constituency members (elected, first past the post voting, single constituencies)	N/A	20 Geographical constituency members (elected, List Voting system operating under the Largest Remainder Formula, 5 constituencies)
10 elected by Election Committee[3]	N/A	10 elected by Election Committee[4]
60	60	60

The relationship between democratisation and the representation of labour is highly complex. The earlier deep political division between the powerful pro-Beijing Federation of Trade Unions (FTU) and the pro-Taiwan Trade Union Council (TUC) was smoothed over to a significant extent in the 1980s with the FTU's adoption of a more public role and the significant increase in the strength and public profile of the independent trade unions (Levin and Chiu 1993: 208–12). However, the emergence of a powerful pressure group both for workers' rights and for greater democracy and civil liberties, the Confederation of Trade Unions (CTU), challenged the dominance of the FTU and became its chief rival as the TUC's support faded (Yeung 1997: 51–2). The CTU leaders initially were supporters of the Democratic Party, but their greater emphasis on the enhancement of workers' rights and more radical view of democratisation caused friction with the Democratic Party and led to the establishment of The Frontier at the end of 1996, a group consisting of CTU leaders and radical independents such as Emily Lau. The FTU allied itself closely with the pro-China DAB and opposed CTU-sponsored legislation to promote greater trade union autonomy and legal support for collective bargaining (see p. 37 below).

The appointment of a heavyweight British politician, Chris Patten, as Governor in 1992 signalled a last-minute reversal in Britain's policy of appeasing China at the expense of Hong Kong in the run-up to the transition (Miners 1995: 29), and considerable momentum was added to Hong Kong's late progress towards a greater representation of its people. Patten's proposals for the 1995 elections were, while perhaps technically consistent with the Basic Law and the Joint Declaration, certainly in breach of their spirit (Miners 1995: 128a). He eschewed the previous practice of secret consultation and negotiations with China and informed the PRC government of his proposals only a week before they were made public. The PRC government bitterly denounced Patten's action. The Chinese and British governments held talks on electoral arrangements between April and October 1993 but no agreement was reached, and the Chinese government broke off the talks when Patten included his proposals in his first address to LegCo. The Electoral Provisions (Miscellaneous Amendments) (No. 2) Ordinance was subsequently passed in February 1994.

Patten's reforms increased both democracy and grass-roots representation in Hong Kong, much more significantly so than did the 1991 reforms. The ten members returned by the Election Committee were elected by the members of the eighteen District Boards, whereas previously Election Committee had been composed of District Boards, Urban Council and Regional Council members, thus refocusing the election on grass-roots issues. The thirty functional constituency members were elected by individuals, whereas previously a number of these had been elected by organisations of some kind (e.g. companies, trade unions), thus increasing the number of registered functional constituency electors to over one million

(Louie 1996: 52). The twenty geographical constituency members (with 2.57 million registered voters) were returned by single-seat constituencies in which each elector had one vote and the successful candidate was the person 'first past the post' (See Table 2.1).

Another significant change was that the Governor no longer held the post of President of LegCo. The LegCo President was now elected from amongst the Legislative Councillors: this had a major impact in time on the ability of LegCo members to introduce Private Bills. The only significant change to ExCo was that Governor Patten severed the link between LegCo and ExCo, making it a policy that membership of the two Councils did not overlap: this diminished the authority and importance of ExCo (Miners 1995: 82c; Lo 1996: 5–6).

The 1995 election was keenly fought, with a record number of both candidates and turnout. China's opposition did not decrease the competitiveness of the elections and, in fact, pro-China supporters actively took part (Louie 1996: 54). During these elections, Hong Kong's political parties achieved a far greater visibility than hitherto (Yeung 1997: 49). After these elections, the balance of political power within LegCo shifted markedly: both the pro-democracy and pro-Beijing groups increased their representation at the expense of independents and business leaders (Lo 1996: 2; Louie 1996: 578; Yeung 1997: 59). The Democratic Party won nineteen seats (compared to fourteen in 1991), including twelve geographical constituencies, while the grass-roots 'fighting-while-talking' ADPL won four. The 'liberal pro-China' DAB/FTU grouping won seven seats and the more recently formed ultra pro-China Hong Kong Progressive Alliance (HKPA) won two seats. In contrast, Liberal Party members were reduced from fifteen to ten.

There was a significant increase in members with a trade union background in 1995 LegCo. Whereas the 1991 LegCo had only one member with a trade union background (a FTU leader), the 1995 LegCo had nine such members and a further two members had strong labour connections. However, these trade union members were split between the pro-democracy and pro-China camps: there were three from the FTU and four from the CTU, together with one from the FLU (a trade union federation affiliated to the CTU but with more moderate concerns) and one from an independent trade union.

In a decision in 1990, the National People's Congress (NPC) of China had made provision for a Preparatory Committee which was to be charged with responsibility for preparing the establishment of the SAR and to prescribe the specific method for forming the first government (Lo 1996: 5). By the same decision the new Chief Executive was to be selected by a 400-member Selection Committee while the members of the last LegCo in the colonial era would become the members of the first LegCo of the SAR – the so-called 'through train'. However, in retaliation for Patten's electoral reforms, the Standing Committee of the NPC decided in August 1994 that the 1995 elected LegCo would come to an end with the transition: the 'through train' was to be derailed. The Preliminary Working Committee, the precursor to the Preparatory Committee, proposed that a provisional LegCo should be set up in order to fill the 'legal vacuum' on 1 July 1997. The Preparatory Committee, which was appointed by the NPC and included fifty-six Mainland Chinese members (out of 150 members), was established in December 1995, and in March 1996 it endorsed the establishment of a Provisional LegCo, which was to operate until the first SAR LegCo elections. Its members were to be elected by a Selection Committee.

This Selection Committee, which was established by the Preparatory Committee in November 1996, consisted of 400 members who had all been appointed by the Preparatory Committee to represent four sectors in Hong Kong including that of labour (Cheung 1997: 2). The members of the Selection Committee were overwhelmingly pro-China with a heavy representation of business interests. The DAB got forty-two seats and the lesser-known HKPA forty-seven; sixteen members were representatives of the FTU (Cheng 1997: xliv). The Selection Committee elected the sixty members of the Provisional LegCo out of 6,000 applicants on 21 December 1996. This election by 400 people contrasts sharply with the election by a much wider franchise in the 1995 LegCo elections. Cheung (1997: 2) describes this as 'a major retrogression in the democratic development of Hong Kong'. Unsurprisingly, there was strong representation of pro-China groups in the Provisional LegCo: the HKPA won six seats, the DAB/FTU grouping got eleven seats, and the Liberal Democratic Alliance got three seats. The Liberal Party retained the ten seats that they had in the 1995 LegCo and the middle-of-the-road ADPL won four. In terms of labour representation, this was confined to pro-China groups: out of the DAB/FTU grouping, four were FTU officials and one was an FLU official. The Provisional LegCo met across the border in Shenzhen, and considered and 'passed' Bills, which were intended to become law as from midnight of 1 July 1997.

The first Chief Executive, Tung Chee-hwa, was elected by the Selection Committee with 80 per cent of the vote on 14 December 1996. While this was the first time the people of Hong Kong had been consulted on the appointment of the chief official, the Democratic Party strongly criticised it as a 'small-circle election' (Yeung 1997: 55). The Chief Executive's powers under the Basic Law are similar to those of the Governor, though a little more trammelled, particularly as concerns dissolving LegCo (Miners 1995: 81). ExCo remains largely unchanged. Cheung (1997: 9) suggested that Tung would discuss his choice of ExCo members with Beijing.

There was strong opposition to the setting up of Provisional LegCo, which had not been provided for in the Basic Law, with Patten arguing for non-cooperation (Cheng 1997: xxxix). The Bar Association of Hong Kong contested the Provisional LegCo's legality and constitutionality (Cheung 1997: 2–3).[2] The Chinese government and its supporters counter-argued that the Preparatory Committee had the power to set up the Provisional LegCo through the Preparatory Committee's mandate to be 'responsible for preparing the establishment of the Region' (Cheung 1997: 2). In terms of public opinion, a survey in June 1996 showed that 56 per cent of respondents had no confidence in the Preparatory Committee.[3]

In the first LegCo of the SAR, there are twenty directly elected members, thirty functional constituency members and ten members elected by an election committee – see Table 2.1. The election procedures are varied and complex,[4] but overall there is a clear reduction in the enfranchisement of the people of Hong Kong compared to the 1995–97 period. Further, the influence of those Hong Kong-belongers who have opted for the safety of a foreign passport was reduced: SAR permanent residents who are not of Chinese nationality, or who have the right of abode in foreign countries, may not exceed 20 per cent of LegCo members.[5]

The twenty directly elected members were returned not as previously by single votes for single constituencies, but from five geographical constituencies using a form of proportional representation – the List Voting system operated under the Largest Remainder Formula.[6] Under this system candidates contest the election in the form of lists and the elector votes by choosing one of the lists of candidates. Each list may consist of any number of candidates up to the number of seats in the relevant constituency. The Largest Remainder Formula favours the relatively weaker groups since the allocation of remaining seats on the basis of the remaining votes can lead to significant differences in the number of votes gained per seat: the lists with the third or fourth largest number of votes can win seats with a lower number of average votes won per seat.[7]

The electorate of the functional constituency members was considerably reduced – returning to these constituencies their élitist character. In a number of constituencies voting by all organisation members was replaced by corporate voting and, in consequence, the number of voters in the functional constituencies was reduced dramatically, from 2.7 million in the LegCo 1995 elections to just over 120,000 in 1998 – the number of voters in the Labour constituency was reduced to 361 compared to 2,001 in 1995. The voting system adopted for the Urban Council, Regional Council, Hueng Yee Kuk,[8] Agriculture and Fisheries, Insurance, and Transport functional constituencies was the preferential elimination system, for the labour constituency (three seats) it was 'first past the post' with each elector casting three votes and, for the remaining constituencies,[9] it was 'first past the post'.

The election method adopted for the members returned by the Election Committee again reduces of the influence of the ordinary Hong Kong-belonger: Patten intended the Election Committee to represent mass interests while China conceived of it as an élitist body representing the interests of the business community.[10] In place of election by the membership of the District Boards, (who in turn were elected by those living in the district), election was by a body composed of 800 permanent SAR residents representing four sectors. Voting for the Election Committee by the different sectors was by 'first past the post' with the elector having the same number of votes as there are seats in that sector. Voting for the ten LegCo members was by block voting and the first ten 'past the post' were elected.

The elections for the first LegCo of the SAR were held in May 1998. Despite worry about the comprehension and enthusiasm of the Hong Kong electorate (who were not encouraged to increase their understanding[11]) the turnout of the May elections was higher than expected: 53 per cent of voters turned out in the geographical constituencies (compared to 36 per cent in 1995) and 64 per cent in the functional constituencies (compared to 40 per cent in 1995). Commentators had argued that the new voting system would have a negative impact on the fortunes of the Democratic Party, which had been predicted to win the overwhelming majority of the geographical constituencies if the 1995 single seat, single vote method had been adopted.[12] In the event, the Democratic Party won thirteen seats (nine geographical constituencies and four functional) demonstrating the continuing public support for civil liberties, law reform and welfare issues. There were nine LegCo members elected with a trade union background evenly split between, on the one hand, the pro-China FTU (five) and, on the other, the CTU and the Professional Teachers' Association (PTA),[13] (four). The FTU won all of the three Labour functional constituency seats; the unsuccessful candidates were a veteran TUC official and an official from a Catholic workers' trade union.[14] FTU officers also won two geographical constituencies. Additionally, a FTU/DAB leader Tam Yiu-chung was appointed to ExCo. He answered criticisms on 'selling out' his working-class principles by sitting on ExCo by emphasising that his presence gave the ordinary person a voice in Tung Chee-hwa's cabinet that would not otherwise be heard.[15]

Both the CTU LegCo victories were in geographical seats. The two members belonging to the PTA won Education seats. A further LegCo member (winner of a geographical seat) was closely allied to the CTU though not himself a trade union activist. A TUC leader standing for an Election Committee Seat lost. Labour issues that were vigorously debated during the electoral campaign were the FTU's lack of support for the introduction of the right to collective bargaining[16] (see p. 37 below), unemployment, and aid to the jobless.[17]

The 1998 LegCo will hold office until 2000. According to the Basic Law, the next LegCo will comprise twenty-four geographically elected members, thirty elected by functional constituencies, and six by the Election Committee.[18] In the LegCo elections after that, there will be thirty members elected on a geographical basis and thirty elected by functional constituencies (no members would be elected by an election committee). Although the intention is that all the LegCo members will be directly elected,[19] the functional constituencies, criticised as 'small-circle elections'[20] and as favouring the business élite at the expense of the grass-roots, will continue for the first decade of the SAR.

Changes in the legal framework for trade unions

The framework in the colonial era

The process of change and counter-change in the composition of LegCo was repeated in the control of trade union organisation and activities, and was again related to the disagreement between the governments of Britain and China over the date from which Hong Kong law should remain unchanged. Trade union organisation and activities in the colonial era were controlled by four Ordinances, the most important of which was the Trade Unions Ordinance (TUO) under which trade unions were required to register with the Registrar of Trade Unions (RTU), who had considerable powers to regulate trade union rules and account-keeping, and to seek the Governor's permission for affiliation with organisations outside Hong Kong. The Societies Ordinance (SO) was a significant source of control over trade unions, since trade union federations whose component unions were drawn from different trades, industries and occupations were not allowed to register under TUO but instead were obliged to register as societies under SO. Controls on their finances and organisation were less stringent under SO but such trade union federations had no immunity from civil suits in trade disputes and registration was with the Societies Officer who was also the Commissioner of Police. The Public Order Ordinance (POO) was also a means of administrative control of trade union activities. Trade unions wishing to hold public activities were subject to its provisions: in particular they had to notify the Commissioner of Police of their intentions to hold public meetings and public processions. POO also gave considerable powers of control of public order to the police. Breaches of the provisions of these three Ordinances were criminal offences, punishable by fines and periods of imprisonment. The last Ordinance giving the government significant control over trade unions was the Labour Relations Ordinance (LRO), which gave the Governor in Council power to order cooling-off periods in trade disputes under certain conditions where the well-being of Hong Kong was concerned.

Amending SO and POO

BORO, introduced in 1991, stated that all pre-existing legislation in Hong Kong that did not admit of a construction consistent with this Ordinance was repealed (s.3(2)). As certain of the provisions of SO and POO did not permit this construction, the government had introduced amendments to SO in 1992, significantly reducing the administrative control of societies in Hong Kong, including the major trade union federations, and to POO in 1995 significantly freeing organisations from police control of public meetings and public processions, including trade union marches and demonstrations.[21] The latter amendments included replacing the requirement for organisations to obtain a licence for public processions from the Commissioner of Police with the requirement merely to notify him.

On 1 July 1997, the SAR government amended SO and POO on the grounds that since the Basic Law was of paramount constitutional importance after the transition, those sections of BORO establishing its overriding status required repealing and, consequently, those amendments introduced to SO and POO as a consequence of the BORO's introduction must be repealed (Chief Executive's Office 1997).

In terms of SO, the SAR has increased government supervision of societies, requiring registration with the Societies Officer rather than notifying him. The Societies Officer has power to refuse to register a society if he reasonably believes that this is necessary in the interests of national security or public safety, public order or the protection of the rights and freedoms of others, or if the society is a political body and has a connection with a foreign organisation or a political organisation of Taiwan (national security being defined as the safeguarding of the territorial integrity and the independence of China). This amendment has implications for two of the major trade union federations: the CTU could lose its registration for criticising China's policies such as that towards Tibet, and the TUC for its links with Taiwan.

In terms of POO, the SAR added the requirement that trade unions must notify the Commissioner of Police of a public procession and obtain a letter of 'no objection' for the public procession from the Commissioner of Police. Again the Commissioner of Police can objects on grounds of national security, protection of the rights and freedoms of others and association with foreign organisations. All the major trade union federations intending to organise public action are affected by this amendment. Further, an increase in the powers of the Police Commissioner to cancel public processions where short notice has been given, up until the start of the procession (rather than only up until 24 hours before as previously) has decreased trade unions' ability to take protest action at short notice in disputes with their employers.

Collective bargaining and amending TUO and EO

While the government was active in the colonial era in ameliorating the restrictive and often harsh provisions in SO and POO as part of its drive to democratise Hong Kong in the run-up to the transition, it showed little interest in introducing changes to TUO despite the inclusion in ICCPR of the right to form and join trade unions (Art. 18). The administration appeared determined to retain its powers to supervise trade union activities and to oppose the introduction of any legal support for collective bargaining despite the significant increase in trade unions' strength, representativeness and role in public life (Levin and Chiu 1993). All the government did was to introduce protection for trade union officers and employees from civil action by employers in trade disputes (new s.43A) with the passage of the Trade Union (Amendment) Ordinance (TU(A)O) on 26 June 1997. While this rectified a long-standing deficiency in Hong Kong trade union law, its practical impact was limited.[22] This amending Ordinance was not repealed by the Provisional LegCo. However, TUO was significantly amended and other important pieces of legislation increasing trade union rights were passed in this period by means of Private Members' Bills introduced by a pro-labour caucus that came together in the 1995 LegCo.[23] This caucus was composed of radical trade union leaders and those with a strong interest in improving people's welfare, particularly that of the working class, but did not include those with FTU and FLU connections (Louie 1996: 62; Ngo and Lau 1996: 2734). There were no changes in the cooling-off provisions of LRO – indeed these (introduced by the administration in 1975) have never been used.

The Employee's Rights to Representation, Consultation and Collective Bargaining Ordinance (ERRCCBO), passed by LegCo on 20 June 1997, was perhaps the most far-reaching of the changes introduced by the pro-labour caucus in the last LegCo of the colonial era. Employees were given rights to representation and consultation through a trade union representative and to be covered by a collective agreement negotiated by a 'representative' trade union (or group of trade unions) (ss.4,7,14,15).[24] Controversially, a trade union (group of trade unions) requesting employer recognition had to satisfy two conditions: its membership must constitute more than 15 per cent of the employees employed by the employer in an undertaking and it must represent more than 50 per cent of these employees (ss.12, 15). Further provisions to help establish collective bargaining practices were added, including the requirement that the employer negotiate in good faith (s.15(5)), the stipulation that collective agreements were legally binding (s.18), and the imposition on employers of a duty to allow trade union representatives paid time-off for representation, consultation and collective bargaining activities (s.23).

There was considerable opposition to ERRCCBO from the Hong Kong Labour Department, employers and the FTU and FLU, mainly on the grounds that collective bargaining was not a tradition in Hong Kong where employers and labour enjoyed a 'harmonious relationship' compared to countries in the West, and that the predominance of small businesses would make such provisions unwieldy. After the transition, this Ordinance was first frozen by Provisional LegCo on 17 July 1997 and then repealed by s.13 of the Employment and Labour Relations (Miscellaneous Amendments) Ordinance (E&LR(MA)O) on 30 October 1997.

The Trade Unions (Amendment) (No. 2) Ordinance (TU(A)(No.2)O), passed by LegCo on 29 June 1997, significantly reduced the government's supervisory powers over trade unions and gave them much-needed opportunities to develop greater solidarity, both amongst themselves and with trade union organisations overseas. After the transition, TU(A)(No.2)) was frozen by Provisional LegCo on 17 July 1997. On 30 October 1997, E&LR(MA)O repealed a number of the new provisions; however, some of the new provisions were allowed to remain and E&LR(MA)O introduced some additional measures.

The restrictions on trade union autonomy in TUO removed by the last LegCo in the colonial era but replaced by Provisional LegCo were concerned first with administrative control of the ways in which trade unions spent their funds. Thus the requirement for trade unions to gain the Governor's approval to expend their funds on contributions to organisations outside Hong Kong, and on any purpose not specifically referred to in the list of approved purposes, again became part of TUO (s.33(1)); thus trade unions did not enjoy the significant relaxation of the financial control exerted by the administration over them as envisaged by the proponents of trade union law reform. The second restriction which was removed and replaced was concerned with the eligibility of individuals to be trade union officers. Thus the requirement for trade unions to obtain the consent of the RTU to appoint officers who were not (or had not been) engaged or employed in a trade, industry or occupation with which the trade union was directly concerned also remained part of TUO (s.17(2)) with the trade unions losing the opportunity to recruit career officers. The third restriction removed by the last LegCo in the colonial era was not simply replaced by Provisional LegCo – the latter substituted a provision which allowed trade unions a modicum of greater freedom in establishing links overseas. Thus, while trade unions were initially relieved from the necessity in s.45 to obtain the Governor's consent before affiliating with organisations outside Hong Kong, a new provision was subsequently introduced which allowed trade unions to affiliate with 'relevant professional organisations' as they pleased, but required them to obtain the Governor's permission to affiliate with other organisations, including political organisations.[25]

Of the restrictions on trade union activities removed by the last LegCo of the colonial era but not replaced by E&LR(MA)O, two were of a minor nature and consisted of reducing the minimum age requirement for a trade union officer from 21 to 18 years (TUO s.17(5)) and the majority needed in a ballot for changing a trade union's name from two-thirds of the trade union's voting members to the majority of members present at a general meeting (s.23(1)).

The permanent removal of the third restriction was more significant. Trade unions were freed from the requirement in s.55 that registered trade union federations must consist of component trade unions whose members were engaged or employed in the same trade, industry or occupation and in s.57 that federation officers must have been (or had been) engaged or employed in the same trade, industry or occupation. However, the SAR government would have been under considerable pressure from the ILO if it had replaced this restriction.

The additional measure introduced into TUO by Provisional LegCo was a move towards a more open system for the administration of trade unions. Thus the RTU was now required to specify in writing his reasons for refusing to register a trade union's rules on registration, or for refusing amendments of such rules after registration (s.18A). An appeal procedure against such refusals to the Court of First Instance was also introduced (s.18A(3)). This move was laudatory, though limited in practice since refusals by the RTU to register or amend trade union rules were rare.[26]

The Employment (Amendment) (No. 4) Ordinance (EO(A)(No.4)O), passed on 29 June 1997, introduced the right for an employee to take action if an employer discriminated against him/her on trade union grounds: the burden of proof was on the employer and the Labour Tribunal could order the reinstatement of a dismissed employee (ss.21D to 21J).[27] EO(A)(No.4)O was frozen by the Provisional LegCo and repealed by E&LR(MA)O. The loss of this valuable protection against victimisation for trade union activists was partly mitigated by the earlier Labour Department-sponsored provision of a right to redress for unfair dismissal (Employment (Amendment) (No. 3) Ordinance (E(A)(No. 3)O)) which was passed on 26 June 1997 but not repealed by the Provisional LegCo.[28]

There have been some recent developments in this now tangled area of labour law in Hong Kong. After the approval by LegCo of E&LR(MA)O, the CTU filed a complaint to the ILO's Committee on Freedom of Association on the grounds that the removal of the right of trade unions to engage employers in collective bargaining, the banning of the use of trade union funds for political purposes and the restrictions on the appointment of trade union officers were a breach of Conventions 87 and 98. The Committee on Freedom of Association considered this in November 1998 and recommended that the Hong Kong government remove the requirement that trade union officers are actually employed in the trade, industry or occupation of the trade union concerned, the requirement that the Chief Executive's approval is obtained for the use of trade union funds in certain instances and the blanket prohibition on the use of funds for political purposes.[29] The Committee also requested the Hong Kong government to review the provisions for employee protection against anti-trade union discrimination and the possibility of a right in such cases for reinstatement not conditional on prior consent of both employer and employee concerned. Finally, the Committee requested the Hong Kong government to give serious consideration in the near future to the laying down of objective procedures for determining the representative status of trade unions for collective bargaining purposes which respect freedom of association principles.

In October 1998, Lee Cheuk-yan, Chief Executive of the CTU and a member of the first SAR LegCo, submitted three Bills to LegCo which, if passed, would reinstate the collective bargaining provisions of the repealed ERRCCBO, the anti-trade union discrimination provisions of the repealed EO(A)(No.4)O, and those amendments removing the restrictions on trade unions spending their funds on political purposes originally contained in TU(A)(No.2)O.[30] The SAR government initially delayed its response on the ground that it needed further time for consideration following the report from the Committee on Freedom of Association. At the time of writing, the government appears set on ruling that the three Bills cannot be submitted as Private Members' Bills on the grounds that they involve government operation and would increase government spending.[31] The government is able to do so since, although according to Art. 74 of the Basic Law LegCo members retain their pre-transition right to submit Bills, such Bills must not relate to public expenditure, political structure or government operation, and the written consent of the Chief Executive is required before Bills relating to any government policies are introduced.

Conclusion: the future for the representation of labour

Democracy, in terms of the representation of the person in the street, has declined in Hong Kong since 1995 with the derailment of the 'through train' for LegCo, with the élite-style elections for the Provisional LegCo, and with the complex List Voting system for the geographical constituencies and the reduced franchise for the functional constituencies for the first SAR LegCo. In terms of controls on trade union organisation, activities, and opportunities to develop, the SAR's amending of SO has increased government control of the activities of cross-trade union federations,[32] while its amending of POO has resulted in tighter controls on trade unions' ability to demonstrate in public. With the repeal of ERRCCBO Hong Kong returns to voluntarism in collective bargaining. Finally, the repeal of most of the last-minute amelioration of government controls in TUO means that the SAR government possesses considerable powers to monitor and supervise trade union activities.

However, assessing the significance of post-transition changes in the representation of labour in Hong Kong is not so simple, on account of the political divisions within the Hong Kong trade union movement. The trade unions had developed more of a common purpose in the 1980s but, with the growing rift in the 1990s between the British and Chinese governments over the transition arrangements, they moved farther apart and now appear to have different future prospects. The FTU appears to be in the ascendancy in the new SAR enjoying a close relationship with the new government: its members were well represented on the Selection Committee, in Provisional LegCo and now in the first LegCo of the SAR. On the other hand, the vibrant and radical CTU is not so favoured and seems certain to endure many clashes: its members were excluded from the Selection Committee and Provisional LegCo but the significant victories of CTU members in the elections for the first SAR LegCo demonstrate its continuing popular support. The two groups also differ in their opinions on the significance of the post-transition changes in the trade unions' legal framework. Drawing here on some in-depth interviews we conducted in January 1998 with FTU and CTU representatives, we found that the FTU representatives considered that the legal changes were minor, representing the proper return of trade union law to the state it was in at the time of the Joint Declaration in 1984. In contrast, the CTU representatives interpreted the reinstatement of most of the repealed restrictions on trade unions in TUO as significant limitations on trade union autonomy, the return of SO and POO to their pre-1990s forms as a significant reduction of trade unions' ability to express their views, and the repeal of ERRCCBO as the removal of a valuable mechanism which trade unions could have utilised to overcome employer indifference and hostility and to increase the limited collective bargaining base. The greater latitude in the amended TUO for trade unions to federate and the greater demands now placed on the RTU for transparency were seen as 'window-dressing for the ILO'.

Notes

1 The authors would like to thank the British Academy and Cathay Pacific for funding this project.
2 The legality of Provisional LegCo was challenged in two cases, one was heard before the transition and the other straddled it, but neither of these succeeded (*Ng King Luen* v. *Rita Fan*, AL No. 39 of 1997 and *HKSAR* v. *Ma Wai Kwan, David and others*, Reservation of Question of Law No. 1 of 1997).
3 Twenty-seven per cent had 'extremely low' confidence in the Preparatory Committee and a further 12 per cent had 'low' confidence (*South China Morning Post* survey quoted in Cheng (1997: xlii)).
4 These are set out in the Legislative Council Ordinance (Ordinance No. 134 of 1997).
5 Foreign nationals may only stand in twelve functional constituencies – these consist of the professional-oriented constituencies such as finance.
6 The total number of votes cast is divided by the total number of seats in the constituency: this is the Hare quota. Each list receives one seat for every Hare quota of votes received. Any remaining votes are awarded to the lists with the largest number of remaining votes.
7 Interview with Lo Hiu-hing, Department of Politics and Public Administration, University of Hong Kong.
8 Rural associations.
9 These are Education, Legal, Accountancy, Medical, Health Services, Engineering, Architectural, Surveying and Planning, Social Welfare, Real Estate and Construction, Tourism, Commercial (First), Commercial (Second), Industrial (First), Industrial (Second), Finance, Financial Services, Sports, Performing Arts, Culture and Publications, Import and Export, Textiles and Garments, Wholesale and Retail, and Technology.
10 *South China Morning Post* (SCMP), 17 April 1998.
11 See for example SCMP, 23, 25 and 28 April 1998. See also the comment by Mr Justice Woo Kwok-hing, the chairman of the Electoral Affairs Commission, that voters will 'cause trouble for themselves' if they attempt to master the LegCo electorial system (SCMP, International Edition, week beginning 21 February 1998).
12 See for example SCMP, International Edition, week beginning 1 November 1997.
13 The PTA is affiliated to the CTU.
14 The Catholic Institution Staff Association (non-affiliated).
15 SCMP, 31 December 1998. See also criticism of Tam by the Catholic Monitoring Group on LegCo members' performance (SCMP, 8 February 1999).

16 See SCMP, 20, 29 and 30 April 1998.

17 SCMP, 25 April 1998.

18 The Executive Council has opted for minimal changes to the election system in 2000 (SCMP, 2 December 1998).

19 The Basic Law provides that all LegCo members will be returned by universal suffrage but stops short of saying when.

20 SCMP, 21 April 1998.

21 The government had been also under considerable international pressure to ameliorate the wide police powers in POO (Human Rights Committee, Summary Record of the 857th Meeting, CCPR/C/SR 857 para. 63, quoted in Chan and Lau 1990: 171).

22 TU(A)O usefulness was limited given the very low strike rate in Hong Kong, the tendency towards informally organised strikes and the fact that most trade union federations are not registered as trade unions.

23 A LegCo member could move a Private Bill but, if it involved public expenditure, the Governor's consent was required before it could be introduced into LegCo. However, a government ruling that a Private Member's Bill had public expenditure implications could be overruled by the LegCo President. Non-official LegCo members rarely exercised their power to introduce Private Bills before the introduction of direct elections in 1991. Between 1991 and 1995 Private Members' Bills proliferated but the government attempted to block many of them on the ground that they would involve public expenditure and hence need the Governor's consent (Lo 1996: 3–4). The first elected President of LegCo shared the government's conservative approach towards interpreting the public expenditure implications of Private Members' Bills but the following President took a much more liberal approach and overrode the government's interpretation a number of times.

24 An employer with less than twenty employees was excluded from the requirement to consult and one with less than fifty employees from the requirement to bargain collectively (s.3(3) and (4)).

25 'Relevant professional organisations' have the objectives of promoting the interests of persons engaged or employed in a trade, industry or occupation with which the trade union is directly concerned.

26 See the Annual Statistical Reports of the Registrar of Trade Unions.

27 Previously, while an employer discriminating against trade union members and activists committed an offence (s.21B), the individual employee had no right of action.

28 However, EO(A)(No.3)O only provides for reinstatement with both employer and employee consent.

29 ILO 311th Report of the Committee on Freedom of Association – Case No. 1942: Complaint against the Government of China/Hong Kong Special Administrative Region presented by the Hong Kong Confederation of Trade Unions (HKCTU), GB.273/6/1 273rd Session, Geneva 1998.

30 SCMP, 2 January 1999.

31 SCMP, 20 and 21 January and 2 March 1999.

32 We note that at the time of writing, December 1998, the major cross-trade union federations remain registered under SO, none so far has elected to register under TUO as the amended TUO allows.

3 The future shape of Hong Kong's economy

Why high-technology manufacturing will prove to be a myth

Howard Davies

Introduction

The future of work and management in Hong Kong depends upon the distribution of the workforce across sectors, the nature of employing organisations, and the postures they adopt in seeking profits. With policy-making now firmly in local hands, there has been considerably more active debate on those issues and on the role which should be played by government intervention. The purpose of this chapter is to examine the view that Hong Kong may, and should, become a 'world class industrial power' (Berger and Lester, 1997: xiii), competing through innovation in high-technology manufacturing. The argument put forward here can be summed up in three statements. First, Hong Kong has no need for a manufacturing sector within the boundaries of the city. Second, Hong Kong firms manufacturing in China and other low-cost locations have no need to reorient themselves towards a more 'high-tech' stance. Third, the Hong Kong environment is poorly suited to innovation, so that the territory's firms would be unable to make such a shift *en masse*, even if it were desirable.

This is not a pessimistic analysis. Hong Kong's people can look forward to well-paid work in the service sector as the territory continues to refocus on its traditional 'merchanting' capabilities, transforming low-value products in one location into higher-value products in another.

The story thus far: from entrepôt to service sector economy via manufacturing

For the first century of the colony's existence the economy was dominated by the trading sector and manufacturing was restricted to a few hundred small factories. By 1941, when war broke out with Japan, only about 90,000 workers were engaged in manufacturing, from a population of 1.6 million.

The territory which returned to British rule was a desperate place in which the options open to the population were highly restricted. The UN/US embargo prevented the return of the entrepôt trade. Agricultural development was prevented by the terrain. Mineral resources were negligible and manufacturing for the domestic market was restricted by its small size. The production of manufactures for export offered the only opportunity available.

Even within that narrow scope prospects were limited. Hong Kong firms could only compete on the basis of cost-leadership, secured through the management of low-cost labour. Geographical, cultural and linguistic distance from markets in the US and Europe made it too costly for manufacturers to identify the needs of consuming households directly, and the technical knowledge needed to translate those needs into product designs was not available. Hong Kong businessmen therefore relied on their customers to provide the product designs and marketing channels, while they themselves focused on procuring inputs, managing production and making sales.

The focus on labour-intensive sectors, and the separation between product design, production and marketing, were efficient responses to the pattern of resource prices and availabilities. As a result, 'low-tech' manufacturing provided the engine of growth for Hong Kong's economy from the 1950s until the early 1980s. At its peak, in 1981, manufacturing employment exceeded 900,000, spread across nearly 47,000 establishments.

Manufacturing began to decline as a source of employment in the early 1980s, following the decision of the Chinese Communist Party to open the mainland to foreign investment. Responding with vigour to the market signal that lower-cost labour was available across the border, Hong Kong's manufacturers transferred production into China, concentrating initially on Guangdong province and the Pearl River Delta in particular. According to Chinese statistics, by 1993 the country was host to more than 100,000 Hong Kong-invested enterprises. Guangdong alone provided the location for more than 40,000 of them, employing in the region of six million workers (MOFERT/MOFTEC 1994). 'Made by Hong Kong' (Berger and Lester 1997) superseded 'Made in Hong Kong' and the reallocation of Chinese labour from low-productivity agriculture into Hong Kong-managed light industry produced huge increases in the mainland's output and exports. These in turn increased demand for 'manufacturing and trade-related' services in Hong Kong, and the territory's pattern of employment shifted dramatically from manufacturing towards services.

As Table 3.1 shows, employment in manufacturing is now very significantly exceeded by that in manufacturing and trade-related services.

This process of de-industrialisation has been almost entirely positive in its impact on Hong Kong's people. National income has grown steadily to US$21,670 per capita at purchasing power parity in 1995, above that of the UK, Germany and Japan. Total employment has grown at least as fast as the population, so that the rate of unemployment has rarely exceeded 2.5 per cent, remaining below 5 per cent even in the 'crisis' conditions of Summer 1998. These figures mask high levels of inequality (Turner *et al*. 1980: 65–8, 1991: 14–17) and there has been persistent unemployment amongst ex-

Table 3.1 Persons engaged, by sector, 1982–97. Manufacturing and 'manufacturing and trade-related services' (MTRS)

Sector	1982	1987	1992	1994	1997
Manufacturing	847,194	867,947	565,137	423,015	288,887
MTRS	386,331	558,384	855,637	1,036,831	1,099,654
of which:					
Import/export	132,629	240,167	395,444	503,039	510,571
Transport, storage and communications	87,578	105,974	145,661	164,198	178,104
Finance, insurance, real estate and business services	166,124	212,243	314,532	369,594	410,979

Source: Hong Kong Government, *Annual Digest of Statistics*, various issues.

manufacturing workers who lack the skills to move into the service sector. Nevertheless, it is undeniable that Hong Kong has a high-performance economy which has served most of its citizens well.

The continuing allure of manufacturing and high technology

Despite the prosperity which has accompanied Hong Kong's de-industrialisation, a conventional wisdom has grown up to the effect that there is something amiss with the city's development. In particular it has become fashionable in academic and policy-making circles to express concern about the increasing dependence upon the service sector, and to call for government intervention in support of high-technology industrial development.

There is nothing new about this call for a higher level of technological sophistication. More than thirty years ago Espy (1965) and Leary (1965) warned that Hong Kong firms were paying insufficient attention to technology, and that the city's economy was vulnerable for that reason. At that time, the Hong Kong government was firmly wedded to the policy of 'positive non-interventionism'. It took no heed of the call for more technology, businessmen wisely ignored the advice proffered, and the economy prospered. By 1977, however, the policy environment had changed. Concern was expressed in official circles that the territory's ability to compete in export markets was being eroded by rising wages, the emergence of lower-cost locations and the impact of protectionist policies in major markets. Government became receptive to the call for technological upgrading and commissioned a study on the diversification of the economy. The resulting Diversification Report (Hong Kong Advisory Committee on Diversification 1979) marked the beginning of a shift away from the policy of 'positive non-interventionism' towards one of 'minimum intervention with maximum support' (Yeh and Ng 1994).

In the event, the concerns which led to the Diversification Report were rendered irrelevant by the opening of the Chinese Mainland, which provided a ready supply of cheap labour. Nevertheless, the arguments in favour of the high-tech vision have retained their currency and they have been pressed with vigour as the city has returned to Chinese rule. Those arguments may be presented as a set of four propositions, which are as follows:

1   Hong Kong 'needs' to have manufacturing within the borders of the SAR.
2   Hong Kong has fallen behind other 'dragon' economies in respect of technological development, and needs to 'catch up'.
3   Hong Kong's manufacturing sector will lose its ability to compete in world markets unless it implements a significant change in its competitive posture, away from cost leadership, flexibility and speed in low- and medium-technology market segments and towards differentiation and innovation in high technology segments.
4   Hong Kong meets the conditions which are required to achieve the shift in posture suggested in Proposition 3.

The argument put forward here is that each of these propositions is false. Hong Kong only needs manufacturing within its borders if the definition of 'manufacturing' is extended so far that it includes most of the service sector. Hong Kong has no need to emulate the technological development activities of its neighbours in the region. The city's manufacturers do not need to shift their competitive stance and they would be unable to do so if it were in fact required. Each of these apparently contrarian assertions may be considered in turn.

Does Hong Kong need to have manufacturing operations within its borders?

The proposition that Hong Kong needs manufacturing activity within the borders of the SAR is articulated by Kwong (1997) and in the collection of studies which make up the recent MIT Report (Berger and Lester 1997). Kwong (pp. 5–6) puts forward three arguments. The first is that services cannot be exported on a massive scale. The second is that even if some services are exportable they will not provide significant additional employment. Third, it is argued that the service sectors (and financial services in particular) do not exhibit sufficient growth in labour productivity to bring rising prosperity.

Every one of these claims is wrong, in principle and in Hong Kong fact. Services can be exported on a massive scale as Hong Kong firms earn foreign exchange through financing trade and investment, insuring goods and property overseas, and brokering trade, as well as hosting tourists. As Table 3.2 shows, Hong Kong enjoys a balance of payments surplus in services, while suffering a deficit in goods.

Table 3.2 Hong Kong's trade in goods and services ($HK billion, 1990 prices)

	1986	1989	1991	1993	1994	1996
Exports of goods	310.5	583.9	750.7	1,021.0	1,127.3	1,322.0
Imports of goods	319.2	579.0	767.8	1,057.5	1,206.0	1,430.9
Balance of trade in goods	−8.7	+4.9	−17.1	−36.5	−79.0	−108.9
Service exports	105.0	137.4	148.9	178.0	189.1	223.5
Service imports	55.8	78.2	97.6	113.3	121.9	133.1
Balance of trade in services	+49.2	+59.2	+51.3	+64.7	+67.2	+90.4

Source: Hong Kong Government, *Annual Digest of Statistics.*

While these figures demonstrate the service sector's ability to export its own output, they also represent a massive underestimate of the sector's contribution to the city's total overseas sales. As the 'manufacturing and trade-related' service industries provide indispensable inputs to the process of exporting manufactures, they are also responsible for a very significant, though unknown, proportion of the value of those exports and re-exports. The city can earn the foreign exchange it needs by servicing the manufacturing sector. It does not need to produce its own manufactures.

The service sectors are also capable of absorbing large amounts of labour, as has already been shown in Table 3.1, and those workers have been employed at higher levels of value-added per person than have obtained in manufacturing. Table 3.3 shows the available data.

Clearly, Hong Kong does not need manufacturing in order to export, to provide employment, or to secure high levels of productivity.

The MIT Report also asserts that manufacturing is needed in Hong Kong, but it approaches the issue in a rather different way. First it is noted that manufacturing and services have been converging (Berger and Lester 1997: 27–30). The service sector provides inputs to manufacturing and the value of manufactures depends increasingly on services which are embodied in the product, including design, customisation, and timely delivery. Many firms in the service industries are closely dependent upon manufacturing and

Table 3.3 Value-added per person engaged in major economic sectors, 1984 and 1995 ($HK,000)

Sector	1984	1995
Manufacturing	55	229
Wholesale/retail, import/export, restaurants, hotels	86	266
Financing	174	450
Business services	136	263
Storage	130	264
Communications	178	650
Transport	101	313

Source: Hong Kong Government, *Annual Digest of Statistics*, various issues.

could not survive without it. Indeed, as a Hong Kong Trade Development Council (1997) report confirms, many companies which were previously classified as manufacturing firms have been reclassified as service sector establishments. The implication of this convergence is that there is significant 'undermeasurement of the real scale and scope of manufacturing industry in Hong Kong' so that the employment and output figures underestimate the importance of manufacturing to the city's prosperity.

This is undoubtedly true. However, it has no bearing on the question of whether Hong Kong needs manufacturing, as conventionally defined, within the boundaries of the SAR. The important debate is not whether the city needs to have manufacturing in the broader sense suggested by the MIT Report. No sensible commentator would ever suggest otherwise, because manufacturing has, in effect, been redefined to include most of the service sector. The debate is about whether the city needs to have the material-cutting and stitching, metal-fabricating, plastic moulding and extrusion activities which once employed so many people and which have now moved to China. The evidence set out above on trade, employment and productivity shows that Hong Kong does not need to have those operations within its boundaries. Manufacturing is important to the city but it does not need to be located inside the SAR. The manufacturing activity which matters is that which takes place elsewhere.

Has Hong Kong fallen behind its neighbours in respect of technology, and does it need to catch up?

The second proposition put forward in support of the high-tech vision has two parts. The first is that Hong Kong has fallen behind other countries in the region, with respect to the resources devoted to technological development. The second is that there is a need to catch up.

There is no doubt about the validity of the first part of this proposition. If attention focuses on the inputs which are applied to technological development in Hong Kong, the immediate outputs of scientific endeavour, or the city's technological infrastructure, then Hong Kong is a 'low-tech' backwater in comparison to countries like Singapore, South Korea or Taiwan. Table 3.4 draws together some of the macro-level indicators.

However, these figures do not themselves demonstrate that there is a need to catch up. If the objective of the economy is to provide growth in the incomes of its residents, then Hong Kong has actually outperformed its more technophile neighbours in important respects (Davies 1996). A whole series of studies on East Asian growth, including those by Young (1994, 1995), Krugman (1994) the World Bank (1993), and the Hong Kong Monetary Authority (Hawkins 1994), reach the conclusion that the Hong Kong economy has delivered higher rates of growth in total factor productivity (TFP) than Singapore, Korea and Taiwan.

At first sight, there appears to be a contradiction between the evidence

Table 3.4 Technological indicators

	R&D as % of GDP 1994	Annual growth rate of scientific publications 1980–95	US-registered design and utility patents 1995	Patents registered per 100,000 residents 1992–3	'Technological infrastructure' indicator [a]
Singapore	1.18	82.85	61	n.a.	40
S.Korea	2.29	280.98	1,240	9.25	41
Taiwan	1.80	83.47	2,087	66.46	35
Hong Kong	0.10	40.41	248	0.20	21

Sources: Amsden 1997: 344–5; *World Competitiveness Yearbook*, 1995, 1996.
[a] An indicator constructed by the US National Science Foundation.

that Hong Kong is technologically backward and the finding that its economy has delivered higher rates of TFP growth than its more technophile neighbours. The complexities of econometric technique certainly provide room for debate over the details (Chen 1997). However, for the Hong Kong case, the central point is clear. The city's economy has delivered rapidly increasing productivity over a period in which activity has shifted dramatically towards the service sector, and when TFP in the manufacturing sector has actually been declining (Kwong 1997: 34). Those facts alone demonstrate that it is the move to the service sector which has been delivering the gains in productivity. Hong Kong's reallocation of resources away from low-productivity manufacturing towards the merchanting function has produced rates of productivity increase which have exceeded those achieved in nearby economies which trumpet their 'high-tech' aspirations and continue to focus on relatively inefficient manufacturing sectors.

The proposition that Hong Kong 'needs' to emulate its more technophile neighbours because it has 'fallen behind' them is false. What matters is not the resources or the publicity devoted to high technology, but the results achieved. Hong Kong has reason to be proud of its record in respect of productivity growth. There has been no falling behind.

Do Hong Kong firms producing in China need to change their strategy?

The third proposition put forward in support of the argument that Hong Kong 'needs' high-technology manufacturing is that the current 'Hong Kong Model' is not sustainable as a means of competing in world markets. The reasoning behind that view has a number of components. On the cost side, the MIT Report (Berger and Lester 1997: 51) points out that Hong Kong firms in China are very heavily concentrated in the neighbouring Guangdong province. In that province both wages and land prices have been rising, so that there is pressure on costs, making it more difficult to compete on the basis of cost leadership. However, the concern over wages is misplaced. Certainly, according to Sung *et al.* (1995), wages in Guangdong province in 1992 were 45–76 per cent higher than in neighbouring provinces, having been roughly comparable in 1978. However, the difference in cost between one Chinese province and another is of very little relevance to firms who are competing in overseas markets. What matters for their ability to compete in world markets through labour-intensive operations is the cost of labour in comparison with other places in the world. The reality in that respect is that labour costs in Guangdong continue to be remarkably low in comparison with labour costs elsewhere. According to Morgan Stanley (*Economist* 1996) the total hourly cost of labour in China, including benefits provided and sick pay, was 25 US cents in 1995. That was the same as the cost in India and compared with 30 US cents in Indonesia, 46 US cents in Thailand, 71 US cents in the Philippines, $US1.59 in Malaysia, $US13.77 in Britain, $US17.20 in the United States, $US23.66 in Japan and $US31.88 in Germany. Even if labour costs in Guangdong were 100 per cent higher than the national average they would still be little more than two-thirds of the cost in the Philippines. Given Guangdong's advantages in respect of its access to Hong Kong's trading infrastructure, and the difficulty of conducting business in other low-cost locations (which has been significantly exacerbated by the Asian financial crisis), there is little reason to fear that the output of Guangdong province will become uncompetitive.

One of the reasons for the continuing low cost of labour in Guangdong province lies in the availability of an estimated 5–6 million migrant workers from other parts of the country. The MIT Report (Berger and Lester 1997: 53) points out that their rootlessness is a source of tremendous local tension and hence a threat to the Hong Kong model. That is certainly true, and industrial development in Guangdong is not a pretty sight. Nevertheless, the presence of these workers, and the tens of millions being made redundant from state enterprises, will keep labour costs in China extremely low for many years to come. Many of these workers are far from Guangdong but improvements in transport and communications are making it much easier for the workers to come to the work and vice versa. With a per capita income of $US424 in 1994, China still has an effectively infinite supply of low-cost unskilled labour. Hong Kong firms producing in China have little to fear in respect of being replaced by lower-cost locations.

In any event, it is myopic to see such competition as damaging to the competitive prospects of Hong Kong firms. If labour becomes available at lower cost elsewhere it will become efficient to transfer some activities to those new locations, especially those which are most labour intensive. Hong Kong firms excel in the management of those processes, and in delivering their outputs to the global market, and they will be well suited to take advantage of the opportunity. This does not imply that there must be a down-turn in the economy of Guangdong. To argue thus is to assume that the amount of work is fixed, so that new jobs created in one location must mean fewer jobs elsewhere. As new manufacturing locations increase their output they become customers as well as competitors, providing new markets for Guangdong products: NAFTA has not resulted in American jobs disappearing to Mexico. Nor would there be a net disappearance of Guangdong jobs and factories. Trade and development is not a zero-sum game in which one region's gain is another's loss but a process of exchange in which all parties may reap gains.

The second set of factors which led the MIT Report (Berger and Lester 1997: 55–7) to doubt the sustainability of the Hong Kong model concerns the effectiveness of the city's competitors, especially the Japanese. Drawing on Hatch and Yamamura (1996) they suggest that Chinese businessmen seek quick profits and therefore fail to acquire the 'dynamic technological efficiency' which results from Japanese long-term investment. They suggest that American business has also been making remarkable progress in managing production in East Asia and that the advantage of Hong Kong firms when operating in China will soon be eroded. A central feature of the argument is that the existing Hong Kong model has led to a 'lock-in to low-wage manufacturing' which has 'retarding effects on technological advance.' (p. 159).

The problem with this assertion is that it assumes erroneously that more advanced technology is essential to competitive success, even where such technology is entirely inappropriate. This is shown most pointedly by the way in which the MIT researchers misunderstand their own example of 'modular manufacturing' in the apparel industry. Modular manufacturing provides a means by which rapid response can be achieved, using teamwork amongst multi-skilled workers (Berg *et al.* 1995) . Attempts were made in Hong Kong to introduce this technology, and a pilot factory was constructed – the kind of government intervention sought by the high-tech lobby. However, modular manufacturing failed to attract interest from Hong Kong manufacturers and today none of them use it. The MIT interpretation is that this demonstrates the weakness of the Hong Kong model by showing how the availability of low-cost labour retards the adoption of technologies which offer productivity gains. The proper interpretation is that modular construction is not appropriate in the Hong Kong/China situation. To introduce a technology which requires multi-skilled team-workers where such workers are not available would be a stupid move, not a wise one. The unquestioned conviction of the MIT researchers that more advanced technology is necessarily better begets the elementary economic error commonly made by 'engineering man' (Wells 1984) when taking decisions in a low-wage environment.

It is certainly the case that Hong Kong firms place great emphasis on 'quick money' which directs them away from spending on research and development. However, that short-term focus is the driver of their superb performance in respect of speed, flexibility and cost. It also directs them into industries and market niches which American and Japanese firms have given up, so that they do not compete with them directly. Hong Kong firms would certainly have difficulty if they tried to compete head-on with the Americans and Japanese. They very sensibly do not. This may limit Hong Kong firms' 'dynamic technological efficiency'. However, if profitability can be sustained by using mature technology developed elsewhere at someone else's expense it is irrational to incur the risk and expense associated with innovation. Only if local technological development is seen as an end rather than a means is this a disadvantage.

While the MIT Report raises doubts about Hong Kong firms' ability to maintain cost leadership, and draws attention to the supposed dangers of retarded technological development, other commentators have cast doubts on the demand side of the Hong Kong model. As one local economist, Tsang Shu-ki, put it: 'Can the world continue to accept so many cheap goods so that the Pearl River Delta can have continual growth?' (Lau 1996: 9).

This seems intuitively appealing but it ignores the fact that it is the market for cheap goods which is expanding most rapidly, while the market for expensive goods is relatively static. Despite the current financial turmoil, most of the world's economic growth in the next two decades is still expected to come from five nations – China, India, Russia, Brazil and Indonesia. These are countries with low per capita incomes whose citizens cannot afford higher-value-added products. What they can afford are the kind of cheap but decent products which Hong Kong firms produce in China. Conversely, the rich countries, whose citizens provide the market for the more expensive products which would result from high-technology manufacturing, are growing slowly. They are also well endowed with firms who are adept enough at the production of innovative and high-value products to be able to pay their workers more than 130 times the cost of a Chinese worker. If we rephrase Tsang Shu-ki's question to ask 'Will the world start to buy expensive goods from the Pearl River Delta?', the fallacy is made clear.

A final consideration in the debate over the sustainability of the Hong Kong model lies in the problem of ensuring a supply of Hong Kong managers to direct manufacturing operations in China. The MIT Report (Berger and Lester 1997: 161) notes that Hong Kong people continue to play a key role in the day-to-day management of Guangdong manufacturing and that the development of PRC managers has been very slow. Growth may therefore be inhibited by shortages of managers, particularly if Hong Kong firms attempt to move further inland in pursuit of cheaper labour.

A number of responses may be made to this argument. First, there are many ways in which Hong Kong firms can economise on managers' time, and economising is something at which they are expert. Improved communications are reducing journey times in China so that managerial resources can be stretched much further. Second, there are hundreds of thousands of PRC nationals in supervisory positions who are now experienced in the manufacturing aspects of the Hong Kong model. If a tiny proportion of them become managers, the problem will be resolved in respect of those functions.

It is certainly true that PRC nationals will have difficulty in fulfilling functions which require regular communication with buyers in sophisticated markets. However, those activities are already carried out in Hong Kong itself.

There is no reason to suppose that the supply of managers in China is inelastic, and the predicted shortage of managers will probably not materialise. Even if it does, and Hong Kong-controlled firms reach the limit of their growth for that reason, the 'high-technology' route does not offer a viable alternative. The pursuit of high-technology manufacturing would create an even greater demand for managers having skills of a much higher order. These are even more scarce, and more difficult to develop, because they are totally different from those applied in Hong Kong and Guangdong over the past forty years. In any event, if Hong Kong-controlled manufacturing firms do reach their limit in this way, that does not preclude growth in the rest of China's manufacturing sector. The city's income can continue to grow by providing the services needed to process the trade arising from PRC-controlled manufacturing. As argued above, Hong Kong 'needs' manufacturing in the sense that manufacturing provides the demand for the city's services. However, that manufacturing does not need to be located in the city, nor does it need to be controlled by Hong Kong firms. As long as Chinese output is growing, so can the city grow.

In summary, there is no convincing reason to suppose that Hong Kong firms need to shift their competitive stance. China contains tens of millions of cheap workers who can fuel the growth of low-cost operations for decades. If other locations do become more attractive in terms of labour costs, Hong Kong firms have well-established advantages in the management of labour-intensive production for sale in world markets, which will allow them to manage and profit from operations in those new locations. The markets for low-end to mid-range products are growing more rapidly than those for top-end products. While this certainly means that the level of technology applied remains low, that is no cause for concern. It simply reflects an appropriate choice of technique in the Chinese circumstances. It might be the case that Hong Kong firms producing in China reach a limit to their growth, set by the limited supply of managerial resources. However, the supply of those resources is probably elastic and in any event Hong Kong's growth could continue with a further refocusing on the services needed to support manufacturing and trade.

Could Hong Kong's manufacturing firms go high-tech if they needed to?

If Hong Kong does not need high-technology manufacturing then it matters not whether the manufacturing sector is capable of taking that route. However, the high-tech lobby's argument is partly based on the contention that Hong Kong's business systems are ready to take up the high-tech 'opportunity'. That idea forms the central thrust of the MIT Report and it is also to be found in Kwong (1997), which recommends a 'design-intensive' version of the 'high-tech' strategy. It also appears in statements and speeches made by leaders of the technophile lobby. Consider the following example:

> Today, I strongly believe that in the next few decades, Hong Kong stands a better chance than any other place in the world of repeating the Silicon Valley story. All the right ingredients are in place. There has been a mushrooming of knowledge or technology based entrepreneurial initiatives in Hong Kong. We see more and more well-educated young Hong Kong people leaving teaching and research posts at universities and technology-oriented jobs in large firms to start up their own businesses. Typically, they are armed with limited personal savings and one bright idea. Importantly, many of them have a good knowledge of the talents available in the various pockets of scientific and engineering excellence in China, where their bright ideas can be complemented at a relatively low price.
>
> (Chi'en 1994)

The first problem with this romantic vision is that it involves a misunderstanding of Silicon Valley (see Florida and Kenney 1990). The second is that it runs counter to the evidence which has been collected on the nature of Hong Kong's environment and the capabilities of its business system. It has been shown above (at p. 48) that Hong Kong lags behind the other 'dragon' economies in respect of the macro-level indicators of techno-logical capability: spending on R&D, patenting and technological infra-structure. That finding is reflected in almost every study carried out on Hong Kong manufacturing. Davies and Whitla (1995) report that the ratio of value-added to gross output in Hong Kong's most successful domestic manufacturing sectors hardly changed at all between 1978 and 1991. Lui and Chiu (1993) found that Hong Kong firms had continued to rely on labour-intensive methods. Leung and Wu (1995) concluded that Hong Kong's 'innovation environment' is not conducive to innovation, because the indus-trial system is dominated by small firms, technology linkages are weak and interactions amongst firms, support organisations and universities are also weak. Kwong (1997: 34) found that the level of technology in manufacturing has been falling, with a particularly rapid decline since 1989. The Hong Kong Industry Department (1996) reported little activity in respect of new products and processes. Yeh and Ng (1994: 466) found that 'when we look at the formidable list of factors for successful high-tech industrial develop-ments, Hong Kong does not seem to stand a good chance of succeeding'.

These findings are reinforced by research and consultancy reports on individual sectors. The MIT Report's own chapter on textiles and clothing confirms an earlier study by Kurt Salmon Associates (1987) with the finding that 'promising areas in new product development and new technologies are barely represented in Hong Kong today' (Berger, Gartner and Karty 1997: 166). A report by P.-E. Consulting (1988: 8) on the metals and light engineering sector found that 'few leading edge technologies are employed in the sector and the general level of production technology is not high'. The MIT Report's chapter on electronics found that there is 'relatively little technology and/or product innovation taking place in Hong Kong today' (Reif and Sodini 1997: 196). In biotechnology, where the Technology Road Map study declared in 1991 that 'Hong Kong is sufficiently innovative, dynamic and intellectually resourceful to become a biotechnology centre in the Asia Pacific region' (Chang *et al.* 1991: 168), MIT found in 1996 that 'one would not expect any drug discoveries or biopharmaceutical manu-facturing to emerge from the territory's industrial sector' and that in the universities 'we were not able to find any new products at the discovery stage' (Wang *et al.* 1997: 258). While the MIT Report went on to identify traditional Chinese medicine as a possible opportunity for biotechnology in the city, it has already been reported that hospitals in Hong Kong lag behind those in the US in its use (Moir 1997).

What is remarkable about many of the studies which have examined Hong Kong's technological capability is that they provide detailed and accurate descriptions of Hong Kong's inadequacies, but then make a contradictory leap of faith to draw the conclusion that Hong Kong therefore both needs and has great potential for technological development. Having found the environment unconducive to innovation, Leung and Wu (1995: 533) assert that because Hong Kong has 'local entrepreneurship, technical ingenuity and an established trading network' the city has the potential to develop an 'indigenous advanced technology base'. How the one set of conditions leads to the other is not explained. Yeh and Ng (1994: 466) follow their description of the territory's technological inadequacies with the assertion that 'we have established that there is an urgent need for Hong Kong to develop high-tech industries'. The only evidence offered in support of that conclusion is the observation that value-added as a percentage of output is relatively low in Hong Kong's domestic manufacturing and the state has done more to support high-tech industry in Japan, Korea, Singapore and Taiwan.

This conflict between evidence and conclusions is most pointed in the main body of the MIT Report. Chapter after chapter explains that Hong Kong faces 'challenges' and 'hurdles' in its attempts to introduce high technology, and yet faith in the high-tech vision never wavers. This is equivalent to examining a desert, finding it dry and then concluding that it provides major opportunities for the development of water-intensive agri-culture! The MIT study does identify a few manufacturing companies who have been successful in following the higher value-added route, and others are exhorted to follow that route with Government help. However, the high-value-added group is very small indeed, comprising perhaps twenty companies, out of more than 100,000 Hong Kong firms producing in China.

Only in Amsden's 'minority report' does the MIT study connect with reality, when she notes that 'Hong Kong's seemingly negligible R&D activity does not inspire hope that manufacturing capabilities will prove an engine of growth in the near future' (Amsden 1997: 332)

This lack of logic might have been avoided if the studies in question had appropriate methodologies, allowing them to proceed in a meaningful way from the evidence to their conclusions. However, the methodology they employ consists of listing Hong Kong's strengths and weaknesses and then recommending that the weaknesses be addressed. What that approach fails to recognise is that the strengths and weaknesses of Hong Kong's manufacturing industry both arise from the same set of characteristics. The features which allow fast response, flexibility and effective cost leadership are the same features which prevent innovation, design leadership and the move into high technology. As Leonard (1992) has indicated, 'core capabilities' often bring with them 'core rigidities'. This can be seen more clearly by returning briefly to the history of Hong Kong manufacturing.

Hong Kong's manufacturing sector came into existence as a response to the geo-political changes of the 1950s, which deprived the city of its entrepôt function. The entrepreneurs who created Hong Kong industry had very limited resources. They had to work within the technical competence available to them, they had to overcome the problems caused by the large physical and psychic distance to their markets, and they had to protect themselves from the impact of unpredictable changes in those markets. They also had to work within the context of Chinese culture within which individuals exhibit low levels of trust towards those outside the family (Carney 1998).

The manufacturing sector which developed from that inauspicious set of circumstances was a miracle of collective ingenuity, having a number of highly idiosyncratic features. First, it was restricted to the low-price segments of just four sectors: textiles and apparel; metal products and machinery; plastic products; and electrical/electronics. Second, it was overwhelmingly made up of small Chinese family businesses who have been well described as 'merchant-manufacturers' (Riedel 1974). These firms had low levels of funding, raised within the family. They focused on quick returns and they carried out vertically very shallow 'single-phase' operations (usually assembly), using limited amounts of general-purpose equipment. The entrepreneurs who owned these firms were expert at controlling cheap labour working at high intensity and adept at avoiding the unnecessary expense of product design, marketing or staff development. If markets changed, they could exit one segment and enter another, using the same low-cost general purpose equipment – sewing machines, simple materials handling equipment, low-tech metal and plastic-working tools. Managerial role definitions, functional structures and hierarchies were non-existent and technical expertise from outside the family was regarded with suspicion. They operated by 'mechanical market response' and their key 'merchant manufacturing' capability lay in taking orders, purchasing inputs at lowest cost and monitoring single-phase production operations.

This population of firms was a highly effective adaptation to a niche in the environment. As a result it has reproduced itself with very little change. Its key capability has persisted (Davies 1998) and Hong Kong manufacturing today retains the characteristics which defined it in the 1950s. However, the attributes which make those firms so effective in that niche are inconsistent with the requirements of a system designed for innovation. The ability to shift rapidly from one supplier or customer to another is a strength but it prevents the development of the intense relationships which are needed for innovation. Vertical shallowness allows the close monitoring of cheap labour which gives low cost, speed and flexibility. At the same time, it restricts the domain of the workers' knowledge base and prevents them from identifying opportunities for innovation which may arise in connection with the inputs to the process, the use of its outputs, or the links between them. High intensity of effort holds down costs but it also limits workers' opportunities for learning. Innovation requires 'patient money', which is not to be found in Hong Kong. It requires investment in specialised assets, the placement of trust in technical experts and the development of close links with the most sophisticated customers, who are still at a long distance from Hong Kong. Innovation requires large-scale spending in pursuit of uncertain returns. None of these requirements are consistent with the objectives and behaviour of the firms which make up the Hong Kong manufacturing sector. If such firms were forced to choose between attempting to compete through innovation and exit from the sector, their most likely response would be to exit, investing their accumulated profits in property, while making use of their well-developed merchanting ability in other activities.

Conclusion: if not high-tech manufacturing, then what?

If Hong Kong's economy is unlikely to shift towards high-technology manufacturing, it remains to consider the shape which the city's economy will take in future. The most likely scenario, disappointing as it may be to the technophile lobby, is a continuation of the current trend. Perhaps the most remarkable feature of the city's economic development has been the persistence of its merchanting capability, built around rapid response to market signals. That capability provided the basis for the entrepôt economy, it determined the nature of the 'merchant manufacturing' sector which grew up in the artificial circumstances of the closed-China period, and it underpins the manufacturing and trade-related service sector which now dominates. The best prediction for the future is that the city becomes increasingly focused on the provision of those services. Its industrial structure will consist of tens of thousands of tiny Chinese family businesses 'doing the deal' and adding value to China's manufacturing output. Those tiny firms cannot fulfil those functions where there are economies of scope or scale. They will therefore continue to operate in an infrastructure of transport, communications and financing provided by the hierarchies of the government, the multinationals, the few large Hong Kong firms and (increasingly) firms from mainland China.

If this prognosis is correct, it is also interesting to ponder the future of the 'Made by Hong Kong' manufacturing sector, made up of Hong Kong-controlled firms producing outside the city. It has been argued here that this sector may prosper and grow by maintaining its current competitive posture in low-cost manufacturing activities. However, faced with more comfortable opportunities in the service sector, the entrepreneurs who own these activities may choose to opt out from the rigours of direct control and management. It is reasonable to speculate that management, and perhaps ownership, may pass to PRC citizens. It would be only natural for the 'merchant manufacturers' of Hong Kong to sell off their manufacturing facilities to mainland interests, invest the proceeds in property, and then continue to make money by organising the sales of their erstwhile establishments and others. Such a prospect may horrify those who believe that owning and controlling manufacturing operations is a must. For the citizens of the city it bodes well. After all, why would any pragmatic Hong Kong businessman, faced with a choice between that comfortable future and addressing the expensive 'challenges' and 'hurdles' associated with the high-tech route, choose the latter?

Part II

Labour market adjustment and inequality in Hong Kong

4 The market at work

Labour market adjustments to the changing environment in Hong Kong

William Chan and Wing Suen

Introduction

It is a straightforward exercise in economic theory to show that, under certain assumptions, a competitive labour market will lead to an optimal allocation of human resources. It is equally straightforward, however, to imagine institutional features of the labour market that seem to undermine the competitive assumptions. Although the Hong Kong labour market is relatively free from the visible hands of the government, one can never conclusively establish that the market is perfectly competitive. For example, in an influential study, Turner *et al.* (1980) argue that, because results of wage surveys are public information, and because of cross-directorship of many large corporations, there is likely to be collusion within the business sector to suppress workers' wages, so that the Hong Kong labour market is far from the competitive model. His view, however, is disputed by Stretton (1981) and by Chau (1988), among others.

One can argue endlessly over assumptions and over which model should better describe the actual situation in Hong Kong, but it would be a pointless exercise. The relevance of a model is determined ultimately by how well its implications conform to and predict empirical observations, not by how closely its assumptions approximate reality. Any theory of the labour market that fails to explain dynamic behaviour in the real world can offer little insight of significance, no matter how plausible it seems on the surface.

Just like any other market, the labour market is constantly subject to exogenous changes in demand and supply. In fact, given its increasing integration into the international economic system and, in particular, its close relationship to China, the labour market in Hong Kong has been perturbed by dramatic and unpredictable shocks in supply and demand over the years. The sheer magnitude of these shocks throws the subsequent responses into sharp relief and offers unique opportunities to study how well the market has worked.

The successive waves of refugees and immigrants from China and the brain drain that saw the emigration of many professionals have had profound effects on the supply of labour in Hong Kong. The acceleration of the economy in the 1970s and 1980s also changed the labour market behaviour of women, with significant realignment of their roles in both the market and the family. These events will be discussed in detail in other chapters. In this chapter we shall focus on how the labour market has responded to the structural transformation of the Hong Kong economy in the past two decades, focusing on the distributional impacts and on the implications for unemployment and labour shortages. While less tangible than the social and economic upheavals that followed mass immigration from the north, the impact of sectoral shifts is no less fundamental. The ability of the market to cope with such a strong disequilibrating force is a test of the efficiency of the labour market.

Structural transformation and sectoral shifts

In the past few decades the economy of Hong Kong has undergone a series of major structural changes. The embargo on China after the Korean War put an abrupt end to entrepôt trade in Hong Kong, and the ensuing rise and decline of manufacturing industries is a well-told story. Within the manufacturing sector, textiles have given way to garments, and plastics have been supplanted by electronics. During the period, commerce and financial services continue to grow until Hong Kong eventually emerges as one of the world's financial centres. The reopening of China in the late 1970s accelerated these changes by offering an abundance of cheap labour as well as an abundance of new business opportunities. Outward processing trade with China was almost non-existent in the early 1980s. In 1994 Hong Kong people sent $181 billion worth of raw materials and semi-manufactures into China for processing, and received $777 billion worth of processed goods. To put these figures in perspective, the total value added from all domestic manufacturing establishments in that year was $112 billion (Census and Statistics Department 1996a). The shift of the manufacturing base is unmistakable.

The movement of employment away from manufacturing industries towards manufacturing- and trade-related services has been discussed in detail in Chapter 3. Less well recognised is the fact that employment fluctuations are equally volatile within broadly defined sectors. For example, while manufacturing employment as a whole experienced a significant decline, employment in printing and publishing industries more than doubled during the past twenty years. As another example, repair service showed virtually no growth in a period when the service sector in general was expanding. The sudden boom and the subsequent bust in wigs production was a well-known episode in the history of Hong Kong manufacturing. At its peak in 1970, the wigs industry employed more than 30,000 people; currently it hires fewer than a hundred (Census and Statistics Department 1993). Real estates brokerage and agencies had about 2,000 employees in 1984. In 1994, this sector had 17,000 people on its payroll (Census and Statistics Department 1984, 1994).

One way to summarise the extent of sectoral shifts is to calculate the following index:

$$\frac{1}{2}\sum_i |s_i - s_i'|$$

In the above formula, s_i is the employment share of sector in one year and s_i' is the employment share of the same sector in another year. The absolute value of the change in employment share, $|s_i - s_i'|$, represents the minimum fraction of workers who have left or joined this particular sector in the interim period. Summing these absolute changes across all sectors would give an indication of the mobility of workers necessitated by sectoral shifts. Since workers who leave one sector will join another sector, the overall sum is divided by two to avoid double counting.

During the early 1980s, the rate of structural transformation in Hong Kong was below that in Singapore and in South Korea, but above that in Japan and in the United States. However, thanks to closer economic links with China, sectoral shifts in Hong Kong accelerated markedly in the late 1980s. The rate of structural transformation surpassed all these four countries in the period 1987–91. Sectoral shifts have decelerated a bit since the early 1990s, but they are still quite sizeable compared to the more mature economies such as Japan and the United States.

Another dimension to the transformation of the Hong Kong economy is the change in its occupational structure. Because of a major reclassification of occupation groups, the occupational structures before and after 1979 and 1991 are not directly comparable. Table 4.1 shows the change in occupational structure between 1976 and 1996 based on a recoding of unpublished census files. As expected, there was a general upgrading in the distribution of occupations. The proportion of workers who were managers and administrators increased by 4 percentage points between 1976 and 1991, and the proportion of professionals and associate professionals rose by 7 percentage points.

Table 4.1 also shows how the changing distribution of occupations varies across industries. Perhaps the most interesting feature of the table is that the increase in percentage of managerial and administrative workers is higher in the manufacturing sector than in other sectors. Moreover, between 1976 and 1991, the proportion of clerical workers in the manufacturing sector increased substantially by 8 percentage points, while the proportion of direct production workers fell by 22 points. This is consistent with the view that many local manufacturers have moved their production facilities to China and used Hong Kong mainly as a distribution and control centre for their regional operations, as portrayed by the expression 'the shop at the front, the factory at the back'. Jobs in manufacturing firms in Hong Kong are therefore becoming less production related. The degree of

Table 4.1 Changes in occupational structure 1976–96

	Manufacturing	*All industries*	*All industries*
Occupation	1976–1991	1976–1991	1991–1996
Administrative and managerial workers	+8.0	+4.1	+2.9
Professionals and associate professionals	+5.6	+7.7	+3.1
Clerks	+7.9	+6.3	+0.9
Service workers and shop sales workers	+0.6	−0.4	+0.6
Craft workers, machine operators and assemblers	−27.2	−20.2	−7.4
Elementary occupations	+5.5	+3.0	+0.1

Source: Census and Statistics Department (1997b, Table 19).

de-industrialisation in Hong Kong, then, is greater than that suggested by the decline in total manufacturing employment alone.

The change in occupational structure after 1991 is shown in the last column of Table 4.1. Although the time span is relatively short, one can already detect a shift towards more skill-intensive and white-collar occupations. The combined share of managers, administrators, professionals and associate professionals rose from 23 per cent in 1991 to 28 per cent in 1996. The share of craft workers, machines operators and assemblers showed a significant drop.

To what extent will the decline of manufacturing and the rise of services continue in the future? A clue can be obtained from the experience of other city economies. As shown in Table 4.2, the manufacturing employment share is considerably lower in Hong Kong than in Singapore. Part of the reason, however, is that the Singapore government deliberately implements policies that favour manufacturing. In the United States, where industrial policy is not widely practised, manufacturing employment share is even lower than that in Hong Kong. At what level manufacturing employment will stabilise will depend on the future direction of the Hong Kong economy. Tsang (1994) depicts a scenario in which Hong Kong becomes the "Manhattan" of South China. If economic integration with China proceeds well, the relevant benchmark for the future structure of the Hong Kong economy is not the United States, but the city of New York. Table 4.2 shows that manufacturing employment in New York is below 10 per cent of total employment. Financing, insurance, real estate and business services constitute a much greater percentage of the workforce in New York than in Hong Kong. Based on this comparison, the structural transformation of the Hong Kong economy does not seem to have reached its end yet. The current Asian financial crisis may have dented local and international confidence in Hong Kong as a regional financial and service centre, but if a much more

Table 4.2 Employment shares by sectors, international comparison 1994

	Hong Kong	*Singapore*	*United States*	*New York*
Agriculture and mining	0.6	0.3	3.5	0.1
Manufacturing	19.6	25.6	16.4	9.1
Construction	7.7	6.6	6.1	1.4
Transport, communication, and public utilities	12.6	11.1	7.1	5.9
Wholesales and retail trade, restaurants and hotels	28.8	22.9	20.9	19.1
Financing, insurance, real estate and business services	11.4	12.0	11.0	33.6
Community, social, and personal services	19.3	21.5	35.1	30.6

Source: Data for Hong Kong, Singapore, and the United States are obtained from International Labour Office (1996). Information for New York comes from US Bureau of the Census (1996).
Note: Numbers in the table are percentage shares.

traumatic shock such as the Great Depression did not change the destiny of New York, we do not see the current problems as more than a temporary setback in the irreversible evolution of Hong Kong.

The wealth and distributional effects of economic restructuring

Changes in the structure of the economy necessitate a constant reallocation of human resources across industry sectors. Such sectoral reallocation is part of the process of economic growth. They should not – and cannot – be resisted. Although the service sector has been hit particularly hard in the latest recession, the renewed calls for government intervention in re-industrialising Hong Kong are surely misplaced. To create and save manufacturing jobs would go against global shifts in production and consumption patterns. Even the much-fancied high-technology manufacturing may prove to be a myth for the future shape of the Hong Kong economy, as Howard Davis argues so persuasively in Chapter 3. In any case, manufacturing jobs are not inherently better than service jobs. There is a common caricature of service workers as low skilled and low paid, typified by the supermarket checkout clerk and the hamburger flipper. In fact, less than a quarter of the service jobs in Hong Kong are in restaurants or the retail sector (Census and Statistics Department 1996a). The fastest growing service jobs are in business and financial services rather than in personal or social services. Using payroll data from 1993, we calculate that 68 per cent of all service workers earned higher wages than the average manufacturing wage. With increasing integration with China and increasing liberalisation of trade, Hong Kong workers will find it more difficult to compete in low skilled manufacturing jobs. The enthusiasm for high-technology industries notwithstanding, the highly skilled are more likely to be in services than in manufacturing. Adapting to the shift away from manufacturing will ultimately pay off the transitional costs.

As workers move away from low-pay sectors towards high-pay sectors, human resources are more efficiently utilised, and average labour productivity and labour earnings will increase. To illustrate this effect, suppose manufacturing workers make up 40 per cent of total employment while the remaining 60 per cent are in service industries. Suppose further, without deviating too much from the facts, that wages in manufacturing are \$9,000 per month and wages in services are \$10,000. The overall average wage is then (\$9,000×0.4+\$10,000×0.6)=\$9,600. If employment in the manufacturing sector declines to 20 per cent, while at the same time employment in the service sector expands to 80 per cent, then the overall average wage will grow to (\$9,000×0.2+\$10,000×0.8)=\$9,800, even if wages in each sector remain unchanged.

According to an earlier calculation based on census data with twenty-five industries (Suen 1995b), the reallocation of labour alone had contributed to a 12 percentage point increase in real earnings in the 1976–91 period, or nearly one-seventh of the total growth in earnings. Using another set of data from the Survey of Employment, Vacancies and Payroll, we update this calculation for the period 1980–93 with a more detailed industry classification (46 industry sectors). We find that average real payroll per person had risen by 66 per cent during that period. Even if real wages in each of the 46 sectors had remained unchanged, the changing composition of labour across the sectors alone would have resulted in an increase in average real payroll per person of 19 per cent. This suggests that the composition effect may have accounted for as much as two-sevenths of the overall growth in earnings. The labour composition effect may not be noticeable to individual workers in the short term, but it is the single most important consequence of sectoral reallocation in Hong Kong.

Although the structural transformation of the Hong Kong economy has brought about significant increases in wealth, there is some evidence that it has also resulted in increasing inequality in earnings. As the economy becomes more sophisticated, tasks that require raw labour power can often been accomplished by machines. At the same time, the increasing use of physical capital induces a greater demand for skilled labour to manage and co-ordinate the production processes. The rise in demand for skilled relative to unskilled labour is partly reflected in an increase in demand for education and partly in an increase in relative wages for skilled workers. In Figure 4.1, we show the real wage index for three classes of workers. Real wage growth for craftsmen and operatives clearly lags behind wage growth for non-production workers and for managers and professionals. Because the level of wages for craftsmen and operatives is below that of other workers to begin with, the differential wage growth also means an increasing disparity of wages.

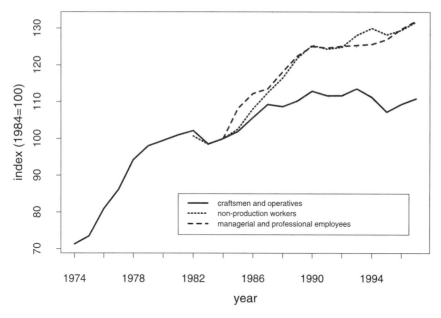

Figure 4.1 Wage and salary indices 1974–97.

The availability of data from population censuses allows us to refine our knowledge about trends in wage inequality. Although Turner *et al.* (1991) report a narrowing of wage differentials between various class of employees between the mid-1970s and mid-1980s on the basis of relatively small-scale surveys, data in Table 4.3 clearly indicate a widening of differentials, apart perhaps from the late 1970s and very early 1980s. This table is based on employment earnings data from a random sample of working men in Hong Kong drawn from the population censuses. Panel (A) shows that the Gini coefficient for male employment earnings rose from 0.39 in 1976 to 0.44 in 1996. Other measures of earnings inequality tell a similar story. For example, the standard deviation of log earnings has increased from 0.64 to 0.73, and the gap between the tenth percentile earnings and median earnings has increased by roughly 22 percentage points. The measures in panel (C) are based on the residuals from human capital regressions. They indicate that, after controlling for observable characteristics such as education and experience, there is still a trend towards greater earnings inequality. House-hold income data confirm the trends shown by wage earnings data. The Gini coefficient for household income distribution is reported to have increased from 0.48 in 1991 to 0.52 in 1996 (Census and Statistics Department 1997b).

This trend towards increasing wage inequality, which will be elaborated upon in Chapter 5, has been observed in the United States and in other countries as well (e.g., Juhn *et al.* 1993; Katz *et al.* 1995; Blau and Kahn 1996). It is part of a global phenomenon involving a shift in demand from

Table 4.3   Measures of earnings inequality

	1976	1981	1986	1991	1996
(A) Raw earnings					
Gini coefficient	0.386	0.382	0.410	0.427	0.438
(B) Log earnings					
Standard deviation	0.637	0.622	0.666	0.698	0.727
90–50 percentile	0.811	0.752	0.833	0.916	1.065
50–10 percentile	0.470	0.552	0.693	0.693	0.693
75–25 percentile	0.606	0.672	0.693	0.750	0.781
(C) Earnings residuals					
Standard deviation	0.492	0.499	0.515	0.532	0.562
90–50 percentile	0.526	0.535	0.545	0.581	0.637
50–10 percentile	0.545	0.574	0.620	0.615	0.640
75–25 percentile	0.519	0.523	0.545	0.571	0.598

Sources: Figures for 1976–91 are reproduced from Suen (1995b, Table 7). Figures for 1996 are computed from unpublished census files.

relatively unskilled labour to more skilled labour. In countries such as Norway, where wage setting is highly centralised and labour market institutions are highly rigid, the demand shift has resulted in increased unemployment for the unskilled. In places such as the United States and Hong Kong, where wage setting is decentralised, the change has not increased the level of unemployment. Instead the bulk of the adjustments occur through changes in the wage structure. There is, however, one crucial difference between the experience of Hong Kong and the experience of the United States: whereas real wages for low-wage jobs in the United States fell in absolute terms, real wages at all levels in Hong Kong increased sharply. For example, real earnings at the tenth percentile of the distribution in Hong Kong grew 39 per cent between 1981 and 1991, even though they fell by 19 per cent relative to the median. Similarly, from 1991 to 1996, median household income among the poorest quintile of the population grew by 59 per cent in nominal terms, though household income among the richest quintile grew even faster. Although the concern about rising wage inequality in Hong Kong is legitimate, changes in relative earnings must not be taken to mask the general growth in actual earnings.

Structural unemployment and worker displacement

Concern over sectoral shifts in Hong Kong has mostly focused on the problems of labour market mismatch and structural unemployment. Structural transformation is associated with the reallocation of workers among sectors. This not only raises the incidence of job separations (i.e., quits and layoffs), but also results in more extensive job search activities in the labour market because workers are not familiar with the industries they

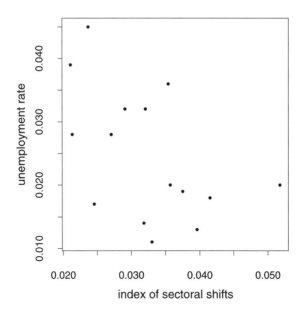

Figure 4.2 Relationship between sectoral shifts and unemployment 1982–1996.

are moving into. In addition, sectoral shifts can also destroy a significant amount of the human capital stock, as skills are often industry-specific and become useless once the workers are made redundant in their original industries. And, without the necessary training, displaced workers may have difficulty securing employment in other sectors. All of these factors can contribute to higher measured unemployment.

Intuitive as it seems to be, the sectoral shift hypothesis has been less than overwhelming. Lilien (1982) offers some evidence for the relationship between sectoral shifts and unemployment in the United States, but his findings are disputed by Abraham and Katz (1986) and by Murphy and Topel (1987). Recently, Chan (1996) constructs a model of short-run adjustments which shows that the theoretical relationship between sectoral shifts and unemployment is not necessarily positive. In Hong Kong, the relevant time series are too short to allow a detailed investigation. Instead, we plot the aggregate unemployment rate from 1982 to 1996 against the index of sectoral shifts (defined above) based on forty-six industries. The result, shown in Figure 4.2, does not suggest any positive relationship between the rate of sectoral shifts and the level of unemployment.

To further test the relationship, we use quarterly data for the period 1983–97 and regress industry-specific unemployment rates for four broad sectors (manufacturing; construction; wholesale, retail, restaurants and hotels; and services) on the change in sectoral employment share and on three sector dummy variables (using manufacturing as the benchmark). The estimated regression is:

unemployment_rate=0.024 −0.071 Δ employment_share
                        (0.002) (0.027)

$$+0.006 \text{ construction}$$
$$(0.003)$$

$$-0.001 \text{ wholesale\_retail\_restaurant\_hotels}$$
$$(0.002)$$

$$-0.009 \text{ services}$$
$$(0.002)$$

The numbers shown in parentheses are standard errors. (If the size of the coefficient is more than twice the size of the standard error, this is generally taken as an indication that the result is not due to sampling error.) This estimated equation indicates that, controlling for the change in employment share, the service sector does have a significantly lower unemployment rate, and the construction sector has a significantly higher unemployment rate, relative to the manufacturing sector. More importantly, higher unemployment is associated with shrinking employment share, even though the effect is not very strong: accelerating the contraction in employment share by one percentage point will only raise the sectoral unemployment rate by 0.07 percentage point. Apparently, many manufacturing workers were able to secure employment in other sectors. It is for this reason that overall unemployment has remained remarkably low despite the drastic sectoral shifts.

Nevertheless, our results so far have focused on aggregate unemployment. An overall bill of health may yet obscure pockets of hardship experienced in more narrowly defined sectors. A more close-up look at the problem is afforded by Table 4.4, which breaks down unemployed persons with a previous job by detailed industry of that job. The data show that, just as for sectoral employment, there is higher variation in unemployment rates within sectors than across, but these differences tend to be grossed over in aggregation. The relatively high unemployment in construction and in wholesale, retail, restaurants and hotels is perhaps more cyclical in nature and may improve as the economy recovers. But the substantial unemployment in manufacturing, particularly in clothing and footwear, which are export-oriented and hence not affected as much by the slowdown in internal consumption in the mid-1990s, is likely to be related to diminished employment opportunities arising from economic restructuring, and, therefore, to be of a more permanent nature. While the published data series on detailed industries (available only since mid-1995) are still too short to clearly disentangle the secular and cyclical components, the high unemployment in

Table 4.4 Unemployment by detailed industries July–September 1996

Previous industry	No. unemployed ('000)	Unemployment rate (%)
Manufacturing	*15.4*	*3.2*
Food and beverage	0.4	1.9
Clothing and footwear	6.5	4.0
Paper and printing	2.5	3.9
Other manufacturing	6.0	2.6
Construction	*10.0*	*3.5*
Foundation/superstructure	6.7	3.3
Decoration/maintenance	3.2	3.8
Wholesale/retail, import/export,		
and restaurants/hotels	*23.0*	*2.49*
Wholesale/retail	9.2	2.4
Import/export	5.0	1.7
Restaurants/hotels	8.0	3.5
Transport, storage, and		
communication	*6.6*	*2.0*
Transport	5.9	2.0
Storage	0.2	5.3
Communication	0.5	1.2
Financing, insurance, real estate,		
and business services	*5.9*	*1.7*
Financing	1.2	1.0
Insurance	0.4	1.4
Real estate and business services	4.2	2.0
Community, social and personal		
services	*6.3*	*0.98*
Public administration	0.4	0.3
Education, health, and welfare	2.0	0.8
Other services	3.9	1.4
Others	*0.2*	*0.6*

Source: Census and Statistics Department, *Quarterly Report on General Household Survey, July to September 1996*, Hong Kong: Government Printer, 1996.

some of the more narrowly defined industries which are known to be in decline is a cause for concern.

Figure 4.3 offers another perspective on this problem. It traces the time trend of long-term unemployment (defined as spells of more than six months) as a percentage of all unemployment spells since the mid-1980s. The initial dip is probably associated with strong secular growth that followed the rapid expansion in the Chinese economy. Since mid-1989, however, there appears to be an increasing prevalence of long-term unemployment in synchrony with the accelerating restructuring of the Hong Kong economy, even when the overall labour market was very tight in the late 1980s and early 1990s. The median duration of unemployment also exhibits a similar increasing trend.

What these data seem to suggest is that, even though the labour force has

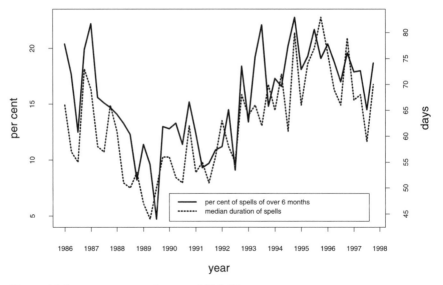

Figure 4.3 Long-term unemployment 1986–97.

adapted very well to the structural transformation, there are some workers who, having lost their jobs in the declining industries, are experiencing difficulties in finding satisfactory employment, either in their initial sector or in another sector. And the longer they stay out of employment, the lower is their probability of finding new employment, since the lack of training for alternative employment, the erosion in confidence with prolonged idleness, and the stigma of long-term unemployment all work against them.

Still, unemployment statistics do not tell the entire story. Apart from those job-seekers who are not able to find employment, there are also some individuals, included in the category of the economically inactive, who would otherwise have been in the labour force if sectoral shifts have not wiped out demand in many sectors. Among them are housewives who would have sought re-entry into the labour market in their middle age. According to Mincer and Polachek (1974), women tend to have interrupted careers, drifting in and out of the labour market as dictated by their family obligations. But when their youngest child reaches school age, many of these by now middle-aged women would tend to seek employment on a more permanent basis. In the past, when the industrial structure was more stable over time, such re-entries would have been relatively easy, as these some-time housewives would still retain some of the skills they acquired in their on-again, off-again career. But with the rapid economic restructuring in the past decade or so, these women find that there are no market opportunities to 'return' to, and end up remaining as home-makers. Not counted as unemployed, this potentially large group of female workers simply disappears among the economically inactive in official statistics. It is, perhaps, for this reason that female labour force participation rate for those aged between 35 and 44 has barely changed in the past decade, as reported in Chapter 6.

Among the displaced or re-entering workers who remain economically active, even if they are able to find a job in one of the expanding industries, it is likely that they will have to accept a substantial pay cut. For skills required in different sectors tend to be very different, and manufacturing workers will find that the human capital they accumulated through learning-by-doing in their previous employment does not have much value in the service industries that place a premium on interpersonal and communication skills. Age also becomes a factor, not only because learning becomes more difficult at a more advanced age, but also because it reduces the workers' incentive to acquire new sector-specific skills, as the period over which the returns from such an investment can be reaped before retirement is now shorter. Stuck with obsolete skills with little market value and having little incentive to invest in new ones, these workers would most likely have to settle for relatively low-paid, unskilled service jobs, and a substantial reduction in living standard.

Because of the lack of disaggregated data, we are not able to precisely estimate these negative effects of sectoral shift. But just as we find little evidence to support the impression of mass structural unemployment, we cannot dismiss the potential problems and difficulties faced by certain segments of the population.

Labour shortage and the increasing demand for professional workers

While sectoral shifts have left redundant labour in some sectors, robust secular growth in the economy has resulted in sustained tightness in the labour market over much of the past two decades. Until the current, sharp downturn as the result of the Asian financial crisis, the situation was particularly acute in the service sectors due to a short-run mismatch in supply and demand. This is illustrated in Table 4.5, which shows the vacancy rate by broad industrial groups in the past ten years.

Two features are immediately apparent from the data in the table. First, the labour market was relatively tight in the early 1990s up until 1994, when vacancies started to fall with the onset of an economic downturn triggered by government intervention in the property market. Second, while the manufacturing vacancy rate dropped by two-thirds in less than six years, the reduction has been milder in the service sectors, particularly in community, social and personal services. This observation reflects the combined effect of both secular and cyclical factors. While both factors are simultaneously negative for declining industries like manufacturing, contributing to the drastic drop in vacancies, the cyclical contraction is partially offset by long-run expansion in the service industries where labour demand remained relatively keen even during the mild recession of 1994–96 .

Table 4.5 Vacancy rate by industry 1988–97

Year	Manuf.	Constr.	Elect./ gas	Who./ret., imp./exp., rest./hot.	Trans. storage/ comm.	Fin./ins./ real est./ busi. serv.	Com./soc./ per services	All
1988	6.12	9.42	1.63	4.69	3.38	4.01	3.37	4.82
1989	5.19	5.66	1.86	3.67	3.56	4.17	3.87	4.17
1990	4.72	2.56	1.80	3.55	2.69	3.24	3.25	3.77
1991	3.44	1.18	1.05	3.11	2.96	2.85	3.09	3.09
1992	3.24	0.85	0.86	3.42	2.66	2.86	3.30	3.15
1993	2.71	1.04	1.14	3.17	2.67	3.23	3.17	2.98
1994	2.68	1.59	0.97	3.19	2.66	3.29	3.50	3.06
1995	1.74	3.73	0.95	2.08	1.80	2.23	2.55	2.13
1996	1.76	2.11	0.20	1.88	1.98	1.76	2.65	2.56
1997	2.21	1.67	0.36	2.21	2.09	3.11	2.57	2.38

Source: Census and Statistics Department, *Quarterly Report of Employment, Vacancies and Payroll Statistics*, various issues.
Note: Vacancy rate is defined as (no. of vacancies)÷(no. of vacancies+no. of persons engaged). Figures are for September of each year and are expressed in percentage points.

When considered by themselves, vacancy rates can, however, be very misleading. Like many statistics, they are sometimes interpreted without regard to the economic content of the underlying concept and are misused in public debate. For vacancies, like unemployment, are a function of wages, actual and expected. Workers become unemployed because actual wage offers fall short of their expectations, while employers fail to fill vacancies because the wages they offer are not up to expectations of the workers for the work involved. High vacancy rates may therefore simply reflect that expectations are temporarily lagging behind reality, or that wages are suppressed below market-clearing levels.

There are a number of reasons for the latter possibility. When the labour importation scheme was first introduced in the early 1990s, quotas were set by the government according to a formula that includes the vacancy rate as one of the considerations. There is, therefore, an incentive for employers to report high vacancies so as to enhance their chances of securing quotas. Indeed, in that period, labour unions had often complained of unreasonably low wages and high qualifications demanded from local applicants for certain jobs. Also, some firms may fail to offer market wages simply because they are no longer competitive in the face of international competition. Constrained by product prices set in the international market and faced with lower-cost alternatives in China, many operations, mostly manufacturing but also some services, are no longer viable in Hong Kong at market wages.

Interpretation of the vacancy statistics should therefore be made in the context of other information. A comparison with sectoral unemployment is particularly instructive. Relative to unemployment in the service sector, the manufacturing unemployment rate has been high. This is true not only in the past few years, when manufacturing vacancies showed a rapid drop, but also in the late 1980s and early 1990s, when manufacturing consistently reported the highest vacancy rates of all sectors. This indicates that there was in fact a rather large pool of idle manufacturing workers who were not taking up the vacant positions in their former industries.

Part of the reason for this phenomenon may be found in Table 4.6, which provides more detailed information on the time trend of wages plotted in Figure 4.1. It further breaks down the real wage indices by industries from 1988 to 1997. Despite the deceptively high vacancy rates and the persistent complaints of employers in the manufacturing industries of escalating labour costs, it can be seen that it is the service industries that have experienced the fastest wage growth. While the data from 1990 onward might have been tainted by the effects of labour importation programmes, manufacturing wage increases have been lagging behind other sectors even in the late 1980s, when the manufacturing industries showed very high vacancy rates. Decomposing the data by broad occupational groups further shows that while wages of non-production workers in manufacturing have managed largely to keep pace with other industries, manufacturing craftsmen and operatives have experienced very little growth in real wages for nine years, and have, in fact, been suffering from a decline in the more recent past. This is all the more remarkable given the almost 27 per cent increase in real wages for operatives in social, community and personal services over the same period. Whether stagnant wages for manufacturing production workers are the result of opportunistic behaviour of employers or, more likely, cost constraints imposed by international competition, the picture presented by proponents of labour importation, of acute labour shortage and spiralling labour costs in manufacturing is an illusion.

This does not mean, however, that there was no overall shortage of labour in Hong Kong in the past decade. After all, an unemployment rate of less than 2 per cent, as reported in Hong Kong in the late 1980s and early 1990s, is extremely low by international standards. What the evidence implies is that, whatever shortage existed, it was concentrated among certain sectors and occupations where rapid expansion outstripped the economy's ability to produce the desired specific human capital. The brain drain in the aftermath of the Sino-British agreement on the future of Hong Kong further reduced the stock of more educated and professional workers. The situation was alleviated with the economic downturn of 1994, and the concurrent wave of returnees from among the many who had emigrated earlier also swelled supply. The onset of the latest recession, which saw the unemployment rate soaring to almost 5 per cent in mid-1998, further shifted social concern away from labour shortage towards unemployment. But cycles come and go. Over the long run, with labour-force participation expected to decrease at both ends of the age distribution, sustained economic growth in Hong Kong continues to depend on whether the secular increase in the demand for professionals and skilled workers will be satisfied.

Table 4.6 Real wage indices by industry

Year	Manuf.	Who./ret., imp./exp., rest./hot.	Trans./ storage/ comm.	Fin./ins./ real est./ busi. serv.	Com./soc./per services	All industries
(A) All workers						
1988	100.0	100.0	100.0	100.0	100.0	100.0
1989	101.8	102.9	107.3	108.1	111.1	102.9
1990	104.1	104.2	111.5	114.7	114.6	105.6
1991	103.0	102.9	113.6	113.9	110.5	104.6
1992	103.4	102.1	115.8	113.9	112.9	104.9
1993	105.3	104.3	118.9	118.5	115.4	107.2
1994	105.1	105.7	121.3	118.8	118.6	108.1
1995	102.0	104.2	118.9	118.2	117.8	106.5
1996	104.2	104.1	121.0	121.8	118.9	107.8
1997	104.2	106.4	123.0	124.3	119.3	109.6
(B) Supervisory, technical, clerical, and misc. non-production workers						
1988	100.0	100.0	100.0	100.0	100.0	100.0
1989	103.8	102.9	108.7	108.1	111.3	104.6
1990	106.8	104.2	113.3	114.7	114.4	107.6
1991	106.2	102.9	116.1	113.9	108.4	106.7
1992	108.1	102.1	116.1	112.9	110.6	107.1
1993	111.5	104.3	119.5	118.5	113.0	110.0
1994	114.1	105.7	126.0	119.0	117.2	111.5
1995	112.2	104.2	125.8	118.4	115.9	110.3
1996	114.7	104.1	128.9	122.0	116.6	111.5
1997	115.5	106.4	126.8	124.4	117.4	113.4
(C) Craftsmen and operatives						
1988	100.0	n.a.	n.a.	n.a.	100.0	100.0
1989	101.2	n.a.	n.a.	n.a.	109.3	101.4
1990	103.4	n.a.	n.a.	n.a.	115.5	103.9
1991	101.9	n.a.	n.a.	n.a.	119.8	102.8
1992	101.8	n.a.	n.a.	n.a.	125.8	102.8
1993	103.0	n.a.	100.0	100.0	130.0	104.5
1994	100.8	n.a.	97.5	94.7	124.8	102.4
1995	97.0	n.a.	93.9	96.1	126.5	98.9
1996	99.3	n.a.	94.7	97.5	129.1	100.8
1997	98.7	n.a.	100.3	99.1	127.3	102.2

Source: Census and Statistics Department, *Monthly Digest of Statistics*, various issues.
Note: Figures are for September of each year. The beginning of each series is rebased to 100 to facilitate comparison.

Is the labour market competitive in Hong Kong?

During the process of economic transformation in Hong Kong over the past two decades, the shortage of labour in some sectors and redundancy in others appear to be a classic case of market rigidity and maladjustment, but it would be a mistake to jump to such a conclusion. After all, an economy that has gone through such drastic restructuring within such a short period of time while maintaining an unemployment rate of around 2 per cent can hardly be considered inflexible. Indeed, Table 4.6 shows that wages for workers in high demand (supervisory, technical, clerical and non-production workers) have experienced much higher wage growth than production workers in the declining manufacturing industries. Over time, this differential in real wages has provided, and will continue to provide, incentives for the reallocation of workers across sectors.

Table 4.6 also shows that, despite the change in the employment share, non-production workers in different sectors have enjoyed similar wage growth. This reflects wage equalisation at the margin, which is further evidence of worker mobility across industries. This observation is confirmed by Suen (1995b), who finds that the relationship between employment growth and earnings growth is weak. According to his estimate, sectors which experience a 1 percentage point increase in employment share (which corresponds to a 25 per cent increase in relative employment level) exhibit only a 1.8 per cent higher growth in earnings. If changes in employment shares are the result of changes in labour demand, the implied elasticity of labour supply (to an industry) is about 14. Such a large elasticity reflects a highly mobile labour force, as the following example will illustrate.

Suppose there is a fall in demand for, say, garment workers, which results in a fall in their wages. The magnitude of the wage reduction will depend on the elasticity of labour supply to the garment factory. If garment workers do not have many other options, their wages will have to fall substantially before some workers will leave the industry. On the other hand, if workers are relatively mobile across industries, their labour supply to the garment industry will be highly elastic. A slight reduction in wages in the garment sector is sufficient to induce workers to leave and therefore restore the balance between labour supply and labour demand. The evidence therefore suggests that Hong Kong workers are highly mobile across industries, so that large shifts in labour demand are associated with only minor changes in relative wages.

Unfortunately, such flexibility does not extend to mobility across occupations. Although expansion of the service sector has offered opportunities for many (particularly skilled) workers, the better positions are filled mostly by the more upwardly mobile younger cohorts. Older manufacturing workers trying to seek alternative careers and home-makers trying to re-enter the labour market often have to compete for low-level, unskilled service jobs. The result is slow wage growth in wholesale and retail, import and export, and restaurant and hotel services, where most of the unskilled service positions are found. In fact, as Table 4.6 shows, wage growth in these industries is not much higher than that for manufacturing operatives.

The lack of mobility across skill levels is, however, consistent with competition in the labour market. Older workers and many home-makers failed to secure highly paid service jobs because of their lack of relevant communication and professional skills. They also tend to have lower incentives to invest in such skills because of shorter horizons and uncertain job attachments. Improvements in welfare benefits, though still not generous by western standards, have also made low-paid employment less palatable, so that many would choose to remain unemployed or economically inactive. The plight of these individuals should not be trivialised. It should, however, be recognised as the consequence not of rigidity in markets, but of rational choice in human-capital investment and labour-force participation.

Many, however, prefer an alternative interpretation. In the debate on the adverse effects of sectoral shift, there has been a particular tendency to attribute higher unemployment among older workers to age discrimination. This ignores that fact that physiological changes over the life cycle imply definite changes in physical and mental strength. Individuals at different points of the life cycle also have different amounts of accumulated experience as well as different incentives to learn. These considerations suggest that it is unrealistic to assume that age is unrelated to productivity. In a detailed study of research publications in science, Stephan and Levin (1992) find evidence that scientists become less productive as they age. In another study using personnel data from one large company in the United States, Kotlikoff and Gokhale (1992) use a present value model to estimate the age-productivity profile. They found that productivity falls with age, with productivity exceeding earnings when young and vice versa when old. For male office workers, for example, productivity rises initially with age until it peaks at age 45 and declines thereafter. The productivity at age 65 is less than one-third of peak productivity.

The reluctance to hire older workers in some jobs then appears to be more a matter of business calculation than a matter of bigotry. Education credentials, test scores, years of experience are all useful but imperfect predictors of productivity. So are age and physical or mental conditions. Any one, or any combination, of these indicators will inevitably yield mistakes. There is always a brilliant computer programmer who has not finished secondary school, or an energetic 50-year old who still can and wants to learn something new every day. Employers who rely on imperfect signals will have to bear the costs of their mistakes, and they will balance these costs with the savings in information costs. Contrary to some recent suggestions (Ngo and Lau 1996), a law that arbitrarily prohibits the use of imperfect signals, whether it is age or gender, will only raise the fixed cost of employment and reduce the flexibility of the market. Such an approach may appeal to those whose distaste for discrimination demands a clear legal statement and penalty against such behaviour, but, given the intrinsic difficulty in distinguishing legitimate from discriminatory decisions, it is not likely to be more effective than the market in promoting equal opportunity for all.

Conclusion: the flexibility of wages in Hong Kong

The generally smooth performance of the labour market over the past two decades showed that market forces are alive and well in Hong Kong. Given the magnitude of the changes, there will inevitably be temporary dislocations in the market, but they are not the results of market rigidity or artificial barriers to mobility. The adaptiveness of the labour market should lay to rest the belief held by some that market signals are not working and that government assistance is necessary to ensure efficiency.

Underlying the flexibility of the labour market is a self-adjusting mechanism that operates through movements in wages. Institutionalised wage rigidities such as union contracts and the minimum wage are virtually non-existent in Hong Kong. The annual civil service pay increase is perhaps the most elaborate ritual in the Hong Kong labour market. Yet even the government pays attention to current market condition in setting its wages. The civil service makes up less than 10 per cent of the working population. In the rest of the economy, changes in wages and benefits are subject to few laws except those of supply and demand.

This flexibility is also reflected at the aggregate level, where changes in the real wage have also proven to be quite responsive to macroeconomic conditions. Figure 4.4 shows the rate of change of real GDP, and the rate of

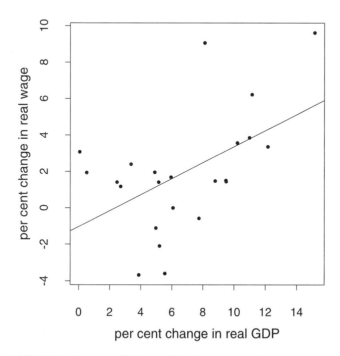

Figure 4.4 Relation between GDP growth and wage growth 1975–97.

change of the real wage index for craftsmen and operatives, in various years between 1975 and 1997. A line of best fit is added to the diagram to emphasise the positive relationship between the two variables. This relationship is statistically significant, although the two series cover only a relatively short span of some twenty years. The slope of the line in Figure 4.5 is 0.44, meaning that a 1 percentage point increase in the rate of GDP growth will raise the rate of real wage growth by 0.44 percentage points on average. In years of strong economic growth, when aggregate labour demand is high, real wages are bid up at a faster rate. When economic growth slackens, wage growth also decelerates and may even become negative. These adjustments help maintain the balance between labour demand and labour supply in the face of economic fluctuations.

A closer look at Figure 4.4 also reveals that real wage cuts are not uncommon in Hong Kong. During the economic slowdown in 1995, for example, real wages for craftsmen and operatives fell by 4 per cent. In the 1975–97 period, there were four years in which real wages registered negative growth, and one year in which real wages registered zero growth. With a moderately high inflation rate, real wage decreases can be achieved without nominal wage cuts. Wage cuts are of course not welcomed by workers, but they also help restore the employment level.

The recession in Hong Kong following the Asian financial crisis of 1997–98 has brought unemployment to reach new heights. Amid waves of business closure and layoffs, downward pressure on wages has mounted. Wages adjustments in this recession will be particularly painful for several reasons. First, this recession is more severe than any other recession Hong Kong has ever seen in the past thirty years. A large drop in labour demand will bring about a large drop in wages. Second, inflation in Hong Kong is already low by historical standards. Thus downward adjustments in real wages can occur only by lowering nominal wages, something which is hard to accept psychologically and is prone to generate labour disputes. Third, the recession takes place at a time when the currencies of most neighbouring countries have devaluated substantially. Labour in Hong Kong has become expensive not only relative to goods, but also relative to labour in other parts of Asia. Significant wage adjustments are needed to bring Hong Kong back to competitiveness. Painful as the wage adjustments may be, they have always been part of the process of economic recovery.

5 Income inequality

The impact on the Hong Kong labour force

Hon-Kwong Lui

Introduction

As explained in Chapter 3, the economy of Hong Kong has developed from an entrepôt to a manufacturing economy and then to a service economy over the last four decades. Recently, international organisations, such as the International Monetary Fund, have classified Hong Kong as a developed economy. As the economy develops, official statistics show that the income distribution amongst households has become more unequal. In December 1996, the Hong Kong government released the summary results of the 1996 Population By-census. A piece of information related to household income has aroused intense public concern. The official Gini coefficient[1] of household income distribution rose from 0.452 in 1986 to 0.476 in 1991, and increasing sharply after 1991 to stand at 0.518 in 1996. As measured by the Gini coefficient, incomes in Hong Kong were among the most unequal in Asia and the Pacific (Deininger and Squire 1996) with an average Gini coefficient for the region of less than 0.4 in the 1990s. Nevertheless, the trend toward higher income dispersion is not confined to Hong Kong. Topel (1997) points out that income inequality has increased in the United States and throughout the developed world with difference in degree and timing.

It is now common knowledge that Hong Kong has undergone rapid economic restructuring, but what is less clear is whether the working population can reap the benefits of economic success.[2] Do local workers face rising income inequality? Does economic transformation widen the income dispersion between workers of different educational levels? Who gains more and who gains less in the changing labour market? These questions have been raised by pressure groups and politicians alike. Unfortunately, official statistics published by the Census and Statistics Department cannot help us to answer these queries. The statistical authority only publishes the official Gini coefficient of household income distribution. The two widely quoted precursors to the present book, Turner (1980) and Turner *et al.* (1991) address these issues in earlier periods. This chapter attempts to bridge the data gap and analyse the income dispersion of the working population in more recent years.

There is a large literature discussing the relationship between economic growth and income distribution. The literature in this area originated from the pioneering work of Kuznets (1955) who proposes that income inequality widens in the early phases of economic growth followed by stabilisation and, as the economy continues to develop, an eventual narrowing of income dispersion. Since the publication of Kuznets' work, the interaction between economic growth and income disparity has remained a topic of active research. In the literature, there is a debate over whether growth affects inequality or inequality affects growth, see for example, Chang (1994), Anand and Kanbur (1993), and Persson and Tabellini (1994). Using household survey data from sixty-seven economies, Ravallion and Chen (1997) find that changes in inequality were uncorrelated with changes in average living standards. Moreover, the experience of East Asian economies shows that we can achieve economic growth with relatively low levels of income inequality (Birdsall *et al.* 1995).

For the case of Hong Kong, various studies analyse the changing patterns of income distribution in different periods. Chow's (1977) doctoral dissertation focuses on the changes in income distribution from the 1950s to the early 1970s. In a report prepared for the International Labour Office, Hsia and Chau (1978) assess the impact of industrialisation on income distribution. Turner *et al.* (1991) suggest that there was significant narrowing of income differentials between different classes of employees between the mid-70s and mid-80s. Chau (1994) suggests that there has been extensive upward mobility of low-income households in Hong Kong especially since the late 1970s. Finally, in an earlier publication, I (Lui 1997) argue that education and public housing policies fail to alleviate the income inequality problem in Hong Kong.

Income growth and labour force upgrading

Before analysing the income distribution of the working population in Hong Kong, I present the basic facts on income growth in the last twenty years. This section also addresses the upgrading of the labour force in the period from 1976 to 1996. Table 5.1 presents the median main employment income for the whole working population and also GDP per capita for the period 1976 to 1996.[3] From the first row of Table 5.1 we can see that the nominal median income of the working population increased 12 times between 1976 and 1996. In order to measure the real increase in main employment income, I adjust the median income by dividing the figures (first row) in Table 5.1 by the corresponding GDP deflator (last row). In the report period, the GDP deflator (1990=100) rose around four times from 30 in 1976 to 150 in 1996. Measured at 1990 constant prices, the median income in 1976 was HK$2,473 increasing to HK$6,333 in 1996. Thus, the median main employment income of the whole working population experienced a real increase of 156 per cent in the period after adjusting for inflation.

Table 5.1 Median income and GDP per capita

	1976	1981	1986	1991	1996
Median income	742	1,516	2,573	5,170	9,500
GDP (HKD billion)	62.8	170.8	312.6	668.5	1,195.3
GDP per capita	14,121	32,942	56,576	116,223	189,402
GDP deflator	30	50	69	109	150

Note: All figures are expressed in Hong Kong dollars at current market prices.
Sources: Census and Statistics Department, Population Census report, various issues. Census and Statistics Department (1997d).

The economic growth of the territory was equally impressive. Nominal GDP rose eighteen times and real GDP increased by slightly less than three-fold in the last two decades. However, absolute changes in GDP tell us nothing about the changes in living standard of an average resident. To address this, we can study the changes in real GDP per capita. From 1976 to 1996, real GDP per capita (measured at constant 1990 market prices) recorded an increase of 170 per cent. In other words, the living standard of an average resident in Hong Kong showed marked improvement in the period. By comparing the growth rate of the median main employment income (156 per cent) and real GDP per capita (170 per cent), it seems that the working population as a whole did enjoy the fruits of economic success. However, workers are not homogeneous and it is natural to expect that the wages of some workers will have risen faster than others. The next section tackles this issue in greater depth and discusses how it affects income distribution. But first, I turn to the distribution of educational attainment of the working population.

Table 5.2 presents the distribution of educational attainment of the working population in the period 1976 to 1996.[4] Until the recent expansion in tertiary education in early 1990, tertiary education was largely restricted to élites. This policy was in line with the British élitist tradition.[5] From Table 5.2 we can see that in 1976 only a small proportion of the working force possessed university degrees or post-secondary qualifications. Additionally, less than 5 per cent of the labour force reached post-secondary or above level, while close to 60 per cent of workers received no more than six years of formal education. However, at that time, the manufacturing sector dominated the labour market and the skill required was relatively low, so that a large supply of low-skilled workers fitted well with the labour demand of the 1970s.

As the economy continued to develop, labour market conditions changed substantially. As the economy moved away from labour-intensive manufacturing to skill-intensive services, employers were looking for better qualified workers. The introduction of free and compulsory elementary and junior secondary education in the 1970s helped upgrade the labour force. Since then, there has been a steady shift in the educational distribution in

Table 5.2 Educational level of the working population

Educational attainment	1976	1981	1986	1991	1996
Degree	3.7	4.0	5.3	7.4	13.3
Post-secondary	1.2	3.8	5.7	6.7	6.2
Matriculation	2.8	3.5	4.9	5.7	6.7
Upper secondary	18.5	22.0	26.8	30.6	32.5
Lower secondary	15.1	19.1	20.0	21.1	20.4
Primary	44.7	36.9	29.2	22.9	18.1
No schooling	14.0	10.7	8.1	5.6	2.9
Total	100.0	100.0	100.0	100.0	100.0

Sources: Census and Statistics Department, *Population Census Report*, various issues.
Note: All figures are in percentage.

Hong Kong. The increasing supply of better-educated workers matched with the changing labour demand. By 1986, the majority of the work force (63 per cent) received lower secondary education or above. Although the full impact of the recent rapid expansion of tertiary education has yet to be felt in the labour market, 19.5 per cent of the working population had received tertiary education in 1996, which was four times that of 1976. At the same time, 79 per cent the labour force went beyond primary school, which was 37.7 percentage points higher than that in 1976. This shows that the quality of the work force was upgraded by a large margin in the last twenty years. In fact, a steady and large supply of well-educated workers is crucial to the successful economic transformation from a manufacturing base to a service economy. As I have pointed out earlier (Lui 1997), the education policy of providing more and better educational opportunities to the general public was well supported by the changing economic environment in Hong Kong. Without the strong government commitment in education, the economic restructuring in Hong Kong could not proceed as smoothly as it did.

Rising income inequality

In the previous section, I showed that the median main employment income rose by 156 per cent in the last twenty years. At the same time, the quality of the work force also improved by a large margin. Human capital theory suggests that one's wage rate is directly related to one's investment in human capital. Economists believe that workers with higher education attainment receive higher earnings than workers with lower education attainment, *ceteris paribus*. Thus the reported income growth may be partly attributable to the general upgrading of the labour force. Turner *et al.* (1991) argue that the high rate of wage advance by international standards in the mid 1970s to mid 1980s was the result of labour force upgrading. Their conclusion may be equally applicable to the wage growth in recent years. In the same study, they also observed that there was a significant narrowing of income differentials between various classes of employees between the mid 1970s and the mid 1980s.[6]

In measuring the inequality of income distribution, researchers and commentators frequently use the Gini coefficient as the only measure of income inequality. However, this inequality index has it limitations (see Lui 1997). In addition to the Gini coefficient, economists also employ the variance of logarithmic income and quantile ratios to analyse income distribution. All three measures of income inequality are employed in this chapter.

In analysing changes in income distribution, it is useful to study the wage growth of workers in different industries and of workers in different occupational groups. Researchers prefer official statistics over private sources because of data credibility and convenience. Unfortunately, the statistical authority in Hong Kong has revised its classification substantially in recent years and direct comparison across industries and occupations over a longer period is impossible. For example, as from March 1991 the Hong Kong Standard Industrial Classification (HSIC) was adopted for the statistical classification of economic activities in place of the International Standard Industrial Classification (ISIC). Moreover, as from March 1993 the occupational classification used in the General Household Survey followed the International Classification of Occupations (1988) with local adaptation for Hong Kong. The statistical authority states clearly that as there are significant differences between the new and old classification schemes, no comparison can be made with earlier years (Census and Statistics Department 1995). I therefore, in common with most other researchers, analyse raw data from 1 per cent random sub-samples of population census and by-census files for the period 1976 to 1991. At the time of writing this chapter, the 1996 1 per cent random sub-sample is not yet available and I have to resort to official statistics when studying the changes in the period 1991 to 1996.

(A) 1976–1991

Table 5.3 presents summary measures of income inequality amongst the working population for the period 1976 to 1991. Basically, four inequality indices point to the same conclusion: that the income distribution of the work force was becoming more unequal throughout the period. The Gini coefficient rose by 12 per cent from 1976 to 1991. The change in the variance of logarithmic income was even more marked, with an increase of 22 per cent in fifteen years. Both measures clearly show that income dispersion in the labour force has widened.

In order to study the changes in income distribution in different segments of the labour force, we can look at the two quantile ratios shown in Table 5.3. If we arrange the main employment income of the working population in ascending order, the P_{90} percentile denotes that 90 per cent of the work

Table 5.3 Income inequality of the working population

	1976	1981	1986	1991
Gini coefficient	0.377	0.384	0.406	0.421
Variance of logarithmic income	0.398	0.406	0.457	0.484
P_{90}/P_{10}	3.750	4.063	4.425	4.643
P_{50}/P_{10}	1.750	1.875	1.917	1.964

Source: Lui (1997).

force have an income below that level. The quantile ratio P_{90}/P_{10} represents the income level at the 90th percentile divided by income level at the 10th percentile of the distribution of main employment income, and the P_{50}/P_{10} ratio represents the income level at the 50th percentile divided by the income level at the 10th percentile. The higher the ratio, the higher the level of income dispersion. From 1976 to 1991, quantile ratios P_{90}/P_{10} and P_{50}/P_{10} experienced an increase of 24 per cent and 12 per cent respectively. These results suggest that income of top earners rose much faster than those who earned less. Workers in the middle-income group did enjoy higher income growth than those at the bottom cohort but their income advancement was not as substantial as those at the higher end of the income distribution. Thus, as I have argued previously (Lui 1997), the increase in income inequality took place at the two extremes of the distribution rather than near the middle. In the following paragraphs, we explore some of the possible explanations for these trends.

Does greater inequality reflect a shortfall of university graduates?

As the economy of Hong Kong has undergone rapid restructuring, the labour demand moved in favour of those with higher skill levels. Moreover, the supply of better-educated workers also increased in the last fifteen years. On one hand, the demand factor pushes up wages of educated workers. On the other hand, the supply factor dampens the wage growth of such workers. Thus, the overall change in income distribution by educational level was the result of the interaction of the changes in supply and demand factors. Table 5.4 presents income ratios by educational level of the working population.

The income ratios shown in Table 5.4 are derived from a fairly complicated method which requires a little explanation. For each 1 per cent sample file, I ran (Lui 1997) ran an earnings regression with the natural logarithm of main employment income as the dependent variable and a set of education dummies together with other socio-economic attributes as independent variables. After running the earnings regression, it is necessary to subtract the coefficient estimate of each education dummy from the coefficient estimate of the upper secondary dummy. Then, the income ratio is computed by taking the exponential of the difference in coefficient

Table 5.4 Income ratio by educational level

	1976	1981	1986	1991
No schooling	0.455	0.480	0.442	0.481
Primary	0.584	0.614	0.552	0.531
Junior secondary	0.738	0.740	0.726	0.693
Upper secondary	1.000	1.000	1.000	1.000
Matriculation	1.340	1.269	1.350	1.359
Post-secondary	1.563	1.748	1.979	1.663
Degree	2.471	2.380	2.714	2.548

Source: Lui (1997).
Note: Upper secondary graduates were used as reference group in computing the income ratios.

estimates. The resulting income ratios can be interpreted as ratios of raw incomes. However, this method has one major advantage in that these ratios are independent of variation in other socio-economic variables. In fact, coefficient estimates derived from an earnings regression can accurately reflect the relationship between dependent and independent variables.[7]

From Table 5.4 we can see that income ratios in the last three rows increased slightly from 1976 to 1991. These figures suggest that workers with higher educational attainment enjoy slightly higher income growth than those workers with upper secondary education. The same phenomenon was also observed in other parts of the world. For example, in the United States, the relative price paid for more educated and experienced workers has increased (Gottschalk 1997), and Juhn *et al.* (1993) argue that rising returns to skill are partly responsible for increasing wage inequality in the United States (see also Topel 1997).

In contrast, workers with lower secondary or primary education experienced slower income growth than those with upper secondary education. A little puzzling is that uneducated workers also enjoyed slightly faster income growth than secondary graduates. One possible explanation is that the supply of uneducated workers was reduced by 8.4 percentage points from 1976 and 1991 (see Table 5.2). The shrinking pool of uneducated workers helped push up their incomes a little. Table 5.4 as a whole suggests that better educated workers enjoyed slightly higher income growth than did less educated workers in the period 1976 to 1991. However, the income growth advantage was relatively small and this indicates that supply and demand forces in the labour market were largely in balance. Moreover, these results are consistent with the results of my earlier work (Lui 1994), where I concluded that there was no major shortfall of university graduates in this period. If the demand for skilled workers outran the increasing supply of such workers in Hong Kong, we should observe relatively higher price paid for skilled workers.[8]

Did economic restructuring cause higher inequality?

When the unemployment rate increased in the early 1990s, the public put the blame on the rapid economic transformation of the late 1980s. Suen (1995) shows that there were clear indicators that Hong Kong had also undergone structural changes in the early 1970s. Although he points out that the rate of economic restructuring has accelerated since the 1980s, he finds no evidence that sectoral shifts led to higher unemployment or underemployment. As official statistics show that Hong Kong has experienced rising income inequality, the public in general, and labour activists in particular, again put the blame on sectoral shifts. However, the relationship between economic transformation and inequality has yet to be established by evidence. For example, Leonard and Jacobson (1990) argue that industrial restructuring has no adverse effect on earnings distributions.

By studying the sectoral shares of 25 broad industries from 1976 to 1991 in Hong Kong, Suen (1995) shows that changes in industrial composition alone accounted for 70 per cent of the increase in income dispersion. In short, sectoral shifts did matter in explaining the overall increase in income inequality in the period 1976 to 1991. In order to take a closer look at the impact of sectoral shifts on Hong Kong workers in more recent years, Suen (1995) narrows down his analysis to the period 1986 to 1991. His analysis indicates that changes in industrial composition explained only 28 per cent of the overall increase in income dispersion (as measured by the variance of logarithmic income). In this five-year period, the within-industry increase in income dispersion was the most important factor in explaining the overall rise in inequality. Although the income dispersion widened, we should not overlook the real increase in actual earnings (Chan and Suen, Chapter 4, above).

Education policy and income inequality

Among redistributive policies, education policy is one of the most frequently used devices to reduce income disparity. For example, O'Neil (1984) shows that education is instrumental in improving one's life and economic status. Earlier I analysed the impact of education policy on income inequality in Hong Kong (Lui 1997). Here I argued that changes in the educational composition of the working population explain almost all the increase in income disparity in the period 1976 to 1991. If the educational composition had remained unchanged, I demonstrated that the variance of logarithmic income would have increased by only 0.005 instead of 0.086. The determination of the government in providing more and better educational opportunities for the public has led to substantial upgrading of the labour force. At the same time, increasing the proportion of more educated workers in the labour market has helped push up income dispersion. I also showed that the income dispersion of highly educated workers is much higher than that of workers of lower education attainment. The recent expansion of tertiary education will increase the supply of graduate workers which in turn will further increase overall income inequality. Thus, far from promoting greater equality, higher levels of education have been associated with greater inequality in Hong Kong during this period.

(B) 1991–1996

Nowadays we seldom describe Hong Kong as a manufacturing-oriented economy. The service industries employ the majority of the labour force and most argue that the service sector demands more educated and experienced workers. However, the brain drain problem posed a serious threat in the early 1990s, although when the world economy became sluggish, the number of returning migrants rose rapidly. Various studies have tried to portray the overall picture of net migration (see, for example, Ho *et al.* 1991 and Chapter 7, below) in Hong Kong. The inflow and outflow of skilled workers has a significant impact on the distribution of income. For example, if the outflow of professionals is large, those professionals who choose to remain in Hong Kong should be able to bargain for higher wages, *ceteris paribus*. On the other hand, as the manufacturing base moved north, we should expect manual workers to suffer most. To understand the underlying changes in the labour market in recent years, I present ratios of median income by occupation in Table 5.5.

In computing the ratios in Table 5.5, the median income of clerks was used as denominator. Clerks were used as a reference group because (i) they accounted for 17 per cent of the work force in 1996 (16 per cent in 1991); and (ii) the required entry qualifications are modest. The median income of clerks was $5,000 and $9,000 per month in 1991 and 1996 respectively. In 1991, the median income of professionals was three times that of clerks. If

Table 5.5 Income ratio by occupation

	1991	1996
Managers and administrators	2.400	2.222
Professionals	3.000	2.667
Associate professionals	1.600	1.556
Clerks	1.000	1.000
Service workers and shop sales workers	1.000	0.944
Craft and related workers	1.000	0.944
Plant & machine operators and assemblers	0.900	0.944
Elementary occupations	0.700	0.611
Overall	1.034	1.056

Source: Census and Statistics Department, *Population Census Report*, 1991 and 1996 issues.
Note: Clerks were used as a reference group in computing the income ratios.

the supply of professionals were insufficient to satisfy the demand, we would expect to see an increased income ratio. However, this ratio dropped to 2.667 in 1996. For managers and administrators, the income ratio decreased from 2.4 in 1991 to 2.2 in 1996. Similarly, the ratio for associate professionals also recorded a decrease. These results suggest that Hong Kong did not suffer from a relative shortage of professionals, managerial personnel or skilled workers. Moreover, the income dispersion among skilled workers seemed to have narrowed between 1991 and 1996. Two possible reasons can explain this phenomenon. First, an increase in the number of returning migrants and the expansion of tertiary education may have provided an adequate supply of highly educated workers to satisfy market demand. Second, it could be argued that the quality of an average university graduate has declined given the marked increase in university enrolment. If so, this might reduce their average productivity, and so their income might also decline.

For semi-skilled labour (such as craft and related workers) and manual workers (such as elementary occupations[9]) the income ratios have decreased in recent years. Contrary to the general expectation, plant and machine operators and assemblers enjoyed higher income growth compared to clerical personnel (and more educated workers). One may argue that those who could secure employment in manufacturing industries were of higher quality than those who were screened out by market forces. Thus, slightly higher income increases may have been a reflection of their productivity *vis-à-vis* an average manual worker. Perhaps surprisingly, given the shift towards the service sector, Table 5.5 shows that the median income of service workers and shop sales workers relative to clerks actually reduced by 5.6 percentage points between 1991 and 1996.

Unlike the period from 1976 to 1991, rising inequality in income distribution did not take place at both ends of the distribution of income. Information gathered in Table 5.5 suggests two important features. While income disparity at the top end of the distribution may have narrowed between 1991 and 1996, income inequality at the low end appears to have widened, at least for craft and elementary occupations. Indeed, employment surveys undertaken by local universities indicated that job markets for fresh graduates were not as good as in the past. The increasing supply of degree holders in the labour market is likely to further dampen the income growth of professionals and managerial personnel in the foreseeable future. Moreover, medical graduates were unable to secure employment to complete their professional training in local hospitals. A sizeable portion of engineering graduates were engaged in marketing and sales positions. In short, university graduates are facing keen competition in the labour market.

At the other extreme, those engaged in elementary occupations received the lowest income increase. In nominal values, their median income increased from $3,500 to $5,500 per month between 1991 and 1996. Their income ratio relative to clerks was reduced by 12.7 per cent from 0.7 in 1991 to 0.61 in 1996. It is the general belief that unskilled workers suffer most from economic restructuring and the results presented in Table 5.5 are consistent with this general wisdom.

Conclusion: rising inequality and the labour market in the twenty-first century

Whilst the economy of Hong Kong has continued to prosper in recent years, the distribution of income has become increasingly unequal since the 1970s. Although the labour force as a whole shared in the benefits of economic success, selected occupations were at a relative disadvantage. This chapter suggests that there is no evidence to support the view that higher inequality during the period 1976 to 1991 reflects a shortfall of graduates relative to other occupations. In the period from 1976 to 1991, the supply and demand of different classes of workers were largely in balance. The income ratio by educational level remained relatively stable over the period. Moreover, Suen (1995) indicates that changes in sectoral composition were significant in the period 1976 to 1986 in explaining rising income disparity. However, economic restructuring only accounted for 28 per cent of the overall increase in income dispersion between 1986 to 1991, with most of the increased inequality being attributable to within-industry changes. The provision of more and better education opportunities to the general public was associated with higher income disparity, *ceteris paribus*, and research results show that income inequality among educated workers was higher than that among less educated workers.

In the years 1991 to 1996, the income advantage of more educated and experienced workers diminished. Professionals and managerial personnel enjoyed lower income growth than that of clerical personnel in these years. As more graduates join the labour market, it is likely that their income advantage will be further reduced in the future. Furthermore, manual workers and those in elementary occupations have had a relatively hard time in recent years. Their median income recorded a slower growth than other workers. Thus, the income distribution at the lower end became more unequal during 1991 to 1996. Regarding the prospects for those at the lower end of the distribution, several important questions should be raised. Are technical changes responsible for the rise in income inequality? Has the relative demand for manual workers reduced? If skills-mismatch is the underlying cause of higher inequality, the solution may be found through effective education and manpower policies. As Topel (1997) points out, the policy options for reducing inequality are severely limited if technical change is the real cause. If the SAR government wants to combat rising inequality, it has to design its education and manpower policies with great care.

Do changing labour market conditions favour skilled workers? The general public seems to agree that skilled workers will dominate labour markets of service economies such as Hong Kong. However, there is a limit to this: the argument is very simple. Information technology improves at a high speed and computer knowledge is no longer the domain of scientists and engineers. Desktop computers are so powerful and user-friendly that high-school graduates can easily master a computer and perform highly productive work. Johnson (1997) argues that unskilled workers can become more efficient in jobs that were formerly done by skilled workers because of technological advancement. For example, publishing jobs that were done by well-trained professionals in the past can now be completed by relatively unskilled workers with knowledge of desktop publishing software. Another example is that in the past, personal financial analysis was performed by professional accountants or financial analysts. Nowadays, any customer service officer in a retail bank can do the same task with the help of a suitable financial analysis software. Hence, at least in cases such as these, the relative demand for skilled labour may fall.

Although a rising return to skill has been observed in developed countries, it is uncertain whether this trend will continue. Advancement in information technology comes into play in shaping the future demand for labour. Nevertheless, the decision made by the HKSAR government to extend computer education to primary level was well taken. If all workers possess marketable skills, the income dispersion can be reduced.

Notes

1 The Gini coefficient is one of the most widely used income inequality index. It takes a value between zero and one. A higher value corresponds to higher income inequality, *ceteris paribus*. See Cowell (1995) for a useful survey of measurements of income inequality.

2 See Chapters 3 and 4 for discussions on economic restructuring in Hong Kong.

3 In 1996, the Population By-census was conducted under the *de jure* enumeration approach whereas the *de facto* enumeration approach was adopted in previous censuses and by-censuses. Thus, data from the 1996 Population By-census were not strictly comparable to those from earlier censuses and by-censuses. However, the statistical authority points out that the problem of incomparability should not be serious (see Census and Statistics Department 1997a for further details).

4 The classification of matriculation and post-secondary courses had changed since the 1991 Population Census and data for 1986 and 1981 have been adjusted to the new classification system to enable direct comparison. However, data for 1976 cannot be adjusted due to insufficient information from published statistics. (See also note 3.)

5 In the United Kingdom, tertiary education also expanded rapidly in the last twenty years. In early 1990s, polytechnics and selected post-secondary colleges in the United Kingdom were upgraded to universities. The development of tertiary education in Hong Kong was very similar to that experienced in the United Kingdom. At the time of writing this chapter, four non-university tertiary institutions in Hong Kong were renamed as universities. It is expected that another tertiary institution, Lingnan College, will be upgraded to university by mid-1999.

6 The Turner *et al.* (1991) analysis was based on data collected from *ad hoc* surveys which exclude managerial or professional personnel.

7 See, for example, Greene (1993) for useful discussions of regression analysis.

8 In the United States, increase in the relative demand for skilled labour has outrun the increasing supply of such labour which has led to increases in inequality (Topel 1997).
9 Elementary occupations include street vendors; domestic helpers and cleaners; messengers; private security guards; watchmen; freight handlers; lift operators; construction labourers; hand packers; agricultural and fishery labourers.

6   Women workers in Hong Kong

Narrowing the gender gap

Hon-Kwong Lui

Introduction

Traditionally, women were expected to take up most of the household responsibilities, whereas men were perceived as providers and protectors.[1] These kinds of gender related social norms and expectations remain fundamental among Chinese as described in Chapter 1. Ng and Chiu show in Chapter 11 that women-friendly human resources policies are not widely adopted in Hong Kong. Nevertheless, as the economy of Hong Kong continues to develop, so the economic status of women improves. Empirical studies on women's economic status in Hong Kong are limited (see for example, Lui and Suen 1993, 1994 and Suen 1995) and most of these studies are conducted by social scientists other than economists.[2] This chapter seeks to address this shortfall by analysing the changing economic status of women and reviewing the narrowing gender gap in the last two decades in Hong Kong.

When studying the economic status of women, we have to rely on a number of indicators, the most widely reported measure being the female–male earnings ratio. Commentators and researchers often cite gender discrimination as the most important source of the earnings gap.[3] Although the gender earnings gap is still quite pervasive and significant, the differential has narrowed by a large margin in the last twenty years.

Other than the earnings gap, indicators of women's economic status include, but are not restricted to, the female labour force participation rate, occupational segregation by gender, and household work done by men and women. Among these four indices, we have quantifiable and reliable data for the first three but as regards information on household work done by men and women, there is no readily available Hong Kong-wide survey data. There are, however, a number of specific studies clearly indicating that women spend more time on household work.

In the next section, I document the female–male earnings gap in different countries. In the last four decades, women workers in different parts of the world have experienced noticeable improvement in earnings relative to men. A similar pattern was also observed in Hong Kong and the female–male earnings differential narrowed by 15 percentage points between 1976 and 1996. I go on to use multiple regression analysis to study the earnings gender gap in Hong Kong. Finally, I consider the economic status of women. The evidence gathered in this chapter clearly shows that the economic status of women workers has risen in Hong Kong in the last twenty years, although as the concluding section points out, whilst women have made impressive economic progress, there are areas for further improvement.

The gender earnings gap in comparative perspective

A considerable gender earnings gap is observed in most parts of the world. Although the gender gap has reduced in many countries in the past few decades, it still exists in all industrialised economies. Table 6.1 presents female–male hourly earnings ratios in manufacturing for selected countries. From the table, we can see that the size of the raw female–male hourly earnings differentials varies considerably.

In analysing the gender gap, we have to consider various socio-economic variables. Among these variables, changes in marital status have a significant impact on the female–male earnings ratio. Single female workers devote a lot of their energy in market activities. However, when they get married, females tend to spend more time on their families and pay relatively less attention to paid work. On the other hand, once a man gets married, he is expected to support his family, so that married men tend to invest more in market activities than single men. Basic economic principles suggest that when workers put more effort on market activities, they receive higher wages. If the above conjecture is correct, the female–male earnings ratio of married workers should be much lower than the earnings ratio of single workers. In Table 6.2, I present female–male earnings ratios (controlling for variations in hours of work) of single and married workers of selected countries. These earnings ratios are imputed by using the regression analysis method with natural log of earnings as the dependent variable.[4]

The gender earnings ratios presented in Table 6.2 demonstrate a clear pattern. The female–male earnings ratio was higher for single workers.

Table 6.1 Female–male hourly earnings ratios of selected economies

	1955	1973	1982	1988	1993
Australia	0.690	0.694	0.782	0.796	0.811
France	n.a.	0.768	0.777	0.792	0.753
Japan	0.447	0.539	0.488	0.485	n.a.
Sweden	0.692	0.841	0.903	0.900	0.900
Switzerland	0.637	0.654	0.670	0.675	0.686
United Kingdom	0.586	0.607	0.688	0.680	0.689
United States	n.a.	0.617	0.654	0.702	n.a.

Source: Blau and Ferber (1992); International Labour Office (1995).

96   *Hon-Kwong Lui*

Table 6.2 Female–male earnings ratio, by marital status, of selected economies

	All workers	Married workers	Single workers
Australia	0.7489	0.6909	0.9144
Norway	0.7308	0.7160	0.9158
Switzerland	0.6174	0.5768	0.9449
United Kingdom	0.6337	0.5966	0.9489
United States	0.6849	0.5944	0.9552

Source: Blau and Kahn (1992).

Apparently there is no reason to believe that women lose their working ability once they get married. The larger gender gap among married workers presumably reflects the fact that working women shift their focus from market activities to household work once they get married. These results confirm the general belief that there is a clear household division of labour even in western countries.

After looking at the female–male earnings patterns of western countries, I now turn to the situation in Hong Kong. Table 6.3 presents the official median monthly income from main employment by sex in Hong Kong.[5] As the median monthly income of women rose faster than the median income of men, the female–male income ratio recorded an increase between the years 1976 and 1996. Before 1981, working women earned about 70 per cent of what men received. A clear jump in income for women was recorded between 1981 and 1986 in which the earnings gap narrowed by 5 percentage points. The latest statistics show that the female–male earnings differential experienced further reduction in recent years and reached 0.8 in 1996. Looking at median monthly income, the gender earnings gap has narrowed significantly in the last twenty years. These ratios, however, take no account of the differences in socio-economic characteristics of working men and women.

When men and women first join the labour market, gender difference in socio-economic characteristics and work ability should be negligible. As age advances, this coupled with changes in life-cycle stages, people are motivated to adjust their work-related attributes, their life-style and their work prefer-

Table 6.3 Median monthly income in Hong Kong

	Female	Male	Income ratio
1976	559	858	0.651
1981	1,165	1,801	0.647
1986	2,143	3,067	0.699
1991	4,250	6,000	0.708
1996	8,000	10,000	0.800

Source: Census and Statistics Department, *Population Census Report*, various issues.

Table 6.4 Female–male income ratio by age in Hong Kong

Age	1981	1986	1991	1996
15–19	0.9701	0.9897	1.0556	1.0000
20–24	0.8000	0.8421	0.9000	1.0000
25–34	0.6500	0.7903	0.7692	0.8547
35–44	0.5000	0.5714	0.5714	0.6667
45–54	0.5556	0.6000	0.5932	0.6500
55–64	0.6000	0.6000	0.6667	0.6494
65 and over	0.6364	0.6000	0.6061	0.7143

Source: Census and Statistics Department, *Population Census Report*, various issues.

ences. Career-minded workers tend to invest more in human capital so as to improve their earnings abilities. In general, the longer the expected work life, the higher the net present value of returns from human capital investment. So, younger workers tend to invest more in human capital than older workers, *ceteris paribus*. Family-concerned people, however, may shift their focus from market work to their families or even quit the labour market. Traditionally, men are more career-minded than women whereas women are more family-concerned than men. Thus, we should expect females to invest less in human capital and the female–male earnings ratio should therefore decrease as age advances.

Table 6.4 presents the female–male median income ratio by age from 1981 to 1996. In Hong Kong the minimum age to enter the labour market is 15 and so the age bracket 15 to 19 in Table 6.4 mainly consists of youngsters who have recently joined the labour market. As discussed earlier, gender difference in earnings ability of those aged 15 to 19 should not be significant. Thus the female–male income ratio for all four census years shown in Table 6.4 was close to one. In other words, young men and women received the same wage rate. Starting from the second age group 20 to 24, gender earnings gap begin to appear. The gender gap widened significantly for workers aged 35 or above in all years. If we study Table 6.4 row by row, we notice that the female–male income ratio rose gradually from 1981 to 1996. For example, in 1981, female workers at prime working age (35 to 54), only managed to get 60 per cent of what men received. By 1996, however, women workers on average earned about two-thirds of what men earned. Female workers in other age groups also experienced substantial improvement *vis-à-vis* male workers. The female–male income ratio narrowed by 20 percentage points for workers aged 20 to 24 and 25 to 34.

Regression analysis of the gender gap

The analysis in the previous section takes no account of the fact that workers are heterogeneous in terms of socio-economic characteristics and earnings ability. A better way to analyse the gender earnings differential is to study the income ratio after controlling for individual differences using regression analysis. As the behaviour of part-time workers is rather different from full-time workers, it is advisable to exclude part-time workers in the analysis. Unfortunately, the 1991 population census did not collect information on hours of work whereas earlier censuses did. In order to have an overview of the impact of including part-time workers in the analysis, I ran several earnings regressions on various 1 per cent random sub-samples of censuses with hours of work information. The regression results with and without part-time workers in the data files differ by a large margin.[6] Whenever possible, I prefer to concentrate on full-time workers in analysing the gender earnings gap. The data sets used in the regression analysis were obtained from population censuses and by-censuses conducted in Hong Kong. From the 1 per cent census samples of 1976, 1981, and 1986, I selected those (i) who were aged between 15 and 64; (ii) who were born in Hong Kong or China; (iii) who were working not less than 35 hours in the census reference week; (iv) who received positive earnings from main employment earnings; and (v) who were not full-time students or unpaid family workers. As for the 1991 population census, I have to include part-time workers in my analysis as these workers cannot be identified in the data set. Thus, the data selection criteria for 1991 census sample are the same as the earlier three censuses except that condition (iii) above does not apply. For comparison purposes, I also use the same selection criteria for the 1986 census sample and repeat the regression analysis. This chapter thus presents two sets of results for 1986: one focuses on full-time workers and the second one includes all workers. The results for 1991 are not strictly comparable to the results of earlier years, but the two sets of 1986 results serve as a bridge in interpreting the results before and after the 1986 population census

In order to control for differences in individual characteristics, economists use multiple regression to estimate the determinants of employment earnings. In this chapter, I use the natural logarithm of main employment income as the dependent variable, so that the estimated coefficients can be interpreted in terms of percentage changes. The independent variables include age, years of working experience (and its square), hours of work, and four sets of dummy variables including (i) marital status, (ii) educational attainment, (iii) place of birth and (iv) gender. The dummy variable 'female' captures the unexplained earnings differential between male and female workers. For example, if the coefficient estimate for the female dummy is minus 0.15, it means that the earnings of an 'average' female worker is 15 per cent lower than that of an 'average' male worker with the same set of socio-economic characteristics.

Economists also provide various methods to decompose the female–male earnings gap (see, for example, Blinder 1973 and Oaxaca 1973). Some researchers, notably some sociologists and economists, describe this unexplained gender gap as 'discrimination', although there is a huge literature analysing this unexplained earnings gap. The most popular theories include discrimination, signaling, differential investment in human capital

Table 6.5 Regression coefficients for the 'female' dummy

	Full-time workers	*All workers*
1976	−0.2911	n.a.
1981	−0.2772	n.a.
1986	−0.2713	−0.2968
1991	n.a.	−0.2914

Note: n.a. means not applicable. This analysis was not carried out, as explained in the text.

and differences in unmeasured earnings ability. The empirical results presented in this chapter do not in themselves allow us to distinguish between these various theories. However, our findings do identify that proportion of the earnings gap which cannot be explained by the other variables included in the analysis.

In order not to over-burden readers with multiple regression results for all data sets used in this chapter, Table 6.5 only presents structural coefficient estimates for the 'female' dummy variable. All other coefficient estimates, though not presented, have the predicted signs and are statistically significant at any practical level.[7] As explained in the previous subsection, the multiple regressions for the 1976, 1981 and 1986 censuses include only full-time workers whereas the results for the 1991 census cover both full-time and part-time workers. For 1976, the estimated coefficient is −0.2911 which means that an average female worker earns 25 per cent (i.e., $1 - e^{-0.2911}$) less than an average male worker after controlling for differences in socio-economic characteristics. Looking at the first column, we can see that the unexplained gender earnings gap was narrowed by 2 percentage points between the years 1976 to 1986. For the period from 1986 to 1991, the earnings gap was further reduced by half a percentage point (the second column). Although the size of the unexplained gender earnings gap was still significant and pervasive in the report period, regression results presented in Table 6.5 indicate that the gap has closed. In fact, evidence gathered in Tables 6.3, 6.4 and 6.5 point in the same direction: that the economic status of women has risen in the period from 1976 to 1991. Moreover, whilst Lui and Suen (1993) argue that the progress made by female workers in earnings relative to men was mainly attributable to the rise in schooling and labour force participation of women, the analysis shown in Table 6.5 suggests that there has been an improvement in the relative earnings of women even after allowing for changes in measured educational attainment, working experience, hours of work and the other independent variables included in my regressions.

The rising economic status of women

In this section, I document stylised facts about women workers from three different perspectives, namely labour force participation, educational attainment and the occupational distribution of women. The results point to the same conclusion – that the economic status of women has risen.

Rising female labour force participation

Other than the female–male earnings ratio, the female labour force participation rate in an economy can also shed some light on the economic status of women. If the economic status of women in an economy is low, the female labour force participation ratio is usually low. If the economic status of women is high, this means that the opportunity cost of non-market activities is higher, leading to a higher female labour force participation rate. In Hong Kong, the labour force participation rate is defined as the proportion of economically active persons, i.e. the labour force, in the total population aged 15 and over.

Table 6.6 presents the labour force participation rates by sex in Hong Kong. The first column indicates that the overall female labour force participation rate rose by 5.6 percentage points from 43.6 per cent in 1976 to 49.2 per cent in 1996. The sharp increase in the labour force participation for women was mainly due to two reasons: (i) the rising economic status of women; and (ii) a large increase in the number of foreign domestic helpers. In 1976, it was unusual for a household to employ a foreign domestic helper, but by 1996 this had become commonplace. If we removed foreign domestic helpers from the labour market, the female labour force participation rate would drop from 49.2 per cent to 46.8 per cent in 1996 (Census and Statistics Department 1997a). Even we take into account the effect of foreign domestic helpers in the labour market, the increase in labour force participation for women is still quite substantial.

In contrast, the overall labour force participation rate for men recorded a decrease of 4 percentage points over the last twenty years. The decrease in overall labour force participation was mainly attributable to rising education opportunities for youngsters. Young men stay in schools or universities for a longer period than ever before. As a result, they join the labour market at a later stage in their life-cycle. In order to take a closer look of the effect of the

Table 6.6 Labour force participation rates by sex

	Female	Male
1976	43.6	80.6
1981	49.5	82.5
1986	51.2	80.9
1991	49.5	78.7
1996	49.2	76.6

Source: Census and Statistics Department, *Population Census Report*, various issues.
Note: All figures are expressed in percentage.

Table 6.7 Labour force participation rates by age by sex

	20–24 Female	Male	25–34 Female	Male	35–44 Female	Male
1976	71.8	87.8	47.8	97.7	42.9	98.4
1981	79.7	90.9	56.8	98.3	53.4	98.6
1986	83.7	88.3	64.8	97.6	57.9	97.7
1991	82.9	84.8	68.4	96.5	57.0	96.9
1996	76.9	79.7	74.8	96.7	57.6	96.7

Source: Census and Statistics Department, *Population Census Report*, various issues.
Note: All figures are expressed in percentage.

recent expansion of tertiary education on the labour market, I present the labour force participation rates by age and by sex in Table 6.7. For prime working age, i.e. aged 25 to 44, most men are economically active. It is usual that once a man joins the labour market, he remains economically active until he retires. From Table 6.7, we can see that in the late 1970s and early 1980s around 90 per cent of males aged 20 to 24 were economically active. However, this ratio dropped to slightly less than 80 per cent by 1996. In Hong Kong, a typical undergraduate starts his/her higher education at the age of 19 and completes his/her bachelor's degree at 22. Hence the provision of more education opportunities at first degree level will lower the overall labour force participation for potential workers in the younger age brackets.

As discussed earlier, women are more concerned with family responsibilities than are men. A significant proportion of women choose to quit the labour market once they get married or have a baby. The results presented in Table 6.7 confirm this conjecture. The female labour force participation rate experiences a sharp decrease between successive age brackets. In earlier years, when the educational attainment for women was relatively low, women tended to leave the labour market at a younger age. In 1976, more than half of females aged 25 and over were economically inactive. By 1996, three quarters of women aged 34 or below stayed in the labour market. If we focus on the age group 25–34, the increase in the female labour force participation rate was very substantial. Between the years 1976 and 1996, the labour force participation rate for women gained 27 percentage points. Although the increase in magnitude was not as great as for the age group 25–34, the labour force participation rate for women for the other two age groups also experienced a marked increase. In short, all these results lead to the same conclusion – that the rising female labour force participation was unmistakable. In other words, the economic status of women has risen in Hong Kong in the last twenty years.

Rising educational attainment of women

In the previous two sections, I argued that women have made substantial

Table 6.8 Educational attainment of population aged 15+ by sex

| | 1976 | | 1996 | |
	Female	Male	Female	Male
No schooling/kindergarten	31.6	9.2	13.8	5.1
Primary	36.1	43.3	22.6	22.7
Lower secondary	12.4	18.7	15.2	22.7
Upper secondary	15.3	19.8	28.8	26.6
Matriculation	1.7	3.7	6.3	5.9
Tertiary (non-degree)	1.0	0.8	4.5	5.1
Tertiary (degree)	1.9	4.5	8.8	12.0

Source: Census and Statistics Department, *Population Census Report*, various issues.
Note: All figures are expressed in percentage.

progress in the labour market *vis-à-vis* men. The female–male earnings gap has narrowed and female labour force participation has risen significantly in the past two decades. Having studied these two phenomena, one would ask what are the major causes of the achievements made by women. I believe that the principal momentum behind the scene was the rising educational attainment of women. Table 6.8 presents the percentage distribution of population aged 15 and above by sex and educational attainment in 1976 and 1996.

From Table 6.8 we can see that the educational attainment of the whole population improved substantially between the years 1976 and 1996. In 1976, slightly more than half of men and 67.7 per cent of females received only primary education or below. The impact of the provision of free and compulsory education up to lower secondary level since the 1970s clearly shows up in the 1990s. In 1996, 72.2 per cent of males and 63.6 per cent of females reached at least the lower level. If we focus on the highly educated cohorts, the improvements made were equally impressive. The proportion of female university graduates increased from 1.9 per cent in 1976 to 8.8 per cent in 1996. Similarly, the ratio of male degree holders gained 7.5 percentage points in two decades.

While Table 6.8 documents the general upgrading of the whole population, it tells us nothing about the corresponding changes in the labour market. In order to analyse the improvements made by woman workers, I present years of schooling of the working population in Table 6.9. In 1976, an average worker received 7.2 years of education, increasing to 9.3 years in 1991. In other words, an average worker had completed lower secondary education in 1991. It is the Chinese cultural tradition that males should receive more education than females. This tradition did exist in the labour market in earlier years but it is no longer true in more recent years. In 1976, an average working man received 7.4 years of schooling which was 0.8 higher than that of an average female worker. The advantage enjoyed by men in earlier years, however, was reversed. In 1991, an average working woman

Table 6.9 Years of schooling of the working population by sex

	1976	1981	1986	1991
Male workers	7.4	7.9	8.7	9.2
Female workers	6.6	7.5	8.7	9.6
All workers	7.2	7.7	8.7	9.3

Source: Lui (1997).

had 9.6 years of education which was 0.4 years higher than that of an average working man.

At first glance, this seems like a paradox especially when we study the results in Table 6.8. Nevertheless, this puzzling fact can easily be resolved. Human capital theory suggests that a worker's earnings is positively related to the investment in education. The theory states that more educated workers receive higher wage rates. The higher the educational attainment, the higher is the opportunity cost of not working in the labour market. I argued earlier that women are more likely to choose to quit the labour market when they get married or they have to take care of children. This stay/leave decision hinges on the associated opportunity cost forgone. Thus, more educated women are more likely to stay in the labour market whereas less educated women are more prone to leave the labour market, *ceteris paribus*. As a result, the average educational attainment of female workers is likely to be higher than the average of all females. On the other hand, most men (no matter whether they are educated or not) stay in the labour market until they reach retirement age. Hence, it is to be expected that the educational attainment of an average working man is lower than that of an average working woman. Nevertheless, the results presented in Table 6.9 indicate that the educational attainment of working women rose faster than that of working men, again pointing to the rising status of women workers.

Climbing the occupational ladder

Over the last two decades, more and more women have come to hold important business and public positions. To name but a few examples, at the time of writing this chapter, the Chief Secretary for Administration (the head of all civil servants), the Chairperson of the Legislative Council, the Chairperson of the Housing Authority and the Chairperson of the Consumer Council are all women. Basing on casual observation, most people would agree that women have climbed upward in the occupational ladder. However, a more systematic analysis of the distribution of occupation by sex is needed to substantiate this claim. Table 6.10 summarises the distribution of the working population by occupation and by sex. Since the 1991 Population Census, the Hong Kong government has adopted a new classification for occupations as promulgated by the International Labour

Table 6.10 Working population by occupation by sex

	1991		1996	
	Female	Male	Female	Male
Managers and administrators	4.9	11.8	7.1	15.4
Professionals	3.0	4.1	4.3	5.5
Associate professionals	11.3	9.7	13.9	11.0
Clerks	28.8	8.0	29.5	8.5
Service workers & shop sale workers	12.5	13.7	13.5	14.0
Craft and related workers	4.4	20.9	3.7	17.9
Plant & machine operators & assemblers	12.7	13.9	4.0	11.6
Elementary occupations	21.7	16.6	23.5	15.3
Others	0.7	1.2	0.5	0.9

Source: Census and Statistics Department, *Population Census Report*, various issues.
Note: All figures are expressed in percentage.

Organisation in 1988 (Census and Statistics Department 1997). Thus Table 6.10 only compares the changes in occupation patterns of 1991 and 1996. Lui and Suen (1993), however, study the changes in the structure of occupations in the period from 1976 to 1986. Using an 'index of occupational position' proposed by Freeman (1981), they show that women had climbed a substantial distance up the occupational ladder between the years 1976 and 1986.

Table 6.10 shows that the proportion of women working as professionals, and managers and administrators, increased from 7.9 per cent in 1991 to 11.4 per cent in 1996. If we include associate professionals, the proportion for women rose 6.1 percentage points from 19.2 per cent in 1991 to 25.3 per cent in 1996. Apparently, more females were engaged in higher level jobs in 1996 than in 1991. Although the percentage share of working men in higher level jobs also increased, the growth was not as fast as that of women. At the lower end of the occupational ladder, we can see that half of women were working as clerks or in elementary occupations.[8] At the same time, about one-quarter of men held similar positions. Another major change in the distribution of occupations is the proportion of women working as plant and machine operators and assemblers. In 1991, 12.7 per cent of working women were employed as plant and machine operators and assemblers, and the percentage share dropped to 4 per cent in 1996. In short, the results presented in Table 6.10 are consistent with the arguments of Lui and Suen's (1993) study. We found that women have moved up the occupational ladder. The economic progress made by women in respect of the distribution of occupations involved: (i) more women holding higher level positions; and (ii) fewer females working as manual workers.

Conclusions: prospects for women in the labour market

In the last twenty years we have witnessed significant economic progress on the part of women relative to men. Various indicators are employed in this chapter to analyse the economic status of women. Evidence gathered supports the view that the economic status of women has risen in the period from 1976 to 1996. The major findings in this chapter are summarised as follows. Firstly, although the unexplained gender earnings gap was quite significant, it has been reduced by a large margin over the last two decades. Secondly, thanks in part to the provision of more and better education opportunities for women, the overall female labour force participation rate has increased by 5.6 percentage points. For women in the age bracket 25–34, the labour force participation rate increased by 27 percentage points from 47.8 per cent in 1976 to 74.8 per cent in 1996. Moreover, the educational attainment of women rose faster than that of men and, by 1997, the educational standard of an average female worker was similar, if not better than, that of an average male worker. Lastly, working women have climbed a substantial distance up the occupational ladder. A much higher percentage share of female workers were working as professionals, and as managers and administrators, in 1996 than in the past. Although women have made impressive economic progress in the last twenty years, the economic status of women is still substantially behind that of men. Not only are the average earnings of women much lower than those of men, the labour force participation rate for women is lower. Moreover, research results presented in this chapter indicate that more than 40 per cent of women were not engaged in market activities after reaching the age of 35. In contrast, for prime age workers (aged 25–44), over 96 per cent of men remained economically active. I believe the economic status of women can be further improved if they are willing to participate more actively in the labour market.

Notes

1 See Becker (1991, Chapter 2) and Bryant (1990, Chapter 5) for formal analysis of the division of labour in households.
2 Those who are interested in gender studies in Hong Kong may consult the bibliographical index compiled by Hong Kong Institute of Asia-Pacific Studies (1991).
3 The first economic analysis of discrimination in the labour market was conducted by Nobel Prize winner Gary S. Becker in his doctoral dissertation in 1955. Several years after he published his dissertation as a book (Becker 1971), economists gradually accepted his economic approach to discrimination and other human behaviour. See Cain (1986) for a survey of economic analysis of labour market discrimination and Becker (1976) for a collection of papers of economic analysis of human behaviour.
4 For details of the derivation of these earnings ratios, see Blau and Kahn (1992).
5 In 1996, the Population By-census was conducted under the *de jure* enumeration approach whereas the *de facto* enumeration approach was adopted in previous censuses and by-censuses. Thus, data from the 1996 Population By-census are not strictly comparable to those from earlier censuses and by-censuses. However, the statistical authority points out that the problem of incomparability should not be serious. (See Census and Statistics Department 1997 for further details.)

6 In fact, including part-time workers in the data files increases the noise in the regressions. The explanatory power (as measured by adjusted R-squared) of the earning regressions reduced by more than 15 per cent when part-time workers were included. When we excluded part-time workers, the lowest adjusted R^2 value was 0.40. On the other hand, when these workers were included in the analysis, the highest adjusted R^2 value was only 0.37.

7 Detailed multiple regression results can be obtained from the author.

8 Elementary occupations include street vendors; domestic helpers and cleaners; messengers; private security guards; watchmen; freight handlers; lift operators; construction labourers; hand packers; agricultural and fishery labourers.

7 Immigration in Hong Kong

A source of labour supply[1]

Kit-Chun Lam and Pak-Wai Liu

Introduction

Since the end of the Second World War, three waves of immigrants from the Mainland have arrived in Hong Kong: in 1948–9 during the civil war in China, in 1959–62 during the collectivisation and the Great Leap Forward, and in 1978–80 after China launched its economic reform and open door policy. In this chapter we evaluate the impact of this immigration on population growth and labour supply in Hong Kong, focusing on immigrants from the Mainland.[2] We will show that as fertility has fallen in Hong Kong, immigration has exceeded natural increase as the major source of population growth.

During the early years of high immigration up until 1980, immigration provided an abundant supply of labour for the labour-intensive manufacturing industries in Hong Kong. The change in immigration policy in October 1980 abruptly stopped illegal immigrants and slowed down the growth of the labour force. This effect was exacerbated by a number of other factors which led to labour shortage in the late 1980s. One of these was emigration. Due to concern over the political future, emigration out of Hong Kong accelerated in the late 1980s and reached a peak in 1992. However, since 1992 emigration has slowed down substantially and return migration has increased. In this chapter we will evaluate the impact of such flows on population growth and labour supply. We will also examine the characteristics of new immigrants to assess their contribution to the labour force in relation to the native-born population. The chapter concludes with a discussion of the possibility of a more active immigration policy which supports population growth and provides skilled manpower to promote economic growth.

Waves of Chinese immigrants

The civil war in China in 1947–9 brought the first wave of Chinese immigrants from the Mainland into Hong Kong since the end of the Second

World War. Hundreds of thousands of refugees entered the territory during 1949 and the spring of 1950 to escape communist rule. In 1950, after negotiation with the Chinese government, the Hong Kong government implemented a quota system, restricting the entry of Chinese citizens. The Chinese government would vet and approve the applications of Chinese citizens for entry into Hong Kong but, in recognition of the population pressure on Hong Kong, would restrict the number of exit permits issued each year. The Hong Kong government would accept all Chinese citizens who have been issued exit permits by the Chinese government for entry into Hong Kong for residence.

In 1958 the failure of the Great Leap Forward and the collectivisation movement in agriculture in China led to widespread starvation (Lin 1990), giving rise to a second wave of immigration from China to Hong Kong. Immigrants in this wave who arrived in Hong Kong were illegal in that they did not have exit permits issued by the Chinese authorities. The Immigration Department of Hong Kong exercised discretion to allow these illegal immigrants to register and stay in Hong Kong. It was reported that as many as 142,000 refugees crossed the border illegally into Hong Kong between 1959 and 1962.

In 1974, the Hong Kong government discontinued the practice of allowing all immigrants from China to stay in Hong Kong and replaced it with what came to be known as the 'reached-base' policy. Under this new policy, those arrested on illegal arrival in Hong Kong were repatriated to China. However, all others who evaded capture and subsequently 'reached-base' were permitted to stay. Reaching base meant crossing the border without being captured and gaining a home with relatives or finding proper accommodation.

In late 1978 China launched its economic reform and open door policy. The barrier, which hitherto had effectively inhibited the flow of capital, people and information between China and the outside world during three decades of isolation under communist rule, was substantially removed. The consequence was dramatic. A third wave of immigration hit Hong Kong in 1978 to 1980 which was in every way more massive than the previous waves. The situation became untenable by August and September 1980 when in each of the two months an estimated 23,000 illegal immigrants arrived in Hong Kong and nearly half of them evaded arrest and reached base. The Hong Kong government, after informing and seeking the co-operation of the Chinese authorities, announced the abolition of the 'reached-base' policy on 23 October 1980. After a grace period of three days, all illegal immigrants would be repatriated to China immediately after capture regardless of whether they had reached base. The door to legal residence in Hong Kong for illegal immigrants was finally closed.

The massive inflow of illegal immigrants had an adverse impact on wages and employment in Hong Kong. The addition of over 300,000 largely unskilled immigrants to the labour market within a short period from 1978 to 1980 depressed real wages. The situation was aggravated as Hong Kong's economy slowed down in 1981–2.

In October 1980 after the 'reached-base' policy was abolished, the governments of Hong Kong and China established an agreement to restrict the issue of one-way permits allowing the holders to enter Hong Kong legally to take up residence. The quota was only raised to 150 in 1995 to clear the long queue of applicants for immigration to Hong Kong, especially Mainland-born children of Hong Kong permanent residents who are entitled to the right of abode in Hong Kong under the 1992 Basic Law.

Natural increase, immigration and population growth

Immigration from the Mainland has always been a major source of population growth in Hong Kong. Since the Second World War, each of the major waves of immigrants swelled the population. After October 1980, only legal immigrants were admitted into Hong Kong. This steady stream of legal immigrants has since become an increasingly important source of population growth in Hong Kong. Its relative importance has grown over the years because the traditional source of population growth, deriving from natural increase, has declined.

In the last three and a half decades, there has been a dramatic decline in the rate of the natural increase in population in Hong Kong from 28.9 per 1,000 persons in 1961 to less than a quarter of that level, 5.1 per 1,000, in 1996. This decline is due to the rapid fall in fertility. The crude birth rate in Hong Kong was 35 per 1,000 persons in 1961. By 1996 it had fallen to less than a third of this level, to 10.0 per 1,000. In fact the fertility rate of Hong Kong is among the lowest in the world. The decline in the total fertility rate of Hong Kong from 1965 to 1990 has been dramatic. In 1965 Hong Kong's total fertility rate was 4.93. By 1990 it has fallen to a low of 1.21 which is lower than virtually all North American, European and Asian countries. For instance, in 1990 the total fertility rate of the USA was 1.88 (1989 figures), Sweden 2.14, UK 1.84, Switzerland 1.59, Australia 1.90 (1989 figures), Japan 1.54 and Singapore 1.83 (Kono 1996).

Legal immigration from the Mainland has, however, increased since the early 1990s. By 1995, for the first time since the abolition of the 'reached-base' policy, the contribution of immigration from China to Hong Kong's population growth exceeded the contribution of natural increase (see Table 7.1). The contribution of legal immigration is expected to remain the *most* important source of population increase, given the present trend of declining fertility.

Immigration and labour supply

Over the history of Hong Kong, the major waves of Chinese immigrants boosted the population and hence the labour supply. The influx of Chinese

Table 7.1 Components of population growth (excluding Vietnamese migrants) 1961–97

Year	Estimated population (end-year)	Births	Deaths	Natural increase	Balance of arrivals and departures[1]	Legal immigrants from China
1961	3,195,300	110,884	19,325	91,559	−15,374[2]	n.a.
1962	3,368,200	112,503	20,933	91,570	81,260	n.a.
1963	3,461,800	114,550	20,340	94,210	−558	n.a.
1964	3,545,100	107,625	18,657	88,968	−5,737	n.a.
1965	3,625,400	101,110	18,150	82,960	−2,638	n.a.
1966	3,679,400	91,832	19,261	72,571	−18,638	n.a.
1967	3,760,600	88,215	20,234	67,981	13,271	n.a.
1968	3,844,500	82,685	19,444	63,241	20,598	n.a.
1969	3,906,100	82,482	19,256	63,226	−1,602	n.a.
1970	3,995,400	79,132	19,996	59,136	30,151	n.a.
1971	4,095,500	79,789	20,374	59,415	40,701	n.a.
1972	4,184,300	80,344	21,397	58,947	29,787	n.a.
1973	4,334,200	82,252	21,251	61,001	88,977	n.a.
1974	4,438,600	83,581	21,879	61,702	42,619	n.a.
1975	4,500,800	79,790	21,597	58,193	4,043	n.a.
1976	4,551,000	78,511	22,633	55,878	−5,711	n.a.
1977	4,631,500	80,022	23,346	56,676	23,809	n.a.
1978	4,769,900	80,957	23,830	57,127	76,117	n.a.
1979	5,024,700	81,975	25,125	56,850	147,388	n.a.
1980	5,145,100	85,290	25,008	60,282	91,708	55,452
1981	5,238,500	86,751	24,832	61,919	39,422	54,249
1982	5,319,500	86,120	25,396	60,724	23,683	53,848
1983	5,377,400	83,293	26,522	56,771	990	26,701
1984	5,430,900	77,297	25,520	51,777	2,690	27,475
1985	5,500,400	76,126	25,258	50,868	2,0991	27,285
1986	5,565,700	71,620	25,912	45,708	2,1059	27,111
1987	5,615,300	69,958	26,916	43,042	4,859	27,268
1988	5,671,600	75,412	27,659	47,753	−8,389	28,137
1989	5,726,500	69,621	28,745	40,876	−15,540	27,263
1990	5,752,000	67,731	29,136	38,595	−9,072	27,976
1991	5,815,300	68,281	28,429	39,852	15,613	26,782
1992	5,887,600	70,949	30,550	40,399	46,621	28,367
1993	5,998,000	70,451	30,571	39,880	83,883	32,909
1994	6,119,300	71,646	29,905	41,741	86,874	38,218
1995	6,270,000	68,637	31,468	37,169	116,322	45,986
1996	6,421,300	62,977[3]	30,641[3]	32,336[3]	132,935	61,179
1997	6,617,100	59,294[3]	31,303[3]	27,991[3]	172,428	50,287

Sources: *Hong Kong Monthly Digest of Statistics*; Demographic Statistics Section, Census and Statistics Department; Immigration Department, Hong Kong, various issues; *Hong Kong – A New Era, A Review of 1997*.

Notes

1 End year comparison. For 1986–97, the figures include an estimate of HK residents away to China/Macau living outside HK.

2 From 7-3-1961 to 31-12-1961.

3 Provisional estimates subject to revision after next population census.

immigrants after the communist takeover of China contained a significant number of industrialists and entrepreneurs from Shanghai who brought with them capital, managerial skills and technical know-how. It also supplied the cheap labour for the early development of labour-intensive manufacturing industries in Hong Kong in the 1950s. Most immigrant labour competed for lower-paid and lower-skilled jobs, and had lower fringe benefits (Turner *et al.* 1991). Each subsequent wave of immigrants boosted the labour supply and sustained the development of labour-intensive industries until the mid-1980s.

Immigration has both an immediate and long-term effect on labour supply. The arrival of immigrants who participate in the labour market immediately adds to the labour force. The impact on the labour supply depends on the size of the flow of immigrants, the proportion that is economically active, their skills and their educational background. Besides the immediate impact, immigration also has a long-term and indirect effect for it increases the population which ultimately determines the size of the labour force.

Slow growth in labour force after the abolition of the 'reached-base' policy

The importance of immigration to labour supply in Hong Kong is just as dramatically evident in periods of low immigration as in periods of high immigration. Since the abolition of the 'reached-base' policy in 1980, illegal immigration has been largely contained and a major source of labour supply has been eliminated. From 1982 to the early 1990s the labour force grew at a slow pace of 0–2 per cent in most years, and actually shrank in some years (see Figure 7.1). The reduction in immigration alone had a major effect in slowing down the growth of the labour force. This was exacerbated by a number of other factors, including the declining rate of natural population increase, the changing age structure of the population, the declining labour force participation rate, and the rising outflow of emigrants.

Declining rate of natural population increase

The decline in the rate of natural population increase has been discussed earlier. The long-term decline in this rate slows down the growth of the labour force in the long run.

Changing age structure of the population

Since the labour force is mainly drawn from the population of working age (15 to 65), a shift in the age composition, in particular, from the younger age bracket to the older age bracket, will have a significant impact on the size of the labour force. To illustrate the shifting age composition, Figure 7.2 shows the population size of two age groups. The age group 15–24 is the youngest

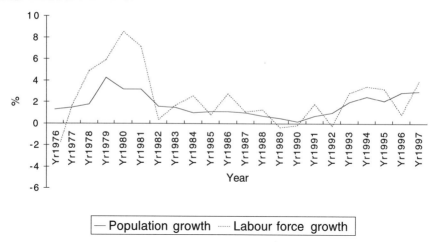

Figure 7.1 Population growth vs. labour force growth, 1976–97.[4]

Source: Hong Kong Monthly Digest of Statistics.

group in the labour force which will provide manpower for the economy for many years to come. It shrank from 1.2 million in 1981 to about 910,000 in 1997. In contrast, the age group 55–64, which is due to retire from the labour force, grew in size from about 410,000 to 522,000 over the same period. The combined effect of these demographic shifts across age groups is to reduce the supply of labour over time.

Declining labour force participation rate

The overall labour force participation rate reached a peak in 1981 because the third wave of illegal immigration in 1978–80 brought a massive influx of young immigrants from the Mainland who by self-selection were mostly potential participants in the labour force. Since 1981 labour participation rates have declined (see Figure 7.3), thus reducing labour supply.

The decline in the overall labour participation rate is mainly due to the fall in the participation rate of the youngest and the oldest age groups in the labour force. The drop in the participation rates among youngsters of age 15 to 24 is the result of the rapid expansion of secondary and tertiary education in Hong Kong in the 1980s, causing many youngsters to defer entry into the labour force. As for workers in the age group 55 to 64, the decline in their participation rate can be attributed to their retiring earlier than before. The rise in real wages of workers increases their income, which induces them to consume more leisure and retire earlier.

Rising outflow of emigrants

Much of the 1980s and the early 1990s were characterised by the rising tide

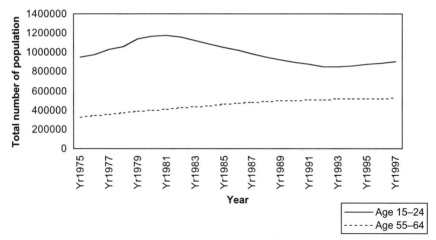

Figure 7.2 Age composition of population, 1976–97.[5]

Source: Hong Kong Annual Digest of Statistics.

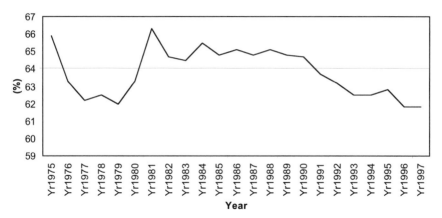

Figure 7.3 Labour force participation rates in Hong Kong, 1976–97.[6]

Source: Economic Database, Department of Economics, CUHK; *Hong Kong Monthly Digest of Statistics.*

of emigration. The number of emigrants was between 18,000 and 22,000 per year throughout the first half of the 1980s. It picked up in 1987, and rose sharply from 42,000 in 1989 to 62,000 in 1990 following the incident of 4 June 1989 in Beijing. The number of emigrants peaked at 66,000 in 1992 before moderating to a lower level following the tightening of quotas in major recipient countries like Canada and Australia (see Figure 7.4).

The number of emigrants rose sharply in 1987 because of the number of individuals applying for emigration and the intake quotas set by the destination countries. As the changeover of sovereignty issue emerged in the early

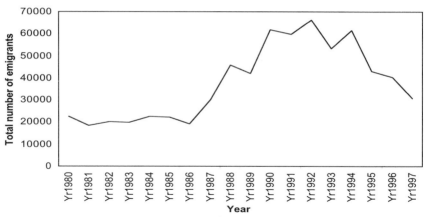

Figure 7.4 Number of emigrants, 1980–97.[7]

Source: Government Secretariat; *Hong Kong – A New Era, A Review of 1997*, 1997.

1980s, Hong Kong people became increasingly concerned over the political future of Hong Kong. At first, most people adopted a wait-and-see attitude on the negotiation that was going on between Britain and China before committing themselves to emigration plans. The outflow of emigrants remained steady in those years. The Sino-British Joint Declaration on the future of Hong Kong was signed in 1984. The initial enthusiasm over the Joint Declaration quickly gave way to scepticism and doubts. A surge of applications for emigration began. The process of application took about a year to complete, so that the increase in outflow was not visible until 1987. Moreover, two major destination countries, Canada and US changed their immigration policies and quotas around this time, thereby providing more opportunities for Hong Kong applicants.

Emigrants are a selected and self-selected group. On the one hand, they are selected by the destination countries as immigrants. The selection criteria of two major destination countries, Canada and Australia, are mainly based on points systems which favour applicants who are young, well-educated, English-speaking, professionals, technicians or managers by occupation, and who have the financial means of either supporting themselves or starting a new business (if they are admitted under the business migration pro-grammes) in the destination countries. On the other hand, individuals self-select in applying for emigration. According to human capital theory, individuals who are young, adaptive to a new culture and who are inter-nationally employable because they possess skills and qualifications that are transferable to other countries are more likely to migrate (Sjaastad 1962). Based on these two considerations, it is not surprising to find that emigrants from Hong Kong are more likely to be in the 25–44 age group, to hold an academic degree and to be employed as a professional, administrator or manager than the general population (see Table 7.2). Not surprisingly, the

Table 7.2 Characteristics of emigrants and the Hong Kong population

Age	Emigrants (1989)	Population (1991)
0–24	13,900 (33.1%)	36.5%
25–34	11,300 (26.9%)	21.1%
35–44	9,200 (21.9%)	16.0%
45–54	3,600 (8.6%)	8.8%
55–64	2,600 (6.2%)	8.9%
65 and above	1,400 (3.3%)	8.7%
	42,000 (100%)	100%
Occupation		
Professional, technical administrative & managerial	9,800 (23.3%)	11.3%
Other workers	13,000 (31.0%)	37.5%
Economically inactive	19,200 (45.7%)	51.2%
	42,000 (100%)	100%
Education		
First degree/ postgraduate	6,100 (14.5%)	4.5%
Post-secondary	4,100 (9.8%)	4.2%
Matriculation (F6–F7)	2,500 (5.9%)	3.9%
Secondary (F1–F5)	18,900 (45.0%)	40.1%
Primary & below	10,400 (24.8%)	47.3%
	42,000 (100%)	100%

Source: Government Secretariat, General Household Survey 1989 and 1991 Census.
Note: The percentages for the emigrants are figures for 1989. The percentages for the population are figures from the 1991 Census.

rising outflow of emigrants has had a detrimental effect on both the quality and quantity of the labour force in Hong Kong in the late 1980s and early 1990s.

The combined effect of the above factors slowed down the growth of the labour force. Since the abolition of the 'reached-base' policy, the growth rate of the labour force declined to less than 3 per cent p.a. in the 1980s (see Figure 7.1). The labour market in the late 1980s to early 1990s was very tight as the unemployment rate fell, reaching a historical low of 1.1 per cent in 1989. In response to labour shortage, the Hong Kong government introduced a modest programme of importation of semi-skilled and unskilled labour in 1990. At the peak of the programme about 27,000 workers were imported, including those working on the construction of the new airport (these figures do not include domestic helpers). However, political opposition made it difficult for government to expand the labour importation programme. By 1995, the labour market had eased and the unemployment rate had risen. The government was obliged to replace the General Scheme of Labour Importation with a Supplementary Scheme in 1996 which imported only 2,000 workers.

Return migration and volatility in population and labour force growth

In the 1990s a new trend of return migration emerged. Over the last few decades there have always been Hong Kong residents who emigrated abroad and returned after obtaining foreign residence status or passports. Return migration abruptly gathered steam in 1992. In Table 7.1 the net increase (decrease) in population due to factors other than natural increase is given by the figures of balance of arrivals and departures. Arrivals include immigrants who are given residence status, return migrants, return Hong Kong residents who used to work and reside in the Mainland, expatriates and foreign workers, whereas departures are due to emigration. These figures of the balance of arrivals and departures are rather volatile. Return migration is the major reason behind the sharp increase in the positive balance of arrivals net of departures which increased from 47,000 in 1992, to 133,050 in 1996. These numbers are substantially above the level of less than 30,000 for most of the 1980s (Table 7.1). Return migration is also responsible for the marked increase in the labour force growth rate in 1993–5. This completely reverses the negative net balance of arrivals and departures in 1988–90 and the corresponding slow to negative growth of the labour force caused by the rising tide of emigration.

Information on return migrants is very scanty. The increase in the number of return migrants since 1992 may be related to the economic recession of major receiving countries of Hong Kong emigrants including the US, Canada and Australia. Hong Kong emigrants were attracted to return migrate by the better economic opportunities in Hong Kong. It is also possible that the number of return migrants increases because the pool of former Hong Kong residents who are living overseas with foreign passports, and who are therefore potential return migrants, has expanded over time.

The large positive balance of arrivals net of departures in 1994 and 1995 could also be due to a return flow of Hong Kong residents who worked in the Mainland. They returned to Hong Kong because of the economic downturn in the Mainland triggered by the tightening of macroeconomic control in 1994.

The demographic statistics collected by the Department of Census and Statistics do not allow us to identify the size of the flow of return migrants or to break down the components of the balance of arrivals and departures. Hence it is difficult to be definitive about the reasons for the volatility of the balance of arrivals and departures over time. What is important is the fact that there are large fluctuations in the balance of arrivals and departures which causes substantial variability in the population growth rate, and correspondingly the labour supply in Hong Kong. In 1979–80 before the abolition of the 'reached-base' policy, the annual population growth rate in Hong Kong was as high as 3 to 4 per cent and the labour force growth rate was 6 to 9 per cent, due mainly to the massive influx of illegal immigrants. After the abolition of the 'reached-base' policy, the population growth rate throughout the 1980s fell dramatically to a low of 0.2 per cent in 1990 on account of controlled immigration, declining fertility and rising emigration. The labour force growth also stagnated. Since 1991 the increase flow of return migration has pushed the population growth rate upward to over 2 per cent again, reaching 2.9 per cent in 1996 (see Figure 7.1).

Characteristics of immigrants

Hong Kong is a society of immigrants. The 1996 By-Census shows that 32.6 per cent of the population are immigrants from the Mainland. Among the native-born, most have parents or grandparents who were immigrants. We define Chinese immigrants to be individuals who were born in the Mainland and at some point in time migrated to Hong Kong to take up residence, and new Chinese immigrants as those who have resided in Hong Kong for six years or less as of a certain date.

The impact of the influx of illegal immigrants in 1978–80 on the gender composition is most apparent among new immigrants. In 1981, the male to female ratio of 58 to 42 is highly skewed in favour of males mainly because of the influx of predominantly male illegal immigrants before it was halted in October 1980. In 1991 the gender ratio is completely reversed to a male to female ratio of 39 to 61. This is mainly attributable to a shift in immigration policy, namely from allowing illegal immigrants to take up residence prior to October 1980 to restricting entry and residence to legal immigrants only. Many of the legal immigrants admitted in recent years are wives of Hong Kong residents who migrated to Hong Kong to join their husbands. The predominance of females among new immigrants in recent years will have important implications for the future labour supply in Hong Kong.

The age pattern of new immigrants and its change over the years from 1981 to 1996 are quite different from the native-born population. Unlike the native-born, the proportion of children and teenagers among the new immigrants increases substantially from 20.7 per cent in 1981 to 25.5 per cent in 1996, reflecting a shift in the selection criteria of the Chinese authorities in favour of family reunion. The percentage of new immigrants of working age of 15–64, fell from 77.2 per cent in 1981 to 73.6 per cent in 1996. The increase in the proportion of children, teenagers and retirees among new immigrants in the recent arrival cohorts will have implications for the labour supply of Hong Kong in both the short run and the long run.

Over the last two decades there has been an improvement in educational attainment levels. There has been a significant reduction in the percentage of the native-born with only primary schooling or lower, and a marked increase in the percentage of those with secondary schooling and first degrees. The educational attainment of the new immigrants also shows an improvement from the 1981 cohort to the 1996 cohort. In contrast to the former cohort, the latter is made up of exclusively legal immigrants. It is clear that legal immigrants are better educated than illegal immigrants. The mechanism through which they are selected is different from the self-selection of illegal immigrants. Despite the fact that the proportion aged 14 and under in the 1996 cohort of new immigrants is significantly higher than in the 1981 cohort, the percentage with only primary schooling or less in the 1996 cohort is only 45.0 per cent as compared to 53.6 per cent in 1981. Correspondingly the proportions with senior secondary schooling, first degrees and postgraduate degrees in 1996 are higher than in 1981.

The labour force participation rates of new immigrants in 1981, both male and female, were substantially higher than those of the native-born. The rate for male new immigrants in 1981 was as high as 95.8 per cent (Table 7.3). This reflects the self-selected nature of the 1981 cohort. The new immigrants then were mostly illegal who left their homeland and risked their lives to cross the border to look for better economic opportunities in Hong Kong. Hence, almost all of them were economically active after arrival in Hong Kong.

However, the labour force participation rates for both male and female new immigrants have experienced a substantial decline from 1981 to 1996, with a drop of 11.6 percentage points and 20.6 percentage points for the males and females respectively. The decline for the females is so large that by 1996 their labour force participation rates had fallen below that of the natives. This substantial decline is due to the drastic change in the composition of new immigrants. Unlike the 1981 cohort, the 1996 cohort of new immigrants is exclusively composed of legal immigrants with an increased percentage of children and married women who came to be reunited with their family. Consequently the percentage of students and homemakers who are economically inactive and therefore do not participate in the labour force increased substantially from the 1981 cohort to the 1996 cohort. Specifically, 24.8 per cent of the female new immigrants in 1981 were homemakers. By 1996 this had increased to 40.6 per cent.

Table 7.3 Labour force participation (ages 15–64)

| | Native-born (%) | | | New immigrants (%) | | |
	1981	1991	1996	1981	1991	1996
Labour force participation						
All	66.5	72.8	72.2	85.3	66.3	61.5
Male	77.4	84.2	83.8	95.8	82.7	84.1
Female	55.7	61.1	60.0	69.9	58.0	49.3

Source: Hong Kong Census and By-Census, 1981, 1991 and 1996.

Immigration as a source of labour supply 119

As discussed in Chapters 3 and 4, the economy of Hong Kong underwent an economic restructuring in the 1980s. The shift in occupational distribution of the natives from 1981 to 1996 reflects vividly the structural transformation of the economy. The skills of the illegal Chinese new immigrants in the 1981 cohort were more likely to be related to agriculture or manufacturing in the Mainland, given the small scale of the service sector. While production skills in manufacturing may be general and therefore transferable from the Mainland to Hong Kong, service sector skills are more country-specific and, even if the new immigrants have such skills, they are less transferable to Hong Kong, especially to jobs which require a good command of English. In short, new immigrants in 1981 were disadvantaged in finding service jobs. A disproportionately large proportion of them became production and related workers, mainly in manufacturing.

The trend has shifted substantially in the 1991 and 1996 cohorts. The new immigrants in these cohorts were better educated than previous cohorts. Unlike the 1981 cohort who were brought up in the Mainland isolated from the outside world, the 1991 and 1996 cohorts left the Mainland after 1985 and 1990 respectively, six to eleven years after China launched the open door policy and economic reform. Since the opening up of China, there has been a massive flow of information between Hong Kong and the Mainland as a result of the flow of investments and visitors across the border, as well as via the mass media. The 1991 and 1996 cohorts of new immigrants must have gained more information on the Hong Kong community in general, and the labour market in particular, than previous cohorts before they migrated to Hong Kong. Their better understanding of the language, culture and ethos of Hong Kong probably helped them in taking up jobs in the service sector. Also the demand for Putonghua speakers in Hong Kong has probably increased over time. The gain in the percentage of service jobs by category from the 1981 cohort of new immigrants to the 1996 cohort is remarkable, while the proportion of production and related workers fell drastically (Table 7.4).

Conclusion: population growth and supply of skilled human resources as objectives of immigration policy

The prevailing immigration policy of the Hong Kong government which the SAR Government inherits is passive. Its objectives have been stated in numerous issues of the *Hong Kong Report*, see for example that for 1996, as follows: 'Policies are framed to limit permanent population growth brought about by immigration into Hong Kong to a level (with) which the territory can cope, and to control the entry of foreign workers.' (Hong Kong Government 1998: 295). The objectives stated are entirely premised on the control of numbers.

Instead of limiting population growth, the immigration policy of Hong Kong should support population growth. With a total fertility rate of about 1.2 which is among the lowest in the world, the population of Hong Kong

Table 7.4 Occupational distribution

	Native-born (%)			New immigrants (%)		
	1981	1991	1996	1981	1991	1996
Professional & administrative worker	10.0	27.4	33.4	2.5	12.9	22.6
Clerical & related worker	20.1	22.7	21.9	3.0	11.3	11.4
Sales & service worker	20.1	22.2	23.4	18.8	28.8	37.2
Agriculture & fishery worker	0.1	0.4	0.5	0.8	0.2	0.9
Production & related worker	48.2	27.2	20.6	74.4	46.8	27.5
Others	1.5	0.1	0.2	0.5	0.0	0.4
Total	100.0	100.0	100.0	100.0	100.0	100.0

Source: Hong Kong Census and By-Census, 1981, 1991 and 1996.

cannot replace itself in the long run by natural increase alone. The shrinking of the labour force will result in severe problems of labour shortage, causing production bottlenecks and bringing the economy to stagnation. The population as a whole will age and the dependency ratio will worsen. Supporting the elderly will become increasingly burdensome for the working young people and the standard of living will decline. An infusion of immigrants is essential to the vitality and viability of the Hong Kong population. Given the important contribution of immigration to population growth, the immigration policy should be framed with the positive objective of supporting population growth rather than the negative one of limiting it.

Together with family reunion, the SAR government should set the supply of skilled human resources to the economy as its objective. Immigration increases the general labour supply. But further, an immigration policy targeted on admission of high-skilled immigrants can relieve bottlenecks which may emerge in the market for skilled workers and professionals, and hence will promote economic growth.

Estimation of an aggregate production function of Hong Kong from 1966 to 1990 by Lau (1994) shows the following elasticities of output:

Capital elasticity	0.465
Labour elasticity	0.399
Human capital elasticity	0.423

In other words, a 1 per cent increase in the labour input will increase GDP by 0.399 per cent. Correspondingly, a 1 per cent increase in human capital will increase GDP by 0.423 per cent. A substantial flow of immigrants that helps to maintain growth in the labour force will make a significant contribution to economic growth. If the immigrants are educated and skilled, the contribution will be even larger.

At present, there are three subsidiary schemes for the immigration of skilled and professional personnel from the Mainland or of Mainland origin. Under the first scheme, Chinese citizens who have resided overseas for two years or more may enter Hong Kong to work with employment visas as long as they possess professional and technical skills which are needed and they are offered employment by Hong Kong employers. Under the second scheme, enterprises of Chinese capital established in Hong Kong are allowed to recruit employees from the Mainland and bring them to Hong Kong to work on employment visas. Under a pilot scheme approved in 1994, Hong Kong employers can apply for a quota, initially set at 1,000, to import professional and skilled employees from the Mainland who must be graduates from one of thirty-six key universities designated by the Commission of Education in the Mainland.

These schemes are targeted towards professional and skilled personnel. They supplement the contribution of immigration to the general labour supply. The numbers admitted are outside the daily quota of 150. The schemes and the numbers admitted under them should be adjusted to the changing economic demands of the labour market. They should be expanded to allow students from the Mainland studying for a degree in Hong Kong to stay in Hong Kong to work after graduation if they are employed. At present these students have to return to the Mainland immediately after graduation.

Overall, population increase in Hong Kong has been rather volatile in the last several decades. Before the abolition of the 'reached-base' policy, the influx of illegal immigrants was the dominant factor that caused substantial fluctuation in population growth and contributed to large growth in the labour force. Since the early 1980s, the uneven flow of emigrants and return migrants has been the principal source of variability. In contrast to the fluctuation associated with the flow of emigrants and return migrants, population and labour force growth in Hong Kong has been underpinned by two steady sources of population increase, namely natural increase and legal immigration. In recent years, legal immigration has overtaken natural increase as the largest steady source of population increase. Since immigration is such an important source of labour supply, the Hong Kong SAR Government should pursue an active immigration policy which targets the supply of skilled human resources from the Mainland, besides facilitating family reunion, as its objective.

Notes

1 This paper is based on a book by the authors, Lam, Kit-Chun and Liu, Pak-Wai. *Immigration and the Economy of Hong Kong*, Hong Kong: City University of Hong Kong Press, 1998.

2 According to the 1996 By-census, 32.6 per cent of Hong Kong's population were immigrants from the Mainland and 7.1 per cent of the population were born in places other than China or Hong Kong. Among the 7.1 per cent most are

expatriate employees and their dependents, foreign workers, and domestic helpers (Lam and Liu 1998), the largest group being the domestic helpers. Most of these foreign-born workers do not become immigrants. They leave Hong Kong after their contracts expire. Since this chapter deals with immigration, the issue of workers born outside China will not be discussed in detail.

3 For a more detailed account of Chinese immigration after 1949, see Lam and Liu (1998).

4 Figure 7.1, showing population growth and labour-force growth, 1976–97, is based on the following data:

Year	Population growth	Labour force growth
1961	n.a.	n.a.
1962	4.3	n.a.
1963	3.5	n.a.
1964	2.4	n.a.
1965	2.7	n.a.
1966	0.9	n.a.
1967	2.6	n.a.
1968	2.1	n.a.
1969	1.6	n.a.
1970	2.5	n.a.
1971	2.2	n.a.
1972	1.9	n.a.
1973	2.9	n.a.
1974	3.2	n.a.
1975	1.9	n.a.
1976	1.3	−3.5
1977	1.5	1.68
1978	1.8	4.89
1979	4.3	5.92
1980	3.2	8.52
1981	3.2	7.15
1982	1.6	0.35
1983	1.5	1.7
1984	1	2.59
1985	1.1	0.79
1986	1.1	2.77
1987	1	1.06
1988	0.7	1.27
1989	0.5	−0.36
1990	0.2	−0.17
1991	0.7	1.84
1992	1	−0.21
1993	2	2.86
1994	2.5	3.47
1995	2.1	3.22
1996	2.9	0.83
1997	3	3.95

5 Figure 7.2, showing the age composition of the population, 1975–97, is based on the following data:

Year	Age 15–24	Age 55–64
1975	945,700	328,500
1976	975,100	338,900
1977	1,028,000	356,700

Year	Age 15–24	Age 55–64
1978	1,059,300	370,200
1979	1,134,200	386,200
1980	1,165,800	397,800
1981	1,177,500	408,800
1982	1,153,700	421,000
1983	1,124,200	433,700
1984	1,087,100	445,400
1985	1,052,000	457,700
1986	1,023,200	469,600
1987	986,400	481,200
1988	950,700	491,200
1989	925,500	497,200
1990	896,100	499,600
1991	872,600	506,800
1992	849,500	509,400
1993	846,600	511,300
1994	860,800	512,600
1995	871,800	511,000
1996	886,400	512,900
1997	907,700	521,600

6 Figure 7.3, showing labour force participation rates in Hong Kong, 1975–97, is based on the following data:

Year	All (%)
1975	65.9
1976	63.3
1977	62.2
1978	62.5
1979	62
1980	63.3
1981	66.3
1982	64.7
1983	64.5
1984	65.5
1985	64.8
1986	65.1
1987	64.8
1988	65.1
1989	64.8
1990	64.7
1991	63.7
1992	63.2
1993	62.5
1994	62.5
1995	62.8
1996	61.8
1997	61.8

7 Figure 7.4, showing estimated emigrants by destination countries, 1980–97, is based on the following data:

Year	Total
1980	22,400
1981	18,300
1982	20,300

Year	Total
1983	19,800
1984	22,400
1985	22,300
1986	18,989
1987	29,998
1988	45,817
1989	42,000
1990	61,700
1991	59,700
1992	66,200
1993	53,400
1994	61,600
1995	43,100
1996	40,300
1997	30,900

Part III
Management in Hong Kong

8 The Meaning of Work

The reconfiguration of work and working in Hong Kong and Beijing[1]

Robert Westwood, Alicia S. M. Leung and Randy K. Chiu

Introduction

Work and working[2] are complex phenomena, being multifaceted constructs which resonate along many dimensions – social, psychological, economic, historical and political. The very notion and definition of work is itself problematical (Hall 1994; Pahl 1988; Thompson 1989). For most people work is the dominating daily activity. It enfolds in complex ways with other spheres of people's lives and has become elementally penetrative in notions of identity, self-worth, belonging and status. Furthermore, the context for work continues, worldwide, to be in a dynamic state. Contemporary contexts, practices and meanings are infused with particular histories and ideologies, but these foundational specificities are constantly reconfigured as new economic exigencies, technologies, organisational forms, managerial practices, job designs and work regimes emerge.

This is nowhere more apparent than in China and its reintegrated Special Administrative Region, Hong Kong. However, the nature of those changes and the context in which they are evolving are very different. In China, the changes are radical at the systemic level as economic, labour market, enterprise and welfare reforms continue and the whole work-related landscape is reconfigured. In Hong Kong, the changing environment for work is less dramatic. There, shifts in organisational form and strategy, managerial outlook and practice, and the technological context for work reflect wider macro-economic and industrial organisation changes as its more mature economy makes the transition into a fuller service economy and a trade hub for its hinterland.

As the nature and context of work alters, so the experience and meaning of work is reshaped. Working for a software company in the Silicon Valley at the end of the twentieth century is radically different from working for a steel mill in Sheffield, England at its beginning. This difference is attributable not only to changes in the way work is performed, but also to radical changes in both the intermediate context of organisation and management, and the wider context of work's place in the social fabric. Differences in both historical and contemporary contexts also mean that work and working are different across cultures.

The analysis of differences in work and its attendant meanings is not only of sociological or historical interest, there are highly pragmatic concerns. The meanings people attach to work have relevance for important outcomes such as motivation, satisfaction and performance and concomitantly for productivity, turnover and commitment. An informed understanding of what work means to people, the values they attach to it, and its perceived significance in relation to other aspects of life, is thus of central importance in managerial, organisational and economic terms.

Whilst the comparative analysis of work from a historical perspective has received significant attention (Godelier 1980; Joyce 1987; Pahl 1988), the same is not true from a cross-cultural perspective. It is as a partial rectification of this deficiency that the studies reported in this chapter were undertaken. The chapter reports on empirical investigations of the meaning of work in Hong Kong and in China via two parallel studies. Both studies made use of the Meaning of Work International Research Team (MOWIRT) (1987) model, modified and adapted to the two different contexts. Core meaning of work variables, such as work centrality and work goals, are discussed and related to the different and evolving contexts in both locations. Furthermore, the results of these studies are put in comparison with results derived from the countries in the original MOWIRT study.

Modelling the meaning of work

The meaning of work has been curiously neglected in management research and theorising, being largely left to sociology. This neglect is particularly acute within organisational behaviour, where the issue has a seeming natural residence. Management and organisational behaviour theory has focused on the more individual level constructs of motivation and job satisfaction which somewhat decontextualises work and its meanings. An exception is the work of England and colleagues in MOWIRT (e.g. England 1986; Harpaz 1990; MOWIRT 1987), which resulted in a comprehensive examination of the notion of the meaning of work and construction of a theorised model applied in an international comparative study.

The original MOWIRT model centres on a set of core meaning of work variables: centrality of work as a life role, valued working outcomes, importance of work goals, work role identification and societal norms about working. Taken together, these variables constitute particular meaning of work patterns. These patterns are shaped by certain antecedent variables: aspects of the respondents' personal and family situation, present job and career history, and factors in the macro socio-economic environment. Personal factors include demographic variables such as age and gender. Family factors centre on the issue of financial dependencies. Job and career issues include habituated working conditions and schedules, and features in a career history such as mobility and the experience of unemployment. The MOWIRT formulation fails to elaborate on macro socio-economic variables and confines itself to values pertinent to the development of societal norms about working – this itself confined to a distinction between obligation and entitlement norms.

The meaning of work variables are held to influence certain consequent variables. Again, in our view, MOWIRT offer a restricted set, focusing only on subjective expectations about future work situations and objective outcomes of working. The former relates to the career recommendations respondents would make to their children and the general importance of working in the future. The latter is pursued in a rather truncated manner through measures of future working hours, future training intentions, and the likely cessation of working.

Figure 8.1 represents our reworking of the MOWIRT model. The changes centre on the antecedent and consequent conditions. It is our view, precipitated by a consideration of the context of our own studies, that the macro-environmental factors need expansion and more intense consideration. The macro-environmental context for work was, and remains, vastly different between Mainland China and Hong Kong. The historical, ideological, economic and political contexts display major differences likely to be of prime significance in shaping work-meaning patterns. The new model also introduces intermediate, organisational level variables. We maintain that the organisational context is significant in shaping work meanings. This would obviously be so in individual cases and at specific points in time, but that would not be relevant in generalised and cross-cultural comparisons. However, organisational contexts – in terms of broad preferences and tendencies for forms of organisational structure and culture, and for styles and modes of management – exhibit systematic differences between countries and in relation to different macro-environmental conditions such that they constitute differential antecedent contexts for the shaping of work meaning patterns.

The model also expands on the consequent variables. This aligns with our view that the meanings people hold in relation to work are deeply implicated in work attitudes, motivation and performance, impacting upon such variables as job satisfaction, organisational commitment, productivity and turnover.

Our prime focus in this chapter will be on reporting the results of the survey in terms of the core meaning of work variables. Space will not permit a full discussion of the expanded model. We will not report empirically on the antecedent and consequent variables, but they will be discussed in general terms and their likely relationship to the meaning of work variables explored. In any case, the MOWIRT authors are correct in asserting that a determining relationship between antecedent variables and meaning of work patterns cannot be effectively established in a cross-sectional study.

The two parallel studies reported here both deployed slightly modified versions – to ensure comprehensibility and relevance to the local context – of the MOWIRT questionnaire. In both cases the questionnaire was translated

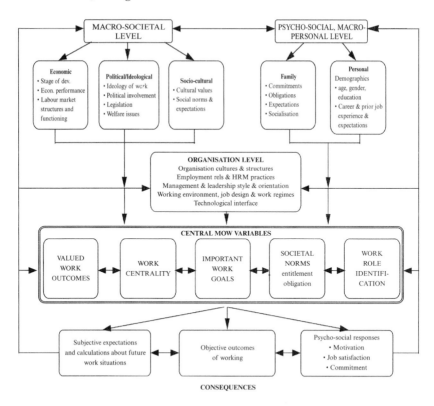

Figure 8.1 Meaning of work model.

into Chinese using the back-translation method and professional translators. The first study was undertaken in the Beijing area. A stratified sample of enterprises was generated and random samples taken from within the strata followed by randomised samples of employees within enterprises. A thousand questionnaires were distributed, the majority administered face-to-face. There were 453 useable returns, representing a response rate of 45 per cent. The second survey was conducted in Hong Kong. In view of the recognised difficulty of obtaining good returns from direct surveys in Hong Kong, a different research strategy was adopted. Students (primarily business students) at tertiary education institutions were each given ten questionnaires and asked to use a convenience/snowballing sampling procedure to generate ten returns each. Two thousand questionnaires were distributed generating 893 useable returns (a response rate of 44.7 per cent).

Basic demographic data are summarised in Table 8.1. As can be noted, the two samples display some differences. The Hong Kong sample, in age terms, is skewed into the lower age groups. The Beijing sample is more evenly distributed, better reflecting the age distribution of a national labour force. There are considerably more married people in the Beijing sample than in

Table 8.1 Sample characteristics

	Hong Kong	*Beijing*
Age		
20 or below	11.3	15.9
21–30	55.2	37.6
31–40	12.3	15.7
41–50	8.5	13.3
51–60	4.5	9.1
61–70	4.8	4.8
70 or above	0.6	3.6
Gender		
Male		55.8
Female		44.2
Marital status		
Married or in relationship	37.9	55.7
Not married or in relationship	62.1	44.3
Working level		
Non-supervisory	73	60.8
Supervisory	15.8	9.1
Managerial	11.2	30.1
Educational level attained		
Primary or below	12.6	14.3
Up to secondary	54.8	45.7
Post-secondary/vocational	17.5	18.5
University degree	15.1	21.5

Hong Kong. This may relate to the age distribution of the Hong Kong sample, and to the tendency for people there to marry later. The educational attainment distribution is not markedly different although the Beijing sample has a larger proportion of more highly educated people than the Hong Kong one. This should be viewed as a skewing of the Beijing sample since it would not reflect the distribution in the population as a whole. There is a higher proportion of managers in Beijing, this may explain the skewed educational distribution, but may also reflect that the interpretation, even given a good translation, of 'managerial' and 'supervisory' may not be equivalent to that in Hong Kong. In addition to demographic factors the survey measured antecedent, core and consequent variables relating to the meaning of work. Not all measures are reported here: the focus will be on the core meaning of work variables.

Work centrality is measured by three items, which can be considered independently or combined into the 'work centrality index'. The first item is a simple question – 'How important and significant is working in your total work life?'[3] – and is responded to on a seven-point scale. The second is a significant item requiring respondents to indicate the importance of work relative to other life spheres by having them allocate 100 points between five life areas.[4] The third item measures centrality indirectly by using the classic 'job lottery' question (Morse and Weiss 1955).[5]

Valued work outcomes were measured by asking respondents to allocate 100 points across six possible work outcomes.[6]

Work goal importance was measured in a somewhat complex fashion. Respondents were presented with eleven work goals such as 'opportunity to learn' and 'good pay'.[7] They were asked to consider the relative importance of each goal to them in their work life and to position each item on a fifteen-point scale ranging from 'extremely important' to 'of little importance'.

Work role identification was measured by having respondents rank order six different aspects of work context and experience in terms of their personal importance and significance.[8]

Societal norms about working focused on two norms: entitlement norms and obligation norms. A four-point scale[9] was used in relation to ten items. A sample entitlement norm question is 'A job should be provided to every individual who desires to work'. One relating to obligation is 'It is the duty of every able bodied citizen to contribute to society by working'.

The context for the meaning of work in Beijing and Hong Kong

This section provides a discussion of some of the differential antecedent conditions that help shape the meaning of work patterns. No attempt is made to explore any systematic or statistical relationship between antecedent variables and meaning of work variables. The intention is to provide some contextualisation of the discussion of the meaning of work responses. Even then, since space does not permit a detailed elaboration, we will only signal some key factors that seem to be different in the two locations and speculate on their likely impact. We are encouraged, however, by the belief that the high visibility of the changes and developments in China and Hong Kong in recent times means that readers will have a common understanding of some of the issues involved.

The macro-societal level: political economy and culture

Macro-societal level factors form the general context within which work and work meanings are framed. For example, and relevantly here, a socialist or communist ideology and political economy constitutes an elementally different frame for work than a capitalist, market-based one. Although China's Marxist-Leninist-Maoist politico-economic ideology is in transformation as Dengist market socialism emerges, it has penetrated systemically into the economic and social fabric, and is at least vestigially present in the management of the economy, the functioning of the labour market, organisational forms, managerial practice and the nature, function and form of work. For those in the workforce prior to the 1978 reform initiative, the memory of a work ethos, regime and attendant structures informed by a rigorous socialist ideology is still relatively fresh. Core principles, such as work as the social obligation of the proletariat and as a role and contribution imbued with significant equalitarianism, will not be set aside easily in the new quasi-market conditions. The central control of economic activity, whilst receding, has not disappeared, and the roles and sentiments that go with it remain entrenched in the minds of many in the workforce.

It cannot be doubted that the politico-ideological trajectory of contemporary China has constituted a unique context for work. It is also clear that current changes are significantly reconfiguring that context in ways likely to impact on people's work meanings. Obviously, the centrally planned nature of the economy, including employment and the labour market, and the political control of organisations and the workplace, is the most significant macro-level feature of the context for work under a communist system. By the same token, it is the gradual erosion of those features in the move to a new form of socialist market economy that is precipitating major changes in the context of work.

By comparison, Hong Kong stands as an exemplar of free-market capitalism. Its economic systems are extremely open and there is widespread endorsement of the capitalist ethos (Lau 1982), in part manifest in rampant materialism, consumerism and entrepreneurialism. Politically, of course, Hong Kong has been subject to British colonial rule, during most of which the Chinese population was largely disenfranchised (refer to Chapter 2 for a discussion of political developments in Hong Kong). It is argued (Lau 1982; Redding 1990) that Hong Kong society is minimally integrated and lacks the accoutrements of a developed civil society. The government has neither sought to engage the local population in political process nor civic responsibilities. Moreover, the provision of welfare has been minimal. A consequence is that the population has remained primarily focused on economic activity and upon gaining and maintaining economic security within the family framework. The Hong Kong government has consistently pursued a *laissez-faire* approach in terms of political economy, adopting what has been called a stance of 'positive non-intervention'. The fiscal system could be described as minimalist, and most trade, financial and labour market activities are only weakly regulated. This again fosters, for all levels of economic actor, a sense of independence, unfettered by government policy or regulation. The labour market is relatively uncontrolled and unplanned. The labour force is very mobile and job opportunities have been plentiful. Hong Kong workers latterly have shown little organisational loyalty or commitment, being readily prepared to move should a better opportunity appear. The recent economic crisis in Asia is likely to bring some changes to this dynamic economic system.

In this type of socio-economic environment it is not surprising that people are motivated primarily by economic advancement and security, as noted in Chapter 1. A culture of hard work and opportunistic entrepreneurialism has developed. As the discussion of culture in Chapter 1 indicated, Hong Kong culture can reasonably be described as family centred (*contra* community, society or civic centred), materialistic, pragmatic, particularistic, adaptive and phlegmatic – encapsulated by Lau's concept of utilitarian familism (Lau 1982). It is reasonable to assume that work-related attitudes are in large part shaped by this milieu. Work is primarily viewed instrumentally as the means to secure the economic return necessary for security and advancement. The added complexity lies in familistic dependencies that obligate members to make an ongoing economic contribution. The prosperity of the family is of significance for the present but also well into the future. Prosperity and independence also brings status and prestige and so there is some pressure to make that obvious through conspicuous consumption. The need for security and independence coupled with materialistic drivers are major stimuli for entrepreneurial activity resulting in the family-owned and managed business being the aspiration of many (see Chapter 13). Work and its meanings need to be situated in this socio-economic context.

During Hong Kong's rapid industrialisation in the 1960s and 70s, the immediate context for work was often extremely tough. There was very little attention to or investment in the physical environment, and conditions were often little above 'sweat-shop' standards. People were prepared to tolerate such conditions provided they could benefit from the rapid rates of growth and economic development and advance their own financial well-being. Physical working conditions have improved considerably along with economic growth, major foreign investment and the turn to a service economy. Working conditions in China remain at an impoverished level. A spartan physical environment is often compounded by low-grade technology, although there are rapid improvements in parts of the economically booming eastern seaboard.

The institutional context for work and working remains radically different as between China and Hong Kong. It is, naturally, the divergent political context that provides the prime source of difference. Hong Kong's *laissez-faire* approach contrasts sharply with China's centrally planned one. However, the notion of Hong Kong's economy being totally free and open is mitigated by the government's control of the territory's most valuable resource, land, and by the subtle, informal relationships between government and business leaders. It can be argued that a powerful elite, composed of members of the government and a small group of influential business-people, effectively controls the economic interests of Hong Kong (refer also to Chapter 2). Government representatives and business investors from the Mainland now also constitute part of this powerful group. The kind of intimate relationship between banks, government and business groups prevalent in Korea or Japan is not present in Hong Kong, but the Hong Kong Shanghai Bank has held a central and special position with respect to the government. Increasingly, the Bank of China is occupying a position of power and influence. In China, that bank dominates but does not enjoy political independence: it is intricately involved in the government's economic policies and reform initiatives. It is also deeply implicated in the state enterprise sector and is presently being asked to prop up a large number of ailing enterprises.

The Hong Kong legal system, until the transition, was firmly rooted in English legal practice, with heavy elements of common law and determinations by precedent. The legal framework for business and employment has largely followed the philosophy of positive non-interventionism. Labour law is rudimentary, compared with most of Europe or the US, and based on the 'voluntarist' model (Williams 1990), although, as Chapter 14 points out, the colonial context entailed important deviations from that model. There are various statutes that are broadly protective in nature, but it is indicative, perhaps, that no equal employment opportunity legislation existed until the mid-1990s (for more detail refer to Chapter 1). The legal system in China remains underdeveloped, including those aspects that apply to business and employment. Even though significant expansions and amendments to labour law were introduced in 1995, much of substance in the law has still not been fully activated.

Regulations with respect to trade unions are also very different in the two locations – indeed, the whole constitution, function and mode of operation of organised labour is vastly different. Details of trade unions and other aspects of organised labour are fully discussed in other chapters in this volume (in particular Chapters 1, 2, 14, 15 and 16).

We have briefly described some features of the macro-environment in economic, political, legal and institutional terms that frame work and its meanings in China and Hong Kong. An important additional feature of the macro-level environment that has a bearing on work is culture. In Chapter 1 we attempted a broad overview of salient features of Chinese culture. It was noted that the cultures of Hong Kong and China, whilst sharing some commonalities resting on a shared heritage, also manifest differences and should not be viewed as homogeneous. Here we will seek to relate some of those aspects of culture to work and its meanings. It should perhaps be recognised that culture represents a force for similarity in this regard and that political, economic and institutional factors are more important in determining differences in the meanings attached to work and working between people in Hong Kong and Beijing.

The large power distance of Chinese societies results, as indicated in Chapter 1, in hierarchical organisation structures that are highly centralised. There is not much delegation from the head, and members have restricted autonomy and discretion. There are expectations that subordinates will be deferential and obedient to the head and will not challenge his authority. The 'paternalistic headship' mode of organisational leadership is distant and aloof, but personalistic in nature. Heads are invested with considerable power and authority, but are expected to be mindful of the well-being of members. Members will have their performance subjectively assessed, and generally need to intuit what the head wants and then act in accordance with that tacit understanding. There is not much recognition or praise for good work.

The familistic collectivism and relationship orientation have four highly significant points of impact on work and work meanings. The first is the paradigmatic family-owned business as a preferred mode for co-ordinated economic activity as noted in Chapter 1. The second is the moral obligation of family members to contribute to the economic well-being and future prosperity of the family. The third is the social ethic of harmony and the need to engage in behaviours that sustain harmony, and which do not generate overt conflict or damage *face*. The fourth is the centrality of relationships in all forms of economic and organisational transactions. This is most acutely captured in the notion of *guanxi*, outlined in Chapter 1. The diffuse (rather than specific) nature of relationships entails, as noted, that work, as a life sphere, is less differentiated from other spheres than is common in western cultures. It also means that work relationships, such as those between peers or between supervisors and subordinates, tend to extend outside of the work domain into other life spheres more than is common in the West.

In terms of the masculinity–femininity dimension, Hong Kong exhibits relatively high levels of materialism, acquisitiveness, competitiveness and other values typical of a moderately masculine culture. Although the Mainland has not shown such strong scores on masculinity, there is increasing evidence that the turn to a market economy away from the equalitarianism and commonwealth ethos of the communist system is precipitating a drift towards more masculine values. In both cases work has a strongly instrumental value orientation.

The two locations currently display the widest disparity in terms of the Uncertainty Avoidance Index. In Hong Kong weak uncertainty avoidance means that organisations and management systems remain more informal, flexible and adaptive. Formalisation is limited and selective (Redding 1990) and job and tasks are less precisely delineated and proscribed. People are less risk averse and there is greater acceptance and tolerance of change. In China uncertainty avoidance remains strong and consequently organisations and management systems are more formalised, rigid and bureaucratised. People are less willing to take risks, to assume responsibilities, and to embrace change.

The implications of the long-term time orientation are mainly in terms of the values of deferment, persistence and thrift. These can each be viewed as important for the constitution of work meanings and motivation and, indeed, as components of a work ethic. There are also implications in terms of planning horizons and problem-solving strategies.

Chinese particularism gives rise to practices which the West views negatively as nepotism, but which in the Chinese context means responding to the needs embodied in *particular* relationships rather than the dictates of some universal principle. Actions and behaviours are judged in the context of the particular, especially relationship, facets of the situation. It is also associated with a high level of pragmatism in which the instrumentality of means to achieve goals provides adequate legitimacy. Furthermore, as noted in Chapter 1, it enables the ready up-take of methods and approaches from outside the system (for example, Western and Japanese management practices).

The 'harmony-with' relationship to the environment may mean that formal planning, particularly of a strategic nature, has less perceived value. At the more personal level the implication may be in terms of the perceived value of matters like career planning and development. It may also lead to what one Chinese psychologist has termed a 'situation accepting orientation' in contrast with a US 'problem-solving orientation' (Leung 1992). Such orientations, if genuine, could be expected to help shape the meaning and experience of work in particular ways.

The psycho-social level: personality, family and career

This part of the model deals with factors that impact more immediately upon individuals and help shape their work meanings. Obviously, previous job history and work experience are instrumental in shaping current work meaning profiles. One would also expect differences in work meanings according to gender, age and socio-economic level, and the MOWIRT study confirms this as does our own research (e.g. see Chapter 12), and other relevant literature. However, space does not permit the analysis of demographic data in relation to other variables and so we will not comment much on them. In the absence of such detailed analysis, we confine ourselves to comments about family relationships and dependencies.

As noted in Chapter 1, familism is a pervasive socio-cultural phenomenon across Chinese contexts where the family is fundamentally an economic unit as well as a socio-emotional one. The interests, welfare and perpetuation of the family take precedence over those of the individual, and each family member is expected to contribute to the economic well-being of the family. Because of the strength of lineal relationships and the importance of ancestry, families have extensionality into both the past and future. Individuals need to be mindful of that and act so as to honour past family members and ensure the future viability and success of the family. Such a familistic orientation provides an elemental backdrop for work and is a significant motivational driver. It was also previously noted that there is less differentiation of life spheres in the Chinese context, and with the family at the centre there may well be a significant admixture of family and work tasks and issues. Family members are influential in shaping the work/career expectations and decisions of children. In Hong Kong it is not unusual for a child's educational and work options to be determined by their parents or elders. When there is a family business, the children, especially boys, are expected to join the business.

Organisational forms, cultures and practices

Naturally, organisations exhibit high degrees of variability in terms of forms, cultures and practices, and individuals' work meanings may be strongly influenced by the particularities of the organisations they associate with. This part of the model is not concerned with the impact of specific organisations on work meanings, but rather suggests that a country or region may have organisational forms, cultures and practices that are distinctive, but with a degree of within-country commonality. As such, these kinds of aggregate organisational effects are relevant to the determination of meaning of work patterns in a generic manner. This is pertinent in the case of Hong Kong and China since there are good grounds for asserting the relative distinctiveness of their organisational forms.

Naturally a wide variety of organisational forms can be found in Hong Kong, ranging from small proprietary enterprises to large multinationals. However, there is a form that is numerically pervasive and paradigmatic: the relatively small, owner-managed, family business (see also Chapter 13). A consensual view of this form's key features has been increasingly documented (Chen 1995; Redding 1990; Westwood 1992; Whitley 1992; Wong 1985). We have previously summarised those key features (Westwood, 1997b):

In terms of business practice:
Family-ownership and non-separation of ownership and control
Small-medium enterprises, or large 'molecular' networks and/or personalistically-linked business group
Individual units highly specialised, diversification through the structural arrangements outlined above
Opportunistic growth strategies through volume expansion or diversification
Maintenance of extensive networks of personal connections to external persons and bodies
Non-formal, personalistic but effective horizontal relationships
Strategically adaptive and 'nimble'
Reliance on informal sources of capital.

In terms of organisation and management:
Highly centralised with clear authority hierarchies and clear control by the 'head'
Limited delegation to a relatively small middle-management group
Paternalistic leadership style and organisational climate
Low levels of formalisation

Reliance on personal/intuitive knowledge for business decisions and for reputation maintenance

Personalistic control and co-ordination mechanisms

Nepotistic employment practices, low reliance on external recruiting for managers

Informal, subjective and personalistic performance appraisal

Relatively closed, controlled and non-formalised information systems

Seniority as a reward criteria, limited performance-reward linkages.

In China, organisations are going through rapid changes as the turn in the political economy has brought into being new forms. In addition to the older-style state-owned enterprises (SOEs) there is a burgeoning private sector and a substantial collective enterprise component. There are also, importantly, numerous international joint ventures. This has opened up alternative employment opportunities and widened the range of work contexts. However, in terms of most people's work experience, the SOE is the forming ground for attitudes and meanings. It represents a distinctive organisational form and environment for working, and a number of elements have been significant in shaping a distinctive work experience. Critical are the notions of guaranteed employment, controlled work and job allocation, and extensive welfarism. The concept of the 'iron rice bowl' has been a catchall for this nexus of practices. The notion of the work unit, or *danwei* system, is more than just a matter of a centralised and controlled work allocation system, it frames many broader aspects of people's work and non-work lives.

For many the *danwei* has been the chief institutional context in which work has been experienced. Within that frame, work is centrally planned and allocated. People were appointed to a work unit and expected to stay with it for most of their working lives. Mobility was highly restricted and developmental opportunities somewhat so. Pay was based on equalitarian principles and linked weakly, if at all, to performance. More broadly, the *danwei* system was also the key vehicle for China's welfare system. As such it constituted much more than just a place of work, taking primary responsibility for the well-being and welfare of employees and their community. It provided a secure job and guaranteed wages, but also a wide range of other welfare and community services including housing provision, health and educational services, transportation and recreational facilities. Managers and political cadres could not help but be involved in a whole range of personal issues including marriages, child-care and illnesses. In this sense the system was highly paternalistic and personalistic. Work unit members had very high dependence on the enterprise, and hence the party and the state. As one commentator puts it, 'Functioning as a self-sufficient "small society" or "mini-welfare state", the SOEs provided comprehensive, non-contributory, and from-cradle-to-grave welfare services to their employees . . . [including] . . . a social security programme, various allowances, and personal and collective welfare services.' (Leung 1994: 383).

We have described the *danwei* in the past tense, but this is misleading since, despite the extensive reforms, the work unit within the SOE remains the primary working context for the majority. The government recognises that the 'iron rice bowl' is not conducive to economic modernisation and has also sought to reform the welfare system so that the burden falls less on its own shoulders. However, so entrenched is the system and so fragile the political sensitivities involved that the actual dismantling of the 'iron rice bowl' and the *danwei* is slow to materialise in practice. There is scepticism about that process 'given the abiding importance of occupational welfare to the maintenance of political stability and legitimacy of the CCP, the "iron rice bowls" will remain largely intact and irreversible.' (Leung 1994: 353).

Nonetheless, the reform process is reconfiguring the organisational landscape and thus the context for working. One notable effect is the decentralisation of organisational power and governance, with enterprise managers/directors having much greater responsibility and autonomy. Thus, leadership and management styles are undergoing change too. The enterprise has also been somewhat depoliticised with a relative diminishing of party and bureaux involvement. The CCP is somewhat less influential and the role and function of the Trade Unions and Worker's Congress is altering (Child 1994; Warner 1991). Other changes have included shifts in the nature of worker participation and in union and works council functioning; an attempted move away from equalitarian to equity-based reward systems with firmer links between performance and reward; and the demise of centrally determined production and output quotas in favour of market determinations. There have also, crucially for the experience of work, been major changes in the terms of employment. Work contracts are increasingly the norm and are enshrined in the 1995 Labour Law. Lifetime employment is no longer a guarantee, firing and other terminations are legitimised (partially), and unemployment is a reality. Recruitment and selection are more open and rational, and greater attention is being placed on skill development and training (Child 1994; Graf *et al.* 1990). These are radical reforms which threaten cherished securities under the old system, and certainly have their detractors. There are important motivational implications here and a likely shift in the conceptions and meaning of work.

Comparative central MOW factors

This section deals with the results of the surveys in terms of the central meaning of work variables. We present this data descriptively, but also include, in most cases, data from the original MOWIRT study to provide a comparative context for the Hong Kong and China material.

Work centrality

The work centrality construct refers to the salience of work for people

Table 8.2 The importance of work relative to other life spheres

	My leisure	My community	My work	My religion	My family
Hong Kong	24 (3)	5.1 (5)	29.1 (2)	8.8 (4)	32 (1)
China	21.0 (3)[1]	9.3 (4)	35.2 (1)	1.8 (5)	32.7 (2)
Belgium	24.6 (3)	6.0 (4)	29.9 (2)	4.9 (5)	34.7 (1)
Britain	22.3 (2)	7.8 (5)	21.5 (3)	8.6 (4)	40.1 (1)
Germany	22.7 (3)	7.3 (4)	28.0 (2)	5.2 (5)	35.7 (1)
Israel	18.2 (3)	4.5 (5)	28.3 (2)	4.9 (4)	43.9 (1)
Japan	19.7 (3)	5.3 (4)	36.1 (1)	3.7 (5)	35.1 (2)
Netherlands	24.2 (3)	7.5 (4)	29.6 (2)	4.9 (5)	33.7 (1)
USA	18.1 (3)	9.9 (5)	24.5 (2)	14.0 (4)	33.6 (1)
Yugoslavia	19.5 (3)	7.5 (4)	36.7 (1)	3.3 (5)	35.3 (2)

Note:
1 Rank order is in parenthesis.

relative to other life spheres. As indicated earlier, it was measured in a number of ways. The perceived importance of work compared with other life spheres was measured with the point allocation question (see Table 8.2 above). The Hong Kong and Beijing samples present a somewhat different profile. Most noticeably, Beijing places 'work' as the most important life sphere and 'family' second, whilst in Hong Kong that order is reversed. Beijing in this regard displays the same profile as Japan and Yugoslavia (still a socialist state at the time of the MOWIRT study). This is interesting given the presumed familistic nature of Chinese culture. The higher preference for 'work' in Beijing either represents the ideological success of Maoism in displacing the 'bourgeois' concept of family from the heart of Chinese culture, or, more pragmatically and likely, is a response to the exigencies of economic life in an impoverished country in which, nonetheless, the reform process has generated new opportunities to be derived from paid employment and the differential earnings embodied therein. Note, though, that the proportional point allocations in the two places are not substantially different. Indeed, all countries, except Britain, have these two items in first and second place. In the majority they are also in close proximity – although wider spread in Israel and the US.

It is perhaps surprising, given the espoused values of a socialist system, that the Beijing sample gives a low allocation to 'my community' (lower than the US for example), but the notion of 'community' is ambiguous, particularly when presented in this abstract form. Both Hong Kong and Beijing allocate over 20 per cent of the points to leisure and rate it the third most

Table 8.3 Inferred centrality score

	% who would continue working
Beijing	87%
Hong Kong	82%

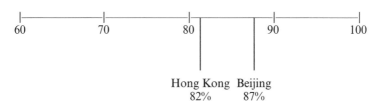

Figure 8.2 Inferred centrality scores.

important life sphere. In this they are in broad alignment with the other countries. The responses to 'my religion' show Beijing with a low allocation (similar to Yugoslavia, but much lower than the 14 per cent in the US) compared to Hong Kong where there is a more tolerant attitude toward religion and a significant Christian community.

The results indicate that work has high salience in people's lives in both Beijing and Hong Kong, although the specific focus and resonance of this cannot be determined from such a general question and may well be different. The inferred work centrality item ('lottery question') confirms high work salience and a level of similarity between Beijing and Hong Kong. Only 13 per cent of Beijing and 18 per cent of Hong Kong respondents indicated that they would stop working. (See Figure 8.2 and Table 8.3). This is very much in line with international results using this question, including the MOWIRT study. For the Beijing sample, almost 40 per cent said they would remain in their existing job.

The MOWIRT analytic allows for the calculation of a work centrality index (using scores from the different questions). Beijing has a score of 7.7 on this index whilst Hong Kong has a score of 7.51. These are compared with the countries from the MOWIRT study in Figure 8.3. This further confirms the high work centrality of the two Chinese contexts. The proximity of Hong Kong and China to Japan on this index, and their distance from the rest, is noteworthy. This may resonate with the strong work ethic commonly presumed to prevail in East Asia. It would, however, be a mistake to conclude that the factors inducing high work centrality, and possibly a work ethic, in China and Hong Kong are the same as those operative in Japan. Indeed, the factors and related conditions may differ between Hong Kong and China.

Valued work outcomes and goals

The kind of goals that people view as important to pursue through working, and the type of outcomes they seek from working, are both significant components of meaning of work patterns. The survey had items relating to both issues.

Table 8.4 details results of responses to the valued work outcomes questions for Beijing and Hong Kong, and for the MOWIRT countries.

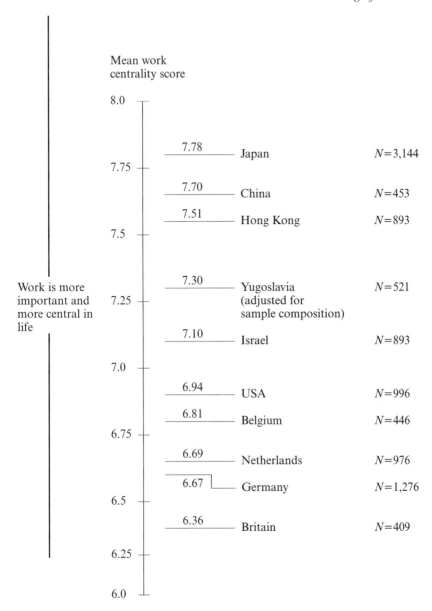

Figure 8.3 Work centrality index, comparative position.

There are some important differences between Hong Kong and Beijing. Whilst both align with the others in allocating most points to 'income derived from working', the Beijing sample – reflecting, perhaps, persisting socialist ideology – rank 'serve society' as second, whereas it is ranked last by Hong Kong. It is also noteworthy that the intrinsic outcome of 'having

Table 8.4 Personally valued work outcomes (mean point allocation and rank)

	Status & prestige	Income	Keeps you occupied	Interesting contacts	Serve society	Interesting & satisfying
Hong Kong	11 (5)[1]	36 (1)	12 (4)	15 (2)	10 (6)	14 (3)
China	12.7 (5)	34.5 (1)	12.8 (4)	14.1 (3)	14.4 (2)	11.6 (6)
Belgium	6.9 (6)	35.5 (1)	8.7 (5)	17.3 (3)	10.2 (4)	21.3 (2)
Britain	10.9 (5)	34.4 (1)	11.0 (4)	15.3 (3)	10.5 (6)	18.0 (2)
Germany	15.7 (5)	41.7 (1)	16.1 (4)	16.8 (3)	13.9 (6)	19.5 (2)
Israel	8.5 (6)	31.1 (1)	9.4 (5)	11.1 (4)	13.6 (3)	26.2 (2)
Japan	5.6 (6)	45.4 (1)	11.5 (4)	14.7 (2)	9.3 (5)	13.4 (3)
Netherlands	4.9 (6)	26.2 (1)	10.6 (5)	17.9 (3)	16.7 (4)	23.5 (2)
USA	11.9 (4)	33.1 (1)	11.3 (6)	15.3 (3)	11.5 (5)	16.8 (2)
Yugoslavia	9.3 (6)	34.1 (1)	11.7 (4)	9.8 (5)	15.1 (3)	19.8 (2)

Note
1 Rank order in parenthesis.

interesting and satisfying work' is rated of least significance in Beijing, but much higher in Hong Kong. Indeed, Hong Kong is more in tune with the wealthier and western nations where intrinsic work outcomes such as satisfaction and self-actualisation typically receive greater weight than in the less developed and/or the Asian contexts. It has to be noted, however, that once the proportional allocation of points to 'income' has been made, there is little spread in the allocation to the other items in either Hong Kong or Beijing.

Looking at the rank ordering for the question relating to work goals, we also see some interesting differences between Hong Kong and Beijing. From Table 8.5[10] it can be seen that, although Hong Kong places opportunities for promotion as the leading work goal, it does not even appear in Beijing's top five. Why promotion has such low resonance in China is hard to determine, but it may simply be that promotion opportunities are perceived to be limited and where they do exist, as subject to factors other than performance and often outside of the employee's control. The data also show a high value placed on 'good interpersonal relations' in China, not a surprising finding in a strongly relationship-centred culture and where *guanxi* is so critical to organisational activity (Chen 1995, Child 1994). It is suggested that in the reform climate – with greater uncertainty than before, less explicit monitoring and control by state and party organs, and where resources are partially subject to markets (and, furthermore, markets that are very imperfect) – personal relationships are even more vital for organisational survival and success than before (Aufrect 1995). Personal relationships are still vitally important in Hong Kong too, reflected in the relatively high ranking of the item there.

The new opportunities and market structures in China have made it apparent to some people at least that the possession of scarce knowledge, skills or expertise is vital to organisational and personal success and survival. Thus, we see 'opportunities to learn' as the third-ranked item in Beijing.

Table 8.5 Work goal importance items

	Rank 1	Rank 2	Rank 3	Rank 4	Rank 5
Hong Kong	Promotion	Pay	Interesting work	Good inter-personal relations	Job security
China	Pay	Good inter-personal relations	Opportunities to learn	Job security	Good working conditions
Belgium	Interesting work	Pay	Job security	Autonomy	Good inter-personal relations
Britain	Interesting work	Pay	Job security	Good inter-personal relations	Convenient hours
Germany	Pay	Job security	Interesting work	Good inter-personal relations	Good match
Israel	Interesting work	Good inter-personal relations	Pay	Autonomy	Oppor-tunities to learn
Japan	Good match	Interesting work	Autonomy	Job security	Pay
Netherlands	Interesting work[1]	Autonomy	Good inter-personal relations	Variety	Pay
USA	Interesting work	Job security	Good match[2]	Opportunities to learn	Variety
Yugoslavia	Interesting work[3]	Good inter-personal relations	Pay	Opportunities to learn	Good match

Notes
[1] Equal first rank with autonomy.
[2] Equal third rank with opportunities to learn.
[3] Equal first rank with good interpersonal relations.

China is also the only country to have 'good working conditions' in the top five. Working conditions in many Chinese factories and offices are still very poor and likely to be a source of discomfort and dissatisfaction. It is not surprising, therefore, those working conditions take on importance.

A final point to note is that, again, Hong Kong gives some value to the intrinsic goal of 'interesting work', whilst it does not appear in the Beijing top five.

'Work role identification' deals with the aspect of the work context and/or experience with which the person has the strongest identification. Table 8.6 presents the means and rank position of the six items for Hong Kong and Beijing, again with comparative data. The two Chinese samples display a high degree of similarity. Both, not surprisingly given the type of orientation

Table 8.6 Most significant aspects of working: means and rank (in parenthesis)

	HK	Chi.	Belg.	Germ.	Isr.	Neth.	US	Yug.
Tasks	3.7 (2)	3.9 (2)	3.5 (4)	3.9 (2)	3.9 (1)	3.9 (1)	3.2 (5)	4.2 (1)
Company	2.5 (6)	2.8 (6)	2.5 (6)	2.5 (6)	2.7 (6)	2.3 (5)	2.9 (6)	2.5 (6)
Product or service	3.0 (5)	3.3 (4)	3.5 (4)	2.8 (5)	3.7 (3)	3.2 (6)	3.8 (2)	4.2 (1)
Type of people	3.7 (3)	3.3 (4)	3.8 (2)	3.7 (4)	3.4 (5)	3.9 (1)	3.8 (2)	2.9 (5)
Type of occupation	3.6 (4)	3.7 (3)	3.8 (2)	3.8 (3)	3.6 (4)	3.9 (1)	3.4 (4)	3.4 (4)
Money	4.6 (1)	4.2 (1)	3.9 (1)	4.3 (1)	3.8 (2)	3.9 (1)	3.9 (1)	3.7 (3)

Note: Data for Britain and Japan was not reported for this item in the MOWIRT study.

that has emerged in earlier parts of this analysis, rank money as the most significant aspect of the work experience. They align next, concretely and pragmatically, with the task and agree in placing the company or organisation they work for last. There is a relatively low level of identification with the product or service they are dealing with, certainly compared with the US. The lack of identification with company or organisation is perhaps worrying in terms of organisational commitment and loyalty, but the Chinese samples are little different from any of the other countries in this regard.

Societal norms about working

This part of the survey deals with respondents' perception of norms within the society relating to work-related entitlements and obligations. The theoretical rationale is that the meanings work holds for people are in part imbued by their understanding of, and socialisation into, prevailing norms within the society.

Figure 8.4 plots the position of Hong Kong and Beijing on some of the key items from this section of the questionnaire. The data reveals very little difference between them: there is a slightly stronger endorsement of the obligation norm in Beijing. This is perhaps in line with persisting socialistic sentiments. What is interesting is that there appears to be a very similar, if weak, endorsement of both entitlement and obligation norms in both groups. This is not the case for other countries where one or other of the norms has greater value (see Figure 8.5). It can be argued that both Hong Kong and Beijing have arrived at a rather balanced position with respect to obligations and entitlements.

These findings are not easy to interpret. We postulate that traditional Chinese values, particularly Confucian, might be expected to have de-emphasised entitlements and promoted obligations. This is strengthened by the previously noted inclinations of Chinese culture towards particularism rather than universalism, and weak inclinations, historically, towards

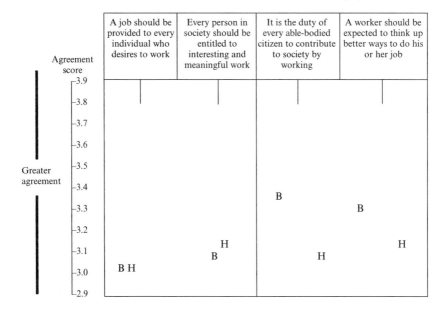

	A job should be provided to every individual who desires to work	Every person in society should be entitled to interesting and meaningful work	It is the duty of every able-bodied citizen to contribute to society by working	A worker should be expected to think up better ways to do his or her job

Agreement score

Greater agreement

B=Beijing
H=Hong Kong

Figure 8.4 Work norm balance

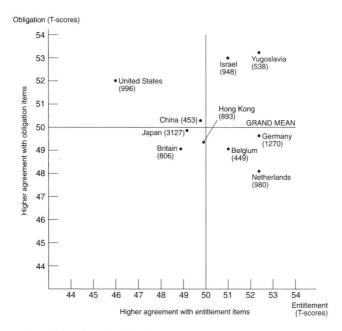

Figure 8.5 Two-dimensional societal norm space

juridical or legalistic outlooks. Certainly, the notion of individual rights has not had great prominence within Chinese social systems. This is bolstered by cultural collectivism under which individual interests are subsumed to that of the collective good. An emphasis on duty and obligation towards the collective good is also, naturally, a precept of communism. On the other hand, under centralist systems of employment there has been a *de facto* guarantee of employment and associated benefits. Chinese workers may have come, over time, to view this as an entitlement. However, the reform context has certainly weakened the message about the entitlement of work *per se*. As unemployment becomes a reality and the demise of the *danwei* accelerates, the right to work becomes an increasingly hollow concept. The emphasis may change; perhaps entitlements will be seen more in terms of opportunity or the provision of training and development.

Conclusion: centrality of work and instrumentalism

The significance and implications of these work-meaning patterns are likely to be consequential at the individual, organisational and economy levels. As noted earlier, we are not dealing primarily with explicit measures of the MOWIRT consequent variables here, rather we will confine ourselves to some more general and speculative relationships. However, before doing so we will briefly present descriptive data on two of the MOWIRT consequent variables by way of illustration.

One question asked: 'If you were to start all over again, would you again choose your occupation or would you choose a different one?' This can be seen as a crude career satisfaction index and Beijing respondents seemed more dissatisfied: only 30.2 per cent said they would choose the same job compared with 43.7 per cent in Hong Kong. In terms of whether they would recommend their own occupation to their children, again 75.5 per cent of the Beijing sample said they would not, compared with 68.4 per cent from Hong Kong.

The link to motivation and performance is potentially the most important implication of the meaning of work patterns, although neither this study, nor the MOWIRT study has any direct bearing on that. It can be argued that the high work centrality in both Hong Kong and Beijing at least signals that work will be taken seriously and that people are prepared to commit themselves to it. Other aspects of the culture and anecdotal evidence do point to a strong work ethic, given a conducive environment. However, the drivers, mechanics, values and outcomes of this work ethic need to be examined and should not merely be assumed. A high work centrality score does not automatically entail high motivation. There is a need for this relationship to be properly theorised and empirically tested.

What is apparent here is that in both Chinese contexts whilst work has high centrality, it is viewed very instrumentally. The low endorsement, especially in China, of intrinsic motivators, such as satisfying and interesting work, and the high endorsement of extrinsic outcomes, such as pay, confirms this. Work has instrumental value as a means to achieve pragmatic and ultimately material outcomes. A significant aspect of this instrumentality is as a means to contribute to and support the family. Both samples defined work in what the MOWIRT group describes as 'concrete' terms.[11]

Thus, both groups currently adopt a highly pragmatic, instrumental view of work. Any managerial motivational strategy needs to take account of this. Strategies that work on intrinsic motivational drivers may be ineffective at this stage. It should be noted, however, that there are significant aspirations for development. In Hong Kong, people are very concerned about their career opportunities and chances for promotion. This may still be instrumentally tied to earnings potential but is a very important human resource management issue – especially given the relative inattention to training, development, and career issues in many Hong Kong organisations. The desire for development opportunities in China is even stronger. The workforce has recognised that things have changed and that to succeed they need the requisite skills. There is tremendous and often unmet demand for training and development in China, at all levels.

The motivational level of Mainland Chinese workers has frequently been questioned, both by foreign business-people and commentators and within China (Deng 1978; Holton 1990; Shenkar and Ronen 1987; Walder 1981, 1987; Wang 1981; Xu 1981). Improving the motivation and productivity of workers in China remains a significant challenge, although factors such as poor technology also affect productivity. The prime causes that are assumed for these problems have been the existence of the 'iron rice bowl', equalitarian reward systems, inappropriate work quota systems, and the failure to link rewards to performance. Even in official circles this has been acknowledged. A policy document in the mid-1980s pointed to the centralised command economy and the reward system dysfunctions just commented upon and concluded that:

> This has resulted in enterprises lacking necessary decision making power and the practice of 'eating out of the same big pot' prevailing in the relations of the enterprises to the state and in those workers and staff members to their enterprises. The enthusiasm, initiative and creativeness of enterprises and workers and staff members have, as a result, been seriously dampened and the socialist economy is bereft of much of the vitality it should possess.
>
> (Communist Party of China 1984: 5–6)

For China, this is a highly significant issue since economic egalitarianism is at the core of socialist ideology, and has been entrenched in policy and practice since the revolution. This principle and the securities of the 'iron rice bowl' are still viewed by many as among the prime achievements of the revolution and essential to social stability (Warner 1987). There is official recognition that the principle, and the reward system accompanying it, are an impediment to the reform process, but the implementation of the necessary changes are highly problematic and fraught with political and social pitfalls (Zhao 1985). There is still support for the 'iron rice bowl' from the labour force and some sections of the Party (Tausky 1991). The notion of wage differentials, contingent upon skills and performance, is also struggling for acceptance (Holton 1990), even though again, there is official recognition that this is vital to the reform process (for example see *Beijing Review* 1988, 1991).

The results of this study indicate that work has high centrality for Chinese workers, but motivational drivers remain highly pragmatic and instrumental. Meeting the needs for appropriate material rewards and for training and development appear to be crucial. Forging clearer links between performance and rewards, and moving to equity-based reward systems would seem to be essential. These are socially and politically sensitive issues and there is considerable inertia, but there are signs that younger members of the workforce are ready to accept such changes.

Notes

1 The authors are grateful for research grants from the Chinese University of Hong Kong and Hong Kong Baptist University which enabled the research on which this chapter is based.
2 'Work' and 'working' are somewhat different conceptually: throughout this paper when the word 'work' is used the notion of 'working' is also implied.
3 1='one of the least important things in my life'; 7='one of the most important things in my life'.
4 The five spheres are: 'my leisure', 'my community', 'my work', 'my religion' and 'my family'.
5 The original question is: 'Imagine that you won a lottery or inherited a sum of money and could live comfortably for the rest of your life without working. What would you do concerning working? 1. Stop working. 2. Continue to work in the same job. 3. Continue to work but with changed conditions.' The wording was altered to reflect local conditions.
6 The outcomes are: 'working': 'gives you status and prestige', 'provides you with an income that is needed', 'keeps you occupied', 'permits you to have interesting contacts with other people', 'is a useful way for you to serve society' and, 'itself is basically interesting and satisfying to you'.
7 The full eleven items were: 'opportunity to learn', 'good interpersonal relations', 'good opportunities for promotion', 'convenient work hours', 'a lot of variety', ' interesting work', 'good job security', 'a match between job requirements and your abilities and experience', 'good pay', 'good physical working conditions', 'a lot of autonomy'.
8 The items were, 'the tasks I do while working', 'my company or organisation', 'the product or services I provide', 'the type of people with whom I work', 'the type of occupation or profession I am in', 'the money I receive from my work'.
9 1='strongly disagree' and 4='strongly agree' with no neutral point.
10 Which shows only the top five of the eleven goals.
11 In Hong Kong the dominant defining quality of work was 'If you get money for doing it'. This was followed by 'If you have to account for it', 'If it belongs to your task' and 'If you do it at a certain time'. In Beijing money came second to the 'If it belongs to your task' definition. Interestingly, the Beijing sample still had contribution to society as the third highest definitional element.

9 Public sector HRM

Vision and reality at the Hong Kong Hospital Authority

David Thompson, Ed Snape,
Clifford Mak Kei-fung and Coryn Stokes

Introduction

The purpose of this chapter is to describe and evaluate the development of the human resource management function in a public sector organisation in Hong Kong. It takes the case of the Hong Kong Hospital Authority (HA), a relatively new organisation undergoing extensive structural and cultural changes. Since it is a heavily labour-intensive organisation, the HA is aware that its human resource management (HRM) policies and procedures are crucial to the success of these changes. These policies and procedures are intended to achieve a decentralisation of the HRM function at the same time as an increase in its professionalism.

The chapter first describes the management reforms in the HA and what they are meant to achieve. The case is then discussed within an exploratory framework derived from the HRM literature and from the published statements of the HA. This provides a basis on which to map the HA's HRM function and to attempt an evaluation of its development so far.

The method of investigation involved a series of interviews and an examination of documents at the HA's Head Office (HAHO) between late 1995 and early 1997. This exercise was accompanied by in-depth case studies in four hospitals to enrich the understanding of the decentralisation process. The research was completed by a questionnaire survey of selected hospitals within the HA to confirm emerging findings. The present work reviews and discusses the findings from the perspective of HAHO.

Management reform in the Hong Kong Hospital Authority

The HA assumed responsibility for the operation and management of Hong Kong's government and voluntary or 'subvented' hospital and healthcare institutions on 1 December 1991. On its establishment, key objectives for the HA included the reduction of patient waiting time, the removal of temporary or camp beds from hospital wards and corridors, the improvement of the general hospital environment, and the development of patient and community feedback and involvement. All these were to be achieved with high quality and cost-effectiveness.

The HA aimed to achieve these objectives by adopting a more decentralised management structure. In December 1991, the Authority launched its 'New Management Initiatives' (NMI), designed to replace the traditional structure which was based on notions of hierarchy and centralised decision-making and inherited from the previous civil service organisation. The new approach emphasised the decentralisation of decision-making responsibilities, with budgetary control to be devolved to hospitals and, ultimately, to individual clinical services and departments within the hospital. Each of the forty or so hospitals was to be headed by a Hospital Chief Executive, fully accountable for its operation and management.

One of the main reasons given by the government for the establishment of the Hospital Authority and the associated management reforms was that they would allow for greater flexibility, particularly on personnel issues such as salary scales, staff benefits, and the use of part-time staff (Yuen 1994).

What was envisaged in the reforms was nothing less than a 'cultural transformation' in public hospitals. The aim was to replace a hospital culture centred on the values of professionalism, specialisation and hierarchical management, with a client- or patient-centred approach, emphasising empowerment of staff, teamwork and the continuous improvement of service quality.

The management reforms initially progressed well, at least in structural terms. The recruitment of Hospital Chief Executives was completed by 1992, a year earlier than planned. The implementation programme for hospital management structures and devolved budgets proceeded ahead of schedule. Encouraging results were claimed in terms of the removal of camp beds from wards and the reduction of patient waiting times. However, there were criticisms of the new regime, with allegations of a failure to reduce bureaucracy, an increase in the amount of time spent by medical staff in management meetings, and a lack of significant improvements in service (see, for example, *Window* 1994). There were also concerns about the continuing staff shortages and poor staff morale. According to one Hospital Chief Executive, the early reforms were of a top-down nature: '. . . most of the changes have been the result of administrative directives from senior managers rather than constructive initiatives by front-line staff.' (Hong Kong Hospital Authority 1992: 5).

What emerged from early 1992 was a realisation amongst senior HA management that the structural reforms could be only one element of the process of organisational transformation, and that there was an urgent need to develop management competencies and to win staff commitment to the new management style and HA mission. Both of these rely heavily on the successful implementation of appropriate human resource strategies.

From the start, the Hospital Authority's Mission Statement contained the commitment 'to provide rewarding, fair and challenging employment to all its staff, in an environment conducive to attracting, motivating and retaining well-qualified staff' (Hong Kong Hospital Authority 1991: 1).

Not surprisingly, given the bid to decentralise management responsibility, the HA aimed to shift key human resource management responsibilities to hospital level. The human resource department of each hospital was given a greater role in recruitment, succession planning, training and development and HRM administration. Furthermore, line managers themselves were to be given greater responsibility for aspects of human resource management. Thus, department heads became responsible for identifying the training and development needs of their staff, in line with changing department requirements, and each hospital was to submit its consolidated training and development plan to HAHO for consideration. The new Staff Development Review (SDR) system, introduced in 1995, was designed to focus line managers' attention on the performance and development of their staff. The move to individual performance-based pay, although proceeding with caution and initially restricted to senior management grades, was to give line managers further responsibility for motivating and rewarding their staff.

Of course, the HA is not unique in developing such a policy of decentralisation. Flexibility and 'getting closer to the customer' has been a common theme in the popular management literature (Peters and Waterman 1982; Peters 1988; Kanter 1988). Decentralisation of the HRM function is being implemented in a growing number of large organisations (IPD 1995; Bevan and Hayday 1994; Storey 1992). Where management responsibilities generally are being decentralised to unit level, similarly, it is often desirable to decentralise HRM decision-making, with the aim of bringing HRM strategies and practices into closer alignment with the needs of business and line management, and so contributing to greater effectiveness (Merchant and Wilson 1994). Whilst there may be HRM specialists at unit level in even the most centralised of organisations, they have often been restricted to a purely operational role. What is now being suggested in many organisations is that unit-level HRM specialists will be required to make a greater contribution to the determination of policy, as well as being responsible for its implementation. At the same time, line managers are to take on more of the day-to-day HRM responsibilities, thus ensuring a closer integration between HRM and business decisions (Storey 1992).

Experience elsewhere has shown that decentralisation is not necessarily without problems. Such problems include a lack of HRM and management expertise, resource constraints, resistance from employees and their representatives, indifference towards HRM issues amongst line managers themselves, and perhaps even a fear on the part of HRM specialists that their own professional standing is threatened (see for example IPD 1995; Bevan and Hayday 1994). However, the effective decentralisation of HRM responsibilities to hospital and line-management level is likely to be a key element in the HA's new approach, relying as it does on the recruitment and retention of high-quality staff, and the winning of their commitment to the HA's mission.

What should a human resources management department do?

The academic literature on personnel/human resources management has identified several role typologies for the function. Building on an earlier typology by Tyson and Fell (1986), Storey (1992) offers a development grounded in his analysis of 15 in-depth case studies. He distinguished between two dimensions in the HRM role. First, HRM functions may be tactical or strategic in terms of their 'contribution to decision making'. Second, they may be characterised in terms of their 'degree of intervention'. '*Handmaidens*' play a purely supporting role, responding to line managers' needs on a tactical basis. '*Advisors*' also take a back-seat role as regards the running of the organisation but they function as internal consultants; they are better informed on the strategic requirements of the organisation and generally show greater professional expertise. '*Regulators*' play a more interventionist role, promulgating, monitoring and even enforcing employment rules, ranging from personnel procedures manuals to collective agreements with unions. The role is one of intervening in the employment relationship to ensure compliance, but the perspective is largely tactical. Finally, the '*changemaker*' is both interventionist and strategic, making a strategic contribution to the development of the organisation in a proactive manner. Such HRM functions are usually at the forefront of organisational change initiatives.

For Tyson and Fell (1986), the problem facing many HRM departments is not so much a need to secure the prestigious changemaker or 'architect' role, but simply to clarify the expectations of their managerial colleagues: only then can the function's contribution be properly evaluated. Others, however, take a more ambitious view of HRM's future. The debates on 'human resource management', for example, clearly espouse the changemaker role as the way forward for HRM, with 'integration' as a key objective of strategic HRM (Guest 1987). According to this view, even the advisor role, whereby line managers are left to define their needs and are able to call on or reject the services of the HRM specialist at will, is insufficient. As Fowler points out:

> The role of the personnel function is not solely to satisfy the heads of various line units. It is also to contribute to the achievement of corporate goals – a role which may sometimes require the stance taken by individual managers to be challenged.
>
> (Fowler 1993: 29)

On this view, HRM needs to transcend the non-interventionary roles. It must make a more strategic contribution, looking beyond its own policies and procedures and meeting the strategic need of the organisation. Only the changemaker role meets these demands. Thus Fowler (1993) identifies three key qualities for an effective HRM department: professional knowledge and expertise; relevance to the achievement of the organisation's objectives; and a proactive approach, initiating proposals rather than simply responding to the demands of line managers or employees.

Fine words! There is, however, a problem. HRM has long been seen as a low-status, reactive function. According to Storey 'personnel management has long been dogged by problems of credibility, marginality, ambiguity, and a trash-can labelling which has relegated it to a relatively disconnected set of activities – many of them tainted with a low-status and welfare connection' (Storey 1989: 5).

The suggestion is that the HRM function in many, perhaps most, organisations has been locked into a tactical role. Even where a bureaucratic or public service tradition, or assertive unions, have demanded a more interventionary approach, this has usually been in the regulatory mode. The challenge facing HRM in many organisations is to escape this legacy as part of the drive towards professionalisation implicit in the ambitious view of HRM espoused by writers such as Guest and Fowler. The issues of professionalising and structuring the HRM function are central concerns of the case under consideration.

Describing and mapping the vision

Prior to the establishment of the HA in 1991, Hong Kong's fifteen government hospitals had been part of the civil service, and the HRM function had operated very much on an administrative-driven model, reflecting the civil service tradition embodied in the Civil Service Regulations. All types and grades of staff were recruited centrally by the civil service Hospital Services Department (HSD) and its predecessor. They were then posted as required to individual hospitals without any local consultation as to their suitability. Such procedures reinforced the tendency of senior staff at hospital level to think of themselves primarily as health care professionals and not as line managers with a responsibility for staff and staffing issues.

Before 1991, staff at the twenty-one voluntary hospitals were employed on non-civil service terms. These varied as to benefits and allowances but were broadly similar in terms of basic salary. Because they were largely funded by subvention from the government, their staff establishment was controlled by the HSD and their recruitment decisions were closely monitored for all but minor staff.

Whilst the HA was quick to develop a range of HRM policy initiatives designed to underpin its key objectives after 1991, it inherited an HRM function which was highly centralised and shaped by healthcare professional influences. Head Office was heavily involved in day-to-day administration of HRM matters and in providing detailed advice to hospitals on policy implementation. The HA also inherited the task of merging together thirty-six (since grown to forty-three) hospitals and 37,000 (since grown to 43,000) staff into an integrated structure with unified terms and conditions of employment.

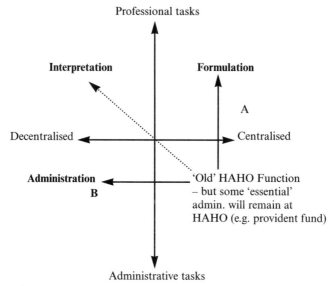

Figure 9.1 Mapping human resource roles.

The drive to improve this inheritance has gone forward under the auspices of the HA's Corporate Vision (Hong Kong Hospital Authority 1995). One of the major strategies in this vision is the *cultivation of organisation transformation and development.* This has been seen to entail:

- a paradigm shift of providers to a patient-centred, outcome focused service;
- a new management culture of decentralisation and empowerment to front-line units;
- a multi-disciplinary team approach to holistic patient care; and
- an environment conducive to continuous quality improvement.

(Weller 1994: 11)

This clearly points out that the development of the HRM function is fundamental to achieving the vision. The direction in which progress is to be made is also indicated.

The analysis of the prior literature and the preliminary interviews and documentary material at HAHO in our research suggested an emerging pattern of HRM at the HA (see Figure 9.1). First, the function involves three roles: formulation of policy, interpretation of policy and administration:

- *Formulation* refers to the creation and explicit revision of HRM policies and procedures. In the HA, many of these are written down, for example in manuals, policy papers and memoranda.

- *Interpretation* refers to the application of policies and procedures to particular cases. Where policies are highly explicit, interpretation may tend to be relatively unimportant, but circumstances can change rapidly and many cases are imperfectly covered so that, in practice, interpretation remains a significant activity in most organisations to such an extent that the difference between policy formalities and interpretation becomes one of degree.
- *Administration* refers to the routine application of policies and procedures, involving little or no scope for autonomous interpretation or discretion beyond the mechanical application of rules and formulae to particular cases.

Second, these three roles were themselves developing on two dimensions: (i) the work was changing from that performed by traditional civil service administrators to that performed by the HRM professional; (ii) the work involved in some of the categories was itself moving from its centralised location at HAHO to decentralised locations in hospitals.

- *Professional/Administrative work*: Professional tasks require expertise founded on specialist knowledge and skills gained through study and/or specialist experience, probably in several organisations. They are performed by following a model of good practice which, whilst applied in a contingent manner, is nevertheless rigorously grounded in expertise and perhaps an ethical code, or set of professional values, that may be independent of the employing organisation.

  Administration depends on expertise founded largely on knowledge of administrative procedures, usually organisation-specific and gained by limited study but mainly by extensive organisational experience. Administration carries with it a notion of efficiency and accuracy in applying regulations impartially and impersonally, but with little or no wider ethical or professional sense.
- *Centralised/decentralised work*: Organisational reform in the HRM function of the HA also consists of changes along the dimension of centralisation–decentralisation. In a *centralised* organisation, the locus of decision-making is at the centre and/or hierarchically senior positions, and local units/junior staff have little autonomy or discretion beyond relatively routine application of rules. Centralisation facilitates greater control leading to consistency in decision-making across the whole organisation. In a *decentralised* organisation the locus of decision-making, for selected decisions, is at local/unit level and/or with more junior positions, and the centre tends to focus on strategic decisions, although even aspects of this may be decentralised. Decentralisation allows for greater flexibility in decision-making at local level resulting in greater responsiveness to 'business' needs.

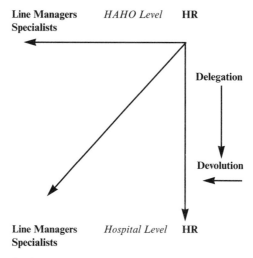

Figure 9.2 Decentralisation of human resource management.

Decentralisation in turn can mean two things, either *delegation* or *devolution*: Where decisions are *delegated*, the locus of decision-making (for selected decisions) moves to HRM specialists at local/unit level and/or to more junior positions in the specialist HRM hierarchy. Such levels are empowered with greater autonomy/discretion to deal with issues more flexibly. Where decisions are *devolved*, the locus of decision-making moves to non-specialist line management. Such staff are empowered with greater autonomy/discretion to deal more flexibly with issues concerning their own staff. The delegation/devolution distinction introduces a third dimension to our map (see Figure 9.2) – the degree of specialist-line involvement in HRM decisions. Whilst centralisation may tend to be associated with specialists, decentralisation may also involve functional specialists at local level, so that delegation to unit level and devolution to line management, whilst possibly correlated, are not necessarily the same thing.

In terms of the above, HA's HRM function had traditionally been heavily centralised, with the centre having a great deal of day-to-day involvement, not only in policy formulation and interpretation but also in routine administration. Our interviews at HAHO clearly pointed to a change of emphasis with a wish to decentralise responsibility for administration to hospitals and even to individual line managers, only retaining those aspects of administration at head office where no benefits accrued from decentralisation.

As the Deputy Director (Human Resources) (DD/HR) put it:

> Our aim was for HRD to focus more on the strategic aspects of policy formulation and not to be 'distracted' by administration. At the same

time, HRD was to develop a stronger HRM-professional orientation, partly by 'upskilling' existing staff and also via judicious recruitment of HRM professionals from outside. In this respect, HRD was to leave behind its former preoccupations with administrative procedure.

All this can be traced out on Figure 9.1 as professionalisation but continued centralisation of policy formulation and a decentralisation of administrative responsibility, as shown by the arrows A and B respectively. Less clear cut is where the responsibility for interpretation will lie. Policies and procedures had traditionally been very detailed and highly prescriptive, leaving little scope for decentralised responsibility and with a focus on the letter of the rule rather than a more flexible notion of good practice or managerial expediency. Our interviews at HAHO implied a management intention to try to avoid the bureaucratisation of HRM decision-making, for example by developing a less detailed set of procedures than hitherto, but at the same time to develop HRM professional skills at hospital level. In this respect, what appears to be envisaged is both a decentralisation and a professionalisation of interpretation decisions.

The above vision clearly has much in common with the shift towards a changemaker role for Human Resources Division (HRD) at HAHO, at the same time reinforcing unit and line-management responsibility for HRM administration and interpretation, subject to the strategic guidance of the central HRD.

The DD/HR was clear that the activities of these HRM experts at HAHO would focus on professional and not administrative functions:

> administration must be pushed down to hospitals where the vast bulk of the staff concerned are working. It must be kept contained at HAHO level only where there are imperatives for coordination or economies of scale, such as the operation of the Provident Fund.

He stressed that administration at HAHO distracts attention from the vital role of policy formulation, the key contribution of the HRM professional.

As formulation has become the priority of HAHO and administration the task at hospital level, interpretation of policy has become the link which fastens the HRM function together. It is clear, however, that the DD/HR intended to encourage hospitals to take interpretation increasingly into their own hands as they accumulated experience and confidence. They were to be helped by the publication of the two Human Resources Policy and Administration Manuals, but would inevitably remain dependent on support and advice from HAHO.

Assessing reality: professionalism

To what extent is the above vision being realised along the two key dimensions of professional/administrator and centralisation/decentralisation? The development of professionalism in the HA is first discussed.

At HAHO, there has been considerable movement from an administrative to a professional HRM approach. There is ample evidence of this from HAHO interviews and documents. A corporate infrastructure is in place which reinforces the priority which the HA Board accords to HRM. The Board has its own specialist Human Resources Committee. Hospitals are involved at HA level through an Human Resources Forum, supported by an Human Resources Policy Group. Measures were taken to restructure the HRM function at HAHO into the HRD to concentrate the availability of professional expertise. In 1991, a Deputy Chief Development Officer/ Human Resources was recruited to take charge of the function. He was subsequently upgraded to Deputy Director/Human Resources (DD/HR) in 1994. He and two of his Senior Human Resource Managers (SHRMs) were HRM professionals recruited from outside the hospital industry. The remaining three SHRMs were HA employees who had undergone a process of 'upskilling' to equip them for their new roles. This produced a team with a blend of hospital, or organisation-specific, experience and HRM professional expertise, although it was acknowledged that there were gaps in both experience and expertise.

Other evidence of professionalism comes from the stream of HRM innovations at the strategic level initiated by the HRD in its major functional areas of human resources systems – manpower planning and resourcing, remuneration and benefits, staff relations and communications and management and staff development. These will be discussed in turn below.

- Major human resource management systems have been developed. A *job evaluation* exercise aimed at simplifying the structure of jobs and identifying clear job families was begun in 1992. It was developed in support of the HA's core values and strategy. The system design and piloting was completed in 1995, leading to an agreed framework for HA wide implementation. The development of an integrated *Human Resource Payroll System* (HRPS) was approved in 1992 and, after considerable systems development, 'rolled out' to hospitals during 1996, giving them on-line, interactive access to payroll and HRM systems. From 1997, the HRPS has generated data for a comprehensive *Human Resources Information System.*
- To provide an infrastructure for manpower planning and resources, a *manpower planning process framework* was agreed in 1995. This sought to establish a relationship between the business, or annual, planning and management planning cycles. In the same year, a conceptual framework for the development of *succession planning* was established.
- With reference to remuneration and benefits, the major strategy since 1991 has been to implement an integrated *Hospital Authority Manage-*

ment Pay Scale (HMPS) and steadily absorb all relevant employees on to it. Performance-based remuneration was examined and a merit-based incremental scheme has been linked to HMPS posts for extension through the management hierarchy. Other incentive schemes such as the *Ten Outstanding Staff Award Scheme* (1994) have been developed and introduced.

- In the area of staff relations and communications, a Hospital Consultative Committee was set up in each hospital during 1991, to discuss matters related to the well-being of staff in the hospital environment and the operational efficiency in the hospital, feeding into the Central Consultative Council at HA level. A *staff development review* (SDR) programme was piloted at two hospitals in 1992. By 1993, the SDR was launched at HAHO and 'rolled out' to hospitals during the year. It focused on individually agreed work objectives, and was designed to manage performance at the individual, departmental, hospital and HA levels and to underpin staff development. New channels of staff communications were introduced, including a staff newsletter *Haslink* (1992) and a programme of *staff opinion surveys* (1993).

- In the area of development and training, strategies have been based on systematic *Training Needs Analysis* (TNA) often conducted by outside consultants. This has led to major programmes for all levels of management provided centrally since 1991. The other thrust in this area is to devolve staff development and training to hospitals by establishing more systematic hospital training budgets linked to hospital annual plans (begun in 1993), and by a programme of *Train the Trainers* (begun in 1994).

This catalogue of innovations is an impressive testimonial to the professional approach of the HRD. Committee papers document a constant process of monitoring of impact and updating where appropriate. Two limitations are noted. One is that there can be a long time-frame for the implementation of large and complex initiatives such as job evaluation and manpower planning in an organisation with this large number of employees, taking into account the need for public accountability and the historically cautious approach to innovation. The second suggests a reason for this drag on professionalism – the continued involvement of the HRD in the day-to-day administration of HRM at hospital level. We turn now to examine the progress of decentralisation in this respect.

Assessing reality: decentralisation

The second development to evaluate is the attempt to decentralise HRM responsibility to hospitals and individual line managers. The DD/HR made the important point that success in the strategy of decentralisation depended on the provision of adequate *infrastructure* at hospital level. In the early years this proved difficult to put in place. In 1991, there were at first few HRM professionals or even HRM administrators at hospital level to take up the challenge, although it is true that ex-subvented hospitals had been accustomed to carrying out much of the basic administration. It was necessary for all hospitals to build up a small team of hospital administrators, under the purview of a general manager for administrative services (GMAS), to be able to handle the *delegated* specialist HRM processes. In parallel, *devolution* was taking place, as 'line managers' were identified from amongst senior service and departmental heads and a sense of responsibility for HRM issues was inculcated (see Figure 9.2). The New Management Initiatives (discussed above, p. 152) were bringing along many other changes for hospitals to absorb, so it is understandable that it took time for the HRM capability to be put in place. GMASs and their teams were not in post until late 1992 and, in some cases, even later.

A basic decision in the process of decentralisation was the choice between the degree of delegation to hospital HRM specialists and of devolution to line managers: this choice could be based on the nature of the particular decisions and priorities. Four examples of programme initiatives are now reviewed, chosen to illustrate the varied ways the choices were made in practice. The programmes are staff resourcing, management and staff development, staff discipline and remunerations and benefits.

The objective and content of the programmes are briefly described, leading to an identification of the choice between delegation and devolution, and an assessment of the successes and limitations of decentralisation.

Staff resourcing

The objective of this programme initiative was to replace the considerable tasks of centralised posting of staff to ex-government hospitals and the close monitoring of appointments in ex-subvented hospitals with a decentralised system whereby all HA hospitals recruited their own staff. It was felt that this would give hospitals the flexibility to acquire the appropriate staff to provide services to meet their patients' needs. HAHO could not be expected to understand these needs so well. The framework for this dramatic change in practices was provided by the Human Resource Administration Manual (HRAM) released in December 1994. Its introduction was supported by a series of one-and-a-half-day workshops held in early 1995. These workshops took hospital staff through the complete process from notification of vacancy, advertising, selection procedures and appointment to commencement.

With the HRAM in place, HAHO freed itself from the burden of day-to-day administration of the recruitment and appointment process. This is now largely performed at hospital level, where the vast majority of staff actually work. One of the respondents estimated that 80 per cent of this administration was currently at hospital level and reported:

Right now we [at HRD] are left with very little say on recruitment activities. At the lowest level, we only act to iron out conflicts between hospitals. We are only involved at high rank through a HAHO representative on the selection panel.

The process is handled by HRM specialists at hospital level. They are involved in advertising, on appointment panels and in selection decisions to assist in the process of skills building, and to ensure consistency in appointments. This represents considerable delegation to them from the specialists in the HRD at HAHO. Line managers in hospitals are also demonstrably taking a much greater part in the process and showing 'ownership' of recruitment decisions. Medical chiefs of service, departmental managers from allied health, departmental operations managers and even ward managers in nursing are routinely involved on appointment panels. Thus there is also substantial devolution to line management. The staffing resource programme initiative, therefore, is seen by HRM specialists at HAHO as an example of a balanced mix of delegation and devolution.

Decentralisation has clearly taken place. Specialist HRM staff at HAHO can now give attention to resourcing policy issues, such as inter-hospital transfer, matters which have corporate implications, such as apparent shortage of nurses, and auditing the process of recruitment rather than administering it. An important Recruitment Quality Review was carried out in December 1995 to monitor consistency of practice between hospitals and compliance by hospitals with the HRAM. Our respondent elaborated:

We are concerned to promote what is fair, what is equitable. Fair, you know, means that everyone can accept the criteria for selection . . . For example, selection by seniority may have been seen as fair, but is also arbitrary . . . we need to review other criteria.

Yet many limitations to decentralisation are apparent. Our respondent emphasised: 'The HA itself is a legal entity and holds all employment contracts. All appointments are formally made by the Hospital Authority even though employees work for individual hospitals.' Unlike the National Health Service Trust Hospitals in the United Kingdom, HA hospitals are not legal employers. The HA, therefore, must remain closely involved in resourcing issues. This is reinforced by the size of the Personnel and Emoluments (PE) budget: some 70 per cent of the HA's total expenditure. All HA functions and activities are affected by decisions about human resources.

For this reason, the HRD remains locked into the interpretation of policy, often on a day-to-day basis. Selected examples presented in August 1997 include a request for support to appoint a Clerk III rather than a health care assistant at one hospital; for advice on the difference between voluntary workers, visitors and clinical attachments; for advice on whether an employee could work part-time at two different HA institutions; and for advice on problems of changing a particular appointment from permanent to temporary status. Given that resourcing still involves a huge volume of work at the HRD, it is not surprising that it pushes more complex and longer-term programme initiatives, such as manpower planning, down the order of priority.

Management and staff development

The key programme initiative in this area was the devolution of training budgets to hospitals, which began in the 1993–4 financial year. The rationale for this was based on several factors. It was in line with the HA's Corporate Vision of organisational transformation. It was aimed at unifying the budgetary arrangements for all hospitals: historically, government hospitals had a more generous allocation than subvented hospitals. It was intended to involve hospitals more closely in the training function and to examine training needs from a hospital perspective. Resource allocation was initially based on a percentage of the PE budget cost of hospitals, on service complexity by hospital categorisation, and on training expenditure in the past year. One of our respondents said: 'We intend to move away from historic and formula budgets to base line budgets based on identified needs and new initiatives . . .'

To assist hospitals to rise to this challenge, a *Train the Trainer* programme was established in 1994. Another respondent explained:

> We want to convince the senior managers that when they develop large training capacity in the hospital, we will provide a supportive training package, so that they can conduct their own training programmes at their own time and at their own pace. It is for their benefit. Otherwise they will wait in a long queue for [external] hot training programmes.

The hospital-level trainers were to come from line managers and supervisors in administration, nursing, allied health and, to a lesser extent, medicine. Although HRM specialists at HAHO recognised that these line managers would also have competing managerial and professional duties, they argued that such trainers would have much more credibility with their professional colleagues than HRM training staff at hospital level. Since line managers were also to be closely involved in preparing training budgets, it was the view amongst HRM specialists at HAHO that the management and staff development programmes represented an area of devolution to line managers, rather than one of delegation to hospital level HRM specialists.

The devolution of budgets and the training of trainers are programmes demonstrating the success of the policy of decentralisation in this area. It represents 90 per cent of the resources devoted to training and development. This especially relates to the professional and vocational (administrative and support staff) training. Less decentralisation is evident in relation to programmes of management development. These continued to be provided by the HRD for all levels of managers from hospital chief executives and HAHO deputy directors to first line nursing officers and supervisors:

> Our [HRD] trainers will conduct this kind of course. So we are not going to employ outside training consultants. Our training department right now is quite well established with enough manpower. So for this kind of core [management] programme, we have our own in-house trainers.

It is clear that HRD will remain a major provider of development programmes: the argument for this rests on 'economies of scale'. While staff development, both professional and vocational, has been devolved, management development remains centralised.

Staff discipline

As a programme area, staff discipline provides an informative contrast to the development programmes discussed previously. The latter was seen to involve devolution to line managers, especially through the training budget. The former may be seen to involve delegation between HRM specialists. The senior specialists in the HRD regarded staff discipline as a sensitive area; the priority objective is to ensure consistency of policy implementation and procedure across the HA's hospitals.

Each staff member is issued with an *Employees' Handbook,* detailing standardised procedures relating to misconduct and disciplinary action: counselling and warnings for minor offences, reprimanding for serious misconduct, dismissal for gross misconduct. Appeals may be lodged through the *Staff Complaints and Appeals Procedure.*

As far as the *Handbook* is concerned, employees will relate primarily to their Heads of Department in disciplinary matters. This disguises a concern at HRD: 'Actually we perceive a lack of skills in handling staff complaints and disciplinary actions in individual hospitals . . . From interactions with hospitals, we do feel that some line managers lack these kinds of skills and they recognise this . . .'

The solution is to target training at the HRM specialists at hospital level. These hospital administrators thus become the experts in disciplinary matters who acquire the expertise and experience to ensure consistent behaviour among line managers. The strategy is therefore to delegate to HRM specialists at hospital level, rather than to devolve to line managers, most of whom will rarely be involved in formal disciplinary action and who thus do not need expertise and do not acquire experience on a regular basis.

Staff disciplinary policy and procedures were put into place early in the existence of the HA. They are clearly spelled out in the HRPM and the HRAM. They have not been an area for further programme initiatives. They do not therefore cast much additional insight into decentralisation of HRM. The roles of the department, hospital and HAHO are clear and understood. While most disciplinary matters are dealt with at hospital level, HAHO would expect to be involved in certain serious cases. The only danger is that, if hospital level procedures lose credibility, the number of individual cases coming to HAHO may get out of control.

Remuneration and benefits

As we have seen, the HA is legally a unitary organisation; its payroll is a large part of its expenditure. One of our respondents explained the standardised nature of remuneration and benefits:

> Actually the Head Office have a set of policies which are supposed to be applicable to all HA employees, no matter which hospital they work in . . . At the hospital level, people in the personnel department have two thick manuals: the Human Resources Policy Manual and the Human Resources Administration Manual . . . When employees have any problems, they should approach their hospital and the personnel people will solve the problem based on the manuals . . . All the conditions and terms are uniform. Every person receives the same package.

In this function, there are no programme initiatives aimed at promoting decentralisation of policy or interpretation, although 70 per cent of the routine administration is seen to be successfully decentralised. The role of hospital level HRM specialists is to assist line managers in routinely administering remuneration and benefits with little flexibility. For example: 'Normally, we have several guidelines on granting salary increments . . . We only grant increments if the hospitals have some difficulty in recruiting people. Those rules and regulations are quite severe.'

There is some talk within HRD about recommending that the rules and regulations might be relaxed a little. But this would be in the context of moving to a performance-based culture:

> We think it is important for the hospitals to learn how to utilise their resources to recruit the suitable person . . . At present, we are trying to promote a performance-based culture in terms of increment . . . We also operate a number of primitive incentive schemes . . .

There is concern to encourage performance but to discourage 'unhealthy competition' in recruitment between hospitals. The efforts of the HRD to ease the rules have to some extent been diluted by the involvement of other HAHO divisions in HRM issues. For example, Deputy Director/Financial Services and Deputy Directors/Operations have legitimate concerns of their own about the costs and deployment of human resource. Mixed messages about remuneration and benefits can go out to hospitals. Programme initiatives are, therefore, proceeding cautiously and under the firm, if sometimes fragmented, control from the centre.

Conclusion: 'two thirds of the way'

There has been considerable progress in attaining the vision of a more 'professional' HRM function. The HRD at HAHO is seen to espouse the role of 'changemaker' and 'architect' identified in the literature (Storey 1992; Tyson and Fell 1986): it makes a strategic contribution to the development of the whole organisation across its five major functions, with policy initiatives aimed at furthering an equitable, developmental and performance-related culture. However, it is clear from the evidence presented in this chapter that the HRD continues to play a strongly interventionalist role in interpreting and administering programmes, and in monitoring compliance with procedures. In this respect, the 'regulator' role is still apparent, in spite of an apparent wish on the part of the HRD to de-emphasise it.

The thrust towards decentralisation has also had its successes. If we review the exploratory framework in Figure 9.1, it may be seen that the 'old' HAHO function has 'exploded' outwards from its 'centralised, administrative' quadrant. Formulation of HRM policy quite properly remains centralised but, as we have seen, this responsibility is now exercised from a more professional perspective. HRM administration has been decentralised to hospital level for the most part. We have also seen how this varies in nature and degree across the HRM functions. Our respondents estimated that between 60 per cent and 80 per cent of the administrative work had been successfully passed to the hospitals.

There have been more mixed results in decentralising the process of policy interpretation, which links together the formulation and administration of policy. The reasons for this include a wariness of setting precedents which have an implication for HA-wide consistency and which take place in a highly visible, publicly accountable organisation. Staff are also fearful of being 'blamed' for 'mistakes' if their interpretation of the policy is seen to be incorrect. Interpretation is seen by some HRM professionals at HRD to be the crucial role, since the development of HRM in the public sector may be seen to be achieved not by changing policies but by reinterpreting them. Progress is made by setting precedents and by developing a body of case law; it can therefore seem to be slow and incremental. While the HRD strategy is still to decentralise interpretation, its members remain involved in the process, often on a day-to-day basis. Whilst this is to some extent understandable, given the wish to maintain equitable treatment of staff across the HA, nevertheless the risk must be that it distracts HRD's attention from the more strategic aspects of the HRM function.

The consensus view among professionals at HRD was that professionalisation and decentralisation had proceeded 'about two-thirds of the way'. In reviewing the substantial progress in the development of the HRM function, the professionals concluded that it had moved from the role of 'security guard or watchman' to that of 'head prefect or arbiter'. They looked forward to further evolution in the role to that of 'changemaker and architect'.

Bach (1995), after Fowler (1992), identifies three options for the structuring of the HRM function in a decentralising organisation. First, HRM can remain centralised, allowing decentralisation units to negotiate with the centre over the cost and provision of HRM services. Second, HRM specialists can be located at unit level, but retain a primary reporting relationship with the HRM centre. Third, units can be fully responsible for their own HRM staff but with a (smaller) central HRM department performing a strategic role. The third option appears to be consistent with the vision espoused by the DD/HR and his senior colleagues, although as we have seen, in practice the HRD has thus far retained a strong 'regulator' role. The extent to which the HRD will be able to relinquish this role and focus more of its energies on strategy depends not least on the extent to which the HRM function within hospitals develops in terms of professionalisation, confidence and hence autonomy. This must surely be one of the key challenges facing the HRM function in the future.

10 Human resource strategy and business performance

Evidence from a survey of multinational firms in Hong Kong[1]

Margaret Shaffer, Ed Snape and Frenda Cheung

Introduction

In recent years there has been a growing recognition of the potential contribution of human resource management (HRM) strategies in meeting organisational goals (Fombrun *et al.* 1984; Pfeffer 1994). Generally this has involved a call for organisations to adopt a *strategic* approach to managing their human resources. HRM is no longer to be seen simply as a staff specialism concerned solely with people-management issues and separate from the management of the business. What organisations must do is to build a coherent package of HRM practices which underpins the achievement of organisational objectives and helps to build sustainable competitive advantage. One implication of this is that much of the research on the effectiveness of specific HRM practices (pay systems, selection techniques, appraisal etc.) misses the point, since what is important is the 'bundle' of HRM policies. It is the overall HRM strategy that matters and the use of a particular technique cannot be evaluated in isolation.

The purpose of this chapter is to empirically investigate the strategic role of human resource management and its impact on firm performance in the context of Hong Kong. After considering why HRM is an important ingredient in a firm's efforts to build sustainable competitive advantage, we outline two models of the HRM strategy–firm performance relationship: (1) a 'one best way' approach in which HRM directly affects employee attitudes and behaviours which in turn affect firm performance; and (2) a 'strategic fit' approach in which firm performance is viewed as a function of both employee attitudes/behaviours and the fit between a firm's strategy and HRM practices. We review the extant literature in this area before presenting the results of our own research, which uses a sample of multinational firms in Hong Kong to test the two models.

Why does HRM matter?

The recent concern with the strategic contribution of HRM raises the question as to why HRM matters: how exactly does it contribute to the pursuit of competitive advantage? Strategic management as an academic discipline has tended to focus on the marketing, financing, and perhaps the operations aspects, leaving HRM as the 'poor relation' of the business functions. HRM's association with worker welfare together with the fact that it has been seen by many as a low-level administrative function, as reflected in Drucker's famous 'trash can' jibe (Drucker 1961), may have contributed to this. All this began to change with the publication in the 1980s of such popular management books as Peters and Waterman's (1982) 'excellence' study and with Walton's (1985) classic *Harvard Business Review* article. There are many accounts of how HRM policies can help build competitive advantage, but the basic idea is that HRM policies influence employee behaviour, for example productivity and turnover, and that this in turn impacts on organisational efficiency and effectiveness.

Theoretical support for the idea that HRM contributes towards the creation of sustainable competitive advantage has come from the 'resource-based' view of the firm (Barney 1991; Wright and McMahan 1992). This perspective sees differences in organisational performance as being attributable to different resource portfolios. Sub-performers may, of course, improve their relative performance by acquiring superior resources. However, where there is imperfect imitability, competitors find it difficult or impossible to copy the resource portfolio of superior performers. The point is that only those resources which are imperfectly imitable provide a basis for sustainable competitive advantage. The usual argument is that HRM policies do provide such a basis, since the 'causal ambiguity' and 'social complexity' involved mean that the link between HRM policies and competitive advantage, whilst genuine, is difficult to understand and hence to imitate (Barney 1991). Furthermore, there are 'time compression diseconomies' involved in implementing HRM policies, in that it may take considerable time for HR practices to have the intended impact on employee attitudes and behaviour (Becker and Gerhart 1996). The TQM literature, for example, suggests that the process of building a culture of continuous improvement, including an open management style and employee empowerment, is a long-term process in which not all firms have been successful but which nevertheless provides the basis for sustainable competitive advantage (Powell 1995).

'Best practice' or 'strategic fit'?

In fact, there are two views on the contribution of HRM. First is what we term the 'best practice' or 'one best way' approach, as best explained by Walton (1985). The argument here is that US firms (Walton is writing about the US context, but his arguments have been taken up in other countries) must move from a 'control' to a 'commitment' strategy, using a strategic bundle of high-performance work practices, aiming to build a committed and empowered workforce. This is apparently necessary if firms are to meet the increasing international competition, particularly on quality differentiation. Such accounts appear to suggest that all firms need to adopt such a sophisticated HRM approach, perhaps even to remain in existence, let alone to win competitive advantage.

Second, we have the 'strategic fit' approach (Boxall 1992). This suggests that it is not enough simply to adopt sophisticated HRM practices, since what is required is to fit or match the organisation's HRM policies with the business strategy. Such accounts have often drawn on the typologies found in the strategic management literature, such as Porter's or Miles and Snow's strategy types (Schuler and Jackson 1987; Arthur 1992; Miles and Snow 1984; Sonnenfeld *et al.* 1992). In this study, we examine the relationship between HRM practices and Porter's competitive strategies of 'cost leadership' and 'differentiation'. Our assumption is that developmental HRM practices will match the requirements of a differentiation strategy, where the emphasis is on quality and innovation, and the requirement is for extensive training and development and relatively high levels of employee involvement (Schuler and Jackson 1987). In contrast, the cost leader strategy will be matched by performance management HRM practices, where the aim is to increase productivity and focus on the achievement of performance targets (Schuler and Jackson 1987). The implication is that there is no one best approach to HRM, but that the task is to 'match' the HRM policies to deliver the particular employee attitudes and behaviours needed to meet the business strategy (Schuler and Jackson 1987).

Research on these issues is still in the relatively early stages, although a body of evidence is now emerging, particularly in the USA (see Becker and Gerhart 1996), supporting the 'best practice' approach. This has usually been operationalised in terms of the extent to which an organisation uses a range of HRM practices which can be labelled as a 'sophisticated' or 'best practice' approach; the term 'high performance work practices' has been used in several of the studies (see, for example, Huselid 1995). The use of such a best practice approach by firms has been found to be positively correlated with employee outcomes such as high productivity and low labour turnover and with various measures of corporate performance (Delaney and Huselid 1996; Huselid 1995; Becker and Gerhart 1996: 783). However, the literature is far from unanimous on what specific HRM practices are included in the best practice model, as demonstrated by Becker and Gerhart's comparison of five recent studies (1996: 785). The role of pay, and whether variable pay is included in the bundle, is especially unclear, suggesting that our understanding of the impact even of individual HRM policies is as yet limited. Theory seems to lag behind testing in this area and authors often appear to select their bundle of HRM practices in a fairly *ad hoc* manner, with only passing reference to underlying theory. It may be that the specification of the best practice bundle would be better done at the level of general principles rather than in terms of specific HRM practices (Becker and Gerhart 1996: 786), or that an empirical approach should be adopted, allowing bundles of practices to emerge from the data (Arthur 1992; 1994; Huselid 1995).

In spite of these shortcomings, the initial findings do appear to be consistent with the view that a more 'sophisticated' approach to HRM has a positive impact on employee behaviour and organisational performance. The findings on the 'strategic fit' view are less clear cut. Several studies examine the interaction between HRM practices and business strategy and find a weak or mixed impact on corporate performance (Huselid 1995; Becker and Gerhart 1996: 783). Youndt *et al.* (1996), however, produce contrary findings, with HRM–business strategy interaction effects dominating the main effect of HRM on operational performance. Similarly, MacDuffie (1995), in a study based on an international sample of sixty-two automotive assembly plants, found that plants which adopted 'flexible production', with team-based work systems, low inventory and repair buffers, and 'high-commitment' HRM practices tended to outperform the 'mass production' plants on productivity and quality. However, the interaction effects between HRM and production practices were even stronger predictors of performance, emphasising the importance of the fit between HRM and production strategies.

The empirical studies have thus often modelled strategic fit as an interaction effect between HRM policies and business or production strategy in regression equations explaining some measure of organisational performance. An alternative is to look at fit as the 'matching' of HRM and business strategy types. An early example of this approach was provided by Arthur (1992), who found some evidence that US steel minimills tended to adopt such a match. In contrast, his subsequent paper provided support for the 'best practice' model (Arthur 1994). In this later study, mills implementing a 'commitment HRM system' had lower labour turnover and superior manufacturing performance (labour productivity and scrap rate) than mills with a 'control HRM system'. Also, the 'commitment' system was associated with a stronger negative relationship between labour turnover and manufacturing performance. Yet Arthur did not directly test the link between HRM–business strategy fit and firm performance in either study. Furthermore, in spite of the interaction effects between HRM and production strategy, there was strong support for a 'best way' approach in MacDuffie's (1995) study, with flexible production consistently outperforming mass production, even where the latter operates with a 'matched' HRM strategy.

In sum, the literature suggests the existence of a link between HRM practices and firm performance, although on balance there is perhaps stronger support for the 'best practice' view than for the notion of 'strategic fit'. Even in the case of the latter, however, the results are sufficiently encouraging to warrant further research in this area. Given that the research to date has focused mainly on the USA, it is particularly important that more such studies are carried out in other locations.

The above discussion leads us to the two models depicted in Figure 10.1, with the following specific hypotheses:

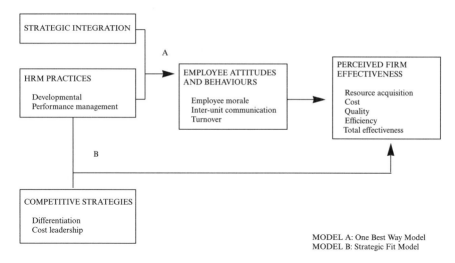

Figure 10.1   The impact of human resource management on firm performance.

1   Employee attitudes and behaviours (i.e. employee morale, inter-unit communication, and turnover) are significant predictors of perceived firm effectiveness (i.e. resource acquisition, cost, quality, efficiency, and total effectiveness). In particular, we expect employee morale and inter-unit communication to facilitate firm effectiveness and employee turnover to inhibit firm effectiveness.

2a Human resource management practices (i.e. developmental and performance management practices) are significant predictors of employee attitudes and behaviours. In particular, we expect that HRM practices will have a positive impact on employee morale and interunit communication and a negative impact on employee turnover.

2b The 'strategic integration' of the human resource management function (i.e. the extent to which management see HRM policies as being important to the success of the firm and as being linked to business strategy) is a significant predictor of employee attitudes and behaviours. In particular, we expect that strategic integration will have a positive impact on employee morale and interunit communication and a negative impact on employee turnover.

3   Employee attitudes and behaviours mediate the relationship between HRM practices and perceived firm effectiveness.

4   The fit between human resource management practices and a firm's competitive strategy is a significant predictor of firm performance. In particular, we expect the fit between (a) a differentiation strategy and HRM developmental practices and (b) a cost leadership strategy and HRM performance management practices to have a positive impact on firm performance.

Hypotheses 1–3 (Model A) test the link between HRM practices and employee attitudes and behaviour and thence to firm effectiveness. The argument is that the greater the extent to which the firm adopts a sophisticated approach to HRM and considers HRM as an important activity which is managed in pursuit of the business strategy, the more favourable employee attitudes and behaviour and the firm's performance are likely to be. This is a 'one best way' model in that the emphasis is on general HRM sophistication and the recognition of HRM's strategic importance, neither of which is necessarily seen to be contingent upon the pursuit of any *particular* business strategy. In contrast, Hypothesis 4 (Model B) examines the importance of the degree of fit between HRM practices and competitive business strategies. This is a 'matching' or 'strategic fit' model. The suggestion is that a developmental HRM approach matches with a differentiation business strategy, given the need for high quality, extra-role behaviours and good customer service, whilst the cost leader is more likely to emphasise efficient performance to specified objectives, which may be facilitated by a performance management HRM approach. Unfortunately, we do not have sufficiently detailed measures to try to link strategies to the specific employee attitudes and behaviours envisaged by Schuler and Jackson (1987), for example, and so we have no alternative other than to hypothesise a direct link from 'fit' to effectiveness.

The HRM survey of MNCs in Hong Kong

Sample

To test the two models and the proposed hypotheses, we conducted a field study in which we mailed separate questionnaires to top managers and human resource managers of 519 multinational firms in Hong Kong. The 519 firms represent those multinational companies with fifty or more employees that are listed in Dun & Bradstreet's *Top 2000 Foreign Enterprises in Hong Kong 1995/96*. Anticipating a lower response rate from top managers, we sent questionnaires to the top three managers listed for each firm. In some cases, only one or two managers were listed, so the actual number of questionnaires mailed to top managers was 1,392. Of these, twenty-one were undeliverable and 151 usable questionnaires were returned, resulting in a response rate of 11 per cent. In a few cases, more than one manager from the same firm returned questionnaires. To create a sample of unique firms, we selected the more senior manager to represent the firm and eliminated others from the sample. This resulted in a reduced sample size of 136. Because the Dun & Bradstreet listing does not include the names of human resource managers, we telephoned each firm to identify who was in charge of its human resource activities. We then sent a personally addressed survey to each of the 519 human resource managers. Four questionnaires were undeliverable and exactly 100 human resource managers returned questionnaires, resulting in a 20 per cent response rate. Considering the notoriously low response rates to cold-call surveys in Hong Kong, these rates are reasonable.

From the questionnaires received, we developed two sets of data: (1) a top manager sample only (n=136) and (2) a matched sample, by firm, of top managers and human resource managers (n=44). The top manager sample was quite diverse in terms of industry and national origin. More than eleven industries were represented: financial services/insurance (20 per cent), manufacturing (19.3 per cent), wholesale, import/export (17.8 per cent), other (14.8 per cent), transport (9.6 per cent), construction (4.4 per cent), business/professional services (4.4 per cent), retail (3.7 per cent), communication (2.2 per cent), agriculture (1.5 per cent), hotels (1.5 per cent), and community/social services (0.7 per cent). Of the twenty different nationalities reported, 24.3 per cent of the firms were from seven Asian countries and 72.8 per cent were from thirteen North American/European countries. Four firms (2.9 per cent) were joint ventures involving both western and eastern partners. Most (97 per cent) of the firms were profit-oriented. The average number of full-time employees in Hong Kong was 390, and the average number of foreign locations per firm was forty-three. As a merged subset of the top manager and human resource manager questionnaires, the firm descriptions for the matched sample were consistent with the larger (top manager) sample from which it was drawn.

Measures

To avoid common method variance, measures were from two different sources (i.e. some were from top managers and some from human resource managers). For the top manager survey, questions focused on the firm in general, including measures of firm effectiveness, employee morale, interunit communication, and competitive strategies. The human resource manager questionnaire was mainly concerned with human resource management issues, including human resource practices and the degree of strategic integration between human resource practices and the firm's business strategy. The measures for the constructs in the proposed models are described below.[2]

Firm effectiveness. Perceived firm effectiveness was measured using scales developed by Miller and Glick (1989). Four subscales of two items each were used to assess firm effectiveness in terms of resource acquisition, cost factors, quality factors and efficiency. To assess resource acquisition, top managers were asked to indicate on a seven-point scale (1=not at all and 7=great extent) the extent to which their firm (1) 'has difficulty obtaining sufficient funds to produce its products and/or services' and (2) 'has easy access to resources for growth and expansion'. The internal reliability of this scale was $\alpha=.64$. The cost ($\alpha=.80$), quality ($\alpha=.62$), and efficiency ($\alpha=.79$) subscales consisted of two items each which requested respondents to compare their firm with what they would like it to be and with other firms in their industry with respect to: 'the cost of producing their firm's products and/or services', 'the quality of their firm's products and/or services', and 'the quantity produced per employee in their firm'. Responses were on a seven–point scale with 1=low, 4=medium, and 7=high. These subscales were also totalled to obtain an overall measure of firm effectiveness (α=.59).

Employee attitudes and behaviours. Employee morale and interunit communication were also measured with two items each from Miller and Glick (1989). On a seven-point scale (1=low, 4=medium, 7=high), top managers were asked to rate their firm in comparison to what they would like it to be and to other firms in their industry with respect to their employees' morale (α=.88) and the effectiveness of communication among subunits (α=.81) of the firm. Turnover was measured by asking human resource managers to indicate the approximate level (per cent) of labour turnover for non-managerial staff per year.

Strategic HRM. Strategic integration was operationalised using the index developed by Buller and Napier (1993). Human resource managers were presented with six human resource functions (e.g. human resource planning, recruitment/selection, compensation/benefits) and asked to rate the import- ance of these functions to firm success and the extent to which these functions are linked to the firm's strategy. Ratings were on five-point scales (1=low and 5=high). The importance and linkage rating for each function were multiplied and these scores were then summed for all activities to obtain an index of the degree of strategic integration of human resource practices and business strategy (α=.82). Human resource management practices were measured using a modified version of the scale developed by Huselid (1995). Human resource managers were asked to indicate the percentages of both non-managerial and non-professional staff (e.g. administrative, clerical, secretarial, manual) who are covered by specified HRM practices. Following the procedures described by Huselid (1995), we subjected the ten human resource practices to a factor analysis. The results, presented in Table 10.1, are consistent with those of Huselid (1995). Two factors emerged, and we labelled the first factor *developmental HRM practices* (α=.65), since it loaded heavily on development and employee involvement items, and the second factor *performance management HRM practices* (α=.78), which loaded on performance appraisal and performance-related pay.

Competitive strategies. Using scales developed by Nayyar (1993), we asked top managers to rate the extent to which their firm emphasises a differen- tiation strategy (ten items) and a cost leadership strategy (six items). Responses were on a seven-point scale (1=no emphasis and 7=major emphasis). Scales were calculated for each strategy by averaging across the relevant items The interitem reliability estimates were α=.79 for the differentiation scale and α=.83 for the cost-leadership scale.

Fit between competitive strategies and human resource practices. We operationalised this in terms of the correspondence between the differen-

Table 10.1 Factor analysis of human resource management practices

Human resource management practices	Factor 1	Factor 2
Receives in-company off-the-job training	.78	
Has access to a formal grievance procedure or complaint resolution system	.75	
Is included in a formal information sharing program (e.g. briefings or newsletters)	.75	
Is administered an attitude survey on a regular basis	.65	
Is involved in regular quality circles or similar problem solving groups	.56	
Is provided with a formal orientation program when they begin their job	.52	
Has a job that has been subjected to a formal job analysis (e.g. with the aim of producing a written job description/ specification)	.37	
Receives a bonus based on the performance of the work group or unit	.34	
Receives formal performance appraisals		.86
Is given performance appraisals to determine their pay		.79

Note: Only loadings greater than .30 are reported.

tiation strategy and developmental HRM strategy on the one hand, and the cost-leadership and performance management HRM strategy on the other. This approach does not imply that firms must necessarily choose between the two strategies; firms may score highly on both; the question is simply to what extent they have in place HRM practices which might be expected to support their business objectives. We measured fit in two ways. First, we included interaction terms (Differentiation × Developmental and Cost Leadership × Performance Management) in our regressions, as has been done in previous studies. Second, we derived two 'fit' indices by standardising the scores on each of the four scales (mean=0 and standard deviation=1) and then calculating the absolute difference between the differentiation strategy and the developmental HRM practices scales and between the cost-leadership strategy and performance management HRM practices scales. Scores were such that *smaller* differences represented a *closer fit* between the business strategy and the HRM practices. We report on each of these approaches in our findings.

Results of the HRM survey of MNCs in Hong Kong

Models A and B were tested using data from the matched sample of top managers and human resource managers. The human resource management variables (i.e. HRM practices and strategic integration) and employee turnover were measured with items from the human resource managers' questionnaire. All other variables were from the top manager questionnaire. Given that the top manager sample was larger, and also to gauge the

Table 10.2 Results of regression analyses for perceived firm effectiveness (Model A): top manager and matched samples

Standardised regression coefficients

Predictors (n=36)	Resource acquisition		Cost		Quality		Efficiency		Total effectiveness	
	Top mgr. (n=113)	Matched (n=39)	Top mgr. (n=113)	Matched (n=38)	Top mgr. (n=114)	Matched	Top mgr. (n=39)	Matched (n=111)	Top mgr. (n=37)	Matched (n=108)
Regressions to test main effects										
Number of employees	.18‡	.23	-.01	.00	.01	-.05	.01	-.14	.05	.01
Number of foreign operations	-.00	-.07	-.05	-.20	-.09	-.14	-.07	-.12	-.05	-.13
West/East	.07	.23	-.16	-.21	.08	-.07	.12	.16	.03	.06
Employee morale	.12	-.03	.01	-.06	.35*	.48‡	.36**	.04	.50***	.35*
Inter-unit communication	.12	.29	-.09	-.00	.08	-.07	.26‡	.64*	.39***	.54**
Turnover		.34‡		-.22		.02		.15		.14
F (full model)	2.04‡	3.03*	.85	0.90	4.58***	1.55	10.61***	4.56**	46.17***	18.92***
R^2	.09	.36	.04	.15	.17	.22	.34	.48	.69	.80
Adj. R^2	.04	.24	-.01	-.02	.14	.08	.30	.37	.68	.75
df	5, 107	6, 32	5, 107	6, 31	5, 108	6, 32	5, 105	6, 30	5, 102	6, 29
Regressions to test mediating effects										
Developmental HRM practices		.03		.30		-.04		-.10		.05
Performance management HRM practices		-.28		-.08		-.35‡		.09		-.16
HRM strategic integration		.03		.05		-.00		-.15		-.01
F (full model)		2.32*		.94		1.59		3.11*		12.97***
R^2		.42		.23		.33		.51		.82
Adj. R^2		.24		-.02		.12		.35		.75
df		9, 29		9, 28		9, 29		9, 27		9, 26

Note
‡p<.10   *p<.05   **p<.01   ***p<.001

comparability of the two samples, Hypothesis 1 was also tested using data from the top manager only sample. All measures had sound psychometric properties in both samples.[3]

Model A: Hypotheses 1–3

We tested Hypothesis 1 using both samples and similar patterns of significance emerged (see Table 10.2). Employee morale was a significant predictor of quality effectiveness and total effectiveness for both the top manager and matched samples. It had a strong impact on efficiency effectiveness for the top manager sample only. For both samples, interunit communication was an important input to efficiency and total effectiveness. Turnover was tested using the matched sample only (this variable was not included in the top manager questionnaire), and emerged as a strong determinant of resource acquisition effectiveness, although in a direction contrary to our expectations.

Hypotheses 2a and 2b, which predicted that human resource management practices and strategic integration would have a direct impact on employee attitudes and behaviours, were also tested using multiple hierarchical regression (see Table 10.3). In support of Hypothesis 2b, HRM strategic integration was an important antecedent of both employee morale and turnover. Performance management HRM practices emerged as a significant positive predictor of turnover, although the positive sign suggests that a greater use of such practices is associated with higher labour turnover.

Hypothesis 3 proposed that employee attitudes and behaviours mediate

Table 10.3 Results of regression analyses for employee attitudes and behaviours (Model A): matched sample

| Predictors | Standardised regression coefficients | | |
	Employee morale ($n=39$)	Interunit communication ($n=39$)	Turnover ($n=40$)
Number of employees	.07	.10	.61***
Number of foreign locations	−.19	−.07	.06
West/East	.02	−.20	.08
Developmental HRM practices	−.15	.04	.05
Performance management HRM practices	−.16	.07	.30‡
HRM strategic integration	.54*	.25	−.39*
F (full model)	1.49	1.13	3.97**
R^2	.22	.17	.42
Adj. R^2	.07	.02	.31
df	6, 32	6, 32	6, 33

Note
‡$p<.10$ *$p<.05$ **$p<.01$ ***$p<.001$

the relationship between the various human resource management variables and perceived firm effectiveness. To test this hypothesis, we first entered the control variables, employee morale, interunit communication, and turnover into the regression equations for firm effectiveness. We then added the HRM practices (developmental and performance management) and the HRM strategic integration index. These results are presented in the lower half of Table 10.2. The addition of these human resource management variables to the basic model did not result in a significant increase in R^2, thus supporting Hypothesis 3 that any link from HRM practices to firm effectiveness is mediated by employee attitudes and behaviours (James and Brett 1984).

The issue of whether or not firms may simultaneously pursue cost leadership and differentiation has been controversial in the strategic management literature. In this study we did not set out with the assumption that firms must necessarily choose between cost leadership and differentiation, nor that developmental and performance management HRM practices are necessarily mutually exclusive. However, it is worth noting that the use of performance management HRM strategies was negatively related to quality effectiveness (Table 10.2) and appeared to contribute to higher labour turnover (Table 10.3). Both findings were significant only at the 10 per cent level, but the suggestion that performance management HRM practices may be inconsistent with a quality-based differentiation strategy and may undermine the

Table 10.4 Results of regression analyses for perceived firm effectiveness (Model B): matched sample

	Standardised regression coefficients				
	Resource acquisition (n=34)	Cost (n=34)	Quality (n=34)	Efficiency (n=33)	Total effectiveness (n=33)
Number of employees	−.12	.08	.02	−.09	−.07
Number of foreign operations	.03	−.26	−.31	−.04	−.13
West/East	.31‡	−.22	.05	.18	.10
Employee morale	.31	−.21	.16	−.04	.33‡
Interunit communication	.03	.14	.25	.74*	.55**
Turnover	.63**	−.32	.10	.17	.22‡
Differentiation/ developmental fit	.15	.27	−.09	−.17	.05
Cost leadership/performance management fit	−.43**	.11	−.30	.02	−.16
F (full model)	3.80**	1.57	1.48	3.29*	11.54***
R^2	.55	.34	.32	.52	.79
Adj. R^2	.40	.12	.10	.36	.72
df	8, 25	8, 25	8, 25	8, 24	8, 24

Note
‡p<.10   *p<.05   **p<.01   ***p<.001

workforce stability which could be important to such a strategy is worthy of further research.

Model B: Hypothesis 4

As mentioned earlier, we adopted two approaches to the measurement of 'fit': interaction terms and fit indices. As regards the interaction terms, these were added to regression equations similar to those reported in Table 10.2, but no evidence of significant interactions was found, thus suggesting that fit does not contribute to effectiveness. Given their lack of significance, we do not report these findings in detail. Second, we included the differentiation/ developmental and cost leadership/performance management difference indices in a hierarchical multiple regression. The results of these regressions, including regression coefficients for the control variables, are presented in Table 10.4. In partial support of Hypothesis 4, the fit between cost-leadership and performance management HRM practices was a significant predictor of resource acquisition effectiveness (recall that higher values on the index signify poorer fit), but in no other case was a fit variable significant.

HRM and firm effectiveness in Hong Kong

The results of this study provide some support for the indirect influence of human resource management on firm effectiveness. Employee attitudes and behaviours clearly have an impact on perceived firm effectiveness. At least one of the attitudes/behaviours was a significant predictor of each dimension of firm effectiveness except cost effectiveness, although turnover had an unexpected sign in the resource acquisition effectiveness equation. The results for HRM practices and strategic integration were less clear cut. For Model A, strategic integration was a significant predictor of both employee morale and turnover, although performance management HRM practices appeared to *increase* labour turnover (a result which might be suggestive of an incompatibility between performance management HRM practices and a quality-based differentiation strategy, as explained above). In the case of Model B, the fit between a cost-leadership strategy and performance management HRM practices significantly predicted resource acquisition effectiveness according to our fit index. This finding, however, was not supported when we measured fit using an interaction term between competitive strategy and human resource practices.

In sum, our study provides at least some support for the 'one best way' model. Firms which see HRM as important and related to their business strategy (strategic integration) had more positive employee attitudes and behaviour, which in turn appear to have a favourable impact on firm effectiveness. However, we found no such positive impact arising from the extent to which firms use either developmental or performance management

HRM practices. The support for the 'strategic fit' model appears rather more tenuous, the only significant relationship being that between cost leader/ performance management fit and resource acquisition effectiveness. However, the lack of significance for the specific business strategy/HRM practices fit variables does not mean that adopting a strategic approach to HRM is unimportant, as the impact of HRM strategic integration on employee attitudes and behaviours in Model A shows. A possible interpretation is that whilst it may not be necessary to match a particular HRM approach (developmental or performance management) with a particular business strategy (differentiation or cost leadership), nevertheless there are benefits in recognising the importance of HRM and in linking HRM decisions to the business strategy. The possibility remains, of course, that we have mis-specified the fit variables.

Conclusion: implications for managers

The results of this study support the contention that HRM is important in building and sustaining a competitive advantage. The implications for managers of multinational firms in Hong Kong are clear: the strategic importance attached to HRM does appear to be significant in influencing employee attitudes and behaviours and firm effectiveness. Firms that recognise the importance of HRM and integrate their HRM practices and business strategies develop employee attitudes and behaviours that translate into effective results for the firm. However, in spite of such a finding, it appears that many firms do not recognise the importance of HRM. As depicted in Figure 10.2, only two human resource activities (staffing and training) were reported to be very important to firm success by more than 50 per cent of the respondents. For all other activities, the majority of respondents indicated that they were only somewhat or not important. The

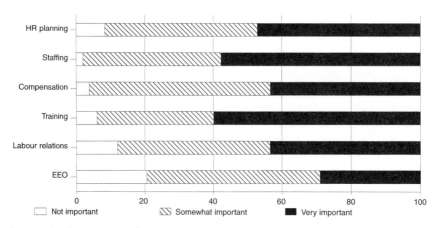

Figure 10.2 Importance of HRM activities to firm success.

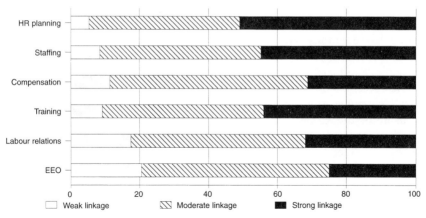

Figure 10.3 Linkage of HRM activities to firm strategy.

perceived linkage of human resource practices to a firm's strategy (see Figure 10.3) received even lower ratings. Only human resource planning was rated by slightly more than 50 per cent of HRM managers as being strongly linked to a firm's overall strategy. These data suggest that firms need to do more to recognise the strategic importance of HRM.

Despite Hong Kong's reputation as a leading business and financial centre, it seems as though the strategic HRM practices of the multinational firms operating in the territory have not kept pace with their sophisticated technological and market advances. To really understand the complex relationship between human resource management and firm effectiveness, however, consideration should be given to factors such as the firm's environmental context. Thus, in response to increased international competition and the recent economic downturn, many firms appear to be increasingly concerned with enhancing productivity and controlling costs. This has often involved either maintaining the status quo or even modifying HRM policies as part of the cost control effort. For example, several firms have implemented pay and hiring freezes, while others have announced pay cuts and layoffs. However, if human resource policies really do make a difference, we anticipate that those firms that maintain a close link between their HRM policies and their business strategies will be successful in sustaining a competitive advantage in the longer term.

In our study we distinguished between 'developmental' and 'performance management' HRM practices. Our tentative conclusion is that a performance management approach, with a strong emphasis on formal performance appraisals linked to pay, might undermine quality effectiveness and increase turnover. This implies that firms should be cautious in the use of such a strategy, particularly where they seek quality differentiation. Given the call from some quarters for firms operating in Hong Kong to move 'up-market' in terms of value added and quality, we might expect greater emphasis on such objectives and on developmental HRM practices. As the authors of an influential report on the future of Hong Kong put it: '. . . the capabilities of Hong Kong's industrial workforce must be upgraded. This means overcoming the widespread lack of commitment to the development of human resources at all levels of Hong Kong industry' (Berger and Lester 1997: xv).

However, we must emphasise that the significant HRM–performance link that emerged in our study involved strategic integration rather than our measure of the extent to which developmental HRM practices were in use. Furthermore, before performance management HRM practice is dismissed outright, firmer findings on the impact of the performance management approach on such goals as quality, differentiation and staff loyalty are needed. Clearly, the precise nature of the link between HRM strategy and effectiveness warrants further research.

Notes

1 Funding for this research was provided by the Department of Management, the Hong Kong Polytechnic University (Grant number 351/177).
2 To control for the possible effects of firm characteristics, we included three control variables in all of our analyses. *Number of employees* was used as an indicator of firm size and was measured by having top managers indicate the number of full-time employees currently working in their firm. *Number of foreign locations* was used as an indicator of scope of operations and was measured by asking top managers to report the number of foreign locations in which their organisation currently operates. Both of these variables were highly skewed, so we transformed them logarithmically. Firm nationality was assessed by classifying the firm ownership as either western or eastern. Thus, all firms of Asian nationality were grouped together as eastern (coded 0) and those from North America and Europe were grouped together as western firms (coded as 1).
3 Descriptive statistics and correlations are available from the authors on request.

11 Women-friendly human resource management in Hong Kong

Concept and practice[1]

Catherine W. Ng and Warren C. K. Chiu

Introduction

This chapter will first highlight the gender stratification phenomenon in Hong Kong's labour market. It then examines some possible explanations for the sex segregation (both vertical and horizontal) phenomenon, and the barriers faced by working women. This is followed by a discussion of women-friendly policies which aim to overcome discrimination and to promote equal employment opportunities. Finally, we detail our own research, and explain how our findings contribute to the literature on women-friendly human resource management.

Hong Kong women at work

The female labour participation rate rose from 43.6 per cent in 1976 to 46.8 per cent (excluding foreign domestic helpers) in 1996 while the corresponding statistic for men dropped from 80.6 per cent to 76.6 per cent (see Chapter 6). The increase in the female labour participation rate can be partially attributed to Hong Kong's declining fertility rate,[2] the increasing number of females in higher education,[3] and the emerging prominence of the service sector.[4] Nevertheless, as discussed in Chapter 6, statistics suggest that women tend to cluster in low-status and low-income jobs, and have difficulties in entering into traditionally male-dominated professions, in getting promotion, as well as in achieving equal pay.

The percentage of Hong Kong female managers and administrators in 1996 was 23.4 per cent (Census and Statistics Department 1997a: 93). Although the figure seems to be ahead of some other Asian countries, such as 2.2 per cent in Japan (Steinhoff and Tanaka 1994: 86), 9.5 per cent in Taiwan (Cheng and Liao 1994: 149), and 16.0 per cent in Singapore (Chan and Lee 1994: 130), the territory still lagged behind some western countries. The percentage of managers and administrators who are female was 41.5 per cent in the United States (Fagenson and Jackson 1994: 389), 33 per cent in Canada (Andrew *et al.* 1994: 378), and 30.6 per cent in Britain (Hammond and Holton 1994: 228). Perhaps the mirror image of the low percentage of women managers is the high proportion of women 'clerical and related workers'. According to government statistics, male workers in Hong Kong outnumbered their female counterparts in seven out of nine occupational groupings, with the female-to-male ratio ranging from a low of 0.14:1 ('Craft and related workers') to a high of 0.83:1 ('Associate professionals'[5]). 'Clerks' and 'Elementary occupations'[6] were the only two occupations in which there were more female than male employees, 2.30:1 and 1.02:1 respectively (Census and Statistics Department 1997a: 93). The above two sets of statistics show that women workers are being segregated both vertically into low-level non-management positions, and horizontally into the 'pink collar' professions. As a result of the segregation, income disparity is quite substantial between male and female employees (see Chapter 6). However, discrimination also contributes to the pay gap. In March 1992, among sixty-four full-time occupations in which both men and women participated, men secured higher wages in sixty of them (Ng 1994).

Barriers to women's labour participation

The reasons for sex segregation, horizontal and vertical, are many. The several areas of research in this regard include tokenism (Kanter 1977), biased human resource management (HRM) policies, procedures and practices (e.g. Alimo-Metcalfe 1994; Payne 1991; Wright *et al.* 1994), work-family interface (e.g. Davidson and Cooper 1984; Emmons *et al.* 1990; Hochschild 1989; Lewis and Cooper 1988), and gender identity (e.g. see Chapter 12).

Research has shown that 'troublesome stereotypical conceptions' about women are still prevalent among members of organisations in Hong Kong (Westwood 1997c: 119). Societies at large still consider that a woman's place is at home as nurturer and carer in the private domestic sphere, while the place of men is at work as breadwinners and decision makers in the public world. Although women's labour participation rates have been steadily increasing over the years (United Nations 1991: 83–6), most women employees do not get relief from unpaid domestic work from their spouses. That is, they are expected to put equal emphasis on work and family, if not putting family before work (Pleck 1977). Locally, according to a survey commissioned by the Equal Opportunities Commission and conducted by the Gender Research Program and the Social Indicators Program of the Hong Kong Institute of Asia-Pacific Studies at the Chinese University of Hong Kong, over 60 per cent of the female respondents considered that women faced more work–family conflict, and that, in comparison to men, married women suffered greater pressure when they worked outside (EOC 1997: 38).[7] Westwood and Leung's (Chapter 12) study of women managers in Chinese contexts also found that female managers face a double burden of managing a career and an unequal share of domestic activities. Without childcare programs, flexible work schedules, cafeteria benefit plans, and other family-friendly organisational policies, working women can find it both physically and emotionally draining to cope with their various implicit and explicit, formal and informal duties and obligations. Hence, work–family stress is one major roadblock to women's entry into the labour force and in their struggle to climb the corporate ladder.

In addition, several studies have established that HRM policies and practices are biased towards men. Back in the 1970s, it was found that interviewers tended to favour men over women when screening job applicants' résumés (Dipboye *et al.* 1975; Zikmund *et al.* 1978). More recently, Collinson *et al.* (1990) studied in depth how informal recruitment and selection procedures discriminated against women candidates. Furthermore, Tharenou and Conroy (1994) found that women were disadvantaged in advancement because they received less training and development and suffered more attendance prevention such as being refused paid study leave. There is however little systematic study of potentially discriminatory HRM policies and practices in Hong Kong; albeit, as discussed in Chapter 12, sex role stereotypes are deeply rooted in Hong Kong, with some jobs considered unbefitting either the femininity or the masculinity concept.

Lastly, no discussion of structural barriers is complete without including Kanter's (1977) contention that opportunities, power and numbers (i.e. majority or minority) shape an employee's attitudes and behaviours. For a lot of 'women of the corporation', three organisational factors – having limited opportunities, lacking power and being in the minority (i.e. being a token) – often limit their career aspirations and advancement, turning notions about women's inability to compete and their lack of ambition and aggression into self-fulfilling prophecies. Worst of all, tokens tend to remain tokens, as the size of the minority group does not get to expand due to the various barriers discussed so far.

Sex discrimination can be blatant and deliberate, or it can be subtle and inadvertent. Underpinning the structural barriers are attitudes towards women, which are, in turn, intricately intertwined with myths and stereotypes (e.g. Crowley *et al.* 1973; Deaux 1985; Snizek and Neil 1992). Study after study, both locally in Hong Kong and internationally, indicate men's attitudes towards women in general and women as managers in particular are less favourable than women's (e.g. Bass *et al.* 1971; Hardesty and Betz 1980; Ng 1993, 1995; Spence *et al.* 1973; Terborg *et al.* 1977; Valentine *et al.* 1975; Yost and Herbert 1985). Given, as shown above, that men dominate in positions of power in the public sphere, their less favourable attitudes towards women will continue to hamper the growth of women's labour participation rates and women's presence at management levels, since negative attitudes are likely to manifest themselves in the formulation and practice of organisational recruitment, selection, training and development, and promotion policies.

Women-friendly HRM concepts

Since the mid 1970s, the understanding of the difficulties working women face on a daily basis has been greatly enhanced by research into their experiences at work. Furthermore, most of these studies of women's work lives lead to recommendations and suggestions that aim to better women's employment opportunity and status. For instance, Kanter (1977), on the basis of her study of Industrial Supply Corporation (Indsco) – a pseudo-named organisation – suggests that in order to enhance opportunity, the rules on hiring, promotion and layoff would have to be reviewed, job descriptions and specifications clearly written to include actual tasks performed and competencies needed, and the philosophy of the performance appraisal system changed to encourage development. She proposes that dead-end jobs such as secretarial positions be redesigned, new jobs developed, and job rotation and job enrichment promoted. Lastly, she supports flexible working hours to allow women to meet family responsibilities. To empower women, on the other hand, requires the hierarchy to be flattened, an increase in decentralisation and a more extensive use of team-based task forces and work groups. 'Sponsorship' (ibid.: 279–80) is also recommended as one strategy for accumulating power. In conclusion though, Kanter contends that 'number-balancing should be the ultimate goal' (ibid.: 283), and to achieve equal numbers of women and men, she suggests batch-hiring of women, establishing role models for women, and developing a women's network. Kanter repeatedly stresses the need to train managers, who mostly are men, and whose support, both in words and in deeds, is germane to the successful implementation of these policies.

More recently, Cockburn (1991) studied four organisations in depth and found that men resisted sex equality in organisations. She then presented two agendas, short-term and long-term, for equal opportunities. In the short run, organisations would have to remove sex-bias from recruitment, training, promotion and other human resource management practices, extend paid and unpaid maternity leave, provide child care, make women's terms of employment more flexible, adopt positive discrimination or affirmative action, re-assess the value of women's low-paid jobs, broach the matter of sexist language and offensive pin-ups, run sexual harassment awareness training to help men learn the required behaviours, and discipline offenders of sexual harassment. These only form the 'minimum position' (ibid.: 216) though, Cockburn argues. The 'long' agenda would involve more substantial kinds of change, such as men sparing some of their time and career priorities to share child care and other domestic tasks with women, democratisation of the organisation to allow greater participation by all, particularly those in the lower grades where women are clustered, and an overhaul of the organisation's masculine cultural hegemony.

Kanter's and Cockburn's recommendations are examples of women-friendly policies and practices, which, generally speaking, aim to offer equal employment and promotion opportunities to female job applicants and members of staff. The organisations that have such policies recognise that sex discrimination, blatant or inadvertent, does exist and espouse ways and means to eradicate unfair practices and to actively promote women. Women-friendliness refers to the degree the policy 'provides . . . women the opportunity to integrate personal, work, marital and family roles success-fully . . . [It] refers to how easy it is for women to work and have a career within the organisation.' (Cattaneo *et al.* 1994: 23) A very comprehensive list of women-friendly organisational policies can be found in *The Best Companies for Women*, which judged an organisation's degree of women-friendliness according to their recruitment and hiring procedures, pro-grammes that aim at promoting women, ways of handling sex discrimination and sexual harassment, training programmes on sexual harassment, attempts to rectify inequality of pay, flextime policies, maternity and paternity leaves, adoption benefits, sick-leave benefits for family illness, leave-without-pay-but-position-assured policy, child care facilities or subsidies, free child care referral services, cafeteria-style approach to benefits, allowance for part-time work, policies on dual-career couples, as well as the percentage of female employees and the number of women in management (Zeitz and Dusky 1988). However, the list misses out on one very important dimension: training and development programmes for women.

Women-friendly HRM in practice

Not only are lists of women-friendly policies and practices seldom complete, they often lack empirical evidence with respect to positive effects on the organisation and its members. For instance, while the number of organisa-tions attempting to find ways of accommodating workers' family obligations is steadily increasing, '[i]n general, there are few hard data on the relationship between family-responsive programs and productivity'. (Zedeck and Mosier 1990: 243) Similarly, Gilbert (1993) comments that although it is well documented that women employees and working mothers are under a lot of stress, '[less] well researched are the effects of work/family benefits on indexes important to employers and employees'. (ibid.: 115) Furthermore, in reviewing the literature on organisational policies to combat sexual harass-ment in the workplace, Livingston (1982) concludes that 'little data is available assessing the extent to which employers have taken these actions, or the effectiveness of the actions'. (ibid.: 9) Hence, most recommendations for preventing sexual harassment and handling such complaints lack any empirical evaluation. In some cases, while the authors are able to conclude that some HRM policies and practices are discriminatory and to explain why, they cannot as convincingly present their case for an alternative mode of HRM operation. Collinson *et al.* (1990), after criticising informal recruit-ment and selection procedures for favouring men over women in general, indicate apprehension about formalisation, as 'it may simply become a more sophisticated means of reproducing and legitimising sex-discriminatory practices through formalised policies'. (ibid.: 81)

Furthermore, what is good for working women in the UK or the US might or might not be entirely applicable or beneficial to their counterparts in Hong Kong. Evaluation of women-friendly policies requires contributions from both scholars and practising HRM professionals. Our research aims first, to find out how commonly is women-friendly HRM being practised in work organisations in Hong Kong; second, to gauge male and female human resource managers' feelings towards the contribution of women-friendly policies and practices to organisation members' quality of work life (QWL); third, to derive clusters of policies and practices that are perceived to be facets of organisational women-friendliness; and finally, using these empirically derived dimensions, to examine the prevalence of women-friendly HRM in local organisations in comparison to organisations which have their national origins outside of Hong Kong, especially in countries where there are longer histories of anti sex discrimination legislation (see Chapter 1).

Research: women-friendly HRM and QWL

Human resource managers who were regular members of the Hong Kong Institute of Human Resource Management (HKIHRM)[7] were invited through mail to participate in the survey. One hundred and forty-eight managers responded, each representing one organisation.[8] Some 28 per cent of the respondents were male and 54 per cent female; i.e. 18 per cent did not indicate gender. One-third of the participants came from organisations with more than 500 employees; about half from companies employing between 100 and 500 employees; and one-fifth from firms of less than 100 employees. More than 60 per cent of the organisations belonged to the commercial sector (e.g. banking, accounting and finance); and about 20 per cent belonged to the engineering and industrial sectors. The rest of the organisations were in sectors such as real estate, education, health services, welfare and utilities. In terms of national origin, Hong Kong firms constituted the largest group (47 per cent). This was followed by American (17 per cent) and European firms (10 per cent). Other major groups were British (8 per cent), Japanese (5 per cent), and PRC firms (4 per cent). Other national origins included Far East and Australia.

The questionnaire administered to these managers consisted of twenty women-friendly organisational policies (see Table 11.1). The HR professional was asked to go through the twenty items one by one and indicate if each one was in practice in his/her organisation. The participant then needed to run through the items again. This time round, for each statement, he/she was to indicate how they felt about the policy's contribution to employees' quality of work life (QWL) based on a seven-point scale (from '1', meaning that the policy severely worsens employees' QWL, to '7', meaning that the policy greatly enhances employees' QWL). Other information pertaining to the background of the respondent and his/her organisation were also collected in the questionnaire.

Table 11.1 Women-friendly human resource management policies

1. Job descriptions and specifications for various positions are written in details and readily available.
2. The organisation has enhanced maternity benefits that more than meet the requirements of labour laws.
3. There is a quota system to ensure a minimum proportion of women in middle and upper managerial grades.
4. Flexible working hours are allowed for women employees who desire such arrangements, e.g. staggered working hours, annual hours, etc.
5. Equal opportunity audits are conducted to ensure quota system is implemented.
6. The organisation has special committees for handling sex discrimination and sexual harassment grievances.
7. The organisation facilitates mentor relationships, both formal and informal, in the workplace.
8. Leave without pay but position assured is an available option for women employees who would like to resume work after an extended leave of absence taken due to family obligations.
9. Women-only training programs are provided to enhance female employees' job skills, interpersonal skills, etc.
10. Voluntary reduced time is permitted for women employees who desire such an arrangement, e.g. working only three days a week.
11. The organisation counsels women employees on career development.
12. The organisation gives training programs to employees on issues of sex discrimination and sexual harassment.
13. The organisation renders advice to women employees on how to combine family and work.
14. Formal job sharing (i.e. two or more employees sharing one job) is permitted.
15. The organisation offers development contracts, e.g. study leave, to women employees.
16. Child care is provided on-site for working mothers, or the organisation gives child care subsidies.
17. Women are promoted over men in cases where the candidates possess same qualifications.
18. The organisation practises cafeteria benefit plan, i.e. employees can pick and choose from available options to develop their own benefit plan.
19. The organisation has policies on rectifying inequity of pay between the two sexes.
20. The organisation has paternity benefits, e.g. male employees are permitted to take reduced-pay leave to spend time with family.

Results indicated that women-friendly policies were not widely adopted in the organisations surveyed. Table 11.2 shows that about half of the policies mentioned in this survey were practised by less than 10 per cent of the organisations. The least practised polices included, for example, a quota system to ensure a minimum proportion of women in middle and upper managerial grades, child care support, and training programmes on issues of sex discrimination and sexual harassment. However, there were items reported to be practised by more than 60 per cent of the organisations. These items were mentor relationships, detailed written job descriptions, and maternity benefits exceeding the minimum requirements of labour laws.

Table 11.2 Women-friendly HRM in practice in Hong Kong

	Proportion of organisations practising the policy (%)
Over 50% of the organisations surveyed practised the following:	
7. Mentorship	67
1. Clear job descriptions and specifications	64
2. Enhanced maternity benefits	61
11%–50% of the organisations practised the following:	
15. Development contracts	44
14. Job sharing	36
11. Career counselling	30
8. Leave without pay	29
19. Pay inequity rectification	29
18. Cafeteria benefit plan	15
20. Paternity benefits	14
4. Flextime	13
10% or less of the organisations practised the following:	
10. Voluntary reduced time	10
17. Affirmative promotion	9
5. Quota auditing	8
6. Committees on sex discrimination and sexual harassment	7
9. Women-only training	7
13. Counselling on family and work	5
12. Training of employees on discrimination and harassment	3
16. Child care	3
3. Quota on gender ratio	0.7

None of the listed policies was perceived by HR managers as being able to greatly contribute to employees' QWL. Most of the policies were rated between 4 (no effect) and 5 (enhance slightly). Items such as promoting women over men with same qualifications, and having a quota system to ensure a minimum proportion of women in managerial grades were even considered to have a slightly negative effect on QWL. In general, the relation between whether a policy was practised and its perceived contribution to QWL was high.[9] The close relationship between the two suggests that the practice of these policies is systematically related to the HR manager's perception of their relative contribution to QWL. A big discrepancy, though, was found in the child care support item. Half of the HR managers found it contributory, either moderately or greatly, to employees' QWL, yet only 3 per cent of the organisations actually provided this benefit. Other than this, the overall results indicated that the more a women-friendly organisational policy was perceived as contributory to QWL, the more likely it was implemented.

Comparing female HR managers' perception of the effect of women-

Table 11.3 Female and male managers' perceptions of the contribution of women-friendly HRM to employees' quality of work life (QWL)

Women-friendly policy/practice	Overall (n=122) Mean	SD	Male (n=42) Mean	SD	Female (n=80) Mean	SD	df	t	eta²
7. Mentorship	5.84	1.12	5.65	1.27	5.94	1.02	116	−1.32	0.015
1. Clear job descriptions and specifications	5.58	1.25	5.34	1.39	5.71	1.17	118	−1.53	0.019
2. Enhanced maternity benefits	5.37	1.20	5.24	1.24	5.44	1.18	117	−0.83	0.006
16. Child care	5.26	1.31	4.98	1.37	5.41	1.26	114	−1.71	0.025
18. Cafeteria benefit plan	5.24	1.24	4.55	1.28	5.61	1.05	113	−4.78*	0.168
19. Pay inequity rectification	5.23	1.19	4.87	1.24	5.41	1.13	112	−2.35*	0.047
15. Development contracts	5.15	1.17	4.95	1.20	5.26	1.15	116	−1.36	0.016
11. Career counselling	4.97	1.16	4.73	1.11	5.10	1.17	115	−1.70	0.025
20. Paternity benefits	4.97	1.18	4.80	1.29	5.07	1.12	113	−1.16	0.012
13. Counseling on family and work	4.85	1.14	4.50	1.16	5.04	1.09	114	−2.48*	0.051
4. Flextime	4.66	1.45	4.30	1.51	4.84	1.40	114	−1.93*	0.032
14. Job sharing	4.64	1.23	4.43	1.20	4.75	1.23	114	−1.36	0.016
6. Committees on discrimination and harassment	4.61	1.05	4.44	1.07	4.70	1.03	111	−1.29	0.015
8. Leave without pay	4.61	1.36	4.45	1.30	4.70	1.30	114	−0.93	0.008
12. Training of employees on s.d.[1] and s.h.[2]	4.52	0.94	4.33	0.98	4.62	0.91	110	−1.53	0.021
9. Women-only training	4.43	1.14	4.08	1.11	4.61	1.13	112	−2.43*	0.050
5. Quota auditing	4.32	1.12	4.05	1.08	4.47	1.12	112	−1.91*	0.032
3. Quota on gender ratio	4.15	1.04	3.97	1.01	4.24	1.05	112	−1.30	0.015
10. Voluntary reduced time	4.15	1.50	3.85	1.31	4.31	1.58	112	−1.56	0.021
17. Affirmative promotion	3.45	1.40	3.54	1.52	3.41	1.33	111	0.48	0.002

Notes
* $p < .05$
[1] Sex discrimination.
[2] Sexual harassment.

friendly HRM on QWL with that of male HR managers, it was found that women had more positive views across almost all the twenty items; the only exception was affirmative promotion, whereby the mean for the women was 3.41, and that for men 3.54. However, the gender difference was only significant for six policies, namely flextime, quota auditing, women-only training, counselling on family and work, cafeteria benefit plan, and pay inequity rectification (see Table 11.3).

All women-friendly policies and practices proposed in this study were conceptually derived from studies of women's work experiences, as discussed in the introduction section. To the best of our knowledge, no research has been conducted to examine how various women-friendly policies and practices relate to one another as per employees' perceptions. In this research, we analysed respondents' ratings on each women-friendly item's contribution to QWL so as to identify the underlying dimensions that represented the interrelationships between the twenty items. Our findings revealed that the HR

Table 11.4 Dimensions of women-friendliness

The seven women-friendly dimensions (WFDs)

Flextime
  14. Job sharing
  4.   Flextime
  8.   Leave without pay
  10. Voluntary reduced time

Training and development
  9.   Women-only training
  11. Career counselling
  15. Development contracts
  17. Affirmative promotion

Anti sex discrimination
  6.   Committees on sex discrimination and sexual harassment
  12. Training of employees on discrimination and harassment
  19. Pay inequity rectification

Family-friendly
  13. Counselling on family and work
  16. Child care
  18. Cafeteria benefit plan

Positive equal opportunities
  3.   Quota on gender ratio
  5.   Quota auditing

Maternity and paternity benefits
  2.   Enhanced maternity benefits
  20. Paternity benefits

Formalised HRM
  1.   Clear job descriptions and specifications
  7.   Mentorship

managers, who themselves were employees of their respective organisations, perceived the twenty women-friendly policies and practices in seven clusters, or women-friendly dimensions (WFDs):[10] 'flextime', 'training and development', 'anti sex discrimination', 'family-friendly', 'positive equal opportunities', 'maternity and paternity benefits', and 'formalised HRM' (see Table 11.4 for details). The results indicated that the concept of women-friendliness is multi-faceted in nature in the minds of organisation employees.

To reflect an organisation's degree of friendliness towards female employees, an index named the women employee assistance programme (WEAP) index was derived by summing across the mean scores of all WFDs. The higher the WEAP value, the more women-friendly the organisation was judged to be. Table 11.5 lists the mean scores of the seven WFDs by national origins of the organisations. Controlling for the effect of organisation size and the gender ratio of employees, a series of analyses of variance were run to examine the effects of origin (i.e. Hong Kong, Asia-Pacific, Europe, Britain and the United States) on WFDs. No significant difference was found on the following WFDs: 'anti sex discrimination', 'family-friendly', 'positive equal opportunities', 'maternity and paternity benefits', and 'formalised HRM'. In contrast, significant differences were found on the two WFDs of 'flextime' and 'training and development'. Further analyses[11] revealed that the mean score of Hong Kong firms was significantly lower than that of Continental European firms. Results show that female employees working for a Hong Kong-based firm might enjoy less flexibility than those who work for a European firm. Also, the mean score of American firms was significantly higher than that of Hong Kong and Asia-Pacific firms. Female employees working for an American firm might enjoy better career advancement opportunity than those working in a Hong Kong or Asia-Pacific-based firm.

Table 11.5 Degree of women-friendliness across organisations of different national origins

Women-friendly dimension	Hong Kong[1] (n=68)	Asia Pacific (n=21)	Europe (n=15)	UK (n=12)	US (n=24)
Flextime	1.17	1.25	1.37	1.23	1.26
Training and development	1.21	1.14	1.28	1.19	1.34
Anti sex discrimination	1.14	1.14	1.15	1.05	1.18
Family-friendly	1.08	1.08	1.11	1.06	1.07
Positive equal opportunities	1.03	1.02	1.07	1.04	1.06
Maternity and paternity benefits	1.34	1.31	1.53	1.42	1.42
Formalised HRM	1.65	1.55	1.63	1.67	1.76
Total	8.62	8.49	9.14	8.66	9.09

Note
[1] At the time of research, Hong Kong was still under British rule, i.e. China had not resumed its sovereignty over the territory.

Conclusion: women-friendly HRM – East and West

Although it was not entirely unexpected, it is still somewhat disappointing to see that quite a number of the women-friendly policies listed in the question-naire are practised by very few organisations in Hong Kong. There are at least two possible explanations. First, women's issues have never been high on the Hong Kong Government's agenda, nor has the general public been keen on discussing them (Ng 1994). Traditionally, the Hong Kong Government's policy towards commerce and trade, finance and economy has been one of non-intervention, i.e. *laissez-faire*, and the general sentiment among the business and commercial sector is that free market forces and strong competition will ultimately ensure efficiency and survival of the fittest; hence excessive governmental regulation is unnecessary. Second, unlike Britain which has an Equal Opportunities Commission (EOC), or the United States which has an Equal Employment Opportunity Commission (EEOC) – both being statutory bodies – at the time of the research, Hong Kong had nothing similar, although such a body has since been established, as discussed in Chapter 1. Two of the functions of the EOC/EEOC are to collect and analyse systematically gender-sensitive statistics and to provide and promote coherent public policies and codes of practice on equal opportunities. Not having such a body might have rendered Hong Kong-based firms both less conversant with the issues concerned, and also less willing to invest in and develop women-friendly HRM. Whether this will now change following the establishment of Hong Kong's EOC remains to be seen.

However, the above points are mere conjectures since the scope of our research does not cover their confirmation or refutation, and since one can argue that women-friendly policies as proposed in Western literature do not suit Hong Kong because of the latter's unique socio-economic fabric. One can go even further to argue that the reason why so few organisations in Hong Kong practise women-friendly policies is that the territory has less of a need to do so in comparison to other countries. A couple of years after our study, Hong Kong entered into a recession partially due to the Asian economic crisis, and in September 1998, the unemployment rate surged to a fifteen-year high of 5 per cent. Cost cutting has thus increasingly become the solution to many businesses' financial conundrums. It is conceivable that women-friendly HRM might have been further downgraded in many local companies' priority lists of organisational changes and developments.

One of the more important findings of this research is the empirical evidence to support our hypothesis that women-friendly policies are multi-faceted in nature. These various dimensions, coined as WFDs in this paper, are extremely useful and meaningful in conceptualising the notion of organisational women-friendliness. Future comparative studies across organisations of different sizes, industry types and national cultures could utilise these dimensions as the basis for comparison, both to rank the subjects of comparison, and to gain insight into why some facets of organisational women-friendliness are more positively or negatively received in different circumstances and situations.

In this study, we have already made a start by comparing the degree of women-friendliness among organisations of different national origins based on their WFD scores. This research has found that both US and European firms are more women-friendly than Hong Kong firms. For US firms, it is the WFD of 'training and development' that stands out when they are compared to Hong Kong-based organisations, while for European firms it is the WFD of 'flextime'. This is a noteworthy finding. It may be that European firms' women-friendly strategies are of a more passive or reactive nature, while that of US firms are of a more proactive and forward-thinking nature. Future research to examine the reactive–proactive difference across nations and/or industries should prove useful in further conceptualising women-friendly HRM.

Notes

1 Parts of this paper have previously been published in the *International Journal of Human Resource Management*, October 1997, vol. 8, no. 5, 644–59.

2 The birth rate in Hong Kong declined from 13 per 1,000 in 1986 to 10 per 1,000 in 1996 (Hong Kong Government 1997: 396). The mean number of children for every married woman decreased from 3.4 children in 1971 to 2.5 children in 1981.

3 The percentage of females amongst students enrolled at universities rose steadily from 26.5 per cent in 1961, 34.4 per cent in 1981, to 42.3 per cent in 1990 (Choi 1995: 102).

4 The service sector has flourished and diversified in its types of activities (e.g. banking, insurance, real estate, and a variety of other professional services). Its contribution in terms of GDP rose from 67 per cent in 1980, 70 per cent in 1985, 74 per cent in 1990, to 84 per cent in 1995 (Hong Kong Government 1997: 50–1).

5 Associate professionals include science technicians, nurses and midwives, dental assistants and other health associate professionals; architectural, surveying and engineering technicians; optical and electronic equipment controllers; ship pilots and air traffic controllers; principals and teachers of primary and pre-primary school; statistical assistants; computer operators; law clerks; accounting supervisors; public relations officers; sales representatives; designers; estate managers; social work assistants; superintendents, inspectors and officers of the police and other disciplined services; performers and sportsmen. (Census and Statistics Department 1997a: 196)

6 Elementary occupations include street vendors; domestic helpers and cleaners; messengers; private security guards; watchmen; freight handlers; lift operators; construction labourers; hand packers; agricultural and fishery labourers. (Census and Statistics Department 1997a: 197)

7 The HKIHRM had approximately 2,700 members, who represented about 1,330 organisations.

8 In the covering letter, we explained to the respondents that we intended to survey only human resource managers, and only one such personnel member per organisation. In other words, should the recipient of the questionnaire not be the human resource manager of his/her company, he/she was requested to pass the mail onto the personnel member most responsible for human resource management in the organisation.

 9 A Spearman rank-order correlation was run to determine the relation between whether a policy was practised and its perceived contribution to QWL. The observed correlation was found to be statistically significant.
10 A principal component analysis using Varimax rotation was employed to examine the interrelationships of the twenty women-friendly items. Seven dimensions were thus obtained.
11 Multiple comparisons between all groups were conducted using least-significant difference (LSD) tests.

12 Women in management in Hong Kong and Beijing

Between pragmatism and patriarchy[1]

Robert Westwood and Alicia S. M. Leung

Introduction

In the west, attention paid to the role of female managers has intensified as increasing numbers of women have entered and progressed in the workforce, and as sexual politics and ideology have altered. However, research and analysis outside of the west or on a comparative basis has been limited (Adler and Izraeli 1994; Chusmir and Frontczak 1990; Davidson and Cooper 1993). In Asia there is little homogeneity with respect to the position, status and experience of female managers, which is due to variations not only in economic development and industrial organisation, but also in culture, ideology and social development. In South Korea, for example, although female labour force participation rates are high, representation in management is extremely low. By contrast, in Singapore and Hong Kong the number of women in management has been more marked, such that the ratio of male to female managers is on a par with that of many Western European economies. The situation in the PRC is more complex. Communist ideology and the exigencies of development again led to large numbers of women entering the labour force, but their participation in management is more difficult to determine, not least because the concept and role of management has been very different, but also because enterprise leadership had until recently been more a political matter with Party officials and cadres occupying leadership roles. Furthermore, the convoluted structure of Chinese bureaux and the lack of accurate records make a clear determination of levels of female participation difficult, even in those terms.

We described Chinese culture in Chapter 1 as having strong patrimonial, patriarchal and patrilineal traditions which are at least vestigially present in contemporary society. Social structures are modelled on familistic forms in which the male head or patriarch has significant power. These social structures have persistently located women in subordinate positions. Gendered structures and differentiations are embedded in family structures and reflexively constituted through family socialisation practices. Such patriarchal systems are transferred into the family businesses that dominate Hong Kong's industrial landscape. These traditional structures and values remain a feature of Hong Kong's social fabric, although progressively weakening. However, whilst women still face considerable barriers to their career development, Hong Kong's economic development has created greater opportunities for females, and business pragmatism and opportunism often overrides gendered ideology and sex bias. The motivation for the studies that inform this chapter was this singular conflation of traditional patriarchy with the pragmatism of modern business in market driven systems. Thus, a spectacularly complex situation, and one that remains in a state of flux and uncertainty, confronts women. Within that framework they seek not only to carve out careers, but also their personal lives, relationships and identity.

This chapter focuses on the status, role and experiences of women managers in Hong Kong. It draws selectively on material from an empirical study of Chinese female managers working in Hong Kong. This was part of a larger study of gender issues in the workplace, but this chapter will draw primarily on material derived from intensive, semi- and un-structured interviews with female managers.[2] Although relatively unstructured, the interviews did revolve around common themes, allowing grounds for comparison. The analysis explores the perceptions and experiences of the respondents in relation to four issues: experiencing stereotyping, discrimination and sexism in male dominated structures and cultures; perceptions of gender differences in the management task; managing gender identity; and coping and succeeding as a female manager.

Encounters with patriarchal structures and masculine cultures: stereotypes, discrimination and sexism

The vast majority of organisations are not gender neutral: they are constituted on and reflexively reinforce masculinist structures, ideologies and values. Organisational cultures are consequently also predominantly male cultures or, as Burton (1991: 3) puts it 'most organisations are saturated with male values'. In addition, the very conception of management, and of the skills, attributes and behaviours deemed necessary for its accomplishment, are also gendered. Indeed, the gendered structuring of organisations and the continued under-representation of women in senior management means that management and leadership persist in being defined in male, if not patriarchal, terms. In many respects when women enter management they are entering an alien terrain and culture. They are expected to assume a role, attitudinal set and repertoire of behaviours that have been constituted by and for men, and are evaluated in those terms. The masculine dominance and culture also means that women often have to contend with sexist attitudes and behaviour. The western literature on women in management makes this very clear (Gutek 1985; Hearn *et al.* 1989; Stockdale 1996).

In the study, we asked about perceptions and experiences of discrimination and sexism. We also attempted to unearth the extent to which respondents experienced the structures and cultures they encountered as in any way difficult, disadvantageous and/or alien. It is fair to say that perceptions of overt discrimination were not extensive. Some women claimed not to have encountered any, whilst for others it was at a minimal level, but a sizeable minority had experienced some form of discrimination. It should be noted that failure to perceive and report discrimination does not necessarily mean that it did not exist. In some cases levels of discrimination become taken-for-granted, in other cases there may be a degree of disingenuousness, or even false consciousness, by which women elide discriminatory experiences (Colwill 1992).

Many women, whilst aware of the male majorities in management in their organisations, had not really entertained the idea that this has a pervasive and insidious influence in terms of perpetuating male definitions, values and cultures. At times such issues surfaced at a more experiential, micro-level; for example, in the discussion of male-female informal groups and networks – we will deal with those aspects shortly. Rosie, who worked in the hotel industry, did comment on the structural male control and culture of hotels. She noted the difficulty of women getting general management positions and that, whilst women may be accepted in marketing, personnel and, to a lesser degree finance, they are not accepted in the management of operations. This represents a general pattern wherein women are excluded from central, strategic and controlling areas of management. There were cases where the organisation had significant numbers, even majorities, of females at the lower levels, but progressively up the hierarchy the proportion drops off. This is true, for example, of the Hong Kong Civil Service where there are female majorities at the executive officer level, but this is not reflected higher up. Mei Ling, commenting on her organisation, noted that at the 'market officer level, the first level of the executive grade, there was a 50:50 gender ratio, but as you move up from the market officer level I would say that you have predominantly male'. She offered an interesting insight into how this came about.

> What happened in this organisation is that you have to be posted overseas for two years at their office before you get promoted, and the current directors and senior managers, a lot of them have gone through that posting. Women have tended not to be able to take those postings or have not been offered them . . . I don't know. But it means that there are simply more men to choose from for the senior positions because of that posting experience.

Carrie, a finance sector manager, commented on the mechanisms leading to structural gender differentiations, implying an occurrence due to market forces. She suggested that men are predominant in corporate banking whereas women are better represented in personal banking. As personal banking is more retail-oriented, it is easier for women to progress because it deals with banking needs at the individual level rather than the corporate level. In corporate banking you have to deal with the 'controllers' of corporations, who tend to be male. She continued:

> When choosing the senior executive, then obviously you are looking at which is the biggest part of your business and, if the major part is corporate banking, then naturally you will find someone who is experienced in that area of your business and because of that . . . the chance of him being a man is higher than of him being a woman. *[note the gendered language]* . . . So I think it is not so much because they want consciously to discriminate against us but it is just a very fair way of choosing their senior executives as the market situation and the job nature demands.

Respondent comments reinforced typical findings in the West where women are placed in less significant, prestigious and visible positions, ones requiring person-related skills but which have restricted career opportunities. There is not only a 'glass ceiling', but also horizontal gender segmentations which confine women to certain organisational functions.

Hitting the 'bamboo ceiling': the experience of discrimination

There were few reports of overt discrimination in areas such as recruitment or performance appraisal. This needs careful interpretation, given that in Hong Kong, as elsewhere, women's earnings are only 70 per cent of that of males and there is some clear discriminatory effect in that figure (see also Chapter 6 and Westwood *et al.* 1995). Indeed, it was only in the early 1970s that basic gender equalities in employment terms were introduced for Hong Kong government employees. The generally slow and belated introduction of equal employment or anti-discriminatory legislation has been documented in Chapter 1. This meant that until 1995, companies were free to specify gender in job advertising and deploy differential contracts and employment practices. The pay issue is interesting since Hong Kong companies tend to have non-disclosed pay systems, so that other employees' earnings are not often known, something respondents, when pressed on the presumption of equal pay, were compelled to admit. In terms of gender-specific advertising and the wider issue of legislating for equality of opportunity, there were mixed feelings. A majority was against such advertising, although some saw it as reasonable business practice. A majority also favoured legislation but was sceptical about its real effect. They concurred with the commonly held view that a change in values, attitudes and behaviours, initiated in societal education, is the only long-term solution.

Some women reported pay differences in the past, but none currently. No woman reported being directly disadvantaged by their gender in the recruitment and selection process, although again, discriminatory practices are not always readily discernible. Interestingly, a minority indicated that they factored gender into their own selection practices. One respondent, Fung Chi, said:

> I'm always caught in a contradiction. Sometimes when I recruit a female I must ask if they have a steady boyfriend or not, whether they are married, even if they are married, when they are going to think about getting a baby – because to me this is very critical. But once they, ah, sort of have these sort of things, like having a baby, I will try to understand their problem, because I, uh, I'm a female and I understand their needs.

Another also inquired about candidates' family situation, was again sympathetic, but very clear that she wanted to know whether work or family came first, and did not want to waste time and money training a woman who would leave to get married or have children.

More women felt they had been, if not actively discriminated against, at least disadvantaged in terms of promotion opportunities. They were aware that women were not achieving senior management positions, and that progression was more likely in some aspects of marketing, corporate communications/public relations, human resources management, and generally in staff functions. They were less likely to get to the top in key financial or strategic areas, or in significant operational or technical areas.

The perceived reasons for the glass ceiling were similar to those reported elsewhere. Obviously there is the general male domination of organisations and the sex stereotypical attitudes that limit opportunity. It was also felt that decision makers still held the traditional view that, even though women are working, the male remains the primary bread winner and is in greater need of promotion. This was made very clear to one respondent seeking a promotion:

> The comment was made that my husband had just been made a partner in a law firm in November, just before I tried for promotion. They (her company's management) said: 'You don't need the promotion, your husband has just been made a partner and he will earn a lot more money'.

Pat, working for a quasi-governmental body, said her overseas posting opportunities were limited since the organisation preferred men representing them at its international sites. A second angle on this is the view that some overseas locations are 'tough' for women. The same respondent said 'For sure they would avoid putting a woman manager in the Japan office'. This was discussed by the women in terms of China postings too, particularly if away from the eastern sea-board in what are seen as 'tougher' environments. This is significant given the volume of trade and investment in the Mainland, and a career in Hong Kong may hinge on experience and exposure there.

Sherry, a hospitality industry manager, noted that there were no general hotel managers in Hong Kong (in fact there was one at the time and now, we believe, two) and doubted that there would be. She also said that men were favoured for the more visible, high-profile projects. This helped groom them for promotion whilst retarding the chances of females. This was another recurrent theme.

A glass ceiling already exists at the entry level, constituted by male prejudices and gendered organisational structures, ensuring limited entry and promotion prospects for women. There were suggestions that male decision-makers viewed women's domestic duties as detrimental to their ability to be good managers. It was also felt that young men rather than women would be selected for important projects, business trips and training. All this exposed men to a wider range of experiences and contacts which would be instrumental in building up leadership credentials. More generally, Chinese management includes respect for age, and moral leadership and authority, which all tend to be based on and equated with inherent patriarchal structures (Westwood 1997a).

'Sit with the ladies please': sexism and sexual harassment

Many more women reported encountering sexist attitudes and behaviour than discrimination. A difficulty here is that the definition, conception and experience of sexism are highly variable. Many women had encountered sexist attitudes. Many had experienced sexist behaviour in the form of comments and jokes. Some were accepting of such 'mild ' sexism, seeing it as 'normal', others were not. Some also felt that sexism in Hong Kong was less of a problem than elsewhere in Asia. On one business trip to Korea Chi Fai, a female executive, was instructed to move to a table with all the other 'ladies and wives' after roundtable discussions, and was not allowed to sit with her business peers. Sexist attitudes in Hong Kong, in terms of not taking females seriously, or treating them without respect, was held to be more prevalent in the traditional, old-style Chinese companies.

It was felt by some that sexist behaviour could be countered and prevented by the woman's demeanour. A woman needs to 'give off the right signals': to indicate immediately and constantly that she is not interested in sexist comments or sexual approaches and that it will not be countenanced. As one woman said, 'they come to see me as masculine, but I don't care, I don't want that nonsense'. This is an additional burdensome self-monitoring and impression-management issue that women have to contend with.

There were only two or three cases of what the women defined as harassment. One woman was basically forced to quit her job because of it. It was apparent from the discussions that sexual harassment was only being considered in its more extreme forms, such as pressure for sexual activity. This restricted view of harassment is a recognised issue and probably means that other forms of harassment were more common, but not defined as such.

The 'Old Boys Club': exclusion–inclusion practices and the power of networking

When women are in a minority in a male-dominated structure and culture, they can be disadvantaged by not being incorporated into central networks, informal groups and channels of influence. As Simpson *et al.* (1987) point out, a variety of practices can signal to females that they are not regarded as full organisational members. Males form into informal groups from which women are often excluded, further enhancing men's interests and occupation of core organisational space. Throughout the analysis this was a recurring theme. Women's exclusion means that they encounter different organisational realities. Such exclusion from networks in which potentially important relationships, information and sources of influence circulate, may be damaging for women's power, their capacity to be involved in decisions, and ultimately for their career progression. Consequently, and for reasons of solidarity, mutual assistance and empowerment, women form their own networks. Much has been made of the value of networking for professional women (Colwill 1995; Ibarra 1993). In Chinese contexts the importance of informal groupings and networks is heightened by the elementally relationship-orientation of the culture. Human transactions are constructed and facilitated by the quality of relationships. The concept of *guanxi*, described in Chapter 1, is a pervasive social practice expressing this. In a collectivist culture, informal interactions and relationship building are critical to success at work because so much of the true work-related requirements are not contained in formal relationships, rules and regulations.

For some women, the formation of groups on gender lines was seen as 'natural' and not problematical. Where it became more of an issue was in those jobs and industries where informal socialising was a normal part of business activity and where foreign business people or locations were involved. Sherry maintained that there were good networks in the hotel industry, but that these were not particularly on gender lines. What she found difficult was when drinking sessions or other night-time social activities were involved, for example, at overseas trade shows.

> All the managers get together and have drinks and in that sense I find it is a little difficult to mix with them . . . [when] we all go to the trade shows all the hotel marketing directors stay in the same hotel and then at night they all go out to . . . you know where to! As a female you get singled out, really you single yourself out. I mean you wanted to meet up with them and it is OK if they sit in a bar and have a drink, but if they go to those other places, we won't go with them . . .

Another woman did actually accompany the men to a 'pick-up joint' on an overseas trip.

They will invite you, but they don't really expect you to go. But this time I said I would go. We went to one of those clubs, you know with bar dancing and girls to pick up. The men sort of showed off, but I could see that they weren't really comfortable. To be honest I wasn't either. I didn't find the experience very pleasant. I even sat there as the men made their choices [of the women]. I left after that.

Other women commented on this type of socialising in Taiwan, Korea and Japan. For some even the drinking regime was a barrier. Others lamented that male networks often formed around sporting activities such as golf, creating another point of exclusion.

This exclusion from the typical after-work social activities of men in the Asian context was a notable sub-theme. Women are compelled to adopt a strategy of pragmatic avoidance. This exclusion can be damaging in career terms, but also socially and psychologically. It is argued that when women are cut off from important groups and interactions in this way they feel isolated and experience exclusion and rejection (e.g. Korabik 1993; Barondi and Igbaria 1995). A number of women pointed out the pragmatic disadvantages of this situation. One noted that without opportunities to talk with leaders personally, women fall behind men in terms of visibility, social contacts and skill development, or they may internalise negative evaluations.

In many cases women's networks are limited to the official occasions and meetings held at work, whereas men's networks transverse the informal–formal boundary and are designed to influence what and how things are done. This encourages (male) leaders to form relationships with them and assign challenging jobs or additional training and development programmes to them. More critically, men's networks tend to be task-oriented – designed to help them get to the top. Women, on the other hand, see the world as a network of connection rather than of competition and confrontation (Tannen 1993). Confronted with exclusion, women seek to share concerns with other women and these same-sex relationships provide them with more satisfying workplace ties than do mixed-sex relationships (see also Maddock and Parken 1993).

Perceptions of gender difference in the management task

Some of the most interesting discussions centred around perceptions of gender difference in managerial style and behaviour, the attributes male and female managers possess, and the advantages and disadvantages that accrue from being either a male or a female manager. This brings to the surface assumptions about gender differences that inform attitudes and behaviour. In these discussions, there was a widespread belief that differences did exist in attributes and styles. There were a diverse range of opinions, but also several recurring themes.

Different attributes and stylistic differences

We will begin with the issue of differences in approach to the managerial task, with a specific focus on perceptions of leadership.

Leadership, power and politics

The literature on male–female leadership style differences is extensive (e.g. Hearn and Parkin 1986–7; Rosener 1990; Rowney and Cahoon 1990). Leadership, like management, has been defined and theorised in a gendered fashion. In Chinese contexts, leadership is perhaps closer to the notion of headship and is rooted in patriarchal traditions (see Chapter 1 and also Westwood 1997a; Redding 1990).

Many women were aware of widely held negative stereotypes about females and leadership. Most did not concur with these, but the issue was viewed in complex ways. Gender differences were generally not attributed to inherent differences but to socialisation and learning. Reference was also made to the 'double-bind' whereby women who act as leaders are perceived as somehow masculinised, but if they fail to behave in 'masculine' ways they are not deemed to be effective leaders. Some pointed to the militaristic metaphors and other masculinist rhetoric by which leadership was commonly discussed. A young respondent, Alice, had a different perspective and a very different metaphor. Nonetheless she still points to differences and the difficulties women have in exercising power and leadership:

> I would like to use Taoism, the Yin and Yang[3] to illustrate the power differences of women and men. Men like to adopt Yang (explicit) power whilst women prefer Yin (subtle) power. A woman may have the power bestowed upon her, but she needs to build up people's confidence in her. Until she gains the recognition, she cannot externally exercise her power. In other words, a woman needs to prove her capability before she exercises her power. But for men, they know how to maximise their power to enable the job to function effectively even if they are incompetent.

There were suggestions that women adopt a different style of leading, one based more on dialogue and mutual understanding, less on directive and autocratic uses of power and position. One might suggest that women deploy more socio-emotional strategies in leading others to task accomplishment whereas men view things more instrumentally, and leadership and task accomplishment as a series of transactions (Bass *et al.* 1993). Male leaders transact with subordinates, providing them with rewards in return for task completion. The style is directive, detached, instrumental, non-inclusive and somewhat combative. The female style is more involving, interactive and inclusive. For females, fulfilling the responsibilities associated with a relationship is more important than being 'on top' or 'in charge' (Belenky *et al.* 1986; Benack 1982). It is interesting to note how the gendered representation of leadership by these respondents resonates with recent theorising on leadership in which the transactional mode is devalued relative to a socio-emotional, transformational one. A transformational mode requires more interactional, relational, and participative approaches (Grant 1988; Aburdene and Naisbitt 1992; Storey 1992; Martin 1993).

Hard-working blues

This represents a recurrent theme in our discussions: namely, women have to work harder than men in order to succeed. Part of the meaning is simply that, given the other duties women typically have to perform, they work harder and longer than male equivalents. Another meaning is that, as a minority and sometimes token in a male domain, women have to work harder in order to establish credibility, and receive respect and authority. Thus: 'Yes, I think women have to prove themselves, that they are capable, whereas for men it seems so natural.' Another, from the banking sector, had an interesting addition: she suggested that in situations where male managers represent well-known and/or large companies to clients it is automatically assumed that, given that background, they are competent. Such allowances are not made for women, they still have to prove themselves. It was also claimed that women worked harder because they had a stronger sense of responsibility and want things done right. Annabell, expressed in stark terms the advantage that men enjoy and the struggle women endure:

> You know, women can't get away with bullshit, not like men. Women have to deliver, they have to show added value and quality. They can't bullshit their way through, they can't make promises to clients and not keep them . . . they have to deliver all the time.

Thus, whether it is objectively accurate or not, women perceive that they must work harder to excel in management and this becomes the reality for them. This is a significant additional burden, especially if they have an uneven share of domestic duties as well. It leads to long hours, stress and the type of sacrifices that we discuss toward the end of the chapter.

Dotting the 'i's' and crossing the 't's'

Another issue that occurred with surprising frequency was the view that women were better at handling detail compared to men – or some variant on that. There are subtle but important implications associated with this. Rose begins to articulate some of these subtleties:

> Men seem to be more hands off and women seem to follow through.

More precisely ... what I mean is, for example, when males are assigning a duty or assignment, they will trust the person and just let it go, but for the female I think they would have more supervision.

This conception of monitoring and maintaining the detail of task accomplishment is echoed by another respondent:

Women feel uncomfortable when they delegate. They carry the burden of the family to the workplace. They pay much attention to detail and as a result everything is under their tight control. Women sometimes falter too much, like me. Women therefore cannot do big things.

Rose expanded, suggesting that for females it was a matter of not having enough confidence to let things go. They feel the necessity of being more careful and patient to make sure that every step is done properly. Others suggested that men provide only the broad task direction and let people get on with things. Women give more detail and this means that a subordinate can learn more from them.

We can begin to see the double-sided nature to this issue. Whilst women are attentive to detail, and this may be positive, the flip side is that they do not always see the strategic implications, the ramifications and long-term impact. Some viewed this as a male skill: they may neglect minor detail, but are more results-oriented and more aware of the wider scheme of things. It is interesting that Rose associates this difference with the aggressive pursuit of career advancement, implying that males are motivated to achieve outcomes in order to progress whereas woman are more focused on actually doing the specific job at hand as well as possible. Another respondent went so far as to generalise this as a paramount gender difference: males are achievement-oriented whereas women are performance-oriented. Still another inferred that a natural division of labour is implied by these presumed gendered differences. She noted that women are more able to handle tedious things. She continued:

This is one of the advantages, because if you need someone to handle the thing step by step in a very detailed way, then it should be a woman who manages that. If you just only come out with the direction, then it should be the man that is the appropriate person ... it's the difference between the nature of the man and the nature of the woman. I can find that for a very senior position in the organisation, most likely it will be a man because they can come out with the direction.

Some related the attention to detail to an orientation acquired in the domestic sphere. Susan provided a clear exposition of what this means:

They (women) tend to be a little more thorough when thinking through problems. Maybe they just tend to be more naturally worried, uh, like a mother, because we are actually moulded to be, uhm, by nature to be mothers and mothers have to be more attentive to details to take care of the babies . . .

This is an example of some of the elliptical reasoning that some women find themselves engaging in. Primal and biological differences surface to account for rather mundane observations of differences in work practice.

The issue of attention to detail also connects to the idea that women can be more demanding as managers, despite the self-attributions of sensitivity and empathy. A number maintained this viewpoint, specifically because women focus on every small detail of others' work. Men, on the other hand, 'give us more allowance'. Another respondent said that women are more focused, vigorous and, again, more demanding. She went on to say that women managers are less liberal with their praise and acknowledgement of subordinates' work.

The perception was that men are more focused on long-term and strategic issues, whereas women are oriented to immediate process and the short term. If this were a real difference it would be a serious impediment to women's success in senior management. However, as with almost all reported differences, it is likely that it is more a function of structural differentiations and learnt behaviours than any inherent difference in skill or attribute. One attribution resonating with some other perceived differences we have discussed is that women are more likely to take account of the personal and family context when dealing with others, and particularly when assessing subordinates' behaviour. More generally, female sensitivity includes concern with context and men are less likely to contextualise things in this way, showing only concern for results and outcomes. On the other hand, women were held to be less likely to place things in strategic context.

Attuned to others

One of the most frequently cited gender differences was that woman are more empathetic, sensitive to others and relationship-oriented. Whether or not this is a mere stereotype, a significant proportion of our respondents made some reference to it. It was referred to not only as a discernible difference, but as something positive for women in the act of managing.

A typical comment was that women are more sensitive to people, and more understanding and open to the issues and pressures facing others. This facilitates better people management. A corollary was that female managers are more able to get others, both men and women, to disclose about personal problems affecting their work. This was also held to be of value in staff appraisals. Other women saw both advantages and disadvantages in female sensitivity. One linked it to emotionality, agreeing that women were more emotional than men. She expanded by saying that being sensitive to others' feelings is positive, but that emotionality can influence decision-making negatively. Eva, a public relations manager, saw things even more negatively, maintaining that women were not more sensitive to others, but *were* more sensitive about the comments of others. Being sensitive to others is helpful in management, but women are actually 'thrown back', as she put it, by being too sensitive about what other people thought or said about them. She implies that males are emotionally tougher and that woman managers also need to be so.

Face and ego

There were comments from the female perspective about managing relationships between the sexes. There was a pervasive opinion that male egos are more fragile than women's, and that this was an issue in managerial relationships. A related meaning is that men's work is often informed by the desire to satisfy ego needs: hence the competitiveness and personal-achievement orientation. A third meaning is that females, aware of male ego sensitivities, make an effort to avoid damaging it. It was argued that men take things too personally, especially if things go wrong or their work is critiqued. The use of 'ego' in this context has associations with the more distinctly Chinese notion of 'face' which is how some respondents couched the issue. It is important in Chinese culture to give face to others and not damage face. But it seems that in the context of Chinese sexual politics, it is more incumbent on women to give and protect the face of men than vice versa. As one woman put it:

> One big difference I noticed is that women are not as face conscious, because men, and especially Asian men, are very concerned with losing face ... I prefer women to work for me because they are not so concerned about losing face and that is good to some extent – your decisions wouldn't be so cluttered by emotion. If you bring in the face element then you have to factor in the emotion element and make the wrong type of decision. Women are able to make the straightforward decision uncluttered by emotions.

This is an interesting antidote to the female emotionality stereotype. She went on to say that male decision-making is informed by the need for social acceptance and face, whereas women's is not: they can therefore be more straightforward and even more 'daring' in their decision-making. Another woman mocked the stereotype and went on to explain the need to protect the male ego:

> The advice our boss got from his predecessor ... was to have a box of Kleenex in the drawer and be prepared when female executives come in. You have to get used to those types of comments. Females need to be

assertive and direct. As to females being more sensitive and cautious, well, I find myself doing that when dealing with the opposite sex. I would be conscious not to hurt the pride of my male counterparts.

In a different voice

That frequent mention was made of perceived gender differences in interaction/communication styles of managers is not surprising. Such differences have become commonplace in the literature (e.g. Tannen 1993). Apart from the general view that women are better communicators, better at managing relationships and more skilled in interactions, the discussions also generated one or two interesting specifics that we will focus on. Respondents, in their role as recruiters, noted that female candidates were generally more impressive in the selection process because they were better communicators, made better presentations and were more skilled at impression management. Another view expressed by Anna was that in a colonial context like Hong Kong, where English is the *lingua franca* of business, woman have an advantage because their linguistic skills are better than males. Good language facility gives confidence and allows women to take initiative: a view endorsed by others. Janice further suggested that woman are better at handling certain types of problems because their sensitivity and interpersonal skills enable them to exercise more tact.

Another common theme is that males are more direct and stunted in their communication style. Women engaged with others and elaborated things more fully. Wei Fung gives an example:

When I ask my subordinate to do something I generally will have to explain to them why I make this decision and then it is easier for them to accept. Whereas, for the man, they will just say 'do this'.

There is still a sense here of having to prove themselves and gain acceptance and legitimacy from others. A different slant on male directness was taken by Pinky, who suggested that men have a more personalistic interactional style: more informal, relaxed and light-hearted. Many women feel they cannot get away with this and endeavour to inject a more serious tone into their communications. Again the pervasive feeling is that women need to be more self-monitoring and to work harder in their communications in order to get the desired responses.

Advantages and disadvantages of being a manager and female

This subsection deals with accounts of what advantages or disadvantages accrued from being either a male or a female manager.

Manoeuvres within the warm embrace of paternalism

A response of several women to questions about the female advantage in management was rather surprising. They said that men often feel protective towards women. This entailed men avoiding open confrontation with women, women being allowed to get their own way more easily than men, and men seeking to protect women from 'difficult' tasks and situations. This latter has a downside since it can mean women's exclusion from challenging assignments, thereby missing exposure and development opportunities. A typical expression of this type of position comes from Melanie:

> It is one thing that we (females) try to use to full advantage. In a male environment they sometimes make life easy, sort of pamper the women. For example, if I didn't want to do a project, I would say 'couldn't you give this to someone else', and usually they would. I can't imagine a man doing that. They couldn't even ask . . . they wouldn't. Such a complaining and whining thing, it's more acceptable for a woman.

A corollary for some is that women's mistakes are more easily accepted and forgiven.

A surprisingly sexist set of attitudes frequently expressed was that women were cosseted because they did not need the job as much as men. The substance of this argument was that men are still considered to be the major family provider and that this creates a significant social pressure. The social pressures on women are less, and certainly so for women with a working partner. Sherry, for example, suggested that:

> Women are less worried about losing their jobs because some of them are married and the husband can take care of the livelihood . . . or the parents are less demanding about a woman excelling in her career. If she excels or she does not excel, she is a girl and, so, they are less afraid of speaking up and speaking their minds.

Other women similarly commented on how the relative lack of financial need for the job made a difference to women's motivation and approach to their work. For men, job security is often a priority, and then money, but for women this isn't always the case. Men have to prove themselves, achieve and advance; they have to keep up with peers. There is less pressure on women in this sense. Anna had a different perspective:

> I don't have to support a husband and child, so the way I look at my task is that I have to do it and do it well so that it will have a good result and then I get personal satisfaction. But a lot of times men, because they have to support the family and look good among peers, will work, not in a manner to do a good job, but to play politics and take credit

from subordinates to get ahead and say 'this is *my* job and *my* performance'.

So not only an advantage for women, but an organisational advantage too, one might suggest.

The positive and negatives of conflict

Strongly related to the above was the widespread view that men were often unwilling to engage women in a conflict. It was argued that women could get their way and get away with things because males backed down in conflict situations. One respondent had an interesting Freudian line on male responses to female verbal assertiveness:

> I think that when a woman gets aggressive, the opposite or counter person, if it is a man . . . tends to back down a little bit because, if you want to be Freudian about it, maybe it reminds him of his mother scolding him and he backs down and shuts up because he does not want to have this noisy woman shouting and arguing in his office, so he will, in the end, let her get away with it. I know, 'everyone laugh', but it is really the case because even in a very senior level, if a woman goes in to argue with the boss more often she ends up winning compared to a man because the man finds that this is irrational behaviour and it is so hard to deal with it or abide it. So just to avoid trouble and to pacify her for a while the man gives in. But a man will never get away with it from another man. I don't think it is really a quality that is positive about a woman.

A perceived disadvantage for women was that, given their sociability and relationship orientation, they do not like to make enemies. This may lead to non-assertive, accommodating or avoiding behaviour that could be sub-optimal in personal and performance terms.

Decisions, decisions

The stereotype that females are less decisive, lack a strong will and are hesitant was expressed by a number of respondents. It was suggested that women put the family before the company. Concomitantly it was held that men are more decisive and risk-taking and that this was their advantage. This was not a unanimous view and there were different perspectives on why women had problems with decision-making. Susanna, talking about the disadvantage of women, said:

> I think decisions, because they are so cautious that they look at details and miss the big picture. And there is a tendency, because they are so

meticulous, they don't find people working for them doing as good a job as they do so they end up not delegating.

Bitchiness and other disadvantages

This refers to a rather miscellaneous set of negative attributions or perceived disadvantages of women managers. Our rather dramatic heading indexes some comments about women being 'bitchy' to and about each other and this being disadvantageous. One woman expressed it in graphic terms:

> I think that women, when they want to, can literally be bitches. They can really think up ways to torture another person. Women are much more effective really at getting revenge and devising ways to torture people than a man is. Men tend to explode and then forget, women store things up and get you later. This is one advantage, a more devious mind.

It is interesting to note that many respondents felt that women were better at politicking than men, but almost all maintained that were not personally interested or good at it!

Additional negative attributions included emotionality, having a narrow perspective, being dogmatic, being unable to keep secrets, and lacking in drive and commitment.

'Bitches', 'strong women' and the feminine: managing gender identity

The literature has suggested that the practice of management is defined in masculine terms. The corollary is that management and leadership is reflexively cast in masculinist terms and thereby the qualities, attributes and skills required for successful management are constructed in ways that resonate with their presumed natural occurrence in males. Since the feminine is elided and excluded from masculinised definitions and conceptions of organisation and management, it is extremely difficult for women to promote an alternative and succeed. Consequently there are intimations that, to be successful, female managers need to masculinise themselves, or at least manage their gender identity.

It has to be said that little homogeneity existed around this issue. Indeed, it had no resonance for many. This does not necessarily imply that the phenomenon was non-existent for them: perhaps they had not conceptualised things in such terms. The issues are, after all, abstract, complex and potentially psychologically unsettling. One would hardly expect women to readily define and articulate themselves as masculinised. However, some confronted the issue head-on whilst others had interesting, indirect comments.

One of the strongest expressions came from a respondent who clearly agreed with the need to masculinise one's style as a female manager: 'Yes, definitely. Sometimes you have to bend your nature.' This included, she continued, not being so attentive to detail as she would normally be, letting certain things go, and being stronger and more direct in verbal style, and even changing the content of conversation:

> You have to talk tougher and act more like one of the boys . . . I avoid discussing certain things when I am with male clients, for example, I always start by talking about something from the newspaper that morning, the latest subjects or banking rates, that type of thing. Sometimes the men are happier talking about more casual things, softer subjects, but definitely for me, I will be talking about hard issues. I will actually make sure that I start out with something that is non-feminine and very hard-nosed. I also pick up a lot of colloquial and rougher language and I think sometimes they (males) buy it if you use that type of language.

There is extensive impression management, and indeed gender identity management, going on here. There is also a surrender to male modes of presentation and communication. Other women concurred with the notion of adopting a more direct and 'tougher' communication style.

Bonnie told us that she was not consciously trying to adopt a masculine style, but that her friends and family informed her that they felt she acted 'more like a man'. She later agreed that her style had become masculinised, in terms of being more assertive than her normal inclination. She expanded:

> I don't think women are in such a defensive position these days. They are more confident and so they can behave more naturally, or in what might be called a more male way. Whereas maybe men feel more threatened today, and they are in a defensive position and behave more womanly . . . you know, indecisive, wavering, can't make up their minds. We call them 'small men'.

Fanny revealed that she was perceived as being very aggressive at work, but even at university she had adopted that style:

> I was told that I am very masculine and that I am a 'tomboy', it used to upset me very much. I think that in my presentation, my style, I'm very masculine. Some women try to get on by using their femininity, exploiting it, but I won't do that, I'm very bad at it anyway.

She explained that in her style of dress she simply tried to look more mature but that her interactive style was natural. In fact, she tried to tone down her assertive and aggressive style because she felt it to be somewhat dysfunctional.

Many respondents were critical of women who exploited femininity to get on. Most said they would not entertain such a strategy: although there were exceptions. There were one or two other cases of women saying that they felt that their natural style was already 'masculine' and so there was no need to consciously adopt a masculine style. This group did not feel that they were compromising their femininity in order to succeed as managers. Others felt that they had to learn certain things that went against their natural inclinations, such as being more aggressive and using more direct communication. There were some who maintained that a distinctive 'feminine' style was discernible and an advantage. Maggie, for instance, felt females were more open and friendly, thus helping to establish better relationships with peers and subordinates.

Agnes took a more critical line in defining the masculinisation of women: 'Masculinity is women who do not have a woman's traits like understanding and collaboration. They want power over people and to control the situation. They won't give leeway to a person to turn back.' Another noted that she was 'very rational, assertive, not emotional and I have a clear picture in mind. Many friends tease me that I am masculine.' Some considered the development of such traits as a loss of womanhood and not appropriate for Chinese culture. As one put it: 'If a woman surrenders her femininity, and ignores the care for the entire group, everyone will dislike her. A woman must "behave like a woman".' She implies that women are supposed to be attentive to the needs and interests of the family and community. The type of traits outlined above are not proper to a feminine woman. Caris reflected on the double-bind that the competing expectations on women in both a social/family role and a managerial role generates: 'My tenderness was always misunderstood as weakness. But when I exhibited my assertiveness I know my female subordinates dislike my direct manner.' She disclosed that being autocratic was the most difficult and the most disliked part of her job. However, if she displayed the culturally defined traits of a woman, she was not respected as a competent individual. This shows that female managers find themselves preoccupied with a female–male dichotomy.

Guilt, sacrifice and stress: coping and succeeding as a female manager

As we have seen, and as noted in the literature, making it as a female manager requires substantial commitment and hard work. For many women, success has a price attached to it. To succeed women often have had to make sacrifices in other areas of their lives. A significant proportion of our interviewees made some reference to this.

A majority of the respondents were not married and some had divorced or separated. Some, clearly with regret, attributed their single status to the pursuit of a career. Others felt that the likelihood of marriage was impaired or relationships had suffered through career commitment. The choice to remain single, in order to pursue their career more vigorously, for some was more or less conscious. A marketing manager in the garment industry felt her single status was partly attributable to her career: 'To be very honest, quite a few of my relationships have not worked because of my career. My feeling is that relationships will come later, at this point my career is important.' Another had split from a long-standing relationship with a boyfriend, who had suggested marriage, in order to continue her career. The age for marriage has risen steadily in Hong Kong over the past three decades, partly reflecting the fact that women are more able, prepared or compelled to pursue a working life. For female managers the perception remained that at times it was difficult to pursue a successful career and have satisfying relationships as well.

Other respondents referred to giving up hobbies, leisure and social time for their careers. The strongest expressions of regret came from those women with children. The failure to spend time with their children was a source of regret for most of these. They expressed feelings of guilt, an additional psychological burden for such female managers. One woman even suggested that her health had been sacrificed to her career and a significant number reported that they often felt stressed, either directly from work-related issues, or from the double strain of trying to handle the family–work dilemma.

Conclusion: commonality and diversity

In exploring the experiences of female managers functioning within a Chinese context we notice both commonality and diversity. Indeed, when these experiences are put into international comparison the same thing holds. There are some experiences and perceptions articulated by these women that are similar to those reported in western studies. It would seem some aspects of the situation for female managers and the experiences they encounter are not substantially different around the world. For example, women remain fundamentally under-represented in management given the proportion of women in the workforce; they confront a glass ceiling which limits progression into senior management; they encounter sex stereotypes and sexist attitudes and behaviour as a matter of routine; they face a double burden of managing a career and an unequal share of domestic activities; they are burdened by the need to be constantly self-monitoring so as to manage their gender identity. We argue that, given that organisations remain primarily male cultures, women face the constant burden of learning to manoeuvre within that culture and to manage their gender identity. The manifestation of these experiences, the specific forms they take, their severity and the factors that give rise to them do exhibit differences in different locations, but some very significant commonalities remain.

The macro-societal context in Hong Kong provides for some of the commonality of experience and, of course, for some of the differences *vis-à-vis* women in other countries. As noted, Chinese societies have strong patriarchal traditions that are still, to an extent, significant. There are clear signs of this weakening as socio-economic conditions, levels of education and sexual politics shift. It was apparent from our discussions and wider observations that business pragmatism means that opportunities are there for women. If a female can demonstrate competence and add value to a business, then this may override any gendered ideology. With the return of Hong Kong to China it is not easy to determine whether this will continue and strengthen or not. We are hesitant because there are some signs in post-reform China of a subtle re-emergence of traditional gender values. There has been some revitalisation of neo-Confucianism and calls from official sources for women to revert back to their traditional reproductive and domestic roles. The new opportunities of the market have created fresh options for some women – as entrepreneurs or in foreign enterprises for example – but for others the new situation is a threat. The old communist ideology of equality, which was never fully actioned, is no longer pursued as much in official rhetoric. Nor is it monitored and policed by the Party since enterprise governance and management has been depoliticised. This opens the door for reactionary and discriminatory practices to be pursued and reinstigated. On the other hand, as China continues to open up – including learning from Hong Kong – the pressures for greater opportunity and equality for women may enter more into the system and constitute a force for change. Undoubtedly the situation will continue to change and unfold in the years to come. We are not, at least in the short term, optimistic that the changes will be entirely beneficial to women in management.

Notes

1 The authors are grateful for research grants from the Hong Kong University Research Council and the Chinese University of Hong Kong which enabled the research on which this chapter is based.
2 Approximately fifty women managers were interviewed, with the interviews usually recorded and subsequently transcribed and analysed.
3 A basic Taoist concept which signals the fundamental interdependency of things, even opposites, within a radical holistic framework.

13 Entrepreneurial and managerial competencies

Small business owner/managers in Hong Kong[1]

Theresa Lau, K.F. Chan, Thomas W. Y. Man

Introduction

Hong Kong has been one of the fastest growing economies in the Asia-Pacific Region. One of the most prominent factors leading to this economic success is its enterprise culture, which encourages and helps a large number of entrepreneurs and industrialists to flourish. In fact, the development of an enterprise culture is the composite result of a high degree of autonomy and a strong profit incentive, as the consequence of a traditional non-interventionist government policy. Consistently over the last few decades, nearly 98 per cent of the firms in Hong Kong belong to a small business sector, which is officially defined as manufacturing firms with fewer than a hundred employees and services firms with fewer than fifty employees.[2] Chinese immigrants constituted the major part of the influx in the 1950s, setting up small enterprises in various industries, in particular the textile and clothing industry (Wong 1988). They grew in size with continuous success throughout the seventies and eighties. Local entrepreneurs have also been tempted to start up business as a result of the government's *laissez-faire* policy.

Stories of successful new ventures and well-known entrepreneurs are often reported in the mass media. Hong Kong is remarked on as a desirable place for establishing small enterprises because it offers ample business opportunities to anyone who likes to take risks and work hard to achieve the goal of running their own business. But, while a favourable environment provides strong support for the initial setting up of a small business, sustainable development depends on the personal qualities, abilities and skills of the entrepreneur. In other words, both the enterprise culture as well as the characteristics of the entrepreneurs themselves help to explain why Hong Kong has been so successful in its economic development.

Many studies have been conducted in the West to explore and examine the personal characteristics of successful entrepreneurs, but very few focus specifically on Hong Kong. The findings of the western studies may not be directly applicable to Hong Kong, given the cultural and contextual differences. It is therefore of particular interest to look at the question of who

Hong Kong entrepreneurs are, and how they compare with their western counterparts. Specifically, our study examines the entrepreneur's behaviour in the process of developing a business, and analyses whether or not they show some consistency in terms of personal traits, skills and competency profiles. A better understanding of existing practices should help us to draw conclusions on how to prepare present and future entrepreneurs better to sustain successful venture development. The study could provide additional information for policy makers on which areas of competence should be developed, especially in Hong Kong and other similar economies, where entrepreneurial training and development remains the main concern of many academics and practitioners.

Founding a business is an entrepreneurial act, but a small business owner/manager cannot be considered as an entrepreneur just by founding a business, since this is not necessarily a reliable predictor of sustained entrepreneurial performance. The small business owner/manager establishes a business mainly to further their own personal goals, and so perceives the business as an extension of their personality, intricately bound up with family needs and demands. An entrepreneur, however, establishes a business mainly for profit and growth, and is characterised by innovative and strategic-orientated behaviour. Strategic-orientated behaviour, growth-orientated behaviour and the control of the growth and development of a business over a sustained period are considered to be the criteria which distinguish entrepreneurs from small business owner/managers (Carland *et al.* 1984; Chell 1986). In this study, all members of our sample of small business owners/managers demonstrate innovativeness and growth-oriented behaviour. Most of all, they have all been managing successful and growing businesses for a number of years. There is no doubt that our sample can be characterised as 'entrepreneurs'.

The background and characteristics of Hong Kong small business

In order to arrive at a profile of entrepreneurs, the environments in which entrepreneurs flourish have to be examined. Hong Kong's economic success depends largely on the contribution from small businesses, which are considered as the backbone of the economy. According to government statistics, the small business sector accounts for 98 per cent of all establishments in the Hong Kong Special Administration Region. In terms of output, the small business sector contributed 44 per cent of the total census value-added in all manufacturing industries in 1996, which amounted to HK$361 billion. In terms of employment, the small business sector was responsible for 69 per cent of total employment in 1997. There is no doubt that the small business sector contributes substantially to employment and total industry output. The large numbers of small businesses indicate a favourable environment for the survival of a large number of entrepreneurs.

Since early 1998, the financial crisis and recession has affected all sectors of the economy. The unemployment rate jumped from 2.2 per cent in 1997 to 5.0 per cent in August 1998. Instead of seeking help from the government, many of those who lost their jobs started up their own businesses. This led to a proliferation of micro-enterprises, especially in the retail sector. Attendance at courses and seminars about business start-ups, franchising and small business survival strategies has become a trend. The universities even provide money for graduates to encourage them to start up their own businesses. No matter whether the recession is a pull or push factor, such a quick adjustment demonstrates the enterprising spirit of Hong Kong people.

This spirit is relatively rare even in other free-enterprise countries (Sit *et al.* 1979). In fact, between 1981 and 1992, Hong Kong had a higher ratio of firms per 10,000 persons than the US. For instance, in 1992, Hong Kong had 618 firms per 10,000 people compared with 344 firms per 10,000 people in the US (Cheah and Yu 1996). Table 13.1 reveals that the small business sector in Hong Kong is characterised by an exceptionally large number of establishments, and a high start-up and failure rate. It is common practice for owner/managers in Hong Kong to close businesses which are no longer profitable and to start something new right away in order to cope with environmental change. This indicates the dynamism of Hong Kong's entrepreneurs and their flexibility in shifting to new activities.

Business in Hong Kong, especially in the small sector, is characterised by family involvement and control. A survey of small-scale industry in Hong Kong in 1987 showed that 60 per cent of the sample were family businesses and partnerships (Sit 1985). A majority of them obtained their initial capital from the personal savings of the owners. Many of the firms were founded by

Table 13.1 Company formation and dissolution in Hong Kong

	1986	1989	1991	1992	1993	1994	1995	1996	1997
No. of companies incorporated during the year	16,743	31,674	43,976	58,110	61,831	42,723	33,008	49,734	49,275
No. of companies wound up during the year	3,094	2,737	5,237	4,804	4,765	6,788	14,821	38,446	57,973
No. of companies registered at the end of the year	161,986	242,709	304,538	358,129	415,911	452,789	471,883	483,181	474,517

Source: Census and Statistics Department 1997c: 1998.

families and remained under family control even when they grew larger. This has resulted in a number of phenomena, according to Enright *et al.* (1997): first, the decision-making power tends to be highly concentrated at the centre of the company, often the owner; second, professional managers and technically expert staff are seldom offered any shareholdings in the company or top executive positions; and third, decisions can be taken extremely quickly, enabling the company to respond with great flexibility to shifts in market circumstances or environmental change. Wang (1977) indicated that family involvement facilitated the pooling and sharing of capital for diversification, and the ownership structure also allowed the building-up of networks which secured supplies and sales, lowered the barrier for risk-taking, and favoured entrepreneurship (Siu and Martin 1992).

Small industrial factories in particular adopt a simple structure, with no or few horizontal divisions. The minimisation of hierarchy facilitates direct and face-to-face control by the owner/managers (King and Leung 1975). The small-scale industry survey conducted by Sit *et al.* (1979) also confirmed the orientation towards simple structure. It was reported in that survey that only 27.2 per cent and 11.8 per cent of the sample employed management staff and technical supervisors respectively. There was generally little division of labour in the upper management levels, and the small business owner/manager usually performed the roles of boss, manager and technician. However, this tendency towards simplicity has changed to a certain extent during the past decade. A recent study by Lau and Snell (1996) has shown that small enterprises in Hong Kong now exhibit a greater variety of structural patterns, including simple structure, machine bureaucracy, professional bureaucracy, divisional form and adhocracy. Many organisations adopt a predominant form with one or two minor ones. With the opening-up of China and the need to cope with an erosion of cost advantage, many Hong Kong manufacturing firms have moved part of their operations to China, where they adopt a predominantly machine bureaucratic structure, while retaining a simple structure at their headquarters in Hong Kong. The adoption of hybrid structures and the engagement of spatial arbitrage reflect the flexibility of small businesses in Hong Kong.

Apart from flexibility, small businesses in Hong Kong are also renowned for their adaptability and responsiveness. These characteristics are linked to the adoption of short-term planning, which is common in many small businesses. Enright *et al.* (1997) refer to this as the use of 'hustle strategies', and this is a major distinction between local small businesses and large corporations. The use of hustle strategies is especially found in the garment, toy and electronic industries as well as in many businesses which emphasise speed, flexibility, quality, delivery and competitive pricing. Such businesses are flexible enough to move from low-end to high-end, from product to product, and even from one industry sector to another. With limited overheads, personnel and machinery, the opportunity costs for the small firm are relatively low.

The result is that small firms often invest little in research and development, and rarely invest in expensive state-of-the-art equipment. Manufacturers usually receive their technical know-how from foreign agents operating in Hong Kong, learn through imitation, and rely on local trading firms to market their products overseas (Cheah and Yu 1996). They also rely heavily on subcontracting systems, which are made possible because of the large volumes required for export. The export activities utilised by many small firms also equip them with transnational skills (Fung 1996).

To sum up, the small business in Hong Kong is characterised by family involvement, simple and hybrid structure, short-term orientation, speed and flexibility of actions, imitation, the use of an extensive subcontracting system, and an export orientation with strong transnational skills. Small business owner/managers in Hong Kong share similar characteristics. Chan and Lau (1993) depicted their behaviour with a COSI scheme – change-orientation, opportunistic-orientation, strategic-orientation and innovativeness. Cheah and Yu (1996) also suggested that they are adaptive, alert to opportunities, flexible and respond rapidly to change. They are, however, not revolutionary innovators, but usually engage in incremental and evolutionary innovations such as product imitation. Redding and Wong (1986) stated that they possess the traits of energy, independence, goal-orientation, lower idealism and flexibility. All of these characteristics are positive influences in the development of entrepreneurship.

Managerial and entrepreneurial competencies

There has been a great deal of research on management and entrepreneurial competencies, and researchers are divided in their opinions as to what competencies should be identified. Boyatzis (1982) defines a job competency as an underlying characteristic of a person, which may be a motive, trait, skill, aspect of one's self-image or social role or a body of knowledge which he or she uses. Because job competencies are underlying characteristics, they can be said to be generic. Woodruffe (1992) has reported nine 'generic competencies' which are clusters of behaviours of high performers. Instead of simply looking at the functions and tasks, he suggested that attention should be paid to the interaction between individuals, tasks and environments. Competencies, according to his view, deal with the behaviours which people need to display in order to do the job effectively, and which are not the job itself. It is therefore necessary to distinguish competencies from job roles.

Focusing on a group of senior executives in small to medium-sized enterprise, Durkan *et al.* (1993) came up with four categories of competencies: intellectual abilities, personal characteristics, social abilities, and managerial abilities. Evers and Rush (1996) also reported on four 'based competencies', which they considered as skills required for advanced-level corporate jobs. While the groupings in the two studies are slightly different, the composite elements within them are largely comparable.

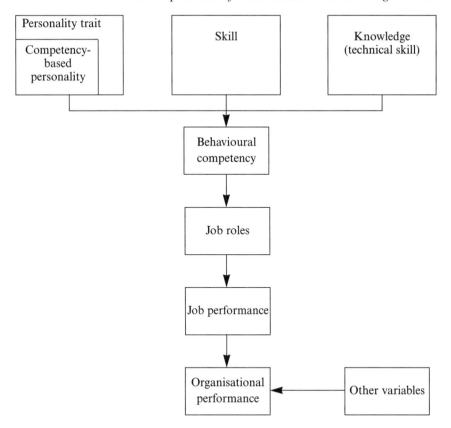

Figure 13.1 The competency model.

Entrepreneurial competencies have been related to business success (McClelland 1987), firm performance (Chandler and Jansen 1992; Chandler and Hanks 1994) and venture growth (Baum 1995). A more comprehensive review of past studies on managerial and entrepreneurial competencies can be seen in Lau *et al.*'s paper (1998). A conceptual model is presented below to illustrate how entrepreneurial competencies contribute to organisational performance.

We can tell whether someone is a good dancer by the way he dances. We can also tell whether someone is a competent manager by the way he manages. The way a manager manages is his/her behavioural competency, which reflects his/her personality traits, skill and knowledge. A manager's behavioural competency would enable him/her to perform his/her job roles such as the ones identified and categorised by Mintzberg (1973). Satisfactory performance of the job role leads to the successful performance of a manager's job and, in turn, contributes to organisational performance. Although an organisation's performance depends on many variables, e.g. environment, strategy and organisational context, it is believed that the small business owner/manager's behaviour will have a stronger impact on the firm's performance as he/she is the one who shapes the culture, value and social behaviour of the organisation. Figure 13.1 presents such integrative competency model. The three elements that comprise behavioural competency are elaborated below.

First, personality trait (T) is a theoretical and unobservable construct which enables us to explain consistencies in observable behaviour (Chell and Burrows 1991). Many studies (Timmons *et al.* 1985; Meredith *et al.* 1982; Brockhaus and Horwitz 1986) have been conducted to identify the personality traits of managers and entrepreneurs. In entrepreneurship research, more empirical studies have been conducted on the characteristics of entrepreneurs than almost any other kind (Herron and Robinson 1993). They explore the personality traits such as locus of control, risk-taking propensity, problem-solving style, opportunism, innovation and so on (Brockhaus 1975; Brockhaus and Horwitz 1986; Collins and Moore 1970; Sexton and Bowman 1985), and these traits were found to be related to entrepreneurial success or organisational performance. It is believed that personality traits are inborn and are stable over time, and they can explain behaviour if the total number of traits is big enough to represent the behavioural patterns (Herron and Robinson 1993).

Second, skill (S) is the ability to demonstrate a system and sequence of behaviours that are functionally related to attaining a performance goal (Boyatzis 1982). In other words, they are the ready abilities that someone brings to a situation at any point in time. They are the results of both the natural aptitudes such as differential intelligence and of the training and practice which the manager has previously had in exercising these skills (Herron and Robinson 1993). Although entrepreneurial textbooks in North America place more emphasis on personality attributes than on skill, that has begun to change (Ray 1993). In fact, skill is more proximal to venture creation process than personality traits, and therefore is more central to entrepreneurship development and easier to train than traits. Typical examples of skills for entrepreneurs are well researched and documented, including communication, leadership, career, problem solving and opportunity skills (Baum 1995; Caird 1992; Durkan *et al.* 1993).

Knowledge (K) is a technical skill. It encompasses specific domains of business and commercial knowledge, including traditional functional areas. Boyatzis (1982) defines specialised knowledge as facts, principles, theories, frameworks or models. Specialised knowledge is often identified as being related to the performance of a manager. It may also relate to the managerial function being performed, the products being produced, and the technology being used. Traditional functional disciplines such as marketing, production, finance and human resources are widely recognised as important knowledge sets that enable entrepreneurs to perform tasks effectively (Adam and Chell 1993; Huck and McEwen 1991).

In sum, entrepreneurial competencies can be conceptualised as the total capability of the entrepreneur to perform job roles successfully. Three distinctive components can be identified in entrepreneurial competencies: personality traits, skills and knowledge. In most cases, business tasks require the small business owner/manager to possess these three components in order for him/her to function effectively. We refer to these components together as the 'composite competency'. In some circumstances, only a 'single competency' (either a specific trait, or a skill or knowledge) is required to achieve good task performance. On the other hand, when two components of the competency are required to perform the job successfully, this may be referred to as 'multiple competency'. The two components can be any combination of the three. For example, a specific personality trait and a specific skill will constitute a multiple competency that the small business owner/manager possesses to perform the job successfully. The last but the most complicated level of ability that the owner/manager may possess we refer to as a 'compound competency'. This refers to a composite competency in which more than one type of personality trait, skill or knowledge is involved. For example, a small business owner/manager might possess a compound competency, which consists of a specific personality trait (relationship orientation), two kinds of skills (marketing and innovation) and a specific knowledge (knowledge on business environment).

Background of owner/managers included in the study

As the successful small business owner/manager in Hong Kong is our target of study, the following criteria were established in selecting our sample:

- The owner/managers started the companies on their own or have made some drastic changes in either the structure or form of the company if it was inherited;
- They have operated and managed the company for at least four years;
- The company is growing either in size or in sales turnover; and
- The company has been established for at least four years.

The best way to approach small business owner/managers is through various business and trade associations. The sample was drawn from the Hong Kong Chamber of Small and Medium Business, the Hong Kong Chamber of Commerce, and the Management Development Centre. Some owner/managers were also selected amongst those featured in *Next Magazine*.

Eighteen small business owner/managers were interviewed with six each in the clothing, food processing and catering industries. Grounded theory was adopted, and the owner/managers were encouraged to talk as freely as they liked and with minimal interruption. However, some probing questions were asked during the interview such as: How and why did the business start? What happened to the business at the start-up stage? What is happening at present? What is likely to happen in the future? How was the business developed and managed? How were problems handled during the business development process? What stage of development is the business in? Who is involved in the business? What has the performance of the business been like over the past few years? What is the business outlook and plan for the future? What are the attributes and skills that you think you possess that contributed to the success and growth of the business?

Interviews were tape-recorded and transcribed verbatim, and were then analysed to identify critical incidents affecting the firm's business development process. The incidents were compiled based on the context, the event and the owner/manager's response to the event. Each of the three researchers then independently analysed the incidents and decided on the personality trait, skill and knowledge that was associated with the behaviour that the owner/managers displayed for each incident. Comparison was made of each researcher's analysis, and if there was no discrepancy, the personality trait, skill of knowledge were ascribed. Where there was a difference in opinion, consensus had to be sought. This usually meant going back to the original transcript and case script to clarify whether there had been any misunderstanding in the scripts, or any misinterpretation of the words used to describe the traits, skills or attributes. In the same way, the definition of the related personality traits, skills and knowledge were discussed, agreed and written down to avoid any further misinterpretation. In cases of discrepancy, only consensus decisions were accepted which meant that the researcher had to justify their analysis and convince others of their viewpoint. In this way, reliability was maintained.

All of the sampled interviewees met our criteria of successful small business owner/managers. Since the clothing, catering and food-processing industries were covered in this study, we use the definition that applies to all three industries. The definition suggested by the Committee on Economic Development (CED) was adopted – a business is classified as small if it meets two or more of the following criteria:

1. Management is independent (usually, the manager is also the owner).
2. Capital is supplied and ownership is held by an individual or a small group.
3. The area of operations is mainly local. Workers and owners are in one home community. Markets need not be local.
4. Relative size within the industry – the business is small when compared with the biggest unit in its field.

Employment is not the only indicator used in defining a small business: employment size is assessed relative to the norm of the particular industry. The six selected firms from the clothing industry are the biggest of the eighteen firms in our study since they belong to a labour-intensive industry. The largest company in this group employs 400 workers in China while keeping eighty workers in Hong Kong to do sampling and design. The firms in food and drink processing are comparatively small, ranging from twenty to sixty employees. Two catering firms employ 400 and 600 employees in their chain of restaurants, while the others have less than 150 employees.

Most of the firms have been in business for less than eight years, except for a few which were founded by a previous generation. The owner/managers in this study followed diverse paths to business development: genuine start-up, buy-in, succession, and joining as a partner. However, they had all managed the successful and growing companies for at least four years. Two of them turned around the companies and a few changed the nature of the business. All of the companies had grown either in size or in terms of sales turnover, and most had grown in both. Therefore, in our definition, all of our sampled interviewees are entrepreneurial managers.

As we mentioned earlier, family involvement is one of the characteristics of Hong Kong firms. Our samples are no exception. Fourteen firms in our study involved partnerships, and more than half of the firms involved family members in their business operations either as partners or managers. Those firms without family involvement were usually run by very young owners and/or those with a western education.

Entrepreneurial competencies of Hong Kong small business owner/managers

From the critical incidents of the eighteen successful small business owner/managers, fifty-nine personality traits were derived from a total of 614 occurrences, twenty-eight skills from 579 occurrences and eight areas of knowledge from 528 occurrences. Due to the large number and similarity of the personality traits and skills, an attempt was made to group the related

Table 13.2 Entrepreneurial personality traits of small business owner/managers in Hong Kong

	Personality traits	Number of occurrences	%
1	Strategic orientation	117	19.0
2	Relationship orientation	78	12.7
3	Reactive change	49	7.9
4	Learning mind	47	7.6
5	Result orientation	43	7.0
6	Innovativeness	41	6.7
7	Commitment	39	6.4
8	Opportunism	39	6.4
9	Risk	38	6.2
10	Quality conscious	35	5.7
11	Proactive change	28	4.6
12	Control	21	3.4
13	Efficiency	14	2.3
14	Integrity	13	2.1
15	Pride	7	1.1

personality traits, skills and knowledge together to form several clusters. In consequence, fifteen clusters of personality traits, twelve clusters of skills and eight clusters of knowledge resulted. Tables 13.2, 13.3 and 13.4 show these three groups of clusters in order of frequency of occurrence.

As shown in Tables 13.2, 13.3, and 13.4, the successful small business owner/managers in our sample demonstrate a diversity of attributes, skills and knowledge. Strategic orientation, relationship orientation, reactive change, and a learning mind are the most often found personality traits. Strategic orientation implies that small business owner/managers in Hong Kong have vision and foresight, set challenging and attainable goals and continue to set goals to challenge themselves. Most of all, they are not content with running just a small business; they tried all means to expand their business – explored new markets, opened up new branches, set up new plants. They were able to plan these strategically. To illustrate, one of our sample, a clothing manufacturer, emphasised the need to diversify the market and product mix, set long-term goals to penetrate into the Chinese

Table 13.3 Entrepreneurial skill of small business owner/managers in Hong Kong

Skills		Number of occurrences	%
1	Planning	162	28.0
2	Communication	83	14.3
3	Marketing	57	9.8
4	Problem solving	43	7.5
5	Organising	42	7.3
6	Human	34	6.0
7	Controlling	31	5.4
8	Learning	30	5.3
9	Adaptation	27	4.6
10	Analytical	23	4.0
11	Innovative	23	4.0
12	Career assessment	17	3.0

Table 13.4 Knowledge of small business owner/managers in Hong Kong

Knowledge		Number of occurrences	%
1	Business and market environment	122	23.1
2	Marketing and public relation	118	22.3
3	Organisational and human resources management	99	18.8
4	Production, operation, purchasing and supply	93	17.6
5	Product and product development	49	9.3
6	Finance	27	5.1
7	Legal	12	2.3
8	Information technology	2	0.4

market, and to develop the company's own brand in order to ensure not only its current but also its future success. Past studies also identify growth-orientated and strategic-orientated behaviour as distinguishing an entrepreneur from a non-entrepreneurial small business owner/manager (Carland *et al.* 1984; Chell 1986).

Relationship orientation is another distinguishing feature of the proto-typical successful small business owner/manager in Hong Kong. They are good leaders, showing concern for employees and getting along well with people. They have pleasant personalities and a sense of humour. They establish and maintain good networks with suppliers, bankers, trade associations and other professionals. As a key partner in a restaurant group noted, although conflicts among partners are unavoidable, his role as a middleman is essential in resolving these conflicts and gaining trust, allowing him to manage the whole group smoothly. Managers who spend more time developing their networks and maintaining good relationships, and seeking assistance, advice, information and other resources from members of the network tend to display more entrepreneurial behaviour.

Consistent with the general belief that entrepreneurs are usually very flexible and positive in dealing with challenges, the behaviour of the Hong Kong small business owner/managers in our study reflected such attributes. As usual, many owner/managers faced a lot of ups and downs in their business development process but, as the analyses show, they maintained a very optimistic view about future results and adopted a very flexible approach that led to results one way or the other. Unfortunately, the results also indicated that Hong Kong owner/managers were more reactive than proactive in making changes. An example of this can be seen from the flexible attitude of the fashion-chain owner in handling business growth:

> The increase in production has resulted in overcapacity. To solve this problem, we increased the number of outlets, but in turn, this led us to expand the production capacity again. Finally, we ended up in having a big factory at Dongguan, China ... The growth is really fast, and we now have to subcontract part of the production to another factory as well.

Table 13.3 shows that proactive change is ranked rather low in the list of personality traits found of Hong Kong owner/managers. Apparently, reactive change is better than keeping the status quo because at least the owner/managers have a receptive attitude when changes are required in dealing with matters. However, in the long run, if Hong Kong owner/managers are not prepared to exploit and initiate changes, i.e. to be proactive, they may not be able to cope with a complex environment, and further business development could be hindered. This particular personality attribute becomes more important when the environment is more dynamic and hostile. In fact, since the financial crisis in October 1997, the competitiveness of small to medium enterprises in Hong Kong has been shrinking. Among many reasons, one is attributed to the deficiency in entrepreneurs' ability to make proactive changes.

A learning mind is another attribute found among small business owner/ managers in Hong Kong but is not typical in entrepreneurs in the western studies. As revealed from the incidents, the Hong Kong owner/managers were capable of learning from experience, were fast and efficient in learning, and were keen on learning. Even when they were performing very well, they were not complacent and tried to prepare for leaner times. That explains why some of them, with very little education and experience, not only managed their business well, but also managed to keep them growing. They learnt management skill as they went along.

With regard to skills and knowledge, small business owner/managers in our study demonstrated a high use of planning, communication, marketing and problem-solving skills and a high application of business and market environment knowledge, as well as marketing and public relations knowledge. As the saying goes, failing to plan is planning to fail. The small business owner/managers proved their competence in the way that they planned. When they saw little progress in their existing business, they exercised their opportunity identification skill to explore different markets. This did not necessarily involve a formal written business plan, but many thought about their businesses all the time. They reported thinking about their businesses when on holiday, on overseas trips, or even whilst having dinner with their partners in their own restaurants. These informal plans resulted in a number of strategic actions, which could bring long-term benefits.

The prototypical small business owner/managers communicated effectively. They were able to explain their visions and ideas in a way that could be easily understood. They presented their proposals clearly and convincingly, influencing bankers and partners to invest money. More importantly, they built up good interpersonal relationships with their customers, as well as negotiating skilfully with their marketing channels. One food manufacturer reported that she had negotiated with a large department store to retain her own brand and the right to set a higher price for selling in their store. While this is a difficult deal for such a small manufacturer, she did it successfully in a 'harmonious atmosphere with mutual understanding', reflecting her exceptional negotiation skills. The prototypical small business owner/managers were able to communicate their vision and mission to their employees, enabling their employees to understand the nature of their jobs and the standards they were expected to meet.

The small business owner/managers had good marketing skills. Not only did they have some typical ways of marketing the product and creative ways of improving it: they were also able to enter into a new market. They had skills in choosing the right locations, finding the different distribution channels, and using the appropriate price strategy to get into the market.

Problems are commonplace for small business owner/managers when starting up a new venture. Problems, challenges and crises can also be found during different stages of business development. The prototypical small business owner/managers demonstrated their ability to select the right course of action to solve a specific problem. They also looked for opportunities and turned problems into opportunities.

Our study reveals that Hong Kong small business owner/managers are able to draw on their knowledge about the general business and market environments in dealing with various incidents. This kind of knowledge is essential when the entrepreneur wants to make a major move. For instance, before one of the interviewees started a vegetarian restaurant, he noticed changes in socio-economic trends. Traditionally most of the vegetarians in Hong Kong belonged to the older generation and they turned vegetarian for religious reasons. The educational standards are generally higher and people are more health-conscious nowadays. As a result, the younger generation have become more receptive to vegetarian food. Therefore, he decided to target non-traditional customers for vegetarian food.

Marketing and public relations knowledge are also often used both at start-up and development stages. Small business owner/managers often rely heavily on face-to-face contacts with customers to build up their market base. This kind of personal marketing is particularly common amongst the restaurateurs in our sample, who stay at work almost every night socialising with their customers. On the other hand, knowledge that must be formally acquired – such as financial, legal and IT – is often less applicable during these stages and therefore not very often found among owner/managers. This was partly due to the lack of formal business-related training in owner/managers, and partly due to the fact that the level and scale of the businesses that the owner/managers had to handle were not sophisticated enough to justify the use of such highly specialised knowledge.

With reference to the competency model that we developed above, we found that small business owner/managers in Hong Kong in fact perform their jobs with four types of competency, i.e. composite, multiple, single, and compound. In total, 624 behavioural competencies were identified from 568 critical incidents. In general, composite competencies were most often found in our study, composed of a single personality trait, a single skill and a single knowledge area (T–S–K). Some of these combinations appear more frequently than others and therefore stand out as more important. The combinations of competencies are also classified into twelve groups. Five of them are trait-based, and seven are skill/knowledge-based competencies. The term 'trait-based competencies' reflects the fact that such capabilities are mainly driven by entrepreneurial personality traits, with the support of skills and knowledge, so that the personality trait is dominant. The strategic-planning competency occurs with the highest frequency within this category. To illustrate, one of the interviewees, a fish ball manufacturer, described how he strategically gained market share:

After around a year of running the business, I had already expanded the market to the whole Hong Kong Island. Then I thought it was about time to expand to Kowloon. I had been considering the exact location in Kowloon that I should start from. I realised that there were many existing fish ball suppliers in Eastern Kowloon, which made it difficult to penetrate into the market. On the other hand, there were very few suppliers in Western Kowloon, and the existing suppliers in the Walled City were a distance away. So I decided to start from West Kowloon first. As a result, I build up the market share in Western Kowloon very quickly.

After independent assessment and joint discussion, the three researchers agreed that a strong sense of *growth orientation* was reflected in this particular incident. At the same time, the interviewee applied his *analytical skill* in the *understanding of the market*. His successful entry into the market indicated that the interviewee achieved a level of competence in this behaviour, which was initiated by his desire to grow, and accompanied his analytical skill and market knowledge. This particular incident was classified under the category of strategic competency.

On the other hand, skill/knowledge-based competencies are more skill/knowledge-dominated, with personality traits playing a supportive role when performing the tasks. Within this category, operational competency has the highest frequency of occurrence. For example, in another incident, the same fish ball manufacturer explained why he operated his production in a seemingly complicated way:

Although I could buy the fish directly from China for processing in the factory there, I decided not do so because it is difficult to control the freshness of the fish in this way. I would rather source the fish in Hong Kong, and then transport them to the factory in China for processing. Here, I have my own buyers who know my requirements well.

Clearly he drew on much of his *knowledge of purchasing and supply* and *controlling skill* in doing so. While he also seemed to be a *quality-minded* person, it was not possible for him to successfully produce the product in this particular way without a strong knowledge and skill foundation.

Tables 13.5 and 13.6 present the two sets of composite competencies which were most often found among small business owner/managers in the study.

Conclusion: what competencies should Hong Kong small business owner/managers develop?

A brief review of the literature reveals that as yet there is no definite answer to the following questions: (i) How could we arrive at a more comprehensive definition of behavioural competency of small business owner/managers, which includes the meaning of personality traits, skills and knowledge? (ii)

What method should we use to explore the job behaviour of small business owner/managers in order to identify their behaviour competency? (iii) What are the actual behaviour competencies necessary for job performance leading to small business success?

Table 13.5 Personality trait-based competencies of small business owner/managers in Hong Kong

	Competency	Occurrence (%)
1	Strategic planning	12.2
2	Relationship	9.0
3	Commitment	7.3
4	Innovativeness	5.0
5	Learning	4.9

Note
The meanings of personality trait-based competencies are as follows:
1   Strategic planning competency: the ability to apply planning skills when dealing with various functional areas with a strategic orientation.
2   Relationship competency: the ability to apply communication, human and organisational skills to maintain good relationships with other people.
3   Commitment competency: the entrepreneurial attitude of determination and consistent effort in achieving the task successfully.
4   Innovativeness competency: the entrepreneurial ability to apply innovative and marketing skills to products, product development and marketing.
5   Learning competency: the entrepreneurial ability to learn effectively.

Table 13.6 Skill-based competencies of small business owner/managers in Hong Kong

	Competency	Occurrence (%)
1	Operational	17.4
2	General planning	15.9
3	Problem-solving	7.9
4	Marketing	7.9
5	Human	5.2
6	Controlling	4.1
7	Career assessment	3.2

Note
The meanings of skill and knowledge-based competencies are as follows:
1   Operational competency: the entrepreneurial knowledge of production and operation when implementing various skills to achieve the task successfully.
2   General planning competency: the ability to apply planning skills in dealing with various functional areas.
3   Problem-solving competency: the ability to apply problem-solving skills in various functional areas.
4   Marketing competency: the ability to apply marketing skills and marketing knowledge to achieve a task effectively.
5   Human competency: the ability to apply human skills and organisational and human resources management skills to achieve tasks effectively.
6   Controlling competency: the ability to apply controlling skills in various functional areas with the objective of achieving better quality.
7   Career assessment competency: the entrepreneurial ability to assess one's own career development path critically and effectively.

To address these questions, we first attempted to develop a comprehensive conceptual framework of how behavioural competencies lead to organisational performance during the business development process. Second, we explained what is really meant by the behavioural competency of small business owner/managers by including personality traits, skills and knowledge. It is believed that the T–S–K scheme is a more effective representation of how small business owner/managers perform their business foundation and development jobs. Based on our grounded field work and the analysis of behavioural incidents, we found four major types of competency: composite, multiple, single, and compound, of which composite competencies, as expected, appear to be the most common. Third, we used a qualitative approach to explore the actual behaviours of small business owner/managers in handling various critical incidents from the start-up to the development stage. Though the critical incident method we used in this study is time-consuming and labour-intensive for the researchers, we believe this is the most appropriate method if we want to examine and identify the real behavioural competencies of small business owner/managers.

The analysis indicates that the most common sets of behavioural competency found in small business owner/managers in Hong Kong are: strategic planning, relationship, commitment, innovativeness, learning, operation knowledge, general planning, problem solving, marketing skills, human skills, controlling skills and career assessment skills. Among these, we found that the first five competencies are dominated by personality traits, while the other seven are skill or knowledge dominated. It is interesting to find these two types of competency in our study, because it does confirm that some of the successful qualities of small business owner/managers are difficult to learn if they are trait-based, while many skills or knowledge based competencies are presumably less difficult to acquire. The implications are therefore very obvious: training and development in behavioural competencies for Hong Kong small business owner/managers should be directed more towards the areas of skill- or knowledge-based competencies. It is envisaged that small business training programmes with emphasis on operation knowledge, general planning, problem solving, marketing skills, human skills, controlling skills and career assessment skills would be the most effective. However, this is not to suggest that it is impossible to develop trait-based competencies. It may be that such competencies could be enhanced through experience in the business development process.

Notes

1 The authors would like to thank the Research Grants Council of the Hong Kong Special Administrative Region for support for this project.
2 The small and medium enterprises homepage, (http://www.info.gov.hk/sme/home.htm), HKSAR.

Part IV

Employee participation and trade unions in Hong Kong

14 Government supervision of trade unions in Hong Kong

Colonial powers, patterns of enforcement, and prospects for change[1]

*Patricia Fosh, Anne Carver, Wilson W. S. Chow,
Ng Sek-Hong and Harriet Samuels*

Introduction

In 1999, Hong Kong has a unique legal framework for trade unions,
bequeathed by the previous government. This framework is a peculiar
amalgamation of nineteenth-century British law and colonial paternalism
with few rights for trade unions and many elements of regulation and
supervision. As we saw in Chapter 2, under the 'one country, two systems'
promise of the 1984 Sino-British Joint Declaration and the 1990 Basic Law,
the distinctive features of the laws governing trade union organisation and
activities are guaranteed to remain unchanged for fifty years, as is the case
with other Hong Kong laws.

However, government control of trade unions has two elements: the first
is its supervisory powers over trade unions established by the legal
framework and the second is its choice as to what extent it enforces its
supervisory powers. The legislation introduced in the colonial era gave the
Governor, the Registrar of Trade Unions (RTU) and the Commissioner of
Police extensive powers to control trade union organisation and activities.
However, the government chose, from the 1970s onwards, to use its supervisory powers benevolently and to achieve trade union compliance with the
administrative requirements by persuasion rather than coercion.

At the time of the return of Hong Kong's sovereignty to China, the
Territory's trade unions were comparatively weak and fragmented, though
they had grown in strength, unity and public role since the 1970s. This
weakness was a result of a combination of factors, such as the economic
structure, the attitudes of employers and political influence from China,
rather than due solely to the legal framework (see Chapter 16). However,
were the trade unions to undertake large-scale industrial action, or voice
extensive criticism of the Special Administrative Region's (SAR) or China's
policies, the SAR government and its Chief Executive Tung Chee-hwa could
utilise the legal powers inherited from the previous government to restrict
their activities severely without introducing any change in the legal
framework.

This chapter undertakes three tasks. First, it examines the extensive powers to regulate and supervise trade union organisation and activities inherited by the SAR government. Second, it presents an analysis on the extent of the use by the government in the colonial era of its powers to supervise trade unions from the introduction in 1948 of the first major piece of legislation to supervise trade unions to the time of the transition, utilising data derived from the Annual Reports of the RTU. Third, it considers what approach the SAR government is likely to take towards the use of its inherited and preserved powers to control trade unions, utilising the results of an interview survey of the opinions of representatives of different interest groups in Hong Kong.

The legal framework for trade union regulation and supervision in Hong Kong

Chapter 2 outlined the legal framework for trade unions in Hong Kong, including the four Ordinances controlling their organisation and activities – the Trade Union Ordinance (TUO), the Labour Relations Ordinance (LRO), the Societies Ordinance (SO), and the Public Order Ordinance (POO). LRO allows the Chief Executive power to order cooling-off periods in industrial disputes under certain conditions of concern for the welfare of Hong Kong and its people. Cross-trade trade unions may register as societies under SO. POO gives the police significant powers of control over public assemblies and requires, *inter alia*, that organisations seeking to hold public processions obtain in advance a 'letter of no objection' from the Commissioner of Police – this provision covers both trade union marches and demonstrations. The most important of these Ordinances is TUO which is the focus of the present chapter.

Trade unions in Hong Kong could lawfully exist as societies in Hong Kong from 1920 but were exposed to 'the full rigours of nineteenth-century judicial interpretations surrounding their activities': on the grounds of public policy their rulebooks were unenforceable and their funds un-protected (England and Rear 1975: 209–10). Following the disruptive 1925–6 Canton Hong Kong Strike Boycott, the government introduced the harsh Illegal Strikes and Lockouts Ordinance in 1927. Its main purpose was to control trade unions' political links, but as well as outlawing political strikes, it also forbade the control of any Hong Kong trade union by a trade union or other overseas organisation, and banned the use of union funds for political purposes outside the territory.

From the beginning of the 1930s, the Colonial Office in London pursued a policy of encouraging responsible trade unions and advised colonial governments to introduce trade union legislation (ibid.: 210). The Butters Report (1939) recommended legislation for Hong Kong along the lines of the Colonial Office's Model Trade Union Ordinance of 1941, but the Second

World War intervened before any action could be taken. The turmoil of the post-war period made it necessary for the government to revive its interest in controlling the labour movement, and the framework for trade union organisation and administration was laid down in 1948 with the Trade Unions and Trade Disputes Ordinance (TU&TDO).

The new Ordinance sought to control trade unions through registration and regulations for trade union funds – in particular trade unions were forbidden to use their funds for political purposes either within or without the Colony (TU&TUO s.22). The post of RTU was established, which was held by the Commissioner of Labour. The government's chief concern was the close involvement of the territory's trade unions with mainland politics, the growth of the communist influence in those unions organising areas of vital economic activity, and unions' infiltration by Triads (England and Rear 1975: 215).

In the mid-1950s, the 1948 Ordinance became increasingly seen as ineffectual: in particular there was a demand to introduce greater controls to prevent trade unions' maladministration and financial laxity. It also proved difficult to have one official holding both the posts of RTU and Labour Commissioner (England and Rear 1975: 211, 215).[2] Following the Houghton Report in 1951, the Trade Union Registration (Amendment) Ordinance was passed in 1961 which repealed and replaced all provisions of the 1948 Ordinance related to trade union registration and administration[3] and established a separate Registry of Trade Unions, headed by the Registrar. A novel feature, not found according to the Colonial Secretary in any other trade union legislation examined, was the power given to the RTU to enforce trade unions' rules at his discretion.[4] TU&TDO now became the Trade Union Registration Ordinance (TURO).

Further substantial amendments to the Ordinance were introduced in 1971: these clarified the details of various provisions and while, on the one hand, they gave the RTU more powers – this time to enforce more effectively the regulations for membership and office holding – on the other, they introduced a system for officers and members to appeal against RTU decisions. TURO became the Trade Unions Ordinance (TUO). The process was completed by minor amendments in 1977 and 1988, easing restrictions on trade unions in the employment of full-time executives and in the spending of funds on local elections.

The government's supervisory powers over trade unions' organisation and administration at the time of the transition are summarised in Table 14.1. This table shows TUO's scope to be both wide-ranging and detailed. Major points to note are the use of criminal sanctions for contraventions, the key role of registration, the RTU's wide powers to ensure that trade unions comply with their rules, the close scrutiny of account-keeping and the demand for a detailed Annual Return, the restrictions on recruitment and office holding, the heavy limitations on expenditure of funds and the ban on political spending, and the limitation on trade unions' affiliating with overseas organisations.

Table 14.1 Major provisions in TUO regulating trade unions' organisation and activities

Registration	A union must be registered with the RTU in order for the union to enjoy those rights necessary for it to function (ss.13, 42–44). Registration must be undertaken within 30 days of a union's establishment and the application must to be signed by at least seven voting members (s.5). The RTU has considerable powers to refuse to register a trade union and to cancel an existing trade union's registration (ss.7 and 10). It is an offence to act as an officer of an unregistered trade union (s.5(5)).
Rules	Every registered union, and every union applying for registration, shall make rules that in the opinion of the Registrar provide adequately for a list of matters specified in Sch. 2 (s.18): these cover, *inter alia,* definition of voting members, discipline procedures, conduct of AGMs and EGMs, members' participation in decision-making, payment of subscriptions, and welfare fund procedures. The Registrar must approve all rule alterations, amendments and additions. To help trade unions, the RTU issues trade unions seeking to register with a set of 'Model Rules'.
Account keeping	The treasurer of a registered union must render, *inter alia*, at least once a year a just and true account of receipts and expenditure: the union's accounts must be audited by a person approved by the RTU (s.35). Any officer or member of a registered union (or any authorised agent) can inspect the account books at such times and in such place as specified in the union's rules (s.37(1)).
Annual Return	Every registered union must furnish annually to the RTU, not more than three months after the termination of each financial year of the union, a statement of account, audited by an auditor approved by the RTU, of all expenditure and receipts and the union's assets and liabilities, together with a copy of the auditor's report (including accounts of every branch and of every undertaking operated by the union (Trade Union Registration Regulations (TURR) s.59(14)) (s.36). In addition each union must furnish the RTU on or before 31 March each year a return showing the union's membership and the names of its officers (s.36(2)). The RTU can inspect union account books at any time, entering any union premises, and he can at any time ask a registered union to give an account of union/any branch's funds for a particular period, together with a statement of its assets and liabilities (s.38). Every member, on application, is entitled to receive free of charge a copy of the union's statement of account and any member can inspect any documents related to a registered union filed with the RTU (s.36(3) & TURR s.59 para.4).
Spending on political objects	A registered union must not spend its funds on political purposes (inside or outside of Hong Kong) (s.34) and a registered union can expend its funds on contributions to a union (or similar organisation) outside Hong Kong only with the approval of the Chief Executive (s.33(1)(j)). However, a registered union may, if it fulfils certain conditions, establish an electoral fund to pay for

various expenses concerned with campaigning for the election of candidates to a District Board, the Urban or Regional council or the Legislative Council (s.33A).

Affiliation   A registered trade union is allowed to become a member of a 'relevant professional organization'[1] established in a foreign country, if authorised to do so by a secret ballot of the voting members of a trade union present at a general meeting. A registered trade union wishing to become a member of another organisation established in a foreign country must obtain the consent of the Chief Executive, as well as authorisation by a members' secret ballot as above (s.45).

Recruitment   No person can be a member of a registered union unless he is ordinarily resident in Hong Kong and is or has been engaged or employed in a trade, industry or occupation with which the union is directly concerned (s.17(1)).

Office holding   No person can be an officer of a registered union (i) unless he is ordinarily resident in Hong Kong and is or has been engaged or employed in a trade, industry or occupation with which the union is directly concerned, unless the RTU consents in writing; (ii) if he has been convicted of the offences of fraud, dishonesty, extortion or membership of a triad society within five years save with the consent of the Chief Executive in Council; (iii) if he is under 18 years of age (s.17).

Amalgamation   The RTU must approve all amalgamations and federations (ss.
and federation   24–31 and ss.53–56).

Enforcement   Contraventions of TUO are criminal offences and punishable by fines of HK$2,000 for the trade union and by fines of HK$2,000 and up to six months' imprisonment for individuals.

Note
1 'Relevant professional organizations' are defined as those with the objectives of promoting the interests of persons engaged or employed an a trade, industry or occupation with which the trade union is directly concerned.

The government's use of its supervisory powers in the colonial era

The government's use of its wide legal powers to regulate and intervene in trade union internal affairs from the passage of TU&TDO in 1948 to the time of the transition is summarised in Tables 14.2 and 14.3. Table 14.2 shows that the government was quick to prosecute trade unions for contraventions of TU&TDO/TURO in the period from the mid-1950s to 1970 and, additionally, the RTU used his power to deregister a significant number of trade unions. Further, the Registry resorted to written notices for trade unions contravening their registered rules.

From 1970 onwards, however, there was a marked change in approach, and the government and the RTU largely refrained from prosecuting and

Table 14.2 RTU's deregistrations of, prosecutions of, and warnings to trade unions for contravening TUO and warnings to trade unions for not complying with their own rules 1948/49 to 1996[1]

	Total no. of TUs on RTU's Register	No. of TUs deregistered for contravention of TUO	No. of TUs and TU officials prosecuted for contravening TUO[2]	No. of TUs and TU officials warned for contravening TUO[3]	No. of TUs warned for contravening their registered rules by written notice[4]	No. of TUs warned for contravening their registered rules by warning letter
1948/49[5]	178	0	0	2	NA	0
1949/50	261	0	0	0	NA	0
1950/51	276	0	0	0	NA	0
1951/52	288	0	0	0	NA	0
1952/53	304	0	0	0	NA	0
1953/54	299	0	0	0	NA	0
1954/55	300	0	0	0	NA	0
1955/56	301	0	34 (34+0)	2	NA	1
1956/57	306	1	25 (25+0)	0	NA	1
1957/58	309	2	16 (14+2)	0	NA	0
1958/59	315	1	38 (23+15)	1	NA	1
1959/60	316	1	13 (3+10)	7	NA	2
1960/61	315	0	20 (1+19)	0	NA	21
1961/62	315	3[6]	12 (4+8)	0	0	5
1962/63	316	0	0	0	36	0
1963/64	313	2	1 (1+0)	At least 3	41	0
1964/65	311	0	5 (5+0)	1	58	Some
1965/66	312	4	13 (5+8)	Some	43	0
1966/67	308	0	2 (2+0)	0	62	0
1967/68	312	1	0	Some	29	0
1968/69	320	1	0	0	22	0
1969/70	321	1	30 (7+23)	7	23	0
1970/71–1974/75[7]	339 (mean pa)	0	0	At least 26 (mean pa)	11 (mean pa)	21 (mean pa)
1975/76–1979/80	379 (mean pa)	0	0	58 (mean pa)	2 (mean pa)	39 (mean pa)
1980/81–1984/85	428 (mean pa)	1 (mean pa)	0	94 (mean pa)	5 (mean pa)	40 (mean pa)
1985–89	459 (mean pa)	3 (mean pa)	0	70 (mean pa)	2 (mean pa)	32 (mean pa)
1990–94	521 (mean pa)	0	0	100 (mean pa)	0	34 (mean pa)
1995–96	571 (mean pa)	0	0	86 (mean pa)	0 (mean pa)	36 (mean pa)

Notes

1   There were no major revisions of TUO after 1961 and the use of the RTU's powers was more consistent after 1970. This allowed the authors to average the statistics in the Annual Reports for five year periods after 1970.

2   The first figure in brackets refers to prosecution of trade unions and the second to prosecution of trade union officials. The first prosecution for contravening TUO was brought in 1955/56.

3 Warnings to trade unions for contravening TUO were sometimes by written notices (which have legal status) but more frequently by warning letters (such warnings did not have legal status). Warnings issued to trade unions were first reported in tabular form in 1975/76. The figures in the column prior to that date are based on textual analysis by the authors. In these earlier reports, sometimes the terms 'reminded' or 'instructed' are used instead of warning but it is clear from the context that the RTU was warning the union.

4 In 1961 TU&TDO was considerably revised and retitled TURO. In s.52 of TUO the RTU was given extensive powers to seek observance by trade unions and officers of the more important rules of a trade union. However, letters advising trade unions to comply with their rules were sent before this date.

5 Model Rules were first issued in this year. Note that information on contraventions of trade unions' own rules was not presented in tabular form in the RTU's Annual Reports in the earlier years and that the data in this table has been derived from textual analysis. Sometimes the reports indicate that RTU in his letters to trade unions 'instructed' or 'strongly advised' rather than 'warned' trade unions to comply with their rules. Where these other words have been used, they have been counted as warnings.

6 The RTU suggested that one of the entries for 1986 was a mistake and that the trade union concerned should have been classified as a voluntary deregistration.

7 Warnings for contravention of trade unions' own rules were first presented in tabular form in the RTU's Annual Reports in 1975/76.

deregistering trade unions. The Registry adopted a benevolent approach to ensuring trade unions' compliance with TUO. The reasons for the change seem to be linked to the 1967 disturbances. Up to 1967, the Colonial Office showed little concern with Hong Kong's internal affairs, being much too busy with the rest of the colonial empire and seeing Hong Kong as a 'shining example' that should be left alone 'to get on with it'.[5] This complacency was shattered by the riots (Miners 1995: 217–18): the Labour government in the UK became sensitised to the dangers of industrial conflict and came under pressure to improve conditions for Hong Kong workers (England and Rear 1981: 20–1, 319–1). Considerable improvements were introduced to protect workers from the harsh logic of *laissez-faire*,[6] the Cinderella Labour Department was doubled in size, labour advisors were brought out from the UK and, most importantly, Labour Tribunals were introduced in 1973 (Labour Tribunal Ordinance)[7] and a framework for the settlement of disputes in 1975 (LRO). These improvements were part of a general campaign on the part of the Hong Kong government to legitimise its rule by winning the hearts and minds of the Hong Kong people.

Table 14.2 shows that, in the 1970s and 1980s and in the run-up to the transition, the RTU substituted written notices and warning letters for prosecution and deregistration when trade unions contravened TUO,[8] and he substituted warning letters for written notices when trade unions contravened their registered rules. This persuasive approach to ensuring compliance with TUO's provisions was particularly marked after 1980. Thus Table 14.3 shows that the RTU gave permission for significant numbers of trade unions to submit their annual accounts late and that Registry officers attended a considerable number of trade union functions. The RTU, however, did refuse a request for federation that suggests some strictness in applying this provision.[9] Thus in 1972/73 an application by the Federation of Hong Kong Civil Servants' Association for registration was refused on the ground, *inter alia*, that members of nine of the eleven component trade unions involved were not engaged in the same industry or occupation.

The attention of the RTU in his supervision of trade union activities, both in the earlier period of more harsh enforcement of TUO and the later more persuasive approach, appears to have been sharply focused on financial administration. Deregistrations, prosecutions and warnings were most frequent for late Annual Returns (eight deregistrations, 110 prosecutions and 455 warnings) and late transmission of accounts (four deregistrations, sixty-four prosecutions and at least 504 warnings).[10] There was also an emphasis on conforming to the requirements for rule changes to be submitted to the RTU for approval (two prosecutions and 344 warnings) and for the exhibition of the list of officers in the trade union's registered office (266 warnings). There were few indications of serious charges having been brought against trade unions by the government. There was only one political charge – a warning for a trade union with an affiliation to a Taiwanese organisation. The most serious financial and administrative charges since 1948 were a trade union certificate being obtained by fraud (one deregistration), a trade union permitting outsiders to operate a fraudulent benefit scheme under its name (one deregistration), trade union officers signing statutory forms containing false statements (or signing statutory forms recklessly) (fourteen warnings), trade unions furnishing false information to RTU (seven warnings), trade union officers failing to render to members just and true accounts (nine warnings), trade union officers using funds improperly and being financially lax (at least four warnings[11]) and improper use of funds[12] (one prosecution and four warnings).

Similarly, with respect to the government's enforcement of trade unions' registered rules, the emphasis was on financial and administrative detail. The most common cause of reprimands from the RTU by far was for holding excessive cash in hand (675 written notices and warning letters).[13] The second most frequent was failure to hold general meetings constitutionally and failure to give sufficient notice for general meetings (219 written notices and warnings).

Considering the period overall since 1948, there are indications that, while the government was willing in the earlier part to deregister trade unions and to prosecute them for infringing TUO's provisions, nevertheless the government did demonstrate a significant acceptance of the trade unions' role and a wish to help them comply with the legislation rather than punish them for failure. Thus Table 14.3 shows that the Governor never refused a trade union application for affiliation with an organisation outside of Hong Kong;[14] that the RTU or the Governor-in-Council on a considerable number of occasions gave permission to a trade union officer to hold his/her position though proscribed from doing so on various grounds (see Table 14.1);[15] and that the Registry provided a large number of courses for trade union officers both on

Table 14.3 Governor's consent to TU affiliation outside Hong Kong, late submissions of accounts granted by RTU, RTU's consent for trade union officers to hold posts, number of social events attended by trade union officers and number of trade union officers attending courses organised by RTU 1948/49 to 1996[1]

	No. of times Governor gave consent to a TU to affiliate with an organisation outside Hong Kong out of number of applications made	No. of late submissions of TU accounts granted by RTU	No. of times RTU or Governor in Council gave consent to a TU officer to hold his post though officer was in a category proscribed from doing so[2]	No. of TU social functions attended by Registry officers	No. of TU officers attending courses organised by RTU
1948/49	NR[3]	NR	7	NR	NR
1949/50	NR	NR	0	NR	NR
1950/51	NR	NR	0	NR	NR
1951/52	NR	NR	0	NR	At least 20 classes held
1952/53	NR	NR	0	NR	Some classes held
1953/54	NR	NR	0	NR	Well over 500
1954/55	NR	NR	0	NR	Over 600
1955/56	NR	NR	0	NR	197
1956/57	1 out of 1	NR	0	NR	About 90
1957/58	2 out of 2	NR	4	NR	About 78
1958/59	2 out of 2	1	2	NR	About 85
1959/60	1 out of 1	NR	0	NR	About 137
1960/61	1 out of 1	NR	0	NR	About 136
1961/62	No applications	NR	0	NR	NR
1962/63	9 out of 9	NR	12	NR	About 264
1963/64	2 out of 2	NR	16	NR	About 134
1964/65	4 out of 4	NR	11	NR	About 124
1965/66	No applications	NR	11	NR	About 33
1966/67	No applications	NR	0	NR	NR
1967/68	No applications	NR	1	NR	NR
1968/69	1 out of 1	NR	0	NR	NR
1969/70	1 out of 1	NR	8	NR	NR
1970/71– 1974/75	8 out of 8 in 5 years	NR	9 (mean *pa*)	NR	NR
1975/76– 1979/80	9 out of 9 in 5 years	NR	3 (mean pa)	NR	NR
1980/81– 1984/85	7 out of 7 in 5 years	26 (mean pa)	5 (mean pa)	15 (mean pa)	186 (mean pa)[4]
1985–89	4 out of 4 in 5 years	19 (mean pa)	5 (mean pa)	24 (mean pa)	288 (mean pa)
1990–94	13 out of 13 in 5 years	22 (mean X pa)	1 (mean pa)	18 (mean pa)	328 (mean pa)
1995–96	2 out of 2 in 2 years	16 (mean pa)	2 (mean pa)	14 (mean pa)	339 (mean pa)

Notes
1 As note 1 in Table 14.2.
2 Note in addition to the prohibitions on office-holding given in Table 14.1 that, until the repeal of the provision in 1971, a person could not hold office if he was an officer of another registered TU unless the RTU consented in writing.
3 NR stands for no record in the Annual Report.
4 Attendance by trade union officers was recorded in the Annual Reports for 1983/84 and 1984/85 only.

the principles of trade unionism and the provisions of TUO, and on practical aspects such as bookkeeping and auditing.[16]

The approach of the Labour Department just before the transition was summarised by two leading officers:[17]

> Punishment of trade unions does not help harmonious industrial relations and that is why the Labour Department chooses the helpful approach towards trade unions.

> We treat trade unions well and make allowances. Hong Kong trade unions are very small. Officers contravene the Trade Union Ordinance mostly due to ignorance. They commit only minor offences so the Registry sees it as its job to help them keep to the Ordinance.

This raises the question of why the government retained these legal controls. While, on the one hand, they may be just an anachronism, on the other hand, there was a long-standing fear of events in China impacting on, and bringing disorder, to Hong Kong. The government may have intentionally retained these controls as a safeguard against trade union unrest (see Chapter 1).

The future for Hong Kong trade unions' legal framework

This leads us inevitably to the question of what the SAR government will do. Will it abolish the legal controls as anachronisms? Will it maintain the present, 'successful' controls? Or will it institute tighter controls in fear of the actions of independent and radical trade union leaders? To answer this question we turn to the results of a survey undertaken by the authors of the views of representatives of different groups of Hong Kong-belongers, interviewed in 1997 and 1998, just before or after the transition.[18] These fifty-two respondents comprised representatives from the Labour Department (five),[19] the leaders of different groups of trade unions – including the traditionally Beijing-oriented Federation of Trade Unions (FTU) (four), the traditionally Taiwan-oriented Trade Union Congress (TUC) (three), the independent and radical Confederation of Trade Unions (CTU) (four), the independent but more conservative Federation of Labour Unions (FLU) (three), and other non-affiliated civil service and professional trade unions (four), representatives of employers' associations and employers from firms with a significant trade union presence (eighteen), judges and barristers (six), representatives of professional and community groups with seats in the Legislative Council (LegCo) (three), and representatives of human rights groups) (two).[20]

The respondents were asked for their opinions on whether the incoming SAR government would chose to alter significantly the trade unions' legal framework, to maintain the inherited framework but to change the pattern of enforcement, or to maintain both the current framework and pattern of enforcement. The major part of the respondents (71 per cent) believed that the SAR government would preserve both the inherited legal framework and the present pattern of enforcement: this view is referred to as 'things will stay the same'. However, a quarter (27 per cent) believed that the SAR government would keep the inherited legal framework intact but would enforce this more vigorously after the transition than the previous government had since the 1970s: this view is referred to as 'tougher treatment for trade unions'. On the other hand, only one respondent (a representative of an employer's organisation with rather untypical views) thought the SAR government would seek to change the present legal framework for trade unions in Hong Kong.

Those who believed that the current pattern of enforcement would continue consisted of all of the Labour Department officials, all of the FTU- and FLU-affiliated officials, the greater part of the employers (83 per cent) and all of the judiciary. Additionally, one of the representatives of the community and professional groups, one of the civil service and professional trade union officials and one CTU-affiliated trade union official were in this group. Those respondents who believed that the SAR government would enforce the trade unions' legal framework more vigorously consisted of all the TUC-affiliated trade union officials, and all but one of CTU-affiliated trade union officials, both representatives of human rights groups, together with three of the civil service and professional trade union officials. Also included was one representative of community and professional groups in LegCo and two employers.

The thirty-seven respondents holding the first view 'that things will stay the same' considered that the SAR government would be concerned to protect Hong Kong's economic prosperity and stability and, consequently, would not wish to change a successful formula: it would continue the previous government's benevolent approach towards trade unions. Most of these respondents held the view that the SAR government was in favour of trade unions and saw them as responsible organisations who would work with other groups to keep Hong Kong's economic success intact. This view is illustrated in the quotes[21] below from an employer and a FLU official:

Why should the government change a successful system? The SAR government understands the present system and will not change it.

Hong Kong should be proud of its achievements in the labour area in these two decades. Therefore the SAR government may not feel obliged to change anything. Trade unions have enjoyed considerable latitude and breathing space . . . Organized labour has been able to challenge or deal with the employers effectively. Labour law reforms are not of pressing urgency on the legislative agenda.

We should note however, that a small subgroup of seven respondents within this group had a less favourable view of the new SAR government. While the respondents in this subgroup felt that the SAR government would exercise its powers under the existing provisions of TUO in the same way as the previous government had done, they were not necessarily optimistic about the future for trade unions in Hong Kong. They simply felt that new Chief Executive would not bother to introduce changes for Hong Kong's small and fragmented trade unions as he would have far bigger problems to deal with, such as health, housing and the elderly. This less optimistic view is illustrated in the following quote from an employer: 'Trade unions are not a major concern for anyone in Hong Kong. They are not a topic of concern for the SAR government. The SAR government is concerned with immigration, housing and hospitals.'

The fourteen respondents with the second view – that is to say those who believed that greater use would be made of the existing legal powers to control trade unions – considered that the SAR government would prove to be much more business-oriented than the previous government and would be quick to control any trade union disorder, or potential disorder, likely to affect Hong Kong industry. These respondents predicted that the SAR government would not tolerate any criticism of its policies, or of China, and that it would clamp down on trade unions' protest activities. The SAR government would use its supervisory powers, such as inspection of trade union accounts, to collect detailed information on trade union activities. There would be less latitude for those trade unions late with their accounts. The RTU would not exercise his permitted discretion to allow those not engaged in the same industry, trade or occupation as the trade union concerned to become trade union officers, and the Chief Executive would subject trade unions wishing to affiliate with foreign 'non relevant professional organisations' to close political scrutiny. The illustrative quotes below are from a CTU official and a representative of a human rights organisation:

> China would like to rule Hong Kong in a way as appealing to employers and capitalists as possible. The major fear of employers and capitalists are trade unions. Trade unions for these are bad news.

> The SAR government will enforce the Ordinances more strongly because they want to make sure that all the organizations in Hong Kong are not critical of the new government.

An important point to note is that the respondents in the second group considered that the provisions of TUO would be enforced more vigorously against certain trade unions rather then others. A particular target of the SAR government was thought to be the CTU and its affiliates, noted campaigners for civil liberties. In contrast, the traditionally Beijing-oriented FTU and its affiliates would be in favour with the SAR government and would not be subject to such increased scrutiny. The respondents also considered that the SAR government might invoke POO's provisions more frequently in order to control trade union public activities such as demonstrations and marches.

The following quote from a CTU officer demonstrate this group's views of the future pattern of enforcement of the provisions of TUO and POO:

> No, the new government will not change the trade unions' legal framework. Hong Kong has the worst system in the world, why change it? Yes, there will be greater enforcement of the Trade Union Ordinance. There will be a bit more supervision of accounts and international affiliations ... Permission [for international affiliations] will depend on which trade union is asking. There will be political scrutiny of the outside organisation. The Public Order Ordinance will be enforced much more vigorously for processions and meetings and these will be made more difficult. Possibly there will be more prosecutions and less just warning of those contravening.

The following quote from a representative of a human rights organisation demonstrates these respondents' expectations of discrimination against certain trade unions:

> The SAR government will use it [TUO] to discriminate against those trade unions which it is not happy with. These trade unions are the ones not controlled by the SAR government or by employers, or refuse to be controlled such as the CTU ... The SAR government will probably use it [POO] on some trade unions, not on those who support Beijing policies though but against those trade unions who do not support the SAR and Beijing.

The two groups of respondents in the survey represented groups with different relationships to administrative power at the time of the transition. Those respondents with the 'things will stay the same' view either expected to be part of the new administration or had developed close links with it. Thus representatives of the judiciary and the Labour Department in the survey were expecting to continue to hold office after the transition. The FTU trade unions were Beijing-oriented in colonial times and the FLU trade unions were a more moderate grouping than the CTU trade unions. Employers were more heavily represented in the Provisional LegCo than in Patten's reformed LegCo elected in 1995, and they were anticipating a fruitful collaboration with the incoming HKSAR government. Those believing that the 'climate will get tougher for trade unions' tended to be in conflict with the new administration. The CTU is an important pressure group for the extension of democracy and trade union freedom in Hong Kong and the TUC is traditionally linked with Taiwan. The human rights and religious groups, together with the community groups represented in the survey, also have a strong commitment to democracy and trade union autonomy that puts them in conflict with the incoming HKSAR government.

Chapter 2 analysed the changes in the trade unions' legal framework introduced both by the previous government and by the pro-labour caucus in LegCo in the run-up to the transition, and the reversal of most of these changes by the incoming SAR government. The respondents were inter-viewed in 1997 when many of these changes were taking place. The conclusion drawn in Chapter 2 was that, after the changes and counter-changes had taken place, the legal framework for trade unions in Hong Kong had more or less returned to its position at the time of the Joint Declaration in 1984. Thus the view of all but one of the respondents that the SAR government would not introduce significant change to the legal framework for trade unions was vindicated at the time of writing in December 1998. So far, there are no indications that the SAR government is enforcing TUO more vigorously than the government had done in the colonial era. However, some interviewees in the minority group, those that believed that there would be 'tougher treatment for trade unions', reported that police supervision and observation of trade union demonstrations and marches was much closer than before the transition.[22]

Conclusion: differing views for the trade unions' future

In post-transition Hong Kong, the legal framework for trade unions is an odd combination of British law of the *laissez-faire* era and colonial paternalistic control: this framework is guaranteed to remain unchanged for fifty years from the date of the transition by the 1984 Joint Declaration. The legal framework gives wide powers of administrative control over trade union organisation and activities. Following its crisis of legitimacy triggered by the 1967 disturbances, and also reflecting the increasingly settled, educated and demanding nature of the Hong Kong-belongers, the previous government chose to administer trade union controls benevolently, seeking compliance through persuasion and help rather than through coercion.

The success of the Democratic Party in the elections for the first LegCo in the SAR, as described in Chapter 2, suggests that the SAR government has its own crisis of legitimacy. Its legitimacy has been further brought into question by the sharp downturn in the Hong Kong economy, accompanied by wage cuts, job losses and increasing unemployment. This uncertainty may lead the SAR government to use a light hand in administering the legal controls on trade union organisation and activity following the colonial pattern: the touch may be light, in particular, given the success of independent trade unions leaders in joining their pro-China FTU colleagues in the first SAR LegCo.

The majority group in the survey, those who are closely linked with the incoming SAR government, expect the administration to continue the previous government's pattern of benevolence towards trade unions. In contrast, the minority group, those who are in a potential position of conflict with the incoming SAR, do not share this optimism and expect the new administration to crack down on criticism from independent and radical groupings. The SAR government may be tempted to do this. But in a society where the enfranchisement of its members is uncertain and the press is considered to be increasingly self-censoring,[23] it is important that groups not part of the elite retain the right to be critical of the government and to act as a check and balance against any arbitrary exercise of power.

Notes

1 We thank the ESRC, the British Academy, the Hang Seng Bank Jubilee Foundation and Cathay Pacific for funding this project and the Hong Kong Labour Department for assistance with preparing Tables 14.2 and 14.3. We are also grateful for help from officers and library staff of the Labour Department, Andrew Byrnes and Johannes Chan of the Law Department, Hong Kong University and all the respondents in our interview survey for their co-operation and help.

2 According to England and Rear (1975: 215) it had been found embarrassing that the same person was responsible for advising and educating trade unions in the principles of responsible trade unionism was also responsible for enforcing TUO.

3 The remaining provisions were concerned with the reference of disputes to arbitration and the 1948 Ordinance became the Trade Disputes Ordinance, which was repealed by LRO in 1975.

4 LegCo. Proc. 1961: 298.

5 Lord Rhodes, House of Lords Debate, 9 November 1967, col. 564 quoted in Miners (1975: 207).

6 There were 150 pieces of legislation of concern to the Labour Department enacted between 1968 and 1979 (England and Rear 1981: 319–20).

7 This was intended to deal, in particular, with employers' shortcomings in terms of arrears of wages, wages in lieu of notice, severance pay and so forth (England and Rear 1981: 320).

8 It is not clear from the text of the Annual Reports when the RTU sent written notices and when warning letters to trade unions in contravention of TUO's provisions. Warning letters appeared to be more frequently utilised than written notices.

9 Until 29 June 1997, TUO s.55 specified that registered trade union federations could consist only of component trade unions whose members were engaged or employed in the same trade, industry or occupation (see Chapter 2).

10 Note that phrases such as 'wilful' and 'after notice' were normally used by the RTU in his reports to describe trade union behaviour that led to trade union deregistration.

11 'At least' is used to indicate that the Annual Report(s) concerned referred to 'some' offences being committed rather than giving a precise figure.

12 Mainly transfer of welfare funds for use as general funds.

13 A limit on cash in hand is one of the RTU's Model Rules and a survey of the rulebooks of the thirty largest trade unions in Hong Kong in 1997 showed that these trade unions had incorporated this Model Rule into their own rulebooks.

14 The number of trade unions with permission to affiliate with organisations overseas was thirty-seven at the end of 1996 (information from Labour Department).

15 It was not possible to determine from the Annual Reports how often the RTU/Governor in Council refused such requests but the Labour Department was of the opinion that these instances were rare.
16 The Labour Department kept no records of trade union courses it held between 1955/56 and 1981 but officials were of the opinion that such courses continued to be held.
17 See the authors' interview survey discussed below, pp. 248–252.
18 Further interviews were conducted in January 1998 including officials from the CTU and FTU and an employer representative.
19 This category includes a spokesperson from the Police Commission who commented on those aspects of POO of relevance to trade union activities.
20 This category included a religious group with an interest in industrial relations.
21 On account of political sensitivities in Hong Kong at the time of the transition, the interviews were not tape-recorded. Instead, the interviewers recorded respondents' answers for key questions in shorthand.
22 Early 1998 interview material.
23 *SCMP Year-End Review*, 12 January 1997: 13.

15 Hong Kong trade unions
In search of a role[1]

Ed Snape and Andy W. Chan

Introduction

The aim of this chapter is to evaluate the role of Hong Kong trade unions during the late 1990s. Following a brief outline of the recent development of trade union functions, we present survey evidence on union functions as seen by leaders of individual trade unions. We then survey recent trends in industrial conflict and, in particular, explore the role played by trade unions in labour disputes. This analysis highlights some of the difficulties facing Hong Kong unions in the effective representation of their members' job-based interests. We conclude with a discussion of the likely implications of our analysis for the future of trade unions in the Hong Kong Special Administrative Region (SAR).

Trade union functions in Hong Kong

We can identify three broad functions typically played by trade unions. First, 'job-based unionism' involves representing the interests of workers in their employment relationship, for example through consultation or negotiation with employers and providing assistance or advice on employment rights. Second, 'services unionism' involves the provision of direct services, cash benefits and retail discounts to members. Finally, 'political unionism' involves political activity, such as lobbying government on members' interests and labour rights. These are not mutually exclusive trade union types. Rather, trade unions emphasise these functions to varying degrees.

In terms of job-based unionism, Hong Kong trade unions have had limited influence in most workplaces, particularly in the private sector (Levin and Chiu 1993). A recent Institute of Human Resource Management survey found that the percentage of private-sector companies determining pay levels through negotiation with trade unions or staff associations was 3.3 per cent in the case of manual workers or technicians, 2.4 per cent for clerical and supervisory workers and 1.9 per cent for managerial and professional staff (Institute of Human Resource Management 1995). Trade union weakness has been attributed to the small size of establishments in manufacturing and private-sector services, to an alleged cultural resistance amongst Hong Kong workers towards joining trade unions and openly challenging their employer (Levin and Chiu 1994: 155), and to employer hostility towards unions (Levin and Ng 1995: 131). Trade unions are more significant in the civil and public services, although the relationship with management tends to be joint consultation rather than collective bargaining, whilst in the private sector even joint consultation is rare (see Chapter 16).

In view of their limited effectiveness in the job-based functions, Hong Kong trade unions have traditionally emphasised alternative appeals to potential members, in particular the direct provision of welfare benefits and other services. The Hong Kong Federation of Trade Unions (FTU) has been particularly active in this field, as have some of the larger public-service trade unions. In addition, the political functions of trade unions have been significant. Traditionally, membership of an FTU, or a Hong Kong and Kowloon Trades Union Council (TUC) union, was an expression of political loyalty to the Chinese Communist Party, or to the Kuomintang. The political complexion of these trade unions traditionally had as much to do with historic political struggles on the Chinese mainland as with representing the immediate interests of Hong Kong workers.

In recent years there has been an increase in the political activity of trade unions, focusing this time on Hong Kong issues. The democratic reforms of the late 1980s and early 1990s led to the emergence of a pro-labour voice on the Legislative Council (LegCo). Whilst the TUC has kept a low profile, others have been more active. Both the FTU and the pro-democracy Hong Kong Confederation of Trade Unions (CTU) have become involved in electoral politics and also in lobbying legislators and the government, overshadowing the long-established consultative devices such as the Labour Advisory Board. Of course, such developments were called into question by the transfer of sovereignty. The labour and pro-democracy forces face some hostility from the new SAR government. However, it is by no means certain that the growth in trade union membership of recent years will be reversed. The FTU has consolidated and strengthened its organisation and the CTU, whilst vulnerable under the SAR, is determined to continue its work (Snape and Chan 1997).

Whilst it is likely that the above pattern of union activity owes much to the opportunities facing trade unions, several commentators have suggested that the trade unions themselves have at times contributed to their own weakness at the workplace by deliberately following a pacifist line in labour disputes and focusing on the provision of services and political representation (England 1989: 116–17; Turner *et al.* 1991: 80–3; Levin and Chiu 1993: 202–3). Indeed, some suggest that the past reluctance of FTU and TUC trade unions to pursue effective representation may have been more important than workers' attitudes to collective organisation in explaining union weakness (Turner *et al.* 1980, 1991; Chiu and Levin 1996: 33). This suggests that whether or not trade unions become more assertive in workplace disputes is likely to be a key factor shaping their future role. In this context, it seems appropriate to reassess the role of trade unions and to ask the question: how do union leaders see the role of their trade unions and how do they see them developing? We attempt to shed some light on this in the following section.

Hong Kong trade unions: some survey evidence

In February 1996 we conducted a survey of leaders of individual trade unions, to try to identify what trade unions were doing, both directly and through their federations, and to explore any expected changes over the next three years. Questionnaires were mailed to the senior official (e.g. chairman, president, etc.) of each union registered with the Registrar of Trade Unions as at the beginning of 1996, a total of 522 trade unions. Completed questionnaires were received from 141 trade unions, a response rate of 27 per cent. The nature of the respondents is described in the Appendix (p. 269).

According to our respondents, the job-based function of representing workers *vis-à-vis* their employer was the area where trade unions were most active (Table 15.1). Collective negotiation and consultation with employers had the highest rating of all. Respondents reported that assisting individual workers with claims at the Labour Department or Labour Tribunal was the least significant activity in this category, reflecting the relative infrequency of such claims in most sectors. Organising social, cultural or leisure activities was the most important services function, whilst the payment of cash benefits was the least. This latter finding is not surprising, given that the percentage of total union revenues paid out as benefits has declined over the years, as state welfare provision has increasingly filled this traditional union role.[2] Instead, unions have tended to emphasise discount purchase deals, and training and education services. Compared to job-based and services functions, respondents rated their organisations as rather less active on political functions. However, most recognised that they had at least some role here, especially in lobbying the government on labour laws and policies.

Comparing trade unions in the community, social and public services with all other (mainly private-sector) trade unions (Table 15.2), the latter claim to be more active in most areas. The exceptions were negotiating and consulting with employers, representing individual workers to employers, offering discount purchase deals and organising social and cultural activities for members, where there was no difference between the two groups of trade unions at the conventional 5 per cent significance level, although the latter two were significantly different at the 10 per cent level.[3] The community, social and public services trade unions cite negotiating and consulting with employers, representing individual workers to employers, and advising workers on their employment rights as their three areas of greatest activity. In contrast, the other trade unions cite advising workers on their employment rights, and representing workers in claims and in disputes as

Table 15.1 'Currently, how active is your union, either independently or through its affiliated federations, in each of the following areas?' (percentage of valid responses)

Function:	Very active		Slightly active		Not at all active	Unsure
Job-based functions						
Negotiating or consulting with employers on terms and conditions on behalf of groups of workers	27	25	17	20	10	2
Representing groups of workers in labour disputes	22	13	22	22	15	5
Representing individual workers to employers	20	21	30	18	12	0
Assisting individual workers in claims at the Labour Department/ Tribunal	15	10	17	13	38	7
Advising individual workers on their employment rights	23	24	26	16	11	0
Services functions						
Payment of cash benefits directly to members	2	6	19	12	53	8
Offering discount purchase deals to members	10	19	30	13	28	1
Organising or providing social, cultural or leisure activities for members	12	19	40	19	10	0
Providing training and education services for members	10	13	24	27	26	1
Political functions						
Lobbying the Hong Kong Government on changes in labour laws and policies	18	10	19	21	30	2
Lobbying the Hong Kong Government on changes in social policies	8	14	18	23	36	2
Lobbying the Preliminary Working Committee/ Preparatory Committee of the SAR	3	11	10	16	52	8
Campaigning in elections to public bodies	13	11	19	13	43	2
Providing support for particular politicians or political parties	7	10	22	16	44	2

Source: Authors' HK trade union survey, 1996 (N=141).

their three main activities, with negotiating and consulting with employers, and representing individual workers to employers ranked fifth and seventh

Table 15.2 Trade union activity by sector (percentage of valid responses)

Function	Community, social and public services unions. (N=87)		All other unions (N=54)		Significance level for difference between the two means*
	Mean	Rank	Mean	Rank	
Job-based functions					
Negotiating or consulting with employers on terms and conditions on behalf of groups of workers	3.43	1	3.38	5	.840
Representing groups of workers in labour disputes	2.77	5	3.48	2	.005
Representing individual workers to employers	3.15	2	3.27	7	.584
Assisting individual workers in claims at the Labour Department/ Tribunal	1.18	12	3.48	2	.000
Advising individual workers on their employment rights	3.13	3	3.63	1	.028
Services functions					
Payment of cash benefits directly to members	1.49	13	2.39	13	.000
Offering discount purchase deals to members	2.53	6	3.00	10	.054
Organising or providing social, cultural or leisure activities for members	2.92	4	3.29	6	.058
Providing training and education services for members	2.27	7	3.03	9	.001
Political functions					
Lobbying the Hong Kong Government on changes in labour laws and policies	2.18	8	3.39	4	.000
Lobbying the Hong Kong Government on changes in social policies	2.13	9	2.71	12	.013
Campaigning in elections to public bodies.	1.93	10	3.08	8	.000
Providing support for particular politicians or political parties	1.82	11	2.78	11	.000

Source: Authors' HK trade union survey, 1996 (N=141).
Notes: Mean is mean score (1 is 'Not at all active' to 5 is 'Very active'); rank is the rank order amongst the functions.
* Independent samples t-test.

respectively (Table 15.2). It may be that private-sector trade unions have come to terms with employers' refusal to recognise them by performing a wider range of functions. However, even here the job-based functions are still seen as the main activity of the union.

Looking at the changes anticipated by respondents over the following three years, the basic pattern was that trade unions were expecting to place more emphasis on areas where they are already most active. The job-based functions in particular emerge as ones which many respondents expected to become more important. Services functions are also expected to become more important, with the exception of the provision of cash benefits. Amongst the political functions, most respondents did not expect their trade unions to become less active in lobbying the government. In this respect, trade unions were expecting to continue to show an interest in the pursuit of their members' interests in the political arena. However, respondents were less clear about their future role in campaigning in elections and in providing support for politicians and political parties; private sector trade unions envisaged some increase in such activities, whereas those in the community, social and public services anticipated being less active here.

Further analysis revealed several differences in the functions performed by trade unions.[4] FTU trade unions tended to place more emphasis on services than did other trade unions, reflecting a long-term strategy to develop such services on the part of the federation. They also rated themselves more highly than non-affiliated trade unions on the job-based and political functions. Thus, in spite of the association of the FTU with services, FTU trade unions show a broader concern and are not simply services-based trade unions, as their rivals have sometimes suggested.

In comparison, CTU-affiliated trade unions rated themselves more highly on job-based functions than did independent trade unions, but less than FTU trade unions on services. This may reflect the ideology and beliefs of CTU leaders, who have shown strong concern for labour rights and interests, rather than for the traditional union services and benefits (Snape and Chan 1997). TUC trade unions also rated themselves lower than did FTU trade unions on services. Independent trade unions in general appeared to be less active than FTU and CTU trade unions across a range of functions. Of course, some of the larger independent trade unions are very active, but this group includes many quite small trade unions with limited resources and this may explain their relative lack of activity.

Trade union subscriptions

The functions performed by trade unions are to some extent reflected in their finances and, in particular, in the level of membership subscriptions. Hong Kong trade unions have a tradition of very low subscriptions and their dependence on income from members is limited, with much of their income coming from trading and other activities.[5] Some union leaders have been

Table 15.3 Trade union subscriptions by federation

Union affiliation	Mean annual subscription rate, $
1 Unaffiliated	94.71
2 CTU	99.65
3 FTU	59.00
4 TUC	43.09
5 Other federations*	347.07

Source: HK trade union survey, 1996 (N=141).
Note: *The high mean for 'Other federations' is due to very high subscription rates for two trade unions in particular. When these two are excluded, 'Other federations' have a mean of $81.46.

critical of this tradition, claiming that low subscriptions and the strong emphasis on direct services fosters inter-union competition, with multiple union membership and 'shopping around' by members. Such competition may thus limit the ability of trade unions to improve their resource base through higher subscriptions. In the longer term, the argument goes, this limits the activities and vitality of the union movement.

Table 15.3 shows that there were differences in average subscriptions according to federation. Whilst the high 'Other federations' figure is inflated by a small number of trade unions with exceptionally high subscriptions, the CTU trade unions in our survey had significantly higher subscriptions levels than either FTU or TUC trade unions. In our interviews, CTU leaders argued that low subscriptions had been a source of weakness and that some CTU affiliates were trying to establish a stronger financial base. Whether the higher subscriptions of the CTU are due to such a policy decision, or whether this simply reflects the higher average wages of some CTU affiliates, is unclear.

Trade unions and labour disputes

Most private-sector workplaces in Hong Kong have no apparent trade union presence. The orthodox view is that industrial relations in such establishments are non-problematic, with a lack of overt conflict and with grievances being dealt with on an individual, face-to-face basis. However, conflicts do emerge and the Hong Kong government provides a voluntary conciliation service to help employees and employers resolve disputes and claims. 'Disputes' involve more than twenty employees and thus represent collective grievances, whilst 'claims' are individual or small-group grievances, usually arising from a breach in the contract of employment or an alleged failure to adhere to the requirements of the Employment Ordinance. Below, in Table 15.5, we attempt to provide an insight into industrial relations issues and conflict resolution in Hong Kong by reviewing the data on disputes for the period 1990 to 1994. The data come from a study of the Labour Department's files on disputes and we also draw on our interviews with Labour Officers and union officials. First, however, we place these findings in context by surveying the overall trend in industrial conflict.

Table 15.4 shows the trend in industrial conflict in Hong Kong since 1980. In general, there have been fewer stoppages since 1982 than in earlier years, with an average of fewer than ten per year since 1983. During this period, there was no discernible trend in the number of stoppages, whilst the numbers of workers involved and working days lost has been affected by occasional large disputes; for example the strike by the Cathay Pacific Flight Attendants' Union accounted for much of the total working days lost in 1993. England (1989), surveying the whole post-war era, identifies a relationship between the economic cycle and the level of stoppages, with an increase in the economic recovery of the late 1970s and a fall after 1982 associated with the recession. However, he also identifies the 'industrial pacifism' of the FTU as a factor in the lower level of stoppages in the 1980s (England 1989: 223). Thus, as the opening-up of China and the approach of the transfer of sovereignty increased China's interest in the economic prosperity and stability of Hong Kong, so the pro-China sympathies of the FTU appear to have favoured a less militant approach to relationships with employers.

Table 15.4 Industrial conflict in Hong Kong

Year	Number of stoppages	Workers involved	Working days lost per 1,000 wage earners and salaried employees	Labour disputes	Claims
1980	37	5,083	10.16	171	14,296
1981	49	7,625	7.18	187	17,035
1982	34	7,262	8.41	176	18,383
1983	11	1,143	1.15	153	19,991
1984	11	2,325	1.37	150	19,905
1985	3	440	0.52	155	20,945
1986	9	2,116	2.10	205	21,608
1987	14	1,661	1.16	140	16,232
1988	8	946	0.97	160	15,434
1989	7	4,059	1.35	130	15,206
1990	15	1,490	1.44	168	16,610
1991	5	127	0.08	169	16,510
1992	11	1,832	1.35	137	17,130
1993	10	1,470	6.37	157	17,866
1994	3	129	0.13	166	20,995
1995	9	1,347	0.37	194	22,180
1996	17	1,763	0.99	226	22,840
1997	7	418	0.28	161	20,404

Source: *Annual Report of the Commissioner for Labour*, various years.

The number of disputes referred to the Labour Department also fell in the early 1980s. However, 1986 saw a short-term increase in disputes, associated with the initial introduction of the Insolvency Fund in April 1985, which provided for the recovery of lost wages for workers in cases of company insolvency (England 1989: 223). The number of disputes then remained at a lower level, increasing markedly only in 1995 and 1996. The number of claims also peaked in 1986, subsequently falling, and then increasing again in the 1990s. The increase in disputes and claims in recent years may owe much to the economic restructuring which has occurred, since the majority of disputes involve cessation of business, insolvency or retrenchment, and over 60 per cent of claims are concerned with termination of contract or dismissal (Commissioner for Labour 1995). Whether the transfer of sovereignty had a 'chilling' effect on disputes and claims in 1997 remains a matter for speculation at this stage, but it seems plausible that trade unions, and indeed workers themselves, may have been distracted by the politics of the handover, thus perhaps explaining the lower recorded level of industrial conflict compared to the previous two years.

So much for the broad trends. We now turn to our in-depth analysis of disputes for the period 1990 to 1994.

The pattern of disputes

It is traditionally argued that Hong Kong employees are reluctant to voice a grievance with their employer, tending to endure the problem or to quit (Turner *et al.* 1991; Lethbridge and Ng 1995: 75). Employee grievances are thus hidden and only become apparent in extreme circumstances. Table 15.5 shows that the great majority of disputes involve an employment relationship which is already at an end due to cessation of business, insolvency, etc. Here, the aim is often to secure unpaid wages or other monies due to employees under the Employment Ordinance.[6]

Almost half the disputes (49 per cent) occurred in manufacturing, a sector which in the early 1990s accounted for 32 per cent of private-sector employment (Labour Department 1991: 36), and 13 per cent occurred in construction, which accounted for only 3 per cent of employment. Another quarter of all disputes occurred in the trade, restaurants and hotels sector (36 per cent of private sector employment). These three sectors, accounting for 87 per cent of all disputes, share several common features – many insolvencies or cessations of business and relatively small workplaces with limited provision for dispute resolution. Notably, these are not the areas of higher union density. In these sectors, the Labour Department conciliators are providing a last-resort service for employees who lack effective representation and dispute-resolution procedures at their places of work.

Our analysis shows that trade unions were involved in 26 per cent of all disputes during 1990 to 1994, although they tend to be involved in the larger disputes, representing 42 per cent of workers involved.[7] The FTU and its

Table 15.5 Labour disputes 1990–4: analysis by cause

Cause	Non-union disputes (%)	Union disputes (%)	All disputes (%)
1 Insolvency/ receivership	28	22	26
2 Cessation of business	38	20	33
3 Removal of factory	2	7	3
4 Redundancy/ retrenchment/ layoff	10	18	12
5 Dismissal	4	5	4
6 Changes in terms of employment	4	14	6
7 Delay or arrears in payment of wages/inability to pay	13	9	12
8 Others	2	3	2
Cause not clearly reported	1	2	2
	n=591	n=206	n=797

Source: Authors' analysis of unpublished Labour Department files.
Note: We have used a slightly different categorisation of causes to that shown in the *Report of the Commissioner for Labour*. Columns may not total 100 due to rounding error.

affiliates were involved in the largest number of union disputes (118 disputes or 15 per cent of the total), followed by the CTU and its affiliates (90: 11 per cent) and the independent trade unions (25: 3 per cent). The TUC and its affiliates were the least active (involved in only two disputes during the period 1990 to 1994). Given that the CTU is rather smaller than the FTU, it had a higher ratio of disputes per member than the FTU. Our earlier research also suggests that the CTU, to a greater extent than the FTU, appears to be responding to non-members who are involved in a dispute rather than simply representing its existing members, and that disputes involving the CTU are significantly more likely to involve industrial action, particularly strikes (Snape and Chan 1997). Union disputes were slightly more likely to involve an ongoing employment relationship but in around half of the cases dealt with by trade unions, at the time of the dispute the employer was no longer operating at the establishment concerned.

England (1989: 224) argues that traditionally, trade unions have usually become involved in a dispute only once it is in progress. However, our interviews with Labour Officers, conducted in 1995, suggest that the pattern had changed somewhat. For example:

> The present scene is quite different from three years ago or five years ago. I can say that the trend is for the involvement of the trade union to be at the early stage right now. Although I agree that say ten years ago maybe the involvement of the trade union is at a later stage, when the dispute was public, such that they got knowledge of it, and they would come along and win the support of the workers involved to join their trade union . . .

The suggestion was that the LegCo elections[8] and greater competition between the CTU and FTU for members were contributing towards a more assertive union stance in disputes. Labour Officers claimed that the CTU had been associated with such an approach since its formation but that, in recent years, the FTU had on occasion adopted a similarly militant stance. The FTU was also developing its organisation and services, for example developing a network of local offices (see Snape and Chan 1997 for a discussion of these developments). It seems likely that such developments are at least partly responsible for the increase in union membership and density during the early 1990s.

Do trade unions make a difference?

Table 15.6 shows that where workers have trade union representation, the dispute resolution process appears to take longer in terms of the number and duration of conciliation meetings and site visits. Also, the dispute is more likely to involve industrial action. All this may imply a greater intransigence on the part of workers with union representation, although it may also be that trade unions are more likely to become involved once a dispute has become prolonged. These findings were replicated in a multivariate context, assessing the impact of union status along with the cause of the dispute, its size and the industry sector concerned.[9]

However, when we compared the conciliated cash settlement per worker involved (only a proportion of disputes result in a conciliated cash settlement, of course), we found that whilst the mean settlement was higher for union than for non-union disputes, it appears that the cause and industry of the dispute were the main factors influencing the size of settlement, rather than union presence, so that when these were controlled for, union presence has no apparent impact on the cash settlement.[10]

Table 15.6 The conduct of disputes by trade union involvement

	Non-union disputes	Union disputes	Sample size
Percentage of disputes involving industrial action (all forms)	8%	30%	797
Mean number of conciliation meetings*	2.23	3.15	281
Mean hours of conciliation*	4.96	9.22	281
Mean number of site visits*	0.13	0.81	281

Source: Authors' analysis of unpublished Labour Department files.
Notes
All differences between union and non-union disputes are significant at 1% level. Row (1) is based on a chi-square test; rows (2), (3) and (4) are based on independent samples t-tests.
*All disputes resolved by conciliation with no further reference (e.g. to Labour Tribunal).

Conclusion: trade unions in the future

In this chapter, we have discussed a range of evidence on the role of trade unions in Hong Kong. In our survey of leaders of individual trade unions, respondents reported that their trade unions were more active in the job-based functions than in providing direct services to members and in political functions. Collective negotiations and consultation with employers constituted the area where union leaders felt that their organisations were most active. Organising social, cultural or leisure activities was the most important services function, whilst the payment of cash benefits was the least. Trade unions were rated as least active on the political function. However, many recognise that they have a role here, especially in lobbying the government on changes in labour laws and policies, and non-public services trade unions rate themselves almost as highly on political functions as on services functions. Officials were expecting this pattern of activities to be consolidated.

Given the traditional weakness of Hong Kong trade unions at the workplace and the lack of established collective bargaining or consultative mechanisms for most employees, the finding of a strong perceived emphasis on job-based functions is perhaps surprising. Of course, this does not necessarily mean that such functions provide the most significant benefits from the point of view of members. The provision of direct services, for example, may be achieved with relatively little effort on the part of the union and yet be of great value to members. However, at least according to our respondents, it seems that job-based functions were the ones which absorbed more of the unions' effort and it was anticipated that, if anything, this emphasis would increase. Even private sector trade unions, which usually lack employer recognition, claim to be most active in the job-based functions, in particular in advising workers on individual employment rights and representing them in claims and disputes. Private-sector trade unions are also relatively active in terms of lobbying government on labour policy. In the face of employers' refusal to negotiate or consult, this may be a second-choice option for trade unions.

As regards the differences between federations, FTU trade unions have been characterised as emphasising direct services, perhaps at the expense of workplace representation (England 1989: 116–17; Turner *et al.* 1991: 80–3; Levin and Chiu 1993: 202–3), whilst the CTU have an image of being a campaigning organisation, active in disputes and in political protest (Snape and Chan 1997). There is partial support for these stereotypes in our survey findings. FTU trade unions tend to place more emphasis on services functions than do other trade unions (CTU, TUC or independent), but they also place more emphasis than non-affiliated trade unions on job-based and political functions. CTU-affiliated trade unions tend to rate themselves more highly on job-based functions than do independent trade unions. Independent trade unions in general appear to be less active than FTU and

CTU trade unions across a range of functions, although there are exceptions to this in the case of some of the larger independent trade unions. TUC respondents did not rate themselves particularly highly on most of the activities. This, along with our findings on disputes, supports the view of the TUC and its affiliates as relatively inactive and low-profile organisations.

Hong Kong trade unions have traditionally had very low subscription rates. Our survey confirms this, although the CTU trade unions tend to have higher subscriptions than either FTU or TUC trade unions. This may reflect the higher average incomes of members of some of the CTU affiliates, although it may also reflect a strategic decision by CTU trade unions to establish a stronger resource base for their representation work, rather than opting for the low-cost, high-benefits approach which has been emphasised by many Hong Kong trade unions hitherto. Certainly, the CTU leaders we interviewed were conscious of the need to build a sound organisational basis for their work, and they recognised that this placed more demands on financial resources than the traditional benefits-based approach. Of course, the ability to raise subscriptions to a more economic level will depend on their ability to demonstrate real benefits to members, and Hong Kong workers' demand for union services may prove to be highly price sensitive, particularly where there are several trade unions competing for membership.

Our analysis of trade union involvement in labour disputes suggests that union representation may make a difference, with trade unions involved in longer disputes. This may reflect union intransigence prolonging the dispute resolution process, although it may simply be that trade unions are more likely to become involved in disputes that last longer. We could not conclude that union involvement necessarily results in better settlements for workers. It may be that there are other dimensions of trade union success which need to be explored. A key question for trade unions is: To what extent does union involvement in labour disputes provide a sound basis for further union organisation? In many cases, such activity involves trade unions representing workers who were not previously members. In this respect, the trade unions, are providing an 'emergency service' to those who encounter difficulties with their employer. The great majority of such disputes involve an employment relationship that is already at an end, so that the direct organising potential of union activity is probably limited, especially when compared to the effort expended. However, as ideology-driven organisations, trade unions arguably do not apply a strict cost–benefit logic to their activities.[11] Furthermore, it may be that such activity has a longer-term value in terms of raising the profile of the trade unions and federations concerned.

Hong Kong trade unions face an uncertain future. They will continue to face the problem of employer hostility and reluctance to recognise them as negotiating partners, and the SAR government has shown, for example in the repeal of the trade union recognition laws (see Chapter 2), that it will continue to follow a strongly pro-business line. However, the Basic Law provides for freedom of association and the relative autonomy of the SAR means that there is likely to be some space for independent trade unions. Since the transfer of sovereignty the trade unions have continued their work, including the CTU, whose leaders have been amongst the most vocal critics of China's human rights and employment policy record. Furthermore, the success of the pro-democracy parties in the 1998 LegCo elections (see Chapter 2), with a significant labour and trade union presence amongst those elected, suggests that welfare and labour issues continue to concern the public.

It may be that the rise in trade union membership and public support for the political causes with which trade unions ally themselves are part of a long-term trend. One reading is that support for independent trade unions and democracy has been growing in other Asian economies as well as in Hong Kong, a reflection of the level of economic and social development (see, for example: Frenkel 1993; Wilkinson 1994; Kuruvilla and Venkataratnam 1996). As economies emerge from the initial phase of low-cost export-oriented industrialisation and diversify into higher value-added and services industries, so skills levels rise and better education and living standards may lead to higher expectations and demands for participation. Such an analysis suggests that rising demands for participation and trade unionisation may be part and parcel of the economic development process and as such will be very difficult for employers and governments to resist in the long term. However, some have suggested that the move to services and to higher value-added industries, whilst consistent with skills development and more positive employment practices, is likely to be associated with a union exclusion strategy based on individualist HRM practices (Kuruvilla 1996). On this reading, Asian trade unions are likely to face similar challenges to those faced by many western trade unions in recent years.

Clearly, the development of Hong Kong's industrial relations system will depend on the pattern of economic development and on government labour market policies in the coming years. Arguably, the trade unions themselves are in a position to influence their own fate, most notably perhaps in the extent to which they are willing and able to approach the job-based functions with greater energy than hitherto. Whilst due moderation and responsible action will be necessary to attract and retain public support, the outright 'industrial pacifism' that has arguably characterised some trade unions is unlikely to secure the future of trade unions in Hong Kong. Trade unions will need to demonstrate that they can secure gains for their members.

Appendix – The survey sample: authors' survey of HK trade unions, 1996

Sample characteristics

	Mean value	*Minimum*	*Maximum*
Membership	2,234	14	100,025
Annual subscription payable	$137	$0	$6,000

Trade union affiliation

	Unions	*% of sample*
CTU	23*	16
FTU	23	16
TUC	12	9
Other federations	28	20
None	55	39
	141	100

Note: *Includes four trade unions affiliated to the Federation of Hong Kong and Kowloon Labour Unions (FLU).

Notes

1 The authors gratefully acknowledge the funding provided for this research by the Hong Kong Polytechnic University (research grant numbers 340/183 and G-S508) and wish to thank the labour organizations, the Labour Department and the officials interviewed for their help.
2 Less than 5 per cent of trade union expenditure now goes on direct cash benefits paid to members (Registry of Trade Unions 1994).
3 These comparisons are based on independent samples t-tests of mean scores on each function, with 5 = very active to 1 = not at all active. All reported differences are significant at the 5 per cent level or better.
4 We scored every union on each of the functions according to a five-point scale (5 = very active; 1 = not at all active), and an average score was calculated for each union on the three groups of functions: job-based, services and political. One-way analysis of variance was then used to test for differences on these average scores according to union affiliation (CTU, FTU, TUC, other federations, and independents). Multiple comparisons tests were used to look for significant pairwise differences (Scheffe tests, 5 per cent significance level).
5 Income from members accounted for only 35 per cent of total income in 1994, with a further 54 per cent coming from 'business undertakings' and 'miscellaneous' sources (Registry of Trade Unions 1994).
6 The Labour Department also dealt with 21,000 claims in 1994, often involving similar issues to disputes but with fewer than twenty workers in each case. Again, claims usually emerge only once the contract of employment is over. In 1994, 61 per cent involved termination of contract or dismissal with another 7 per cent involving retrenchment and 5 per cent involving layoffs, cessation of business, insolvency or removal of factory (Commissioner for Labour 1995: 61).
7 This suggests that the level of union involvement in claims is likely to be even lower since claims involve fewer workers.

8 As we have seen, the CTU was associated with the Democrats and the pro-democracy forces, and the FTU with the DAB and pro-China camp.

9 We estimated ordinary least squares regressions for the dependent variables number of conciliation meetings, hours of conciliation and number of conciliation visits. Whether or not the dispute involved industrial action was coded as a dummy variable ($0 = $ No; $1 = $ Yes) and so logistic regression was used in this case. Independent variables in all regressions were: union status ($0 = $ No; $1 = $ Yes), dummy variables for the causes of disputes (based on Table 15.5) and for industry sector, the number of workers involved in the dispute and the number involved as a percentage of total workplace employment. In each case, the coefficient on the union variable was positive and significant at the 5 per cent level or better.

10 This analysis involved regressions similar to those referred to in note 9, with the cash settlement per worker as the dependent variable. The union dummy was not significant. We repeated the analysis, replacing the single union variable with separate dummy variables for each of the federations (CTU, FTU, TUC, Independent and Joint cases; with non-union status as the residual case). The only significant finding on union status was that FTU disputes appear to result in significantly higher per capita cash settlements than non-union disputes, although this was only significant at the 10 per cent level. Whether this reflects more effective representation by the FTU or whether they are choosing only the more 'winnable' cases, we cannot be sure.

11 Recall the political origins of the FTU and TUC, and the CTU's origins in the Christian campaign for workers' welfare.

16 Joint consultation in Hong Kong

Employee participation or trade union exclusion?[1]

Andy W. Chan and Ed Snape

Introduction

The extent to which employees have a say in the decisions affecting their working lives and livelihood is an issue which confronts all societies. In spite of its economic success, Hong Kong has been seen as being relatively backward in terms of the development of 'industrial democracy' (Chiu and Levin 1996). Trade unions remain relatively weak at the workplace, especially in the private sector, and collective bargaining is rare (see Chapter 15). In general, workplace industrial relations show a low level of institutionalisation (Ng and Cheng 1993). However, government and some large employers have sought to provide for some form of employee representation, and joint consultation has emerged as the preferred model in the civil service and in some of the large public utilities.

There appears to be significant support amongst employees for some form of joint consultation or employee representation. Turner *et al.*'s (1980, 1991) surveys of employees across the Hong Kong economy, both public and private sector, found that in 1985, 31 per cent preferred 'joint consultation with workplace representatives', 32 per cent legislation, and 12 per cent trade union negotiation as a means of winning improved working conditions. The figures for their comparable survey in 1976 were 36, 25 and 10 per cent respectively, suggesting a decline in the popularity of legislative methods and a slight increase in the popularity of joint consultation between the two surveys. Turner *et al.* (1980, 1991) interpreted their findings as evidence of a gap in terms of employee representation at the workplace, and urged the government to consider requiring large and medium-sized firms to set up an elected JCC.

In this chapter we examine the practice of joint consultation in Hong Kong and evaluate its significance as a channel for employee representation. Whilst we survey developments in the public sector, our main focus is the private sector, seen as the more problematic for effective employee representation. In particular, we present a case study of the use of joint consultation in a private-sector company.

What is 'joint consultation'?

The precise form taken by joint consultation may vary from company to company, but it is usually taken to involve some form of committee or discussion forum, with members drawn from both management and employees, the aim being to provide for more effective management–employee communication. Marchington *et al.* define it as follows:

> A mechanism for managers and employee representatives to meet on a regular basis in order to exchange views, to utilise members' knowledge and expertise to deal with matters of common interest which are not the subject of collective bargaining.
>
> (Marchington *et al.* 1992: 11)

Thus, in a UK context, the process of joint consultation is usually distinguished from collective bargaining, and emphasises the exchange of information rather than negotiation. Collective bargaining, at least in its more adversarial forms, has been characterised as a 'distributive' process, whilst joint consultation is more likely to be 'integrative' with non-zero sum outcomes (Hyman and Mason 1995). This is attributable to the underlying assumptions and to the nature of the issues with which each has traditionally been concerned. Collective bargaining has usually been seen as a process of negotiation between two 'equal' parties in pursuit of agreement on terms and conditions of employment and related matters. Joint consultation has been seen as a process of management providing information to employee representatives and receiving their views; in the last analysis, however, the assumption has usually been that management prerogatives are maintained. Furthermore, joint consultation tends not to be centrally concerned with terms and conditions, indeed in some organisations joint consultation committees are not allowed to discuss pay.

However, it is possible to draw too clear a distinction between collective bargaining and joint consultation. The distributive–integrative distinction can be seen as a continuum. Collective bargaining can take on integrative characteristics, while the distinction between the two processes can become blurred, for example when issues which are the subject of collective bargaining are raised during joint consultation (Hyman and Mason 1995). Indeed, where the two processes co-exist in an organisation, both sides may use joint consultation to 'sound out' the other on issues which may later become the subject of negotiation. Where joint consultation exists in the absence of collective bargaining, it is likely that employee representatives will seek to influence decisions on pay and conditions, even where these issues are specifically excluded from the formal scope of the consultation process. Such qualifications aside, however, the usual assumption is that collective bargaining is the 'harder' form of participation, affording greater employee influence, while consultation is essentially a communications mechanism which leaves management prerogatives largely intact. Indeed, joint consultation may be used by management as a means of marginalising or excluding trade unions (Marchington 1994).

Joint consultation in Hong Kong is a legacy of British rule. However, as we shall demonstrate in this chapter, the form and significance of joint consultation in Hong Kong differs significantly from the British pattern, not least because of the relative weakness of unions and the limited development of collective bargaining in Hong Kong.

Joint consultation in the public and social services

As the largest employer in the territory,[2] the government has attempted to set a good example in providing channels of employee representation (England 1989: 82). Consultation between management and staff is well established at central and departmental levels. In light of the government's growing awareness of the need for formal channels of employee representation in the aftermath of the 1967 riots, the Senior Civil Service Council (SCSC) was formed in 1968 to facilitate communication between the government and white-collar (Master Pay Scale) civil servants. The Model Scale 1 Staff Consultative Council was set up in 1982 to provide similar channels for blue-collar staff. There are also joint consultation committees (JCCs) for the police and the disciplined services, the latter including Immigration, Customs and Excise, the Fire, Correctional and Flying Services. In addition to these central JCCs, there are JCCs at departmental level, with over eighty departmental consultative committees. The JCCs are made up of 'official' (management) and staff sides. For example, the SCSC has up to six officials appointed by the Chief Secretary, with up to nine staff representatives nominated by three staff unions and each side also appoints a secretary. Staff representatives are nominated by recognised trade unions, as shown in Table 16.1.

The civil service JCCs have rather broader terms of reference than is typical in the UK model of joint consultation. In the absence of separate collective bargaining machinery, they cover all issues of concern to staff including pay and conditions. The Standing Commission on Civil Service Salaries and Conditions of Service, consisting of members drawn mainly from the business sector, advises the government on civil service pay and conditions, and there is an annual comparability survey conducted by the Pay Survey and Research Unit under the administrative control of the Standing Commission. The staff sides of the four central JCCs are involved in the commissioning and analysis of the survey through their representation on the Pay Trend Survey Committee. The survey provides the basis for the annual pay adjustment, although changes in the cost of living, the state of the economy, the budgetary situation and the pay claims put forward by the staff sides of the central JCCs are also taken into account by the government in determining the adjustment.

Table 16.1 Nominated trade unions in the central consultative councils of the Hong
Kong civil service

Senior Civil Service Council
Association of Expatriate Civil Servants of Hong Kong
Hong Kong Chinese Civil Servants Association
Senior Non-expatriate Officer Association

Model Scale 1 Staff Consultative Council
Agriculture and Fisheries Department Staff Association
Government Employees Association
Government Municipal Staff General Union
Government Property Attendant Association
Government Staff Union
Hong Kong Chinese Civil Servants Association
Hong Kong Civil Servants General Union
Hong Kong Government Waterworks Chinese Employees Union

Police Force Council
Expatriate Inspector Association
Junior Police Officer Association
Local Inspector Association
Superintendent Association

Disciplined Services Consultative Council
Association of Customs and Excise Service Officers
Hong Kong Customs Officers Union
Correctional Services Officers Association (Junior Section)
Correctional Services Officers Association (Senior Section)
Government Flying Service Air Crewmen Union
Government Flying Service Aircraft Engineers Union
Government Flying Service Aircraft Technicians Union
Government Flying Service Pilots Union
Hong Kong Fire Services Control Staff's Association
Hong Kong Fire Services Department Ambulance Officers Association
Hong Kong Fire Services Department Ambulancemen's Union
Hong Kong Fire Services Department Staff's General Association
Hong Kong Fire Services Local Officers Association
Hong Kong Immigration Service Immigration Assistants Union
Immigration Service Officers Association

Source: Staff Relations Division, Civil Service Bureau, Hong Kong SAR Government,
September, 1997.

The typical mode of operation in the SCSC, for example, is to seek
agreement between the official and staff sides. Both sides have accepted that
such agreements are then binding on all parties. However, the government
reserves the right not to implement such agreements where this is in conflict
with the public interest and similarly, in spite of the undertaking to consult
with staff associations before making changes in conditions of service, the
government reserves the right to initiate changes in conditions of service if
this is judged to be in the public interest. Where no consensus can be reached

between the official and staff sides within the SCSC, this is recorded in the minutes, along with details of the differing viewpoints. There is provision for a committee of inquiry to be set up to deal with failures to agree on terms and conditions of employment; it has been suggested that this may act as a bargaining tool for the staff side, since the official side has an incentive to reach an agreement rather than face the uncertain outcome of an inquiry (England 1989: 85). However, neither side is bound to accept the findings of an inquiry.

Thus, whilst the SCSC and other councils give the appearance of a British-style Whitley Council, and these arrangements are probably Hong Kong's 'closest approximation to modern collective bargaining in the Western sense' (Ng and Sit 1989: 91), in fact the government 'escape clauses' mean that the arrangements stop far short of full-blown collective bargaining. Indeed, one commentator has referred to the 1968 agreement which established the SCSC as an 'unequal treaty' between government and civil servants (England 1989: 84–5). The Hong Kong government has historically resisted trade union calls for full bargaining rights, and departmental managers, in particular, have often been less than enthusiastic about setting up JCCs in their departments. Furthermore, it appears that many JCC staff representatives feel that the committees lack real impact on key issues of concern (Cheek-Milby 1984), and a survey of civil servants showed that 93 per cent of respondents wanted to have full collective bargaining over pay and working conditions in preference to the consultative arrangements (Cheek-Milby 1988: 112).

Even so, joint consultation in the Hong Kong civil service amounts to rather more than simply a communications device; there is scope for trade unions to exert a degree of influence. Thus: '. . . there has developed over the life of the [SCSC] council a certain amount of "horse trading" for the line between consultation and negotiation invariably becomes blurred when employees have strongly organised associations behind them.' (England 1989: 85).

The nomination of staff representatives by the trade unions has been criticised as being rather unrepresentative, particularly in the past when the unions accounted for a minority of staff, whilst some have accused the government of seeking to exclude the more militant organisations, such as the Federation of Civil Service Unions, in spite of their having more members than some recognised trade unions (Cheek-Milby 1984). Nevertheless, the participation of trade unions in these formalised JCCs appears to be at least one of the factors explaining the steady increase in civil service trade union membership since the 1970s. Internal and external pay differentials are amongst the issues fuelling significant discontent amongst rank and file civil servants at various times during the last two decades, and the existence of the JCCs at central and departmental levels has afforded trade unions an opportunity to demonstrate that they can have an impact in furthering the interests of civil servants.

Aside from the civil service, joint consultation is also widespread in other parts of the social and public services. The Hospital Authority (HA), for example, has JCCs at corporate and hospital levels and also for the six 'staff groups' (administrative staff, doctors, nurses, allied health professionals, supporting staff, and supervisory/clerical and general staff). All HA JCCs are specifically excluded from discussing personal and disciplinary cases and the annual pay rise. Management's intention was that Hospital Consultative Committees would focus on operations, productivity, training and staff welfare, whilst the Staff Group CCs would focus more on the interests of their particular group. Staff representatives on the hospital CCs are usually directly elected on a department or staff-group basis, the HACC has a staff representative from each hospital CC, whilst the staff group CCs have a mix of trade union-nominated and directly elected members. The HA approach thus differs from the civil service in placing less emphasis on trade union representation. Indeed, in recent years the HA has developed a direct employee communications strategy involving staff newsletters, opinion surveys and hospital visits by senior corporate managers, and placing less emphasis on trade union representation as the main communications channel. There has been some questioning amongst staff and their representatives about the ability of the JCCs to resolve issues of concern, and some have argued that directly elected representatives in particular may face difficulties in communicating effectively with their constituents due to a lack of time and resources.

Some government-aided social services organisations are known to operate formal staff consultation mechanisms. For example, one of the authors' recent study of eight government-aided social service organisations found that, in addition to communications channels such as staff bulletins, two had established formal staff consultative committees. The staff side of the JCC in the larger organisation was represented by an in-house staff association, which was a registered trade union. In the smaller one, there was no trade union representation on the JCC, but staff representatives were elected according to a written constitution to discuss issues relating to their work, welfare and benefits, as well as the service provided to clients.

Hong Kong schools, whether government, government-aided or private, tend not to have formal joint consultative committees. However, some schools do have regular dialogues between school management board members and teachers. With the inception of the School Management Initiative Scheme in 1991, teachers in those schools implementing this school-based management reform programme can elect their representatives to sit on the school management committee, equivalent in a sense to having 'employee directors'. By the end of 1995, some 220 out of a total of 1,200 primary and secondary schools had adopted the School Management Initiative Scheme, and the Education Department wished all schools to implement it by the year 2000 (*Ming Pao Daily*, 20 December 1995).

The development of joint consultation in the private sector

The riots and labour unrest of 1967 also influenced the government's thinking on policies for the private sector. In addition to the enactment of the Employment Ordinance as a means of safeguarding employment standards, the Labour Department launched a campaign to promote 'good' workplace relations. A key element in this was the promotion of joint consultation, especially in larger enterprises (Yeung 1988; Pong 1990).

Some large employers established such committees, but the development of JCCs in private enterprises is limited compared to the public sector in terms of coverage and also in the degree of influence afforded to employee representatives. In Kirkbride and Tang's survey of large private-sector companies (1989: 40), 13 per cent had a JCC and 8 per cent had formal meetings between management and trade unions or staff associations.[3] According to the Labour Department, JCCs covered almost 77,000 employees in the private sector in 1993, up from 62,000 in 1984 (Table 16.2). Most were in the utilities and services, including power supply, transportation and telecommunications. Significantly, joint consultation committees were very rare in those sectors exposed to strong market competition.

Several reasons have been suggested for the limited development of joint consultation in the private sector, including the small average size of workplaces in manufacturing (which arguably limits the need for formalised communications devices), high labour mobility (which suggests that where grievances exist employees and employers accept the principle of 'exit' rather than 'voice'), and employer reluctance to implement JCCs for fear of limiting management prerogatives (Yeung 1988: 56).

The Labour Department has maintained its official policy of encouraging employers to set up joint consultation arrangements, with the Promotion Unit of the Labour Relations Service and Labour Officers proposing this to employers as a way of improving communications and helping to avoid

Table 16.2 Joint consultative committees in the private sector 1984 and 1993

Sector	Number of establishments with JCCs		Total number of JCCs		Estimated number of employees covered	
	1984	*1993*	*1984*	*1993*	*1984*	*1993*
Manufacturing	6	4	11	5	6,100	1,950
Construction	1	–	1	–	1,200	–
Services	17	22	32	47	19,640	39,790
Utilities	6	6	31	78	32,460	27,900
Education and welfare	2	4	2	6	2,150	7,330
Total	32	36	77	136	61,550	76,970

Source: Chiu and Levin (1996: 28).

disputes. In fact, the approach is a flexible one, as one Labour Officer explained it to us:

> We haven't made a very formal or systematic evaluation of this policy, but still it is our department's stance to promote Joint Consultation. If there are some other means whereby employees and management can communicate with each other, whether this is formal joint consultation machinery or not is not essential. To us, they have achieved the purpose of consultation with each other.

However, our interviews with Labour Officers suggest that most employers are sceptical and that, even where employers express initial interest perhaps following a dispute, this usually soon wanes. Thus, the Labour Relations Service continues to deal mainly with 'casualty-type' work, helping resolve disputes that have already become conflictual, rather than working on helping employers to develop sound long-term employee relations.

Having surveyed the extent of joint consultation in Hong Kong, in the remainder of the chapter we present a private-sector case study. The aims in so doing are to provide some insights into management strategy in maintaining a JCC and to evaluate the extent to which JCCs can afford effective employee involvement in the private sector.

Joint consultation at the Hong Kong School of Motoring

The Hong Kong School of Motoring is jointly owned by the Cross Harbour Tunnel Co. Ltd and Wilson Parking International Holdings Ltd. It provides driving tuition for the general public. There are courses covering private motor car, light goods vehicle, motor cycle, commercial vehicle and bus training. The School of Motoring employs around 700 full-time staff, of which 500 are driving instructors, the rest being management and support staff. There are another 120 part-time instructors, along with a smaller number of part-time car cleaners, telephone operators and refuelling assistants. The company operates on three main sites, located at Wong Chuk Hang on Hong Kong Island, and at Yuen Long and Shatin in the New Territories.

JCCs have been in operation at the company since its establishment in 1983, the principle of joint consultation having been introduced from the parent company. The objectives are set out in the JCC constitution as follows:

a To give the employees a wider interest in the day-to-day activities of the company.
b To provide a recognised and direct channel of communication between the employees and the management on matters affecting their joint or several interests.

    c To promote throughout the Company a spirit of cooperation and securing the contentment of the employees.

    d To help employees have a wider interest in, and a greater degree of responsibility for, the conditions under which their work is performed.

(The Hong Kong School of Motoring Ltd.
Joint Consultative Committee – Constitution)

Thus, the stated aim is to enhance communication between employees and management and to underpin positive employee attitudes towards the company.

There are committees for each of the three sites. Employee representatives are elected, normally for a term of two years, with half being replaced each year so as to ensure a degree of continuity. Each employee who has completed their probationary period of employment is eligible to vote in the election and is entitled to nominate one fellow employee as a candidate. Candidates for election must themselves be eligible to vote in the group for which they are being nominated, must have at least one year's service, have no disciplinary record in the preceding six months, and be at least 21 years old. Contested elections are the norm, although on occasions supervisors have had to encourage employees to stand for election. Retiring representatives are allowed to stand again, although this is not usual. At the time of our interviews, the longest serving representatives had been in position for only three years and the Human Resources (HR) Manager expressed a

Table 16.3 Organisation of the JCCs and corresponding employee representatives at the Hong Kong School of Motoring

Group/Staff covered	*No. of employee representatives*
Shatin Operations JCC	
1 Operations private car groups	6
2 Commercial group, support group and duty officers group	1
3 Senior driving instructors	1
4 Motorcycle group	1
Wong Chuk Hang JCC	
1 Operations private car groups	4
2 Motorcycle	1
3 Support group and senior driving instructors	1
Yuen Long JCC	
1 Operations private car groups	3
2 GADC/ MGV/ bus group	1
3 Support group/ senior driving instructors and motorcycle	1

Source: The Hong Kong School of Motoring Ltd. Joint Consultative Committee – Constitution.

preference for revolving the role amongst as many different staff as possible. Employees vote for the representative(s) for their own group (Table 16.3). The annual elections take place during July or August by secret ballot and a turnout of at least 60 per cent is required for a valid election. The company provides training for elected employee representatives, covering such issues as communications, presentational and problem-solving techniques.

There are three appointed management representatives on each committee: the Operations Comptroller (a senior manager with overall responsibility for operations, who only normally attends when major company-wide issues are discussed), the site Operations Manager, and the company HR Manager. One of the management representatives is Chair of the JCC, usually selected for the three-year term of office. An HR Officer or Assistant acts as secretary

JCCs must meet at least quarterly, but not normally more than once a month. In practice, meetings are usually around once every six weeks, lasting for around two to two and a half hours, and are held during normal office hours. JCC meetings are minuted by an HR Officer and the minutes are circulated to all members and then posted on employee notice boards. Employees who are not elected representatives are allowed to attend the meetings as non-participant observers, an attempt to increase employee interest in and understanding of the JCC.

Representatives meet informally with their constituents before the meeting to discuss possible agenda items. A few days before the JCC, a short 'agenda meeting' of employee representatives is held. This is described by the JCC representatives we interviewed as a democratic process, with an elected chairman and, where necessary, voting on the priority issues to put forward. The suggested agenda is then forwarded to the HR Manager, who must decide whether issues fall within the remit of the JCC and whether certain issues can be resolved prior to the meeting. Management also put forward agenda items, particularly to sound out employee opinion on new policies, and may brief representatives on key issues. Management's aim is to gather employee opinions and to win their acceptance of management decisions. The final agenda is circulated to all members at least two days before the JCC meeting.

The JCC Constitution defines the 'scope for discussions' as 'any matters that are pertinent to the general well being of the employees', although 'salary and monetary benefits' and 'individual cases' are excluded. The JCCs focus mainly on conditions of work, including physical conditions and work rules. Benefits, including working hours and fringe benefits, were also discussed, but there was no minuted discussion of pay. Other items included, for example, appraisal and promotion policies and the increase in the social club membership fee (Table 16.4).

Discussion at JCC meetings usually involves the originator of the agenda item explaining the issue, prior to a general discussion. In essence, JCC meetings involve an exchange of opinions, with employee representatives

Table 16.4 Analysis of the items discussed in the Hong Kong School of Motoring JCCs during 1996

Subject category	Number of items	Management clarification of query	Management agree to implement	Management reject the proposal	Other actions (e.g. noted)
Working conditions	37	8	13	4	12
Welfare and benefits	14	9	3	1	1
Miscellaneous	14	1	10	3	0

Selected issues

a Working conditions
Change of shift of instructors and subsequent compensation to company
Avoidance of last-minute message on change of shift
Ventilation, cleanliness and pest control of the workplace
Noise-proof wall for lecture room
Change of the vehicle licence position
Traffic congestion
Arrangement of work after typhoon signal is hoisted
Handling students' absence due to illness
Safety award
Quality of woollen vest
Company's new products

b Welfare and benefits
Change of meal hours
Rest period of lecturers
Overtime pay for senior driving instructors
Award of five-year full attendance
Ten-year service award
Annual leave arrangement and its calculation
Arrangement of medical benefits and comments on doctors
Amendment in retirement fund
Confidential and private mails for staff
Birthday card for staff
Staff purchase uniform and shoes
No-smoking areas
Suspension of canteen operation on Sunday
Scholarship for children of the staff

c Miscellaneous
Appraisal and promotion of staff
Printing of salary slip and its format
Salary increment when under warning
Company policy on drunk driving
Courtesy campaign
Follow-up on sexual harassment case
Penalty of loss of staff card
Increase of social club membership fee
Bus training course
Duty change affecting attendance on training courses

Source: Human Resource Department, Hong Kong School of Motoring.

raising questions and airing their views and with management supplying information, giving clarification or perhaps even responding to employee suggestions. Certainly it is a two-way discussion, but it is not a decision-making forum and there is no voting or passing of resolutions. Whilst management often follow up issues after the meeting and take the views of employees into account in formulating or amending policies, the JCC stops short of being a negotiating body.

Where employee representatives raise issues which relate to particular individuals, the HR Manager may try to resolve the matter with the representative concerned or pass the case on to the departmental manager. Other than individual cases, matters which are formally beyond the terms of reference of the JCC are occasionally discussed at the end of the formal meetings – 'off the minutes'. As the HR Manager put it to us:

> I feel that the only effective way is to let them voice their concern and not to suppress them. If you suppress them they will say 'Where else can I go?', and then they will start to write things on the toilet doors.

However, there would be no question of management representatives entering into any kind of dialogue or negotiation on pay or monetary benefits, not least because such matters as the annual pay increase are beyond the discretion of the managers who sit on the JCC.

JCC representatives take on a broader employee communications and involvement role within the company. Regular 'Open Forum' meetings are held for employees, in groups of twenty or so, at which JCC employee representatives brief them on JCC discussions and on the follow-up on issues raised. In addition, JCC employee representatives are included on panels for disciplinary hearings, management's concern here being to demonstrate the fairness of the procedure.

Employee representatives vary in the extent to which they are able and willing to speak up in the JCC. It may be that some employees still feel intimidated about speaking up in front of management, particularly on more controversial issues, in spite of the following 'guarantee' in the JCC Constitution:

> Each representative shall be free to discharge the duties of his office in the Committee with the assurance that his personal standing with the company will in no way be affected by any action he may take in good faith while acting in the capacity of a representative.

Management were aware of no trade union members amongst the workforce at the time of our research. However, there have been two key incidents of industrial relations conflict in the past: a strike in February 1992 over the annual pay rise and a conflict over the retrenchment involving twenty-seven staff in March 1995. The February 1992 incident involved unsuccessful attempts to recruit by both the Confederation of Trade Unions (CTU) and the Federation of Trade Unions (FTU). In the wake of this episode, management took steps to improve employee communications, including the more effective communication of JCC deliberations and outcomes to the workforce, and to reform the election process in order to ensure that JCC representatives were seen to be truly representative.[4] The second incident led to a high-profile campaign by the FTU to recruit at the School of Motoring, with leaflet distribution at site exits and at Tai Wai station to try to encourage employees to join a trade union, with rallies outside the main building and with the blocking of the exits from the Shatin site. However, the FTU's bid eventually failed. As the HR Manager explained:

> I think we survived the second trial because after 1992 we really took all our efforts to improve communications and all of us knew why these 27 people had been laid off, because after they were given the letter we [were all] briefed properly . . .

Thus, the JCC can be seen as part of an employee communications strategy aimed at avoiding industrial conflict and minimising employee support for trade union representation. Management appear to have concluded on the basis of the 1992 and 1995 episodes that communication and effective consultation are necessary if employee commitment and harmonious relations are to be maintained. As the HR Manager put it:

> Sometimes you will know that we have done something wrong; we have made some mistakes . . . We have to be brave enough to admit it; to fix it with some concessions. Sometimes I have a difficult time to persuade the management to give the concessions. But with the JCC we have the groundwork for fixing things.

Judging from our interviews with employee representatives, they are reasonably positive about the JCC and some feel that they are genuinely able to influence management decisions on some issues, citing specific examples to us.[5] There is also a recognition that communication can help to contain conflict. Thus, in the busy summer period of 1997, high staff turnover and shortages led to instructors being asked to limit their leave and the JCC provided management with an opportunity to explain the situation:

> The JCC can reduce workplace conflict because there is communication or clarification before the issues become too serious. One example was to clarify to us the difficulty management face with the work schedule . . . we accepted their explanation . . .

However, others noted the limits to their role and even raised the possibility of their being incorporated into management's point of view. As one of them explained:

> We, as JCC representatives, just transmit colleagues' views to management but we cannot participate in decision-making . . . Maybe after being JCC representatives for some time, we know more about the practical problems management face and become more considerate than before . . .

There was a feeling amongst some employee representatives that the annual pay increase should be included in the terms of reference of the JCC, since this was the key concern of employees, who were requesting greater management transparency on this issue. The employee representatives we interviewed expressed considerable frustration, having had requests to discuss the annual pay adjustment turned down by management, and they intimated that they found it very difficult to explain to their colleagues their lack of impact on management decisions. Some employee representatives suggested that, in spite of the JCC, management decision-making lacked transparency and that, in practice, management tended not to change their predetermined policy. The danger is that JCC representatives will lack credibility with employees to the extent that they are seen as having little or no influence on key issues.

Conclusion: future prospects

In Hong Kong, joint consultation is the norm in the public sector. Especially in the civil service, trade unions are afforded a degree of recognition by management as providing the basis for employee representation. Indeed, civil service joint consultation has arguably developed into a form of 'quasi-collective bargaining' and Turner *et al.* (1980, 1991) argue that when Hong Kong workers express a preference for JCCs, it is this model which they appear to have in mind. In the private sector, things are rather different, and joint consultation is found mainly in the public utilities, transport and communications, apparently covering fewer than 80,000 employees. Even here, the pattern differs from that of the public sector, with JCCs functioning more as a communications device and with trade unions marginalised. Indeed, there appears to be an element of a 'trade union substitution' strategy here in some companies.

At the Hong Kong School of Motoring, the JCC was part of a broader communications strategy aimed at the management of employee attitudes. The avoidance of overt conflict and trade union activity was a key aim of the consultative arrangements and management sought to avoid a repeat of earlier industrial action by bolstering the credibility of JCC representatives amongst staff. This meant that management had to be prepared to make concessions to employee opinion on occasions, but the JCC was clearly a communications rather than a decision-making forum, and pay and monetary benefits were excluded from the agenda. Staff representatives agreed that they were able to influence management decisions to some extent, but many recognised that their impact was ultimately limited, and there was a desire amongst representatives and employees for pay to be included as an item for discussion. However, employees had in the past eventually refused the involvement of outside trade unions in the face of management resistance.

Perhaps not surprisingly, the CTU's stance is that, particularly in the private sector, joint consultation has been used by management to resist trade union involvement and that JCC agendas are deliberately limited to discussions of less controversial issues, leaving employees without a voice on the key issues which concern them (*CTU in Solidarity*, No. 26, December 1996, p. 1). Our case study provides some evidence of this. Management was using the communications strategy, of which the JCC was part, to avoid a situation where employees turn to a trade union for help. The exclusion of pay from the JCC agenda also provides support for the CTU view.

It seems that employees are prepared to become involved in their JCCs, perhaps because this is often the main source of information and influence available to them. Our case suggests that JCCs can afford employees a degree of influence over management decisions, even in the private sector, but that this is very much on management's terms, and is limited in scope. The approach in our private-sector case study was one of management communicating policies to the JCC, of listening to employee questions and opinions, and then either providing further information or reconsidering decisions accordingly. There was no evidence of bargaining or of trying to reach any agreement. This differs from the civil service, where more emphasis is placed on trade union representation and on trying to reach a consensus, but even here management prerogatives are maintained, for example with the presence of many 'escape clauses' available to the government following a resolution from the JCC.

The relationship between joint consultation and trade union growth is a complex one. The experience of the civil service suggests that where unions are seen to have an influence, then staff will join. Elsewhere, and even in parts of the public sector, joint consultation is seen by management as an attempt to limit trade union growth and influence. There may be some trade-offs for management: insisting on a non-union approach and treating the JCC as a rival to trade union representation is the essence of the trade union substitution strategy, but basing staff representation on trade union channels may make for more effective representation of employee opinions and more effective dissemination of the deliberations of the JCC. This may help build employee commitment to the process. Where such commitment is lacking and where staff representatives lack credibility in the eyes of employees, there may be a risk that employee grievances are seen to be ignored by management and so provide fertile ground for disruptive action of either a collective or individual nature.

Industrial relations in the majority of Hong Kong workplaces is characterised by a lack of effective means of employee representation and dispute resolution (Turner *et al.* 1980, 1991; Chiu and Levin 1996). JCCs are well established in the public sector, but recent years have seen little evidence of growth in the number of private-sector companies implementing joint consultation and the institutionalisation of workplace industrial relations remains weak. Indeed, the trend may be the reverse. Compared to other sectors of the economy, public utilities have had more institutionalised forms of industrial relations, including JCCs. However, deregulation and restructuring has been associated with job losses and new policies designed to improve efficiency and customer service. Such developments by definition reduce the number of employees covered by these JCCs, and new strategies may call into question the previous industrial relations arrangements.

Clearly, the Labour Department's long-standing policy of urging employers to consider joint consultation on a voluntary basis has had little direct impact. Turner *et al.* (1980) came to a similar conclusion in an earlier period and suggested that the way forward was to require employers by law to establish elected JCCs, at least in large and medium-sized firms. The success of the pro-democracy candidates in the 1998 LegCo elections and the possibility of public support for pro-labour policies offer some hope for those who would champion an extension of the rights to employee representation. However, the removal of the laws passed during the last weeks of British rule, affording rights to trade union representation, consultation and collective bargaining, as discussed in Chapter 2, demonstrates employer and government opposition to such forms of industrial relations. If the employer lobby has its way, then we are unlikely to see a significant increase in the private-sector incidence of joint consultation or similar forms of participation in the foreseeable future.

Notes

1 The authors gratefully acknowledge the funding provided for this research by the Hong Kong Polytechnic University (research grant number G-S508) and wish to thank the Hong Kong School of Motoring for their help..
2 There were 185,442 civil servants in October 1997.
3 The large company survey was aimed at companies with more than 200 employees. These percentages are based on a sample of 143 companies.
4 During the 1992 incident, JCC representatives addressed the workforce on the company's behalf to try to dispel rumours and explain the company's position. However, they lacked credibility and management report that at that time the election process was not taken very seriously by employees. Management were concerned that informal and unnamed strike leaders emerged.
5 Table 16.4 suggests that the JCC exerts a degree of influence on management decisions.

Part V
Hong Kong in East Asia

17 Hong Kong in context

Employment relations in East Asia

Chris Leggett

Introduction

The purpose of this chapter is to survey the East Asian employment relations context of Hong Kong in the last decade of the twentieth century. At
the beginning of the decade there were signs that Japan might not be able to
sustain its economic dynamic. However, observers were still confident that
the Asian economic 'miracle' would be extended through the 'generations' of
industrialisers; that it would only be a matter of time before Vietnam and
other late industrialisers caught up with the 'tigers', and the 'tigers' with the
'newly industrialised economies' (NIEs). Towards the end of the decade,
East Asian countries were in a major recession precipitated by a rapid
transfer of capital out of the region in 1997, the transfer facilitated by the
forces of globalisation that most East Asian countries were eager to
embrace. In the same year, Hong Kong, which had been singled out from
among the Asian NIEs because of its apparent *laissez-faire* economy and
employment relations, was joined as a Special Administrative Region (SAR)
to the People's Republic of China (PRC) ruled by a communist government
that was once dedicated to highly regulated employment relations. It is from
this central perspective of Hong Kong, then, that employment relations in
the countries of East Asia are surveyed.

In discussing the contexts for employment relations, Dore (1979) demonstrates how they reflect the different stages of development through which
the economies pass. Hence it is possible to classify the economies of East
Asia as they stood before the financial crisis began in 1997 (Leggett and
Bamber 1996). In the lead was Japan. Since the mid-1970s, there has been a
substantial interest in Japanese employment systems, and in the transferability of Japanese management styles and practices abroad, including to the
East Asian region where Japanese company subsidiaries began to be estab-
lished earlier than in Europe and North America. Next were NIEs of Hong
Kong, Singapore, Taiwan and South Korea, followed by a third generation
of industrialisers comprising Malaysia, Thailand and the Special Economic
Zones (SEZs) of the PRC, and by a fourth generation including Indonesia,
Vietnam, the Philippines and provinces of the PRC.

Hong Kong has a long tradition of bureaucratic personnel management. Such practices had characterised the British joint stock companies or 'hongs', the Civil Service, and, to some extent, the *émigré* Shanghai capitalist-owned textile companies (England 1989). However, democratisation in the 1990s and a partial dependence on foreign labour had oriented Hong Kong's policy-makers and corporate managers towards a more strategic and flexible application of human resource management (HRM) (Levin and Ng 1995), a development echoed in South Korea (Kim 1995), in Taiwan (Farh 1995), and of course in Singapore (Wilkinson and Leggett 1985). Meanwhile trade unionism in Hong Kong was resuscitated, perhaps by democratisation, by the bargaining opportunities created by labour market shortages, and by apprehension over the colony's impending restoration to Chinese sovereignty. Elsewhere in the region, some other countries have also seen growing union autonomy.

This chapter provides a comparative perspective on employment relations in Hong Kong, by providing an overview of developments in selected East Asian economies. The chapter begins by reviewing the various frames of reference that have been used to examine the rapid industrialisation of the region. Next, it investigates what constitutes the regionalisation and globalisation dimensions of the East Asian context before proceeding to an overview of the distinctive features of employment relations development in East Asian countries, selected according to their position in the industrialisation chain. Attention is paid to the employment conditions of women workers, especially in the export processing zones (EPZs), and, where possible, to the effects on employment relations of the ongoing Asian financial crisis. The chapter concludes with a summary which highlights the main characteristics of Hong Kong's East Asian context and their relevance to Hong Kong itself.

Frames of reference for East Asian industrialisation

In the second half of the 1970s Hong Kong, together with Singapore, Taiwan and South Korea, was recognised as one of the Asian NIEs. Among the frames of reference adopted to try to account for the economic achievements of the Asian economies have been the geopolitical (Borthwick 1992), the region as a complement to European and North American trading blocs (Petri 1995), and the region as a source of developmental inspiration for underdeveloped or stagnant economies (Wilkinson 1994; Lee and Park 1995). There has been consensus among academic economists that East Asian industrialisation was exceptional, but they were divided over whether it amounted to the success of free markets or of government intervention. Of the explanations themselves, these more or less conform to the five approaches identified by Verma *et al.* (1995: 336). There is the socio-economic view, which stresses how a combination of chance and latent Confucianism facilitated industrialisation (Vogel 1991: 8–12). Then there is a mainly political explanation of the state orchestrating an environment conducive to multinational corporate investment, a condition of dependent development (Deyo 1981). Related to this there is the administrative competence of government in setting imperatives and building infrastructure (Riedel 1988: 37). Another approach hypothesises that a collectivist rather than an individualist culture has been conducive to economic growth (Vogel 1991: 92–101). Finally, there is the influence of institutional forces, which include business family groupings ranging from the Korean *chaebol* (Kwon and Leggett 1994: 804–35) to the overseas Chinese family networks (Redding: 1990). With regard to the last two explanations – which are subsumed in some of the others – Paik *et al.* (1996) caution against the assumption of homogeneity across ethnic communities, although Hofstede (1984) maps clusters of countries according to national similarities in organisational behaviour. Other explanations combine the above approaches. Whitely (1992), for example, argues that a combination of historical factors and industrialisation explain the distinctive character of Asian business systems.

Deyo (1989) focused on labour in the Asian NIEs, in particular its 'subordination' by the ruling élites through their exercise of power, which has varied from persuasive to coercive. As Taylor (1996: 7) has put it:

> The characteristics of such regimes, until now, include a relative absence of pressure groups, weak oppositional parties, policy informational rather than policy critical media, an emphasis on group rather than individual rights, reinforced by socializing programs at various points in the education and social system. Moreover, such regimes often came into existence in a period of political upheaval. The ruling elite is almost exclusively comprised of males and in many instances over time has been closely linked to military interests: in some cases, it might be said, there is a dynastic flavour to the style and history of the elite. Leaders of organized labour are either intimately linked with the ruling elite in a state corporatist arrangement, or effectively excluded from political processes through restrictive industrial regulation and extremely limited access to formal political channels. Where they do exist opposition political parties find electoral success almost totally elusive.

Taylor's observations were made in the context of the effects of regionalisation and globalisation on employment relations, and it is to these and their place in the East Asian context that this chapter now turns.

The significance of regionalisation

The Association of Southeast Asian Nations (ASEAN) and the Asia-Pacific Economic Co-operation forum (APEC) became significant regional forces in world trade in the 1990s. ASEAN was established in 1967 to promote the economic and social development of, and maintain a balance of power among, Indonesia, Malaysia, the Philippines, Singapore and Thailand. These were joined by Brunei in 1984 and by Vietnam in 1995. ASEAN's Labour Ministers meet as a separate group from its Economic Ministers to co-operate on matters of common interest, such as the regulation of migrant workers (Castro 1982: 78). APEC, on the other hand, includes ASEAN members and is an Australian-initiated trade forum that got off to a slow start, having been conceived in 1989 but not born until 1993. As well as the ASEAN countries, it comprises Japan, South Korea, the People's Republic of China (PRC), Taiwan, Hong Kong, the USA, Canada, Mexico, Chile, Australia and New Zealand. Consistent with developments generally, the agenda of both ASEAN and APEC, where they concern employment relations, are inclined more towards HRM than towards traditional institutional industrial relations matters. Skills training and development are of concern, although APEC's primary focus, like that of the North American Free Trade Agreement (NAFTA) of 1992–3 is on achieving trade liberalisation. APEC in particular, and ASEAN less so, are looser groupings of heterogeneous countries than is the European Union (EU).

The rapid industrialisation of many East Asian countries sensitised their industrialising élites to the global effects of their economies and to their need to be responsive to global and regional developments in trading relationships. Not least in importance here is the determination of the character of employment relations in each of the countries. To take Indonesia as an example, employment relations in the archipelago were of global interest, at least until the financial and political turmoil of the late 1990s, because of a number of factors. Of these, among the more important was the linking of trade preferences with the reform of human and worker rights. Also important were the role of labour in the socio-political control of the country, the need for Indonesia to decide where to position itself *vis-à-vis* globalisation, and the link between the struggle for independent trade unionism and democratisation. From a regional perspective therefore it might be concluded that the future of employment relations in Indonesia and other East Asian economies may be looked for as much in the agendas of ASEAN and APEC as in the historical development of the individual countries themselves.

On regionalisation in Asia, Peter Drucker (Drucker and Nakauchi 1997: 42), observing from a prescriptive management perspective notes:

> The most important emerging regions will not be able to follow the examples of others. These are the regions of Asia, and no one can know how many regions tomorrow's Mainland Asia will have. Coastal China by itself is certainly big enough to be a region of its own, and distinct enough. South East Asia and the ASEAN countries together, are also big enough to be a region, but, unlike Coastal China, they are extremely diverse – culturally, socially and politically. Half, for instance, have a Confucian tradition; the other half are Muslim. The relationship of

Japan to either of these two regions still has to be worked out and cannot even be guessed at.

Globalisation and East Asian employment relations

There are alternative conceptualisations of globalisation which as yet remain theoretically weak. Further, whether globalisation is a tendency towards one global economy or whether it is just another stage in the internationalisation of capital remains contested. Gollan (1995: 1–2) tries to clarify the concept by dividing definitions of globalisation into three integrated elements: the integration of 'capital accumulation or technological expansion', 'political action beyond the jurisdiction and scope of individual states', and 'accessibility of ideas and information' resulting from advances in communications technology.

From the global restructuring consequent upon the processes associated with these elements, pressures have arisen for the restructuring of employment relations. However, there appear to be two opposed views as to the economic and social outcomes of globalisation in East Asian countries: one emphasising positive outcomes, the other negative impacts. The positive is the neo-liberal view which claims that free trade and export-oriented production and trade result in improved socio-political conditions and recognition of basic rights. Riedel (1988: 21), for example, suggests that the quality of life in the East Asian countries improved significantly through the 1970s and the 1980s and, except in Thailand and Indonesia, proportionately more than in other developing countries on average. The negative view is that competition in the global economy undermines labour standards. Governments may use 'the compete or perish' argument to justify the dilution of protective labour legislation, shore up managerial prerogatives, and cut social spending to accelerate their economies' integration into the world economy. For example, compliance with the Singapore government's imperatives for employment relations was largely achieved by the incorporation of the trade union movement into the Peoples' Action Party (PAP) hegemony. The spearhead of the PAP-endorsed labour movement was, and is, the National Trades Union Congress (NTUC). However, the curtailment of collective bargaining lost trade union members. The decline in membership was eventually turned around, mainly through the NTUC's role in centralised wage determination, to peak in 1979. Since 1979, membership decline has re-emerged, albeit slower than in the earlier period, and may be attributed to changes in values, occupational structure and, anecdotally, to the non-charismatic leadership of the NTUC (Leggett 1988).

National and regional pressure groups in the developed countries have called on their governments to insist on political democratisation in the East Asian region. In parallel, there have been pressures to improve human and trade union rights – from Australia, New Zealand and via the International Labour Organisation (ILO). However, the most powerful pressures have come from North America, including the US government and the AFL-CIO, and from the European Union (EU). These have been linked to trading arrangements within and between the major trading blocs. The model of the transformation of an industrial relations system was developed with reference to the USA by Kochan *et al.* (1986), and the USA's industrial relations institutions are offered as an example to democratising countries such as Korea and Taiwan. Nevertheless, the transformation of American industrial relations has not been attributed to an increase or decrease in the degree of democratisation. Rather it has been explained in terms of the changing strategies of management in the face of increasing international competition: employers have sought to minimise labour costs and maximise control over their workforces by maintaining a 'union-free' environment. Nevertheless, while Japanese employment practices have a strategic component, it was found that Japanese company subsidiaries in their Southeast Asian subsidiary operations were more inclined to accommodate local practices than were those of other countries, thereby gaining cheaper labour costs and justifying their not interfering in local ways (Hutchings 1996).

The remainder of this chapter will identify and discuss some of the distinctive employment relations developments in East Asia, on a country-by-country basis. The significance of such developments for Hong Kong is reflected upon. We begin with Japan, the first East Asian country to industrialise and continue down the industrialisation chain.

Japan at the point of convergence

Following his study of technologically similar electrical manufacturing companies in Britain and Japan, Dore (1973) suggested that Japan had leapfrogged the stage of pluralistic industrialism typified by the USA and was itself the model for others' industrial futures. By being a 'late' developer Japan had more effectively than elsewhere adapted through 'welfare corporatism' the modern bureaucratic equivalent of paternalism. Regular Japanese employees in the large corporations, but not women, migrants or workers in dependent companies, enjoyed lifetime employment, age-based promotion and seniority wages, which had the effect of encouraging the incorporation of these employees into the enterprise culture, resulting in turn in strong employee commitment.

Many explanations for the extraordinary growth of several East Asian economies since the early 1960s begin with Japan (Fruin 1992). Since the mid-1970s there has been a global interest in Japanese management (for example Suzuki 1995) and in the transferability of Japanese management styles outside of Japan (for example, Oliver and Wilkinson 1992). This interest has been informed by experiences of Japanese companies in other parts of East Asia (Hutchings 1996). As has been noted, some Japanese companies began to establish subsidiaries in East Asia before they ventured to Europe and North America and one study of such experiences has found that the differences between management styles in Japan and elsewhere are declining (Shadur *et al.* 1995: 735ff.). Important now, however, are the Japanese approaches to employment relations as they are challenged by the changing economic and political context following economic recession and regional instability in the 1990s. In any case, notwithstanding its corporate presence in Hong Kong, the immediate importance of Japan to Hong Kong is with Japan as an investor which sees Hong Kong as a gateway to China rather than as a model for employment relations *per se*.

Singapore: the other city state

Soon after its economic take-off Singapore's industrialisation became dependent on multinational corporate investment, with the PAP government supplying infrastructure development. Through the 1960s, the PAP government regulated employment relations, with legislation covering trade unions, collective bargaining, dispute settlement and terms and conditions of employment. From 1972 the size and scope of wage increases were regulated by a tripartite National Wages Council (NWC) and, in the 1980s, amendments to trade union and employment legislation emphasised labour-management co-operation in the pursuit of productivity in an economy restructured towards high technology and high value-added enterprise (Leggett 1993).

In parallel with the legislation, the NTUC was, at different stages, transformed into something of a transmission belt for the values the government deemed appropriate for a disciplined workforce. Singapore's unions were prepared for a workplace focus and a greater flexibility in enterprise bargaining which has accommodated the variable needs of individual companies. HRM, rather than conflict management, was, and is, propagated and diffused throughout management and the workforce in the public and private sectors, by the universities and polytechnics, the management institutes, unions and employers' associations, and the network of corporations through which Singapore is regulated. Thus, the circumstances of Singapore's dependence on multinational investment led the PAP government to take the initiative in human resource planning and development on a national scale, only cautiously moving the locus of control to the workplace with its decision to restructure the economy. This caution, and the government's capacity to fine tune Singapore's employment relations in response to changes in the environment, have enabled the city state to weather the current Asian economic crisis better than any of its neighbours. For example, the maintenance of a high level of national savings through compulsory employer and employee contributions to the state-run Central Provident Fund (CPF) has provided leverage on employer costs which it has used in times of recession, including the present one. The HRM orientation of Singapore's employment relations too may be a complementary asset to government levers such as the CPF in the current circumstances.

In East Asia generally, human resource managers are involved in devising strategies for corporate survival involving layoffs, whereas two years ago their attention was focused on recruitment, retention and productivity. In Hong Kong, a city state both compared and contrasted with Singapore, a recent survey of 300 multinational and local employers found that in the following three months 20 per cent expected to lay off employees and 65 per cent to reduce wage bills; whilst 37 per cent considered 'low morale' to be their biggest HRM problem (*Far Eastern Economic Review*, 21 January 1999: 43). Hong Kong's uncertainties have at times benefited Singapore, the government of which is quick to exploit opportunities to improve the quality of its labour force. Thus, in 1989, when emigration from Hong Kong was at its height, Singapore made special efforts to recruit potential citizens from what, for cultural reasons, was already a preferred source.

South Korea and *Chaebol* relations

The character of South Korea's employment relations has been largely determined by successive governments having chosen the family conglomerates, the *chaebol*, as their vehicle for industrialisation. Although these governments sponsored a compliant Federation of Korean Trade Unions (FKTU or Daehan Nochong), adopted well-defined labour codes and directed investment policies, it has been the *chaebol*, such as Hyundai and Daewoo, which have developed the policies and practices of South Korean employment relations.

South Korea, like Singapore, Hong Kong and Taiwan, began to industrialise rapidly in the 1960s and the prevalent theme of most analyses of employment relations has been the central role of the state rather than the role of the *chaebol*. However, since the mid-1980s, many *chaebol* employees have organised themselves within an alternative trade union federation (since registered as the Federation of Korean Democratic Trade Unions FKDTU or Minju Nochong), thereby making the managerial approaches of the *chaebol* towards trade unionism significant in shaping the future of South Korean employment relations (Chun 1989: 318–21).

Several factors have contributed to the importance of the *chaebol*. It was the *chaebol* under government patronage that initiated the industrialisation of South Korea and they have played a dominant role in the country's economic development ever since. In 1990, it was reported that the total earnings of Korea's top thirty *chaebol* contributed about 95 per cent of South Korea's GNP (Bank of Korea 1990). Further, there was reportedly a high concentration of large single firms within the *chaebol*; in 1990, the top fifty-three *chaebol* included the 797 largest of these (Korean Economic Planning Board 1990). Empowered by the sheer size of their conglomerates and through intermarriage with the families of the military élite, the *chaebol* families had by the 1980s established themselves as South Korea's capitalist class, employing a substantial proportion of Korea's workers.

When they were confronted by independent trade unionism in the mid-1980s, the *chaebol* employers initially resorted to unlawful tactics to contain it. Since the early 1990s, however, a greater reliance on strategic HRM has prevailed. In 1996, President Kim Young-sam announced a New Conception of Industrial Relations (NCIR) with the purpose of reform through the deliberations of a multi-representative Industrial Relations Reform Commission (IRRC). There immediately followed a dramatic increase in the number of trade unions, in trade union membership and in trade disputes, but only minor amendments to labour laws which continued to recognise only the FKTU and locked out 'third parties' from collective bargaining (*Far Eastern Economic Review*, 3 February 1994: 54).

In December 1996, against expectations, the Kim Young-sam government amended the Trade Union Act largely in favour of employers, deferring major reforms into the new millenium. An ensuing general strike forced the government to compromise by making the FKDTU lawful and revising the amendments. Since then, South Korea, along with other Asian nations, has experienced a reversal of its economic fortunes such that union power will be substantially weakened by layoffs and the strict application of International Monetary Fund (IMF) requirements.

On a comparative note then, the circumstances of Singapore's dependence on multinational corporate investment led the PAP government to take the initiatives in configuring and reconfiguring employment relations on a national scale, only cautiously moving the locus of control to the workplace with its decision to restructure the economy in 1979, a process which it has continued with typical pragmatic accommodation to changes in the economic environment. This contrasts with the predominance in South Korea of the *chaebol* in the development of employment relations policies and practices For instance, whereas in Singapore the state provides and regulates workers' housing and other facilities, in South Korea, company towns such as Woosan (Hyundai) and, in the public sector, Pohang (POSCO), house and service employees. In contrast, in Hong Kong union division and weakness has meant that there has arguably been less need to control unions by incorporation along the lines of the other three NIEs.

Although company welfarism and state regulation are found in Hong Kong and Taiwan, Poon (1996) sees the flexibility derived from sub-contracting, (i.e. quite different working conditions from South Korea and Singapore) as underwriting their dramatic economic growth since World War II. However, she envisages changes in the operation of the sub-contracting networks in both countries – as a result in Taiwan of government intervention and in Hong Kong of the relocation of labour-intensive manufacturing to Mainland China – and uncertainty for the employment of manufacturing workers unless they are able to upgrade their skills. Particularly vulnerable are full-time women workers whose dislocation from manufacturing has been by the use of part-time married women workers, and by foreign workers. Since the economic crisis began in 1997, women workers have been among the first targets for dismissal.

The Asian economic crisis has affected South Korea more than most East Asian countries. The cost to South Korea of being bailed out by the IMF is the economic restructuring conditions imposed by the IMF. Restructuring has meant massive layoffs by the *chaebol* and South Korea has experienced an unemployment rate comparable to that in western industrialised countries where, unlike South Korea, there is at least some entitlement to unemployment benefit. Migrant workers from Vietnam, Mongolia and Bangladesh have been repatriated (*Asian Labour Update*, February–May 1998).

Taiwan: the Kuomintang in residence

Robins (1998) traces the stages of Taiwan's economic development through the following stages: 'import substitution, 1950–60'; 'export-led industrialisation (1960–73)'; 'deepening of the industrial base, 1973–80 (secondary import substitution)'; and 'towards innovation, higher technology and higher value, 1980–present'. Taiwan's first EPZ was established in 1966, at Kaohsiung. Others were established in 1969. Most EPZ employees in Taiwan have been women, in the past sometimes pressured to remain single by employers. Because labour costs rose as Taiwan successfully industrialised, many factories relocated to EPZs in cheaper labour countries, and those remaining keep their costs down by employing migrant labour.

Throughout its industrialisation Taiwan, like South Korea, has had state-controlled trade unions. The Kuomintang government-endorsed Chinese Federation of Labour (CFL) and its enterprise affiliates came to fulfil a paternalistic welfare function but, as in South Korea, an independent labour movement emerged in the mid-1980s. The effect of labour legislation (the Labour Standards Law, and the Arbitration Disputes Act 1988) and the new-found strength of the labour movement, demonstrated as much by the capture of executive committees with allegiance to the Kuomintang as by forming new union federations in the 1980s, have contributed to a new climate of industrial relations in Taiwan (Wilkinson 1994: 144–9). However, in the 1990s the fortunes of a labour movement involving a Labour Party and a Workers' Party declined, although in 1994 pressure for reform of labour legislation came from a Committee of Action for Labour Legislation which included in its representation the National Federation of Independent Trade Unions (NAFITU).

The difficulties Taiwan's trade unions have in maintaining the momentum of the late 1980s have been attributed to the structural characteristics of the Taiwanese economy:

> Despite these new developments, the unique characteristics of the Taiwan economy, such as the predominance of small businesses and the heavy involvement in international trade, the seniority wage system, and

the economic superiority of white-collar workers, have made it difficult for trade unions to make significant inroads into workplaces. If there is any role for trade unions in Taiwan's future, it will be in the area of employee training and employee benefit coordination among small firms as workers move frequently from firm to firm. The movement towards capital- and skill-intensive industries will make human resource management increasingly important as workers develop more specific skills, require more training, and cost more to retain. Trade unions can also play an important role in the area of occupational safety and health by serving as a watchdog and making sure their employers comply with the safety standards set by the government.

(Lee 1995)

Taiwan's Council of Labour Affairs (CLA) was established in 1987, and, according to its Chairman, adheres to the ideal of 'labour-management cooperation, co-existence and co-prosperity' (Chan 1998: 2). Its emphasis is still on welfare but there is acknowledgement that socio-economic change, globalisation, regional alliances and information technology have an impact on the government's labour policy. Its priorities for the twenty-first century are listed as follows:

First, strengthening the work safety of labourers and boosting the benefit of occupational disaster in insurance [*sic*]. Second, increasing the job opportunities for aborigines and women. Third, establishing a sound employment security system. Fourth, working out a reasonable and also feasible labour retirement system. Fifth, fortifying the management on alien labourers and reducing their negative effects. Sixth, resolving effectively labour-management disputes. Seventh, tightening the legal system of the labour to thoroughly protect their rights and interests.

(Chan 1998: 3)

Managing foreign workers has preoccupied the Taiwan government for a number of years. As with the other Asian NIEs, the tight labour markets of the 1980s and 1990s have attracted migrant workers from within the region.

An important and substantial labour migration in the East Asian region has been of female domestic helpers from the Philippines – and to a lesser extent from Thailand, Indonesia and the Indian sub-continent – to the NIEs, especially to Hong Kong and Singapore. The supply of overseas domestic helpers enabled mothers to join the labour market; indeed, it was public policy in government-interventionist Singapore to encourage well-educated women both to have families and to apply their qualifications to the economy (Wilkinson and Leggett 1995: 11–12). However, the Asian economic crisis has reduced the demand for domestic helpers and led to pay cuts, such that in February this year Filipina domestic helpers in Hong Kong publicly protested at a 5 per cent drop in their minimum wage (*Far Eastern*

Economic Review, 18 February 1999: 18–19). Hong Kong's Filipina domestic helpers have a visible presence in Hong Kong and, in contrast to their compatriots working in Singapore, an audible one as they have campaigned for improved working conditions in the 1990s.

Taiwan's migrant workers have come from Thailand, Malaysia, the Philippines and Indonesia, mainly as unskilled workers in construction, manufacturing, seafaring and domestic service. The NIE governments have regulated the supply of migrant labour through visa and employment passes, through the licensing of labour agencies and, in the case of Singapore, severe punishments for migrants overstaying and employers for illegal hiring. The policy is to supplement the national workforce, not to replace it. The Taiwan authorities appear to share their Singaporean and South Korean counterparts' concern that foreign workers from sources which are culturally very different may disturb the social homogeneity of their own countries.

Malaysia's way

The employment relations policies of the East Asian industrialisers, including Malaysia, Thailand and the People's Republic of China, have attracted attention in the 1990s as they have echoed the experiences of the region's NIEs. These countries were seen as caught in a low-wage trap with competition from below and exclusion from higher value-added markets above (Deyo 1995: 23). Both Malaysia and Thailand have been severely affected by the 1997 Asian financial crisis, but the Malaysian government has reacted by resisting rather than complying with IMF formulae for recovery, a response which has resulted in a serious political crisis.

Before the 1997 Asian financial crisis, the Malaysian government, following Singapore's example, sought to avoid the low-wage trap by attracting high-technology, high-value-added production through national employment relations policies. The intention was to develop Malaysia into an industrialised economy by 2020 (Kuruvilla and Arudsothy 1995: 184). To this end, competition in the private sector and revitalisation in the public sector were having an impact on employment relations practices (Kuruvilla 1995: 59–61). Unlike Singapore, Malaysia does not have a single union federation to act as a transmission belt to inform and mobilise the workforce to meet national industrial imperatives. Traditionally, the Malaysian Trades Union Congress (MTUC) and its affiliate, the National Union of Plantation Workers (NUPW) had been the face of manual workers and the Congress of Unions of Employees in the Public and Civil Services (CUEPACS) of white-collar workers in Malaysia. However, the Malaysian government initiated the Malaysian Labour Organization (MLO) with a view to it becoming more occupationally representative of Malaysia's industrialised future than were the traditional federations (Ramachandran 1994; Kuruvilla 1995: 55–6). Electronics workers, as employees of the industrial future, had only been permitted to unionise in 1988, when they quickly formed the National Union of Electronics Workers.

The MTUC did attempt to organise women EPZ workers but has not been so successful because it is not itself structured to represent women workers' interests. Most of Malaysia's EPZ employees (about 150,000) are unmarried Malay women, often from rural communities who, as in Indonesia, see their employment as a liberating opportunity. However, the cultural dislocation and repetitive, monotonous work can be stressful and has at times resulted in mass hysteria (*Asian Labour Update*, May–July 1995: 12–13). Foreign workers in export-oriented industries in Malaysia are to be allowed to stay, although, as a result of the Asian economic crisis, some 850,000 out of two million foreign workers in Malaysia are not getting their work permits renewed (*Far Eastern Economic Review*, 22 January 1998: 23).

Thailand's labour intensive industrialisation

In the late 1980s and early 1990s the Thai economy was achieving an annual average growth rate of about 10 per cent, mostly driven by export-oriented manufacturing, especially of textiles. However, liberalising trade in ASEAN and within APEC, among other developments, exposed Thailand's labour-intensive manufacturers to cheaper labour competition resulting in the short run in the adoption of a range of cost-cutting measures. Moreover, the 1997 Asian financial crisis can be expected to prolong these initially short-run measures. Among the measures have been mechanisation and diversification, relocation to cheap-labour sites, non-compliance with minimum wage and standards legislation, casualisation and subcontracting to households. Although some employers adopted long-term strategies of flexibility and quality enhancement, these were confined to a few companies – mainly in engineering – and are unlikely without the government's backing to be carried over to other sectors (Deyo 1995: 26–36).

Thailand has been among the locations for Hong Kong manufacturers seeking cheaper labour. Hong Kong entrepreneurs became the world's leading producer of toys in the 1980s, but in the 1990s they were sub-contracting the manufacture of globalised favourites such as Batman figures, Barbie Dolls and Ninja Turtles, to local factories in China, Thailand, Malaysia, the Philippines, Macao and Indonesia. Employment standards are not always enforced by the local governments and working conditions in the factories are often hazardous; in the case of a toy factory in Bangkok in 1993 this resulted in the deaths of 189 workers, mostly young women, in a fire.

In the 1990s Thai workers have been restricted from forming trade unions and taking industrial action and, in tripartite institutions, the government representatives tend to side with the employers. Thus pay cuts were achieved by the employers' Federation of Thai Industries in designated areas along the borders with Burma and Laos, areas intended to attract migrant workers.

These migrant workers are now being repatriated as a result of the Asian economic crisis. In June 1998 it was estimated that Thailand was host to one million illegal workers, most from Burma, but also from Cambodia and Laos (*Far Eastern Economic Review*, 22 January 1998: 22–3).

As with most other countries in this survey, Thailand's economic growth has depended on export-oriented manufacturing and, in the EPZs, electronics is the most common industry. The composition of the workforce in Thai export-oriented manufacturing is 90 per cent female and is not inactive in campaigning for benefits and wage increases in spite of the threat by employers to move their operations to China or Vietnam.

In the 1980s professional employment relations management was infused into medium-sized and larger business establishments in Thailand, particularly among foreign-owned companies (Supachai 1993: 265). When, in 1989, Lawler and Atmiyanandana (1995: 302–15) conducted a survey of firms in Thailand, the results enabled them to classify HRM strategies according to companies' countries of origin, including Thai-owned companies. They found that western subsidiaries of multinational firms had structured internal labour markets, paid relatively high wages, avoided unionisation and aimed at rational control and efficiency. Japanese subsidiaries, on the other hand, were more concerned with acculturation, had relatively unstructured internal labour markets, and emphasised training and employee involvement. The larger Thai family enterprises were generally owned by ethnic Chinese entrepreneurs whose control of employees was through the management of the deference that is observed to be a part of Thai interpersonal relations. In contrast, publicly held Thai corporations were nurturing a young equitable managerial élite equipped with North American MBAs, who nevertheless also exploited traditional values to control lower-level employees.

People's Republic of China SEZs

In the People's Republic of China (PRC), the central planning priorities determined the state-level employment relations policies which shaped those at the enterprise level. However, subsequent reform has meant that 'the HR [human resource] policies of Chinese enterprises are driven by product-market considerations and by state-level HR policies which are being adjusted to a market-driven economy' (Verma and Yan 1995: 317–18). Labour reform has not been straightforward. For example, disputes arising from the rapid transfer of workers from lifetime to contract employment appeared to provide the trigger for about 50 per cent of all labour disputes in the late 1980s and early 1990s. Moreover, rural migration, in spite of restrictions, has created heavy urban unemployment (Jackson 1994). Although it was once claimed that the PRC provided some of the cheapest labour in the world to the factories being developed by expatriate, mainly Hong Kong Chinese, entrepreneurs in the special economic zones (SEZs) along its coast (O'Leary 1994: 51), this is no longer the case. Consequently, Hong Kong and other Asian entrepreneurs have been moving inland from the coast and the Pearl River delta and into Northern China in search of cheaper labour. One study of pay policy and wage determination in Hong Kong and Guandong concluded that despite important differences there are now sufficient similarities to suggest an element of convergence in the region (White *et al.* 1998: 363–73).

According to the Hong Kong Christian Industrial Committee (*Asian Labour Update*, May–July 1995) there are between 60 and 70 million workers employed in the PRC's five SEZs and fourteen 'open cities'. Despite the element of convergence mentioned above, approximately 80 per cent of SEZ workers are young, unmarried women who are housed in dormitories, as they usually are in other EPZs in East Asia. Working conditions are said to be poor, especially in terms of health and safety; for example, a fire at a toy factory in Shenzhen adjacent to Hong Kong in 1993 killed eighty-four workers. However, few workers are unionised. Attempts to organise unions independent of the All China Federation of Trade Unions (ACFTU) in the Shenzhen SEZ in 1993–4 were suppressed. However, in Zhuhai SEZ in 1995 Matsushita employees, aggrieved at the cancellation by management of their Chinese New Year leave, successfully organised a strike and picket.

Indonesia's failed new order

Indonesia's economic development under Suharto's New Order government, which had been in office since 1968, had been predicated on the supply of cheap labour to complement heavy investment in manufacturing with an increasing export orientation. The quality of employees' working lives was largely determined within a labyrinthine complexity of relationships involving the ruling elite, the military and ethnic Chinese entrepreneurs, and underpinned by the *Pancasila* (Five Principles) state ideology. As elsewhere in East Asia, the US government and labour groups had pressured Indonesia to reform its labour practices by threatening to revoke tariff concessions.

The official view of employment relations in Indonesia before the economic and political crises that have challenged and continue to challenge the structure of the society since 1997 is that they should be non-confrontational, and this is consistent with the tradition of *musyawarah-mufakat* (discussion leading towards consensus). Dispute resolution tribunals were established by Law No. 22 of 1957 as the Panitia Peneyelesaian Perselisihan Perburahan Daerah (Regional Mediation Body for Labor Conflict or P4D) and the central body, the Panitia Penyelesaian Perselisihan Perburuhan or P4P, but served the corporatist policies of the New Order government.

Pressures for labour reform in Indonesia came from the USA, the World Bank and the ILO. In 1994 the International Confederation of Free Trade Unions (ICFTU) complained to the ILO Committee on Freedom of

Association of Indonesia's infringement of Conventions, and the ILO censured the country 'for violations of trade union rights including suppression of independent unions, intimidatory use of the military, and restrictions on collective bargaining and strike action' (Upham 1995: I-31). Although in January 1994 the government repealed a decree (Regulation 342/1986) which allowed military intervention in disputes, army intervention continued, as at Medan later that year.

Labour standards in Indonesia were perceived as a problem before 1997. Although larger firms had complied with protective labour codes, small and medium enterprises in general had not, so that labour welfare provisions had lagged behind development. In any case, labour standards were unlikely to follow the trends in other industrially more advanced countries in Asia, such as Taiwan and Korea because a much higher proportion of Indonesian workers were outside the formal sector – as much as 80 per cent – and Indonesia never had the tight labour market typical of the Asian NIEs (Manning 1996: 263–8).

Restrictions on foreign investment in Indonesia were lifted in 1993, but the country has experienced capital investment from Japan, South Korea, Taiwan and Hong Kong since the 1970s and into EPZs since the first one, the Nusantara Bonded Zone, was opened in 1986. Manufacturing in the EPZs has been mostly of garments and shoes, by young unmarried women workers. Before the economic and political crises hit Indonesia, protests over pay and working conditions broke out from time to time in the EPZs and other industrial areas of Indonesia but were suppressed, usually by military intervention. A military-organised crackdown on striking workers involving the torture and horrendous murder of a woman workplace representative in Medan in 1994 demonstrated the extent of the New Order government's intolerance of labour activists and the resentment by ethnic Malay workers of ethnic Chinese entrepreneurs. Ethnic Chinese Indonesians make up about 3 per cent of Indonesia's population but are said to control about 70 per cent of the economy (*Asiaweek*, 24 January 1997, 28 February 1997).

Since 1985, the only officially recognised trade union federation, apart from the 1.3 million-member Indonesian Teachers' Association, has been the Serikat Pekerja Seluruh Indonesia (All Indonesian Workers' Union or SPSI). In 1991 environmental and human rights groups organised Serikat Buruh Merdeka Setiakawan (Solidarity Free Trade Union or SBMS), in effect challenging the corporatist and unitarist model of *wadah tunggal* which had permitted only one organisation for each sector of society. SBMS was banned, but in 1993 the Serikat Buruh Sejahtera Indonesia (Indonesian Prosperous Labour Union or SBSI) was formed with support from the American and European unions. It too was banned but survives, and SPSI, in a tactical move, was restructured as an industry-based federation to give it a more respectable face internationally, in particular in a bid to achieve the sought-after recognition from the ICFTU.

Social unrest remains endemic in Indonesia in spite of the resignation of

President Suharto and the prospects for economic recovery are poor, according to the IMF, until institutional reforms are undertaken. (*Far Eastern Economic Review*, 4 March 1999: 44). In this uncertainty, it is unlikely to be a favoured location for investment by Hong Kong entrepreneurs who may also be deterred by the anti-Chinese sentiment of labour and political protest demonstrations.

Vietnam on the margin in East Asia

Structural reforms in the 1990s in Vietnam were directed towards making the transition from a centralised planned economy to a market economy. A labour code was enacted in 1994. It distinguished between industrial relations in the state sector, in the non-state sector. and in foreign-funded establishments. The new structures led to new types of employment relations. The role of trade unions was limited and the Vietnam General Confederation of Labour (VGCL) has had to adjust its Marxist principles to the Vietnamese Communist Party's economic restructuring imperatives. Under the new labour code the capacity to strike has been constrained, the VGCL's monopoly of representation broken, and employers' prerogatives extended (Lansbury 1994). Although the concept of tripartism was established and institutionalised in Vietnam, both employers and employees have had difficulty in understanding it and, as a result, disputation and strikes over pay and conditions increased.

Vietnam has not been very successful in developing EPZs. Only Tan Thuan is functioning and it employs only just over 1,000 workers, all of them women. The enterprises in Tan Thuan are mostly joint ventures, and it was in joint-venture enterprises in Ho Chi Minh City that strikes occurred in the early 1990s. Since the Asian financial crisis began, Vietnamese workers have been laid off by foreign investing companies, including the Hong Kong-owned Kollan Company, which in 1998 was unable to pay all their wages to those laid off. Hong Kong manufacturing companies had been competing with investors from Taiwan and South Korea and with state-owned companies in Vietnam subcontracting from East Asian countries (*Asian Labour Update*, February–May 1998).

Disunity in the Philippines' labour movement

As with other less developed countries in East Asia in the 1990s, the Philippines was faced with the requirement to accommodate to globalisation. However, the role of labour in this accommodation has been hampered by lack of unity within the labour movement. The 'moderate' Trade Union Congress and the 'progressive' Kilusang Mayo Uno (KMU) appear to be beset with political infighting, which inhibits their effectiveness as a labour movement. Consequently, one might expect a diversity of employment-relations practices according to the national or ethnic ownership of the employing company as has been observed in Thailand and Hong Kong. However, hypothesising that in the Philippines historical and structural factors have shaped a convergence of employment relations, Amante (1995), after comparing pay and employment in Japanese-owned, western-owned and Filipino-owned firms, concluded that 'it is quite meaningless to attach [these ethnic-ownership terms] to universal concepts like IR [industrial relations] and human resource approaches'.

An important characteristic of Filipino labour is its employment overseas, such that a significant component of the Philippines economy is net factor income from abroad, consisting mostly of foreign exchange remittances by overseas Filipino workers. In 1995 it was estimated that overseas Filipinos numbered 4.2 million (Department of Labour and Employment 1995). Filipina domestic helpers, as has been observed, make up a significant constituent of the workforce in Hong Kong.

In the EPZs of the Philippines, as elsewhere in East Asia, female workers are expected to be single and, although also required to be college-educated, are mostly allocated the unskilled jobs, the higher-skilled ones being allocated to men. Hiring for less than six months as a means of avoiding the regularisation of employment is common among employers. Nevertheless, women workers in the EPZs have had some success at organising themselves – as the Kilusang ng Manggagawang Kababaihan (KMK) in 1984 – to pursue women's specific demands at work, and KMK was instrumental through striking and picketing in forcing union recognition by a joint Korean–Philippine shoe manufacturer in the Bataan EPZ (*Asian Labour Update*, May–July 1995).

People's Republic of China beyond the SEZs

The impact of globalisation on the PRC's economy has deepened regional income disparities. A difficulty is that, although the ACFTU has a long history, there is no labour organisation that can independently represent workers' interests or bargain effectively with management. In addition, Chinese labour legislation is basic and is not systematically enforced. Meanwhile, the government has sought to transfer workers to contract employment. The transfer of workers to contract employment is one of three reforms (the others being of payments and social insurance systems) of state-owned enterprises introduced in North East China in the early 1990s. The employment relations implications are discussed by Warner (1996), who concludes that the labour contracts have served mainly to clarify duties and responsibilities and that the introduction of social insurance is intended to provide protection to workers on contracts.

Structural reforms to state enterprises, especially their reorganisation into shareholding companies, has been accompanied by large-scale layoffs – about 17 million by the end of 1998 (*Far Eastern Economic Review*, 18 February 1999: 12), and workers still employed are in some cases not getting paid. Worker grievances are not without protest and labour unrest is reported to be rampant but not mobilised (*Far Eastern Economic Review*, 25 February 1999: 46–8).

Conclusion

The economies of the East Asian countries whose distinctive employment relations are described above have moved, or are moving, through the process of industrialisation, with Japan as the first country to industrialise followed by the NIEs including Hong Kong, the third generation of industrialisers such as Malaysia, and then the fourth generation of more diverse industrialisers such Indonesia and the provinces of the PRC. However, although the employment relations in these countries have undergone this process of industrialisation and are located in the same region, their employment relations are not the same. It is possible to discern a number of differences between the characteristics of Hong Kong described in the preceding chapters of this book and those of its close neighbours surveyed in this chapter. Indeed, Hong Kong employment relations differ significantly even from those of the other NIEs, namely Singapore, Taiwan and South Korea. Many factors account for these differences, including political history, culture, technology and government ideologies and policies. The role of the state has almost everywhere been important in defining the parameters of workers' organisations and determining the legal framework of employment relations, but its approach has varied from the central planning priorities of the PRC government, through the corporatist strategies of the Singapore government, to the selective *laissez-faire* of the Hong Kong government. The varying nature of the employer, ranging from multinational to backyard workshop, to homegrown family conglomerate, has also been important. Likewise, the history and quality of trade unionism differs from one country to another in spite of affiliation to regional and international federations – thus the militancy of trade union leaders in Taiwan has not been matched in Malaysia for several decades, that of Korean unionists has no parallel in Singapore, and the enterprise union structure in Korea is currently a cause of tension in that country's industrial relations but of industrial harmony in Japan.

However, these countries also share a number of similarities. They all shared to some extent in the Asian economic miracle based, *inter alia*, on cheap and comparatively quiescent labour. The resultant rising cost of this labour has led to its substitution by capital in production systems. To organise this on a national scale was a priority of the Singapore government from 1979; the Korean government through its relationship with the *chaebol* moved the country's economy from labour-intensive activities in the 1960s to heavy industry in the 1970s and towards electronics and service industries in the 1980s and 1990s. The rising labour cost also led employers to search for cheaper labour to maintain cost competitiveness, either by relocating production overseas to the less industrialised countries in the group – to the PRC, Vietnam, Indonesia, the Philippines and now Cambodia – or retaining production within the country by the import of cheap labour – from Indonesia to Malaysia, from the Indian sub-continent to Korea, and from Thailand, the Indian sub-continent and the Philippines to Singapore and Taiwan. These countries are also all suffering from the current Asian economic crisis, although some, such as Indonesia and South Korea, have suffered more than others. Additionally, these East Asian countries have all experienced rising levels of education and skills, and increased economic and political roles for women.

This comparison helps us to understand some of the features of Hong Kong's management and labour at the end of the twentieth century and to catch a glimpse of future developments in the new SAR. On the other hand, certain features of Hong Kong are distinctive, such as its largely British legal framework and its peculiarly uncertain future given its close dependence on political events in the PRC. Particularly important will be the extent to which the SAR government adopts a planned high-tech profile for Hong Kong.

References

Abraham, K. G. and Katz, L. F. (1986) 'Cyclical unemployment: sectoral shifts or aggregate disturbances?', *Journal of Political Economy*, 94, June: 507–22.

Aburdene, P. and Naisbitt, J. (1992) *Management for Women*, New York: Villard.

Adam, E. and Chell, E. (1993) 'The successful international entrepreneur: a profile', paper presented at the 23rd European Small Business Seminar, Belfast.

Adler, N. J. and Izraeli, D. N. (eds) (1994) *Competitive Frontiers: Women Managers in a Global Economy*, Cambridge, Massachusetts: Blackwell.

Alimo-Metcalfe, B. (1994) 'Gender bias in the selection and assessment of women in management', in Davidson, M. J. and Burke, R. J. (eds) *Women in Management: Current Research Issues*, London: Paul Chapman.

Amante, M. S. V. (1995) 'Employment and wage practices of Japanese firms in the Philippines: convergence with Filipino–Chinese and Western-owned firms', *International Journal of Human Resource Management*, 6(3): 642–55.

Amsden, A. (1997) 'Manufacturing capabilities; Hong Kong's new engine of growth?', in Berger, S. and Lester, R. (eds).

Anand, S. and Kanbur, S. M. R. (1993) 'The Kuznets Process and the inequality-development relationship', *Journal of Development Economics*, 40, February: 215–52.

Andrew, C., Coderre, C. and Denis, A. (1994) 'Women in management: the Canadian experience', in Adler, N. J. and Izraeli, D. N. (eds).

Arthur, J. B. (1992) 'The link between business strategy and industrial relations systems in American steel minimills', *Industrial and Labour Relations Review*, 45(3), April: 488–506.

Arthur, J. B. (1994) 'Effects of human resource systems on manufacturing performance and turnover', *Academy of Management Journal*, 37(3): 670–87.

Aufrect, S. E. (1995) 'Reform with Chinese characteristics: the context of Chinese civil service reform', *Public Administration Review*, 55(2): 175–82.

Bach, S. (1995) 'Restructuring the personnel function: the case of NHS Trusts', *Human Resource Management Journal*, 5(2): 99–115.

Bank of Korea (1990) *Economic Indicators*, Seoul: Bank of Korea.

Barney, J. (1991) 'Firm resources and sustained competitive advantage', *Journal of Management*, 17: 99–120.

Barondi, J. J. and Igbaria, M. (1995) 'An examination of gender effects on career success of information systems employees', *Journal of Management Information Systems*, 11(3): 181–201.

Bass, B. M., Avolio, B. J. and Atwater, L. (1993) 'The transformational and transactional leadership of men and women: an extension of some old comparisons', Report 93–6, The Center for Leadership Studies, School of Management, State University of New York at Binghampton.

Bass, B. M., Krusell, J. and Alexander, R. A. (1971) 'Male managers' attitudes toward working women', *American Behavioral Scientist*, 15, 2: 221–36.

Baum, J. R. (1995) 'The relationship of traits, competencies, motivation, strategy and structure to venture growth', *Proceedings of the Fifteenth Annual Entrepreneurship Research Conference*, Centre of Entrepreneurial Studies, Babson College, Massachusetts.

Becker, B. and Gerhart, B. (1996) 'The impact of human resource management on organizational performance: progress and prospects', *Academy of Management Journal*, 39(4): 779–801.

Becker, G. S. (1971) *The Economics of Discrimination*, second edition, Chicago: University of Chicago Press.

Becker, G. S. (1976) *The Economic Approach to Human Behavior*, Chicago: University of Chicago Press.

Becker, G. S. (1991) *A Treatise on the Family*, enlarged edition, Cambridge, Massachusetts: Harvard University Press.

Beijing Review (1988) 15–21 August: 4.

Beijing Review (1991) 15–21 April: 5.

Belenky, M. F., Clinchy, B. M., Goldberger, N. R. and Tarule, J. M. (1986) *Women's Ways of Knowing: The Development of Self, Voice, and Mind*, New York: Basic Books.

Benack, S. (1982) 'The coding of dimensions of epistemological thought in young men and women', *Moral Education Forum*, 7(2): 297–309.

Berg, P., Applebaum, E., Bailey, T. and Kalleberg, A. (1995) 'The performance effects of modular production in the apparel industry', *Industrial Relations*, 35(3): 356–73.

Berger, S. and Lester, R. K. (eds) (1997) *Made by Hong Kong*, Hong Kong: Oxford University Press.

Berger, S., Gartner, D. and Karty, K. (1997) 'Textiles and clothing in Hong Kong', in Berger, S. and Lester, R. (eds).

Bevan, S. and Hayday, S. (1994) *Helping Managers to Manage People*, Institute of Manpower Studies Report, University of Sussex, Brighton, April.

Birdsall, N., Ross, D. and Sabot, R. (1995) 'Inequality and growth reconsidered: lessons from East Asia', *The World Bank Economic Review*, 9, September: 477–508.

Blau, F. D. and Ferber, M. A. (1992) *The Economics of Women, Men, and Work*, second edition, Englewood Cliffs, NJ: Prentice Hall.

Blau, F. D. and Kahn, L. M. (1992) 'The gender earnings gap: learning from international comparisons', *American Economic Review*, 82, May: 533–8.

Blau, F. D. and Kahn, L. M. (1996) 'International differences in male wage inequality: institutions versus market forces', *Journal of Political Economy*, 104, August: 791–837.

Blinder, A. S. (1973) 'Wage discrimination: reduced form and structural variables', *Journal of Human Resources*, 8: 436–55.

Bond, M. H. (1986) *The Psychology of the Chinese People*, Hong Kong: Oxford University Press.

Borthwick, M. (1992) *Pacific Century: The Emergence of Modern Pacific Asia*, Boulder, Colorado: Westview Press.

Boxall, P. (1992) 'Strategic human resource management: beginning of a new theoretical sophistication?', *Human Resource Management Journal*, 2(3), Spring: 60–79.

Boyatzis, R. E. (1982) *The Competent Manager: A Model for Effective Performance*, New York: John Wiley and Sons.

Brockhaus, R. H. (1975) 'I-E locus of control scores as predictors of entrepreneurial intentions', *Academy of Management Proceedings*, New Orleans.

Brockhaus, R. H. and Horwitz, P. S. (1986) 'The psychology of the entrepreneur', in Sexton, D. L. and Smilor, R. W. (eds), *The Art and Science of Entrepreneurship*, Cambridge, Massachusetts: Ballinger.

Bryant, W. K. (1990) *The Economic Organization of the Household*, New York: Cambridge University Press.

Buller, P. F. and Napier, N. K. (1993) 'Strategy and human resource management integration in fast growth versus other mid-sized firms', *British Journal of Management*, 4: 77–90.

Burton, C. (1991) *The Promise and the Price: The Struggle for Equal Opportunity in Women's Employment*, Sydney: Allen and Unwin.

Butters, H. R. (1939) *Report on Labour and Labour Conditions*, Legislative Council Sessional Papers No. 125, Hong Kong.

Cain, G. C. (1986) 'The economics analysis of labor market discrimination: a survey', in Ashenfelterm, O. and Layard, R. (eds), *Handbook of Labor Economics*, vol. 1, Amsterdam: North Holland.

Caird, S. (1992) 'Problems with the identification of enterprise competencies and the implications for assessment and development', *Management Education and Development*, 23(1): 6–17.

Carland, J. W., Hoy, F., Boulton, W. R. and Carland, J. A. C. (1984) 'Differentiating entrepreneurs from small business owners: a conceptualization', *Academy of Management Review*, 9(2): 354–9.

Carney, M. (1998) 'The competitiveness of networked production: the role of trust and asset-specificity', *Journal of Management Studies*, 35(4): 457–79.

Castro, A. (1982) 'ASEAN economic co-operation' in Broinowski, A. (ed) *Understanding ASEAN*, London: Macmillan.

Cattaneo, R. J., Reavley, M. and Templer, A. (1994) 'Women in management as a strategic HR initiative', *Women in Management Review*, 9(2): 23–8.

Census and Statistics Department (1984) *Employment and Vacancies Statistics (Detailed Tables)* 1984, Hong Kong: Government Printer.

Census and Statistics Department (1993) *Hong Kong – 25 Years' Development*, Hong Kong: Government Printer.

Census and Statistics Department (1994) *Employment and Vacancies Statistics (Detailed Tables)* 1994, Hong Kong: Government Printer.

Census and Statistics Department (1995) *Hong Kong Annual Digest of Statistics: 1995 Edition*, Hong Kong: Government Printer.

Census and Statistics Department (1996a) *Hong Kong Annual Digest of Statistics: 1996 Edition*, Hong Kong: Government Printer.

Census and Statistics Department (1996b) *Report on 1996 Annual Survey of Industrial Production*, Hong Kong: Government Printer.

Census and Statistics Department (1997a) *Hong Kong 1996 Population By-Census: Main Report*, Hong Kong: Government Printer.

Census and Statistics Department (1997b) *Hong Kong 1996 Population By-Census: Summary Results*, Hong Kong: Government Printer.

Census and Statistics Department (1997c) *Hong Kong Annual Digest of Statistics : 1997 Edition*, Hong Kong: Government Printer.

Census and Statistics Department (1997d) *Estimates of Gross Domestic Product: 1961 to 1996*, Hong Kong: Government Printer.

Census and Statistics Department (1998) *Hong Kong Monthly Digest of Statistics*, August, Hong Kong: Government Printer.

Chan, A. and Lee, J. (1994) 'Women executives in a newly industrialised economy: the Singapore scenario', in Adler, N.J. and Izraeli D.N. (eds).

Chan, H.S. (1998) *Executive Yuan Republic of China*, Council of Labor Affairs, Taipei.

Chan, J. (1977) 'Human rights: from one era to another', in Cheng, J.Y.S. (ed), *The Other Hong Kong Report 1977*, Hong Kong: Chinese University Press, 137–66.

Chan, K.F. and Lau, T. (1993) 'Are small business owner/managers really entrepreneurial?', *Entrepreneurship and Regional Development*, 5: 359–67.

Chan, W. (1996) 'Intersectoral mobility and short-run labor market adjustments', *Journal of Labor Economics* 14, July: 454–71.

Chan, J. and Lau, V. (1990) 'Some reflections on the Human Rights Committee's hearing of the United Kingdom Second Report on dependent Territories held November 4–5 1988 in Geneva', *Hong Kong Law Journal*, 20(2): 150–77.

Chan, W. and Suen, W. (1999) 'The market at work: labour market adjustments to the changing environment', in Chapter 4 of this book.

Chandler, G. N. and Hanks, S. H. (1994) 'Founder competence, the environment, and venture performance', *Entrepreneurship Theory and Practice*, 18(3): 77–89.

Chandler, G. N. and Jansen, E. (1992) 'The founder's self-assessed competence and venture performance', *Journal of Business Venturing*, 7(3): 223–36.

Chang, H., Cheung, P., Ho, W., Lee, L. S., Ma, C. and Wong, J. (1991) 'Bio-technology', in Kao, C. K. and Young, K. (eds) *Technology Road Maps for Hong Kong: An In-depth Study of Four Technology Areas*, Hong Kong: Chinese University Press.

Chang, R. (1994) 'Income inequality and economic growth: evidence and recent theories', *Federal Reserve Bank of Atlanta Economic Review*, 79, July/August: 1–10.

Chau, L. C. (1988) 'Labour and labour market', in Ho, H. C. Y. and Chau, L. C. (eds) *The Economic System of Hong Kong*, Hong Kong: Asian Research Service.

Chau, L. C. (1994) 'Economic growth and income distribution in Hong Kong', in Leung, B.K.P. and Wong, T. Y. C. (eds).

Cheah, H. B. and Yu, T. F. L. (1996) 'Adaptive response: entrepreneurship and competitiveness in the economic development of Hong Kong', *Journal of Enterprising Culture*, 4(3): 241–66.

Cheek-Milby, K. (1984) 'Staff relations', in Scott, I. and Burns, J. P. (eds) *The Hong Kong Civil Service: Personnel Policies and Practices*, Hong Kong: Oxford University Press.

Cheek-Milby, K. (1988) 'Identifying the issues', in Scott, I. and Burns, J. P. (eds) *The Hong Kong Civil Service and Its Future*, Hong Kong: Oxford University Press.

Chell, E. (1986) 'The entrepreneurial personality: a review and some theoretical developments', in Curran, J., Stanworth, J. and Watins, D. (eds) *The Survival of the Small Firm, Volume 1: The Economics of Survival and Entrepreneurship*, Aldershot: Gower.

Chell, E. and R. Burrows (1991) 'The small business owner-manager', in Stanworth, J. and Gray, C. (eds) *Bolton 20 Years On: The Small Firm in the 1990s*, London: Paul Chapman Publishing.

Chen, E. K. Y. (1997) 'The total factor productivity debate', *Asian-Pacific Economic Literature*, 11, May: 18–38.

Chen, M. (1995) *Asian Management Systems*, London: Routledge.

Cheng, J. (1997) 'Introduction', in Cheng, J. (ed.), *The Other Hong Kong Report 1997*, Hong Kong: Chinese University Press.

Cheng, W. and Liao, L. (1994) 'Women managers in Taiwan', in Adler, N. J. and Izraeli, D. N. (eds).

Cheung, C.Y. (1997) 'Constitution and Administration', in Cheng, J. (ed.) *The Other Hong Kong Report 1997*, Hong Kong: Chinese University Press.

Chief Executive's Office (1997) *Civil Liberties and Social Order: Consultation Document*, Chief Executive's Office, Hong Kong Special Administrative Region Government.

Chi'en, R. (1994) 'Do we still love laissez-faire? Hong Kong's new industrial policy', speech given at Hong Kong Economics Association, March.

Child, J. (1994) *Management in China During the Age of Reform*, Cambridge: Cambridge University Press.

Chiu, S. and Levin, D. A. (1996) 'Prosperity without industrial democracy? Developments in industrial relations in Hong Kong since 1968', *Industrial Relations Journal*, 27(1): 24–37.

Choi, P. (1995) 'Women and education in Hong Kong', in Pearson, V. and Leung, B. K. P. (eds) *Women in Hong Kong*, Hong Kong: Oxford University Press.

Chow, K. K. and Ng, S. H. (1992) 'Trade unions, collective bargaining and associated rights: the case of Hong Kong', *Hong Kong Law Journal*, 22(3): 293–318.

Chow, S. C. M. (1977) 'Economic growth and income distribution in Hong Kong', unpublished Ph.D. Dissertation, Boston University.

Chun, N. D. (1994) *Minjunochong Geonseoleul Wihan Jae 1cha Josayeonku Bogoseo (The First Report for Organization of The Democratic Federation of Korean Trade Unions)*, Chonnodae, Seoul.

Chusmir, L. H. and Frontczak, N. T. (1990) 'International management opportunities for women: women and men paint different pictures', *International Journal of Management*, 7(3): 295–301.

Cockburn, C. (1991) *In the Way of Women: Men's Resistance to Sex Equality in Organisations*, Basingstoke: Macmillan.

Collins, O. F. and Moore, D. G. (1970) *The Organisation Maker*, New York: Appleton-Century-Crofts.

Collinson, D. L., Knights, D. and Collinson, M. (1990) *Managing to Discriminate*. London: Routledge.

Colwill, N. L. (1992) 'Why does the phenomena of women's denial of personal discrimination exist', *Women in Management*, 3(1): 4–5.

Colwill, N. L. (1995) 'Understanding aspects of networking', *Women in Management*, 5(1): 18–23.

Commissioner for Labour (1995) *Report of the Commissioner for Labour 1994*, Hong Kong: Government Printer.

Communist Party of China (1984) *China's Economic Structure Reform: Decision of the CCP Central Committee*, Beijing: Foreign Languages Press.

Cowell, F. A. (1995) *Measuring Inequality, second edition*, Hertfordshire, UK: Prentice Hall/Harvester Wheatsheaf.

Crowley, J. E., Levitin, T. E. and Quinn, R. P. (1973) 'Seven deadly half-truths about women', *Psychology Today*, March: 94–6.

Davidson, M. J. and Cooper, C. L. (1984) 'Occupational stress in female managers: a comparative study', *Journal of Management Studies*, 21: 185–205.

Davidson, M. J. and Cooper, C. L. (eds) (1993) *European Women in Business and Management*, London: Paul Chapman.

Davies, H. (1996) 'High IQ and low technology: the key to Hong Kong's success', *Long Range Planning*, 29(5): 684–90.

Davies, H. (1998) 'The persistence of key capabilities in flexible production networks; the watch industry in Switzerland and Hong Kong/China', in Strange, R., Slater, J. and Wang, L. (eds) *Trade and Investment in China: The European Experience*, London: Routledge.

Davies, H. (1999) 'The future shape of Hong Kong's economy: why high-technology manufacturing will prove to be a myth', in Chapter 3 of this book.

Davies, H. and Whitla, P. (1995) 'The competitiveness of Hong Kong's domestic manufacturing operations', in Davies, H. (ed.) *China Business: Context and Issues*, Hong Kong: Longman.

Deaux, K. (1985) 'Sex and gender', *Annual Review of Psychology*, 36: 49–81.

Deery, S. J. and Mitchell, R. J. (eds) (1993) *Labour Law and Industrial Relations in Asia: Eight Countries Study*, Melbourne: Longman Cheshire.

Deininger, K. and Squire, L. (1996) 'A new data set measuring income inequality', *The World Bank Economic Review*, 10, September: 565–91.

Delaney, J. T. and Huselid M. A. (1996) 'The impact of human resource management practices on perceptions of organizational performance', *Academy of Management Journal*, 39(4): 949–69.

Deng, X. (1978) 'Greeting the great risk', *Peking Review*, 21: 5–8.

Department of Labor and Employment, Philippines (1995) *White Paper on the Overseas Employment Program*, Manila: Department of Labor and Employment.

Deyo, F. C. (1981) *Dependent Development and Industrial Order: An Asian Case Study*, New York: Praeger.

Deyo, F. C. (1989) *Beneath the Miracle: Labor Subordination in the New Asian Industrialism*, Berkeley and London: University of California Press.

Deyo, F. C. (1995) 'Human resource strategies and industrial restructuring in Thailand', in Frenkel, S. and Harrod, J. (eds).

Dipboye, R. L., Fromkin, H. L. and Wiback, K. (1975) 'Relative importance of applicant sex, attractiveness, and scholastic standing in evaluation of job applicant resumes', *Journal of Applied Psychology*, 60(1): 39–43.

Dore, R. (1973) *British factory–Japanese factory*, London: Allen & Unwin.

Dore, R. (1979) 'Industrial relations in Japan and elsewhere', in Craig, A. (ed.) *Japan: A Comparative View*, Princeton, NJ: Princeton University Press.

Drucker, P. (1961) *The Practice of Management*, London: Pan.

Drucker, P. and Nakauchi, I. (1997) *Drucker on Asia: A Dialogue between Peter Drucker and Isao Nakauchi*, Oxford: Butterworth-Heinemann.

Dun and Bradstreet Information Services (1995) *Dun's Guide: Top 2000 Foreign Enterprises in Hong Kong 1995/96*, Hong Kong: Dun and Bradstreet.

Durkan, P., Harrison, R., Lindsay, P. and Thompson, E. (1993) 'Competence and executive education and development in an SME environment', *Irish Business and Administrative Research*, 14(1): 65–80.

Economist (1996) 'Sliding scales', 2 November: 95.

Emmons, C., Biernat, M., Tiedje, L. B., Lang, E. L. and Wortman, C. B. (1990) 'Stress, support, and coping among women professions with preschool children', in Eckenrode, J. and Core S. (eds) *Stress between Work and Family*, New York: Plenum.

England, G. (1986) 'National work meanings and patterns – constraints on management action', *European Management Journal*, 4(3): 176–84.

England, J. (1989) *Industrial Relations and Law in Hong Kong, second edition*, Oxford: Oxford University Press.

England, J. and Rear, J. (1975) *Chinese Labour under British Rule*, Hong Kong: Oxford University Press.

England, J. and Rear, J. (1981) *Industrial Relations and Law in Hong Kong*, Hong Kong: Oxford University Press.

Enright, M. J., Scott, E. E. and Dodwell, D. (1997) *The Hong Kong Advantage*, Hong Kong: Oxford University Press.

Equal Opportunities Commission (1997) *A Baseline Survey of Equal Opportunities on the Basis of Gender in Hong Kong, 1996–1997*, Hong Kong.

Equal Opportunities Commission (1998) *Code of Practice on Employment under the Family Status Discrimination Ordinance*, Hong Kong.

Espy, J. L. (1965) 'Not wanted: experts?', *Far Eastern Economic Review*, XLVII: 66.

Evers, F. T. and Rush, J. C. (1996) 'The bases of competence: skill development during the transition from the university to work', *Management Learning*, 27(3): 275–300.

Fagenson, E. A. and Jackson, J. J. (1994) 'The status of women managers in the United States', in Adler, N. J. and Izraeli, D. N. (eds).

Far Eastern Economic Review, Hong Kong.

Farh, J. L. (1995) 'Human resource management in Taiwan, the Republic of China', in Moore, L. F. and Devereaux Jennings, P. (eds).

Florida, R. and Kenney, M. (1990) 'Why Silicon Valley won't save us', *California Management Review*, 33, Fall: 68–88.

Fombrun, C. J., Tichy, N. M. and Devanna, M. A. (1984) *Strategic Human Resource Management*, New York: John Wiley & Sons.

Fowler A. (1992) 'How to use quantity management in personnel', *Personnel Management*, October: 29–30.

Freeman, R. B. (1981) 'Black economic progress after 1964: who has gained and why?', in Rosen, S. (ed.) *Studies in Labor Markets*, Chicago: University of Chicago Press.

Frenkel, S. (ed.) (1993) *Organized Labor in the Asia-Pacific Region: A Comparative Study of Trade Unionism in Nine Countries*, New York: ILR Press.

Frenkel, S. and Harrod, J. (eds) (1995) *Industrialization and Labor Relations: Contemporary Research in Seven Countries*, New York: ILR Press.

Fruin, M. (1992) *The Japanese Enterprise System*, New York: Oxford University Press.

Fukuda, K. J. (1993) *Japanese Management in East Asia and Beyond*, Hong Kong: Chinese University Press.

Fung V. (1996) 'Hong Kong competing into the 21st Century', Speech at the Hong Kong Management Association Theme Year Evening Talk, 4 July.

Gilbert, L. A. (1993) *Two Careers/One Family: The Promise of Gender Equality*, Thousand Oaks, California: Sage.

Godelier, M. (1980) 'Work and its representations: a research proposal', *History Workshop Journal*, 10.

Gollan, P. (1995) 'Global overview of conference proceedings', in Gollan, P. (ed.) *Globalization and its Impact on the World of Work*, Sydney: Australian Centre for Industrial Relations Research and Teaching.

Gottschalk, P. (1997) 'Inequality, income growth, and mobility: the basic facts', *Journal of Economic Perspectives*, 11, Spring: 21–40.

Graf, L., Hemmasi, M., Lust, J. and Liang, Y. (1990) 'Perceptions of desirable organisational reforms in Chinese state enterprises', *International Studies of Management and Organization*, 20(1/2): 47–56.

Grant, J. (1988) 'Women as managers: what they can offer to organizations', *Organizational Dynamics*, 16(1): 56–63.

Greene, W. H. (1993) *Econometric Analysis*, second edition, New York: Macmillan.

Guest, D. (1987) 'Human resource management and industrial relations', *Journal of Management Studies*, 24(5), September: 503–22.

Gutek, B. A. (1985) *Sex and the Workplace: Impact of Sexual Behaviour and Harassment on Women, Men and Organisations*, San Francisco, California: Jossey Bass.

Hall, R. H. (1994) *The Sociology of Work*, Thousand Oaks, California: Pine Forge.

Hammond, V. and Holton, V. (1994) 'The scenario for women managers in Britain in the 1990s', in Adler, N. J. and Izraeli, D. N. (eds).

Hardesty, S. A. and Betz, N. E. (1980) 'The relationships of career salience, attitudes toward women, and demographic and family characteristics to marital adjustment in dual-career couples', *Journal of Vocational Behavior*, 17: 242-50.

Harpaz, I. (1990) 'The importance of work goals: an international perspective', *Journal of International Business Studies*, 21(1): 75–93.

Hatch, W. and Yamamura, K. (1996) *Asia in Japan's Embrace*, Cambridge: Cambridge University Press.

Hawkins, J. (1995) 'The best of times. The worst of times: developments in productivity', *Hong Kong Monetary Authority Quarterly Bulletin*, August: 11–21.

Hearn, D. L., Sheppard, P, Tancred-Sheri, P. and Burrell, G. (1989) *The Sexuality of Organisation*, Newbury Park, California: Sage.

Hearn, J. and Park, P. W. (1986–7) 'Women, men, and leadership: a critical review of assumptions, practices, and change in industrialised nations', *International Studies of Management and Organization*, 16(3/4): 33–60.

Herron, L. and Robinson, R. B. (1993) 'A structural model of the effects of entrepreneurial characteristics on venture performance', *Journal of Business Venturing*, 8: 281–94.

Hiu, C. H. and Tan, C. K. (1996) 'Employee motivation and attitudes in the Chinese workforce', in Bond, M. H. (ed.) *The Handbook of Chinese Psychology*, Hong Kong: Oxford University Press.

Ho, L. S., Liu, P. W. and Lam, K. C. (1991) *International Labour Migration: The Case of Hong Kong*, Occasional Paper No. 8, Hong Kong Institute of Asia-Pacific Studies, Chinese University of Hong Kong.

Hochschild, A. (1989) *The Second Shift: Working Parents and the Revolution at Home*, New York: Viking Penguin.

Hofstede, G. (1980) *Culture's Consequences: International Differences in Work-Related Values*, Beverly Hills, California: Sage.

Hofstede, G. (1984) 'Cultural dimensions in management and planning', *Asia Pacific Journal of Management*, 1(2): 81–99.

Hofstede, G. (1994) *Cultures and Organisations: Intercultural Cooperation and its Importance for Survival*, London: Harper Collins.

Hofstede, G. and Bond, M. H. (1988) 'The Confucius connection: from cultural roots to economic growth', *Organizational Dynamics*, 17: 4–21.

Holton, R. H. (1990) 'Human resource management in the People's Republic of China', *Management International Review*, 30: 121–36.

Hong Kong Advisory Committee on Diversification (1979) *Report of the Advisory Committee on Diversification*, Hong Kong: Government Printer.

Hong Kong Confederation of Trade Unions (1996) *CTU in Solidarity*, No. 26, December.

Hong Kong Government (1974) *White Paper: The Further Development of Medical and Health Services in Hong Kong*, Hong Kong: Government Printer.

Hong Kong Government (1993) *Green Paper on Equal Opportunities for Women and Men*, Hong Kong: Government Printer.

Hong Kong Government (1996) *Hong Kong 1996 – A Review of 1995*, Hong Kong: Information Services Department.

Hong Kong Government (1997) *Hong Kong 1997 – A Review of 1996*, Hong Kong: Information Services Department.

Hong Kong Government (1998) *Hong Kong – A New Era, A Review of 1997*, Hong Kong: Information Services Department.

Hong Kong Government Industry Department (1996) *Hong Kong's Manufacturing Industries*, Hong Kong: Government Printer.

Hong Kong Hospital Authority (1991) *Newsletter Issue 1*, May, Hong Kong.

Hong Kong Hospital Authority (1992) *Newsletter Issue 7*, December, Hong Kong.

Hong Kong Hospital Authority (1995) *Annual Plan 1995–1996*, Hong Kong.

Hong Kong Institute of Asia-Pacific Studies (1991) *A Bibliography of Gender Studies in Hong Kong*, Hong Kong: Chinese University of Hong Kong.

Hong Kong Trade Development Council (1997) *Profile of Hong Kong's Major Services Industries*, Hong Kong: Trade Development Council Research Department, July.

Houghton, R. (1951) *Confidential Report to the Commissioner of Labour on the Labour Problems of Hong Kong* (CO 129/626/3).

Hsia, R. and Chau, L. (1978) *Industrialization, Employment and Income Distribution: A Case of Hong Kong*, London: Croom Helm.

Huck, J. F. and McEwen, T. (1991) 'Competencies needed for small business success: perceptions of Jamaican entrepreneur', *Journal of Small Business Management*, 29(4): 90–3.

Huselid, M. A. (1995) 'The impact of human resource management practices on turnover, productivity, and corporate financial performance', *Academy of Management Journal*, 38(3): 635–72.

Huselid, M. A. and Becker, B. E. (1996) 'Methodological issues in cross-sectional and panel estimates of the human resource-firm performance link', *Industrial Relations*, 35(3): 400–22.

Hutchings, K. (1996) 'Workplace practices of Australian multinational corporations operating in Singapore, Malaysia and Indonesia', *Human Resource Management Journal*, 6(2): 58–71.

Hyman, J. and Mason, B. (1995) *Managing Employee Involvement and Participation*, London: Sage.

Ibarra, H. (1993) 'Personal networks of women and minorities in management: a conceptual framework', *Academy of Management Review*, 8(1): 56–87.

Institute of Human Resource Management (1995) *Human Resource Management Practices in Hong Kong: Survey Report*, Hong Kong: Institute of Human Resource Management/Ashridge Management College.

Institute of Personnel and Development (1995) *Personnel and the Line: Developing the New Relationship*, London: IPD.

International Labour Office (1996) *Yearbook of Labour Statistics: 1995*, Geneva: International Labour Office.

Jackson, L. (1980) 'Prostitution', in Libra, J. and Paulson, J. (eds) *Chinese Women in Southeast Asia*, Singapore: Time Books International.

Jackson, S. (1994) 'Labour issues in China', in Jackson, S. (ed.) *Contemporary Developments in Asian Industrial Relations*, Sydney: Industrial Relations Research Centre, University of New South Wales.

James, L. R. and Brett, J. M. (1984) 'Mediators, moderators, and tests for mediation', *Journal of Applied Psychology*, 69: 307–21.

Jao, Y. C., Levin, D. A., Ng, S. H. and Sinn, E. (eds) (1988) *Labour Movement in a Changing Society: The Experience of Hong Kong*, Centre of Asian Studies, University of Hong Kong.

Johnson, G. E. (1997) 'Changes in earnings inequality: the role of demand shifts', *Journal of Economic Perspectives*, 11, Spring: 41–54.

Joyce, P. (1987) *The Historical Meanings of Work*, Cambridge: Cambridge University Press.

Juhn, C., Murphy, K. M. and Pierce, B. (1993) 'Wage inequality and the rise in returns to skill', *Journal of Political Economy*, 101, June: 410–42.

Kanter, R. M. (1988) *When Giants Learn to Dance*, New York: Simon & Schuster.

Kanter, R. M. (1977) *Men and Women of the Corporation*, New York: Basic Books.

Katz, L., Lovemen, G. W. and Blanchflower, D. G. (1995) 'A comparison of changes in the structure of wages in four countries', in Freeman, R. and Katz, L. (eds) *Differences and Changes in Wages Structures*, Chicago: University of Chicago Press.

Kim, T. (1995) 'Human resource management for production workers in large Korean manufacturing enterprises', in Frenkel, S. and Harrod, J. (eds).

King, A. Y. C. and Leung, D. H. K. (1975) *The Chinese Touch in Small Industrial Organisations*, Social Research Centre, the Chinese University of Hong Kong.

Kirkbride, P. S. and Tang S. F. Y. (1990) 'Personnel management: challenges and prospects for the 1990s', *The Hong Kong Manager*, March/April: 3–11.

Kirkbride, P. S. and Tang, S. F. Y. (1989) *The Present State of Personnel Management in Hong Kong*, Hong Kong: Management Development Centre.

Kirkbride, P. S. and Tang, S. F. Y. (1994) 'From Kyoto to Kowloon: cultural barriers to the transference of quality circles from Japan to Hong Kong', *Asia Pacific Journal of Human Resource*, 32 (2): 100–11.

Kirkbride, P. S. and Westwood, R. I. (1993) 'Hong Kong', in Peterson, R. B. (ed.) *Managers and National Culture: A Global Perspective*, London: Quorum Books.

Kono, S. (1996) 'Relation between women's economic activity and child care in low-fertility countries', in *Population and Women*, New York: United Nations.

Korabik, K. (1993) 'Women managers in the People's Republic of China: changing roles in changing times', *Applied Psychology: An International Review*, 42: 353–63.

Korean Economic Planning Board (1990, 1992) *Major Statistics of Korea*, Seoul.

Kotlikoff, L. J. and Gokhale, J. (1992) 'Estimating a firm's age-productivity profile using the present value of workers' earnings', *Quarterly Journal of Economics*, 107, November: 1215–42.

Krugman, P. (1994) 'The myth of Asia's growth', *Foreign Affairs*, November/December: 62–78.

Kurt Salmon Associates (1987) *Final Report on the Techno-Economic and Marketing Research Study on the Textiles and Clothing Industry*, Hong Kong.

Kuruvilla, S. (1995) 'Industrialization Strategy and Industrial Relations Policy in Malaysia', in Frenkel, S. and Harrod, J. (eds).

Kuruvilla, S. (1996) 'National industrialisation strategies and their influence on patterns of HR practices', *Human Resource Management Journal*, 6(3): 22-41.

Kuruvilla, S. and Arudsothy, P. (1995) 'Economic development strategy, government labor policy and firm-level industrial relations practices in Malaysia', in Verma, A., Kochan, T. A. and Lansbury, R. D. (eds).

Kuruvilla, S. and Venkataratnam, C. S. (1996) 'Economic development and industrial relations: the case of south and southeast Asia', *Industrial Relations Journal*, 27(1): 9–23.

Kuznets, S. (1955) 'Economic growth and income inequality', *American Economic Review*, 45, March: 1–28.

Kwon, S. H. and Leggett, C. (1994) 'Industrial relations and South Korean Chaebol', in Callus, R. and Schumacher, M. (eds) *Current Research in Industrial Relations: Proceedings of the 8th AIRAANZ Conference*, Sydney, February 1993.

Kwong, K. S. (1997) *Technology and Industry*, Hong Kong: Hong Kong Economic Policy Study Series, City University Press.

Labour Department (1991) *Labour and Employment in Hong Kong*, Hong Kong: Government Printer.

Lam, K. C. and Liu, P. W. (1998) *Immigration and the Economy of Hong Kong*, Hong Kong: City University of Hong Kong Press.

Lam, K. C. and Liu, P. W. (1999) 'Immigration as a source of labour supply in Hong Kong', in Chapter 7 of this book.

Lane, H. W., DiStefano, J. J. and Maznevski, M. L. (1997) *International Management Behaviour*, third edition, Cambridge, Massachusetts: Blackwell.

Lansbury, R. (1994) 'Will Vietnamese workers profit from "The Last Gold Rush"' *Southland Magazine*, 4: 12-13.

Lau, A. and Snell, R. (1996) 'Structure and growth in small Hong Kong enterprises', *International Journal of Entrepreneurial Behaviour and Research*, 2(3): 29–47.

Lau, C. K. (1996) 'Boom or bust in the delta growth zone', *Sunday Morning Post*, 18 February: 9, Hong Kong.

Lau, L. J. (1994) *Sources of Long-term Economic Growth: Empirical Evidence from Developed and Developing Countries*, Stanford University, May.

Lau, S. and Kuan, H. (1988) *The Ethos of the Hong Kong Chinese*, Hong Kong: Chinese University Press.

Lau, S. K. (1982) *Society and Politics in Hong Kong*, Hong Kong: Chinese University Press.

Lau, T., Chan, K. F. and Man, T. W. Y. (1998) 'The entrepreneurial and managerial competencies of small business owner/managers in Hong Kong: conceptual and methodological considerations', paper presented at the Fourth International Conference on Competence-Based Management, Oslo, Norway, 18–20 June.

Law, P. (1988) 'White-collar unionism: the case of teachers', in Jao *et al.* (eds).

Lawler, J. and Atmiyanandana, V. (1995) 'Human resource management in Thailand', in Moore, L. F. and Devereaux Jennings, P. (eds).

Leary, R. H. (1965) 'Technical trouble', *Far Eastern Economic Review*, XLVII: 111.

Lee, C. K. (1994) 'Lao zi xie shang huo dong (The practice of joint consultation in Hong Kong)', *Labour Relations Newsletter*, 35, December 2, Hong Kong: Labour Department.

Lee, J. (1996) 'The emergence of party politics in Hong Kong 1982–92', in Leung, B. K. P. and Wong, T. Y. C. (eds).

Lee, J. S. (1995) 'Economic development and the evolution of industrial relations in Taiwan, 1950–1993', in Verma, A., Kochan, T. A. and Lansbury, R. D. (eds).

Lee, J. S. and Park, Y. B. (1995) 'Employment, labor standards and economic development in Taiwan and Korea', *Labor, Special Issue of Tenth IIRA World Congress*, 31 May–4 June.

Leggett, C. (1988) 'Industrial relations and enterprise unionism in Singapore', *Labour and Industry*, 1(2): 242-57.

Leggett, C. (1993) 'Singapore', in Deery, S. J. and Mitchell, R. J. (eds).

Leggett, C. and Bamber, G. (1996) 'Asia-Pacific tiers of change', *Human Resource Management Journal*, 6(2): 7–19.

Leonard, B. D. (1992) 'Core capabilities and core rigidities: a paradox in managing new product development', *Strategic Management Journal*, 13: 111–25.

Leonard, J. S. and Jacobson, L. (1990) 'Earnings inequality and job turnover', *American Economic Review*, 80, May: 298–302.

Lethbridge, D. G. and Ng, S. H. (1995) 'Labour and employment', in Ng, S. H. and Lethbridge, D. G. (eds) *The Business Environment in Hong Kong*, third edition, Hong Kong: Oxford University Press.

Leung, B. K. P. and Wong, T. Y. C. (eds) (1994) *Twenty-five Years of Social and Economic Development in Hong Kong*, Hong Kong: Centre of Asian Studies, University of Hong Kong.

Leung, C. K. and Wu, C. T. (1995) 'Innovation environment, R&D linkages and technology development', *Regional Studies*, 29(6): 533–46.

Leung, H. H. (1992) 'The growth of white-collar unionism in Hong Kong', in Chen, E. K. Y., Lansbury, R., Ng, S. H. and Stewart, S. (eds) *Labour-Management Relations in the Asia-Pacific Region*, Hong Kong: Centre of Asian Studies, University of Hong Kong.

Leung, J. C. B. (1994) 'Dismantling the "iron rice bowl": welfare reform in the People's Republic of China', *Journal of Social Policy*, 23(3): 341–61.

Leung, K. (1992) 'Decision making', in Westwood, R. I. (ed.) *Organisational Behaviour: Southeast Asian Perspectives*, Hong Kong: Longman.

Leung, S. H. (1983) 'Industrial relations in Cable and Wireless: a unionist's view', in Ng, S. H. and Levin, D. A. (eds).

Levin, D. A. and Chiu, S. (1993) 'Dependent capitalism, a colonial state, and marginal unions: the case of Hong Kong', in Frenkel, S. (ed.).

Levin, D. A. and Chiu, S. (1994) 'Hong Kong's other democracy: industrial relations and industrial democracy in Hong Kong', in Leung, B. K. P. and Wong, T. Y. C. (eds).

Levin, D. A. and Ng, S. H. (1995) 'From an industrial to a post-industrial economy: challenges for human resource management in Hong Kong', in Verma, A., Kochan, T. A. and Lansbury, R. D. (eds).

Lewis, S. N. C. and Cooper, C. L. (1988) 'The transition to parenthood in dual-earner couples', *Psychological Medicine*, 18: 477–86.

Libra, J. (1980) 'Immigration to Southeast Asia', in Libra, J. and Paulson, J. (eds) *Chinese Women in Southeast Asia*, Singapore: Time Books International.

Lilien, D. M. (1982) 'Sectoral shifts and cyclical unemployment', *Journal of Political Economy*, 90, August: 777–93.

Lim, L. and Gosling, P. (eds) (1983) *The Chinese in Southeast Asia*, Volume 1 and 2, Singapore: Maruzen Asia.

Lin, J. Y. (1990) 'Collectivisation and China's agricultural crisis in 1959–1961', *Journal of Political Economy*, 98(6), December: 1228–52.

Lin, T. B. (1985) 'Growth, equity, and income distribution policies in Hong Kong', *The Developing Economies*, 23, December: 391–413.

Livingston, J. A. (1982) 'Responses to sexual harassment on the job: legal, organisational, and individual actions', *Journal of Social Issues*, 38(4): 5–22.

Lo, C. K. (1996) 'Constitution and administration', in Nyaw, M. K. and Li, S. M. (eds) *The Other Hong Kong Report 1996*, Hong Kong: Chinese University Press.

Lo, S. H. and Yu, W. Y. (1996) 'The electoral system of Hong Kong's Legislative Council: results under different proportional representation formulae', in Kuan, H. C., Lau, S. K., Louie, K. S. and Wong, K. Y. (eds) *The 1995 Legislative Council Elections in Hong Kong*, Institute of Asia-Pacific Studies, Chinese University of Hong Kong.

Louie, K. S. (1996) 'Election and politics', in Nyaw, M. K. and Li, S. M. (eds) *The Other Hong Kong Report 1996*, Hong Kong: Chinese University Press.

Lui, H. K. (1994) 'The expansion of tertiary education in Hong Kong: an economic perspective', *Higher Education Review*, 27, Autumn: 23–33.

Lui, H. K. (1997) *Income Inequality and Economic Development*, Hong Kong: City University of Hong Kong Press.

Lui, H. K. and Suen, W. (1933) 'The narrowing gender gap in Hong Kong: 1976–1986', *Asian Economic Journal*, VII, July: 167–80.

Lui, H. K. and Suen, W. (1994) 'The structure of the female earnings gap in Hong Kong', *Hong Kong Economic Papers*, 23: 15–29.

Lui, T. L. and Chiu, S. (1993) 'Industrial restructuring and labour-market adjustment under positive non-interventionism', *Environment and Planning A*, 25: 63–79.

McClelland, D. C. (1987) 'Characteristics of successful entrepreneurs', *Journal of Creative Behaviour*, 21(1): 18–21.

MacDuffie, J. P. (1995) 'Human resource bundles and manufacturing performance: organizational logic and flexible production systems in the world auto industry', *Industrial and Labor Relations Review*, 48: 197–221.

Maddock, S. and Parken, D. (1993) 'Gender cultures: women's choices and strategies at work', *Women in Management Review*, 8(2): 3–9.

Mak, H. W. (1988) 'White-collar unionism: the case of social workers', in Jao *et al.* (eds).

Manning, C. (1996) 'Labor standards and economic development: the Indonesian case', in Lee, J. S. (ed.) *Labor Standards and Economic Development*, Taipei: Chung-Hua Institution for Economic Research.

Marchington, M. (1994) 'The dynamics of joint consultation', in Sisson, K. (ed.) *Personnel Management: A Comprehensive Guide to Theory and Practice in Britain*, Oxford: Blackwell.

Marchington, M., Goodman, J., Wilkinson, A. and Ackers, P. (1992*)* *New Developments in Employee Involvement*, London: Department of Employment Research Series.

Martin, P. (1993) 'Feminist practices in organisations', in Fagenson, E. (ed.) *Women in Management: Trends, Issues, and Challenges in Managerial Diversity*, Newbury Park, California: Sage.

Meaning of Work International Research Team (1987) *The Meaning of Work*, London: Academic Press.

Merchant, G. and Wilson, D. (1994) 'Devolving HR in the civil service', *Personnel Management*, January: 38–41.

Meredith, G., Nelson, R. and Neck, P. (1982) *The Practice of Entrepreneurship*, Geneva: International Labour Office.

Miles, R. E. and Snow, C. C. (1978) *Organizational Strategy, Structure and Process*, New York: McGraw Hill.

Miles, R. E. and Snow, C. C. (1984) 'Designing strategic human resources systems', *Organizational Dynamics*, 13(1), Summer: 36–52.

Miller, C. C. and Glick, W. H. (1989) *Code Study of Organizations: UT Extended Local Study Procedures and Instruments*, CODE Technical Report 12, Department of Management, University of Texas.

Mincer, J. and Polachek, S. (1974) 'Family investments in human capital earnings for women', *Journal of Political Economy*, 82: S76–S110.

Miners, N. (1975) *The Government and Politics of Hong Kong*, first edition, Hong Kong: Oxford University Press.

Miners, N. (1995) *The Government and Politics of Hong Kong*, fifth edition, Hong Kong: Oxford University Press.

Mintzberg, H. (1973) 'Strategy-making in three modes', *California Management Review*, 16, Winter: 44–58.

MOFERT/MOFTEC (1994) *International Trade News*, 16 May.

Moir, J. (1997) 'Hospitals "lag behind US on Chinese medicine"', *South China Morning Post*, 9 October: III.

Moore, L. F. and Devereaux Jennings, P. (eds) (1995) *Human Resource Management on the Pacific Rim: Institutions, Practices, and Attitudes*, Berlin and New York: Walter de Gruyter.

Morse, N. C. and Weiss, R. S. (1955) 'The function and meaning of work and the job', *American Sociological Review*, 20: 191–8.

Murphy, K. M. and Topel, R. H. (1987) 'The evolution of unemployment in the United States, 1968–1985', *NBER Macroeconomics Annual*, 2: 11–58.

Nayyar, P. R. (1993) 'On the measurement of competitive strategy: evidence from a large multiproduct U.S. firm', *Academy of Management Journal*, 36(6): 1652-69.

Ng, C. W. (1993) 'Attitudes toward women as managers in some male-dominated professions in Hong Kong', *Proceedings of the First International Conference on Women in Management in Asia*, Hong Kong: Chinese University of Hong Kong.

Ng, C. W. (1994) 'Hong Kong women in organisations', in Welsh, A. (ed.) *The Hong Kong Manager's Handbook*, Hong Kong: Longman.

Ng, C. W. (1995) 'Hong Kong MBA students' attitudes toward women as managers: an empirical study', *International Journal of Management*, 12(4): 454–9.

Ng, C. W. and Chiu, W. C. K. (1999) 'Women-friendly human resource management in Hong Kong: concept and practice', in Chapter 11 of this book.

Ng, S. H. (1997) 'Reversion to China: implications for labour in Hong Kong', *International Journal of Human Resource Management*, 8(5): 660–76.

Ng, S. H. and Cheng, S. M. (1993) 'Transition to more cooperative and consensual patterns of labour-management relations: Singapore and Hong Kong compared', *Asia Pacific Journal of Management*, 10(2): 213–27.

Ng, S. H. and Levin, D. A. (eds) (1983) *Contemporary Issues in Hong Kong Labour Relations*, Hong Kong: Centre of Asian Studies, University of Hong Kong.

Ng, S. H. and Sit, V. F. S. (1989) *Labour Relations and Labour Conditions in Hong Kong*, Basingstoke: Macmillan.

Ng, S. H., Stewart, S. and Chan, F. T. (1997) *Current Issues of Workplace Relations and Management in Hong Kong*, Hong Kong: Centre of Asian Studies, University of Hong Kong.

Ngo, H. Y. and Lau, C. M. (1996) 'Labour and employment', in Nyaw, M. K. and Li, S. M. (eds) *The Other Hong Kong Report 1996*, Hong Kong: Chinese University Press.

Oaxaca, R. (1973) 'Male–female wage differentials in urban labor markets', *International Economic Review*, 14, October: 693–703.

O'Leary, G. (1994) 'The contemporary role of Chinese trade unions', in Jackson, S. (ed.) *Contemporary Developments in Asian Industrial Relations*, Sydney: Industrial Relations Research Centre, University of New South Wales.

Oliver, N. and Wilkinson, B. (1992) *The Japanisation of British Industry*, Oxford: Blackwell.

O'Neil, D. M. (1984) 'The quiet revolution in education attainment', *Challenge*, 27, September/October: 57–61.

Pahl, R. E. (ed.) (1988) *On Work: Historical, Comparative and Theoretical Approaches*, Oxford: Blackwell.

Paik, Y., Vance, C. and Stage, D. (1996) 'The extent of divergence in human resource practice across three Chinese national cultures: Hong Kong, Taiwan and Singapore', *Human Resource Management Journal*, 6(2): 18–29.

Payne, J. (1991) *Women Training and the Skills Shortage: The Case for Public Investment*, London: Policy Studies Institute.

P-E Consulting Services (1988) *Techno-Economic Study of Hong Kong's Metals and Light Engineering Industries, 1987–88*, Hong Kong: Hong Kong Government.

Persson, T. and Tabellini, G. (1994) 'Is inequality harmful for growth?', *American Economic Review*, 84, June: 600–621.

Peters, T. J. (1988) *Thriving on Chaos*, New York: Alfred A. Knopf.

Peters, T. J. and Waterman, R. H. (1982) *In Search of Excellence: Lessons from America's Best Run Companies*, New York: Harper and Row.

Petersen, C. J. (1997) 'Hong Kong's first anti-discrimination laws and their potential impact on the employment market', *Hong Kong Law Journal*, 27(3): 324–55.

Petri, P. A. (1995) 'The interdependence of trade and investment in the Pacific', in Chen, E. K. Y. and Drysdale, P. (eds) *Corporate Links and Foreign Direct Investment in Asia and the Pacific*, Pymble, New South Wales: Harper Educational.

Pfeffer, J. (1994) *Competitive Advantage Through People, Unleashing the Power of the Workforce*, Boston: Harvard Business School Press.

Pil, F. K. and MacDuffie, J. P. (1996) 'The adoption of high-involvement work practices', *Industrial Relations*, 35(3), July: 423–55.

Pleck, J. H. (1977) 'The work-family role system', *Social Problems*, 24: 417–27.

Pong, B. K. (1990) 'Joint consultation: an effective communication channel between labour and employers', *Labour Relations Newsletter*, 16: 1, Hong Kong: Labour Department.

Poon, T. S. (1996) 'Dependent development: the subcontracting networks in the Tiger Economies', *Human Resource Management Journal*, 6(4): 38–49.

Powell, T. C. (1995) 'Total quality management as competitive advantage: A review and empirical study', *Strategic Management Journal*, 16: 15–34.

Ramachandran, S. (1994) *Indian Plantation Labor in Malaysia*, S. Abdul Majeed, Kuala Lumpur.

Ravallion, M. and Chen, S. (1997) 'What can new survey data tell us about recent changes in distribution and poverty?', *The World Bank Economic Review*, 11, May: 357–82.

Ray, D. (1993) 'Understanding the entrepreneur: entrepreneurial attributes, experience and skill', *Entrepreneurship and Regional Development*, 5: 345–7.

Redding, G. and Wong, G. (1986) 'The psychology of Chinese organisational behaviour', in Bond, M.H. (ed.) *The Psychology of the Chinese People*, Hong Kong: Oxford University Press.

Redding, S. G. (1990) *The Spirit of Chinese Capitalism*, Berlin: Walter de Gruyter.

Registry of Trade Unions (1994) *Annual Statistical Report*, Hong Kong: Government Printer.

Reif, R. and Sodini, C. (1997) 'The Hong Kong electronics industry', in Berger, S. and Lester, R. (eds).

Riedel, J. (1974) *The Industrialisation of Hong Kong*, Tübingen: J. C. B. Mohr (Paul Sieback).

Riedel, J. (1988) 'Economic development in East Asia: doing what comes naturally?', in Hughes, H. (ed.) *Achieving Industrialization in Asia*, Cambridge: Cambridge University Press.

Robbins, F. (1998) 'Taiwan's economic success', in Sheridan, K. (ed.) *Emerging Economic Systems in Asia: A Political and Economic Survey*, Sydney: Allen & Unwin.

Rosener, J. (1990) 'Ways women lead', *Harvard Business Review*, November/December: 119–25.

Rowney, J. I. A. and Cahoon, A. R. (1990) 'Individual and organisational characteristics of women in managerial leadership', *Journal of Business Ethics*, 9: 293–316.

Saporito, B. (1994) 'The world's best cities for business', *Fortune*, November 14: 68–91.

Schuler, R. S. and Jackson, S. E. (1987) 'Linking competitive strategies with human resources management practices', *Academy of Management Executive*, 1(3), August: 207–19.

Segal, Quince and Wicksteed (1995) *Hong Kong Science Park Study*, Stage 2, Hong Kong: Segal Quince Wicksteed (Asia) Ltd.

Sexton, D. L. and Bowman, N. (1985) 'The entrepreneur: a capable executive and more', *Journal of Business Venturing*, 1(1): 129–40.

Shadur, M. A., Rodwell, J. J. and Bamber, G. J. (1995) 'The adoption of international best practices in a Western culture: East meets West', *International Journal of Human Resource Management*, 6(3): 735–57.

Shenkar, O. and Ronen, S. (1987) 'Structure and importance of work goals among managers in the People's Republic of China,' *Academy of Management Journal*, 30: 564–76.

Simpson, S. M., McCarrey, M. and Edwards, H. P. (1987) 'Relationship of supervisors' sex-role stereotypes to performance evaluation of male and female subordinates in nontraditional jobs', *Canadian Journal of Administrative Sciences*, 4(1): 15–30.

Sit, V. F. S. (1985) 'Small-scale industries within laissez-fairism: a Hong Kong case study', in Sit, V. F. S. (ed.) *Strategies for Small-Scale Industries Promotion in Asia*, Hong Kong: Longman.

Sit, V. F. S., Wong, S. L. and Kiang, T. S. (1979) *Small Scale Industry in a Laissez-Faire Economy – A Hong Kong Case Study*, Hong Kong: Centre of Asian Studies, University of Hong Kong.

Siu, W. S. and Martin, R. G. (1992) 'Successful entrepreneurship in Hong Kong', *Long Range Planning*, 25(6): 87–93.

Sjaastad, L. A. (1962) 'The costs and returns of human migration', *Journal of Political Economy*, October: 80–93.

Snape, E. and Chan, A. W. (1997) 'Whither Hong Kong's unions: autonomous trade unionism or classic dualism?', *British Journal of Industrial Relations*, 35(1): 39–63.

Snizek, W. E. and Neil, C. C. (1992) 'Job characteristics, gender stereotypes and perceived gender discrimination in the workplace', *Organization Studies*, 13(3): 403–27.

Sonnenfeld, J. A., Peiperl, N. A. and Kotter, J. P. (1992) 'Strategic determinants of managerial labour markets', in Salaman, G. *et al.* (eds) *Human Resource Strategies*, London: Sage.

Special Broadcasting Service (1998) *World Guide*, Melbourne: Hardie Grant Publishing.

Spence, J. T., Helmreich, R. and Stapp, J. (1973) 'A short version of the attitudes toward women scale (AWS)', *Bulletin of the Psychonomics Society*, 2(4): 219–20.

Steinhoff, P. G. and Tanaka, K. (1994) 'Women managers in Japan', in Adler, N. J. and Izraeli, D.N. (eds).

Stephan, P. E. and Levin, S. G. (1992) *Striking the Mother Lode in Science*, Oxford: Oxford University Press.

Stewart, P. L. and Cantor, G. (1982) *Varieties of Work*, Beverly Hills, California: Sage.

Stockdale, M. (ed.) (1996) *Sexual Harassment in the Workplace*, Thousand Oaks, California: Sage.

Storey J. (1989) *New Perspectives on Human Resource Management*, London: Routledge.

Storey J. (1992) *Developments in the Management of Human Resources*, Oxford: Blackwell.

Stretton, A. (1981) 'Is the Hong Kong labour market competitive? A comment on Turner's thesis', *Hong Kong Journal of Public Administration*, 3, June: 110–18.

Suen, W. (1995a) 'Gender gap in Hong Kong: an update', *Asian Economic Journal*, 9, November: 311–19.

Suen, W. (1995b) 'Sectoral shifts: impact on Hong Kong workers', *Journal of International Trade and Economic Development*, 4, July: 135–52.

Sung, Y. W., Liu, P. W., Wong, R. and Lau, P. K. (1995) *The Fifth Dragon: The Emergence of the Pearl River Delta*, Hong Kong: Addison-Wesley.

Supachai, S. (1993) 'Thailand', in Deery, S. J. and Mitchell, R. J. (eds).

Suzuki, S. (1995) 'Tradition and modernity in Japanese management: on industrialization and the groupism management in Japan', in Hing, A., Wong, P. and Schmidt, G. (eds) *Cross Cultural Perspectives of Automation*, Berlin: Sigma.

Tang, S., Lai, E. and Kirkbride, P. (1995) *Human Resource Management Practices in Hong Kong: Survey Report*, Hong Kong: Institute of Human Resource Management/Ashridge Management College.

Tannen, D. (1993) 'Men talk; women talk: do they really understand each other?', *HR Focus*, 70(6): 12-24.

Tausky, C. (1991) 'Perestroika in the USSR and China: motivational lessons', *Work and Occupations*, 18(1): 94–5.

Taylor, V. (1996) 'East Asian labour and globalization', paper presented at the 10th Annual Conference of the Association of Industrial Relations Academics of Australia and New Zealand (AIRAANZ), Perth, Australia, 8–10 February.

Terborg, J. R., Peters, L. H., Ilgen, D. R. and Smith, F. (1977) 'Organizational and personal correlates of attitudes toward women as managers', *Academy of Management Journal*, 20(1): 89–100.

Tharenou, P. and Conroy, D. (1994) 'Men and women managers' advancement: personal or situational determinants?', *Applied Psychology: An International Review*, 43(1): 5–31.

Thompson, P. (1989) *The Nature of Work*, second edition, Basingstoke: Macmillan.

Timmons, J. A., Smollen, L. E. and Dingee, A. L. M. (1985) *New Venture Creation: A Guide to Entrepreneurship*, Illinois: Irwin.

Topel, R. H. (1997) 'Factor proportions and relative wages: the supply side determinants of wage inequality', *Journal of Economic Perspectives*, 11, Spring: 55–74.

Trompenaars, F. (1993) *Riding the Waves of Culture: Understanding Cultural Diversity in Business*, London: Nicholas Brealey.

Tsang, G. (1995) 'The women's movement at the crossroads', in Pearson, V. and Leung, B. K. P. (eds) *Women in Hong Kong*, New York: Oxford University Press.

Tsang, S. K. (1994) 'The economy', in McMillan, D. H. and Man, S. W. (eds) *The Other Hong Kong Report 1994*, Hong Kong: Chinese University Press.

Turner, H. A., Fosh, P. and Ng, S. H. (1991) *Between Two Societies: Hong Kong Labour in Transition*, Hong Kong: Centre of Asian Studies, University of Hong Kong.

Turner, H. A., Fosh, P., Gardner, M., Hart, K., Morris, R., Ng, S. H., Quinlan, P. and Yerbury, D. (1980) *The Last Colony: But Whose? A Study of the Labour Movement*, Labour Market and Labour Relations in Hong Kong, Cambridge: Cambridge University Press.

Tyson, S. and Fell, A. (1986) *Evaluating the Personnel Function*, London: Hutchinson.

United Nations (1991) *The World's Women: 1970–1990 Trends and Statistics*, New York: United Nations Publication.

Upham, M. (1995) *Trade Union and Employers' Organizations of the World*, London: Longman.

U.S. Bureau of the Census (1996) *Country Business Pattern 1994*, Washington: U.S. Government Printing Office.

Valentine, D., Ellinger, N. and Williams, M. (1975) 'Sex-role attitudes and the career choices of male and female graduate students', *Vocational Guidance Quarterly*, September: 48–53.

Verma, A., and Yan, Z. (1995) 'The changing face of human resource management in China: opportunities, problems and strategies', in Verma, A., Kochan, T.A. and Lansbury, R.D. (eds).

Verma, A., Kochan, T. A. and Lansbury, R. D. (eds) (1995) *Employment Relations in the Growing Asian Economies*, London: Routledge.

Verma, A., Kochan, T. A. and Lansbury, R. D. (1995) 'Lessons from the Asian experience: a summary', in Verma, A., Kochan, T. A. and Lansbury, R. D. (eds).

Vogel, E. F. (1980) *Japan as No. 1: Lessons for America*, Tokyo: Charles E. Tuttle.

Vogel, E. F. (1991) *The Four Little Dragons: The Spread of Industrialization in East Asia*, Cambridge, Massachusetts: Harvard University Press.

Walder, A. G. (1981) 'Some ironies of Maoist legacy in industry', *Australian Journal of Chinese Affairs*, 5: 21–38.

Walder, A. G. (1987) 'Wage reform and the web of factory interests', *China Quarterly*, 109: 22-41.

Walton, R. E. (1985) 'From control to commitment in the workplace', *Harvard Business Review*, 63, March–April: 77–84.

Wang, D. (1981) 'Behavioural sciences can be used to improve workers' motivation', *Jinji Guanli (Economic Management)*, 7: 77–8.

Wang, D., Leung, J., Wu, I. C. and Gao, N. (1997) 'Biotechnology and Hong Kong', in Berger, S. and Lester, R. (eds).

Wang, G. (1991) *China and the Overseas Chinese*, Singapore: Times Academic Press.

Wang, S. H. (1977) 'Family structure and economic development', *Bulletin of the Institute of Ethnology*, 44: 1–11, *Taipei, Taiwan*.

Warner, M. (1987) 'Industrial relations in the Chinese factory', *Journal of Industrial Relations*, 29(2): 217–32.

Warner, M. (1991) 'Labour-management relations in the People's Republic of China: the role of trade unions', *International Journal of Human Resources Management*, 2(2): 205–20.

Weller, D. R. (1994) 'The Hospital Authority's corporate human resource strategies and activities', *Hong Kong Manager*, 30(2): 11–14.

Wells, L. T. (1984) 'Economic man and engineering man', in Stobaugh, R. and Wells, L. (eds) *Technology Crossing Borders*, Boston: Harvard Business School Press.

Westwood, R. I. (1992) *Organisational Behaviour: Southeast Asian Perspectives*, Hong Kong: Longman.

Westwood, R. I. (1997a) 'Harmony and patriarchy: the cultural basis for 'paternalistic headship' among the overseas Chinese', *Organization Studies*, 18(3): 445–80.

Westwood, R. I. (1997b) 'Culture, business organisation and managerial behaviour in East Asia', in Safarian, A. E. and Dobson, W. (eds) *The People Link: Human Resource Links Across the Pacific*, Toronto: University of Toronto Press.

Westwood, R. I. (1997c) 'The politics of opportunity: work and gender in Hong Kong, part 2: the vertical dimension and theoretical accounts of the sexual division of labour at work', in Cheung, F. M. C. (ed.) *Engendering Hong Kong Society: A Gender Perspective of Woman's Status*, Hong Kong: Chinese University Press.

Westwood, R.I., Mehrain, T. and Cheung, F. (1995) *Gender and Society in Hong Kong: A Statistical Profile*, Hong Kong: Institute for Asia-Pacific Studies, Chinese University.

Westwood, R. I., Ngo, H. Y. and Leung, S. M. (1997) 'The politics of opportunity: work and gender in Hong Kong, part 1: the gendered segmentation of the labour market', in Cheung, F. M. C. (ed.) *Engendering Hong Kong Society: A Gender Perspective of Woman's Status*, Hong Kong: Chinese University Press.

White, G., Luk, V., Chiu, R. and Druker, J. (1998) 'Pay policy and wage determination in Hong Kong and Guangdong: a case of regional convergence', *Proceedings of the 6th Annual Conference of the International Employment Relations Association*, July 15–17, University of Wollongong, Wollongong.

Whitley, R. (1992) *Business Systems in East Asia: Firms, Markets and Societies*, London: Sage.

Wilkinson, B. (1994) *Labour and Industry in the Asia-Pacific: Lessons from the Newly-Industrialised Countries*, Berlin: Walter de Gruyter.

Wilkinson, B. (1994) 'The Korea labour "problem"', *British Journal of Industrial Relations*, 32(3): 339–58.

Wilkinson, B. and Leggett, C. (1985) 'Human and industrial relations in Singapore: the management of compliance', *Euro Asia Business Review*, 4(3): 9–15.

Williams, K. (1990) *Hong Kong Employment Law*, Hong Kong: Oxford University Press.

Window (1994) 'A hospital case', Hong Kong, 13 May: 34–7.

Wong, S. L. (1985) 'The Chinese family firm: a model', *British Journal of Sociology*, 36(1): 58–72.

Wong, S. L. (1988) *Emigrant Entrepreneurs: Shanghai Industrialists in Hong Kong*, Hong Kong: Oxford University Press.

Wood, S. (1996) 'How different are human resource practices in Japanese "Transplants" in the United Kingdom', *Industrial Relations*, 35(4), October: 511–25.

Woodruffe, C. (1992) 'What is meant by a competency?', in Boam, R. and Sparrow, P. (eds) *Designing and Achieving Competency*, McGraw-Hill.

World Bank (1993) *The East Asian Miracle: Economic Growth and Public Policy*, Oxford: Oxford University Press.

Wright, I., Bengtsson, C. and Frankenberg, K. (1994) 'Research note: aspects of psychological work environment and health among male and female white-collar and blue-collar workers in a big Swedish industry', *Journal of Organizational Behavior*, 15: 177–83.

Wright, P. M. and McMahan, G. C. (1992) 'Theoretical perspectives for strategic human resource management', *Journal of Management*, 18: 295–320.

Xu, J. T. (1993) *Xu Jia-tun Xianggang Hui Yi Lu (Xu Jia-tun's Memoirs of Hong Kong)*, Hong Kong: United Daily News Limited.

Xu, L. (1981) 'Behavioural sciences and the reform of economic systems', *Jinji Guanli (Economic Management)*, 3: 57–76.

Yeh, A. and Ng, M. (1994) 'The changing role of the state in high-tech industrial development: the experience of Hong Kong', *Environment and Planning C: Government and Policy*, 12: 449–72.

Yeung, C. (1997) 'Political parties', in Cheng, J. (ed.), *The Other Hong Kong Report 1997*, Hong Kong: Chinese University Press.

Yeung, C. K. (1988) 'Joint consultation, collective bargaining and trade union recognition: status and prospects', in Jao *et al.* (eds).

Yost, E. B. and Herbert, T. T. (1985) 'Attitudes toward women as managers (ATWAM)', in Goodstein, L. D. and Pfeiffer, J. W. (eds) *The 1985 Annual Developing Human Resources*, San Diego: University Associates, Inc.

Youndt, M. A., Snell, S. A., Dean, J. W., Jr. Lepak, D. P. (1996) 'Human resource management, manufacturing strategy, and firm performance', *Academy of Management Journal*, 39(4): 836–66.

Young, A. (1994) 'Lessons from the East Asian NICs: a contrarian view', *European Economic Review*, 38: 964–73.

Young, A. (1995) 'The tyranny of numbers: confronting the realities of the easy Asian growth experience', *Quarterly Journal of Economics*, August: 641–80.

Yuen, P. P. (1994) 'The corporatisation of public hospital services in Hong Kong: a possible public choice explanation', *Asia Journal of Public Administration,* 16(2): 165–81.

Zedeck, S. and Mosier, K. L. (1990) 'Work in the family and employing organization', *American Psychologist*, 45(2), February: 240–51.

Zeitz, B. and Dusky, L. (1988) *The Best Companies for Women*, New York: Simon & Schuster.

Zhao, L. (1985) 'The problem of reforming the wage system in our country', *Chinese Economic Studies*, 18: 38–9.

Zikmund, W. G., Hitt, M. A. and Pickens, B. A. (1978) 'Influence of sex and scholastic performance on reactions to job applicant resumes', *Journal of Applied Psychology*, 63(2): 252-4.

Index

Asia–Pacific Economic Co-operation forum (APEC) 291–292
Asian financial crisis 1997–8 80
Association for Democracy and People's Livelihood (ADPL) 27, 32
Association of Southeast Asian Nations (ASEAN) 291–292
Australia: immigration criteria 114

'bamboo ceiling' for female managers 202–204
Bank of China 134
barriers to women's labour participation 16, 186–187
Basic Law 1990 25, 27, 32, 36
Becker, G.S. 105
behavioural competency of small business owners: elements 225–227; major types 227
Beijing meaning of work survey 130, 140–148; demographic data 131; *see also* MOWIRT
Bill of Rights Ordinance 1991 (BORO) 27, 35–36
biotechnology 55
British citizenship 27
British colonial rule: end of 3
bureaucratic personnel management 290
business strategy: interaction with HRM practices 172

Canada: immigration: criteria 114; policy change 1987 114
capitalism: unions perceived as threat 250
case study of private sector joint consultation 278–284; agenda 280; analysis of items discussed 281; attitude of representatives 283–284; constitution of committee 282; election of representatives 279–280; industrial relations conflicts 282–283; joint consultation objectives 278–279; organisation of committees 279; role of representatives within firm 282

civil liberties: union campaigners 250; Public Order Ordinance 251
civil services joint consultation committees 273; lack of impact 275; nominated unions 274; operation 274; terms of reference 273; union participation 275
chaebol: anti-union tactics 297; vehicle for industrialisation 296–298
Chief Executive: powers under Basic Law 32
China: centralised command economy 149–150; economic reform 108; employment relations 302–303; growth of contract employment 302, 306; impact of globalisation 306; information flow since open-door policy 119; labour costs and supply 50; migrants 107–109; social structure and values 135–136; socio-economic reform 127, 132, 133, 139, 140; special economic zones (SEZs) 302–303, 306; state-owned enterprises 139; unmet demand for training 149; urban unemployment 302; worker motivation 149
Chinese immigrants: definition 117; new *see* new Chinese immigrants
Chinese patriarchal system in Hong Kong 199–200
Chinese values and culture 10; labour organisation 10
clerical personnel: income 89, 91
collective bargaining 36–37; contrast with joint consultation 272; opposed by FTU 34, 37; provisions repealed 39; rareness 17, 20, 256
collectivism 10–11
colonial era 26
colonial law on trade unions 239
'commitment' or 'control' strategy in HRM 170, 172
communism: refugees 108; women in labour force 199
company formation and dissolution 222
competencies of managers and entrepreneurs